THE KASHMIR DISPUTE 1947–2012

Volume I

THE KASHMIR DISPUTE 1947–2012

Volume I

A.G. NOORANI

When the ambivalence of one's virtue is recognized, the total iniquity of one's opponent is also irreparably impaired.

– George F. Kennan, *Russia and the West*

Tulika Books

Published by **Tulika Books**
No. 44, first floor, Shahpur Jat, New Delhi 110 049, India

First edition (hardback) 2013
Second edition (paperback) 2013
Third edition (paperback) 2015
Fourth edition (paperback) 2017

Fifth edition (paperback) 2019

ISBN: 978-93-82381-65-5

Printed at Repro Knowledgecast Limited, Thane

TO

the people of Kashmir who, having suffered for long under Mughal, Afghan, Sikh and Dogra occupation, rejoiced on Independence Day, only to suffer betrayal by the tallest leaders of India and Pakistan and their own leaders – from Jawaharlal Nehru, Mohammed Ali Jinnah and Sheikh Mohammed Abdullah down to this day

AND

to the memory of Jayaprakash Narayan who spoke up for the people

And I say with all respect to our Constitution that it just does not matter what your Constitution says; if the people of Kashmir do not want it, it will not go there. Because what is the alternative? The alternative is compulsion and coercion – presuming, of course, that the people of Kashmir do not want it. Are we going to coerce and compel them and thereby justify the very charges that are brought by some misguided people outside this country against us? . . .

Do not think you are dealing with a part of Uttar Pradesh, Bihar or Gujarat. You are dealing with an area, historically and geographically and in all manner of things, with a certain background. If we bring our local ideas and local prejudices everywhere, we will never consolidate. We have to be men of vision and there has to be a broadminded acceptance of facts in order to integrate really. And real integration comes of the mind and the heart and not of some clause which you may impose on other people.

– Jawaharlal Nehru in the Lok Sabha on 26 June 1952

As for plebiscite, we were absolutely, absolutely dishonest.

– V.P. Menon to H.V. Hodson, September 1964

Contents

Preface

This is a collection of articles on the Kashmir dispute which I wrote since 1964. The Introduction, based on recently published documents, highlights some important episodes – to wit: Mohammed Ali Jinnah's approval of the tribal raid into Kashmir and his rejection of India's written offer, made at Lahore on 1 November 1947, based on plebiscite in Kashmir, Junagarh and Hyderabad, which would have settled the dispute and altered the course of history; Jawaharlal Nehru and Vallabhbhai Patel's attempts to secure Kash-mir's accession to India before the raid, using a particular Standstill Agreement as a cloak for the Instrument of Accession proper; Sheikh Abdullah's reluctance to accede to India or, for that matter, to Pakistan; his second thoughts soon after the accession to India; Nehru's intrigues against the Sheikh; his prime responsibility for ordering in 1953 Sheikh's dismissal from office as Prime Minister of Kashmir, for his arrest and long imprisonment, and for launching a false case of conspiracy with Pakistan on charges he knew to be false; his use of the army in 1953 and his false statements on the arrest to the President, Parliament and even to Indira Gandhi; her desire to meet him shortly after the arrest; Nehru's calculated and determined 'erosion' of Article 370; the reasons for the Sheikh's espousal of a Kashmir set-tlement in 1953 and his acceptance of accession to India in private parleys (1965–68) unknown to his followers and, not least, Nehru's decision in private in 1948 to rule out a plebiscite while promising publicly and repeatedly right till 1954 to hold one; Nehru's secret plans in 1948 for an alliance with the United States; the fundamental difference between Nehru's secular outlook and Patel's communal outlook. Nehru resisted Patel's agenda but his policy on Kashmir contributed to the growth of the very forces he had valiantly fought and continued to fight till he died.

I wrote *The Kashmir Question* in 1964. It is being reprinted here since it is out of print. Also included is an essay which surveys bilateral negotiations between India and Pakistan on Kashmir from 1947 to 2006. It was published in *Criterion*, a quarterly edited by the veteran diplomat S. Iftikhar Murshed and published from Islamabad. I should like to thank him and the editors of the journals/newspapers in which the articles appeared; namely, *Opinion, The Indian Express, The Statesman, Hindustan Times* and *Frontline* in which a good many of them appeared. Two friends who are, sadly, no more, deserve particular mention: A.D. Gorwala, ICS, Editor of *Opinion*, and Cushrow R. Irani, Editor of *The Statesman* who was extremely generous in the space he provided.

Nor must I omit to record my debt to Ved Bhasin, founder and former Editor of *Kashmir Times;* Fayaz Ahmad Kaloo, Editor of *Greater Kashmir*; Shujaat Bukhari, Editor of *Rising Kashmir;* and Taher Mohiuddin Editor of *Chattan*, an Urdu daily (formerly a weekly published from Srinagar), for keeping me informed. I owe the same to my friend S. Iftikhar Gilani. I cannot thank my friend M. Saleem Beg enough for providing me with a copy of Hafiz Jalandhari's immortal poem on Kashmir's tragic fate: *Pachattar Lakh ka Sauda* (*The Sale for Rs 75 Lakh*). I am responsible for errors of fact or interpretation exclusively.

I should very much like to thank Noor Zaheer for the pains she took in translating, at my request, the poem of the Urdu poet, Hafiz Jalandhari, on the failed deed of 1846. I bear exclusive responsibility for the revised, final version.

I thank Maya John and Rakhi Sehgal at Tulika Books for their impeccable work on the manuscript. If I reserve for the last my expression of gratitude to Indira Chandrasekhar, it is because her contribution to this book is the greatest – in patience, understanding and all the qualities one would expect in a publisher who is as highly respected as she is.

Mumbai A.G. NOORANI
16 September 2012

INTRODUCTION

These few stanzas are from Hafeez Jalandhari's long and highly controversial poem on Kashmir, *Pachattar Lakh ka Sauda* (*The Sale for Rs 75 Lakh*). The complete poem will soon be published in book form.

Roared a lion in the valley, resonated the mountains
Came alive the workers and woke up the peasants

Hearing from all directions freedom of the people's call
Vanished the intoxicated pride of the feudal lord

In the ears of luxury carried the message of death
Creating hurdles in the abundant life of luxury

Gathered the old gamblers of the markets of theft
Known recognized thugs, cunning clever forgerers

And amongst them that paunch seated on the couch
Vain in pride to be called 'Paunch son of paunch'

Problem of Kashmir was brought into argument
Paunch it was who initiated the discussion

Why have those people created such a halaboo?
Why have animals begun resisting their own slaughter?

Call some of their females and a few males too
Blind their eyes and break open their skulls

Teach them a lesson for saying 'Leave Kashmir!'
Go set them free from the imprisonment of life

'Leave Kashmir' meaning we let go Kashmir
To beggars hand this hereditary kingdom of Kashmir

Should we plan something new to feed our gluttony?
And give away the rich sweetmeats to these dogs

They have set their eyes on our appetite and hunger
This quarrel must be resolved at once, 'Kaak-ji'

The deal of trade worth seventy-five lakhs
Accepted and patented by none other than 'Company'

Devalue the market these destitutes would
Why the hearts not break of the capitalist would

If this cry of 'freedom freedom' be raised
Our dominance in the market would be erased

Valleys, mountains, forests, rivers, fruits, flowers and grain
Cattle, sheep, humans and their work and labour

All traditions inherited by us from our forefathers
Look at the sale deed, everything is in black and white

Ownership of a country bought for seventy-five lakhs
Confiscated all this booty in seventy-five lakhs

Be it cattle or humans to be bought, all for sale
Their sons, daughters and progeny all for sale

None can ever be free, all are up for sale
Homeless till doomsday, ruined, forever on sale

The foreheads of grass blade and moon carry our stamp
Babies in the wombs of mothers carry our stamp

Ravaged stands man's destiny for seventy-five lakhs
Sold is Kashmir's paradise for seventy-five lakhs

Work and strength, a man's treasure for seventy-five lakhs
The jewel of woman's chastity for seventy-five lakhs

Country, nation, race, possession, life in seventy-five lakhs
Yes for only seventy five lakhs, just seventy-five lakhs!

> There is a very big question, Kashmir. Perhaps. Why 'perhaps'? – certainly, that is the most difficult of all these problems as between India and Pakistan. I say problems between India and Pakistan, certainly, but we must always remember Kashmir is not a thing to be bandied about between India–Pakistan. *It has a soul of its own; it has an individuality of its own.* We cannot, certainly much less can Pakistan, play with it as if it were something in the political game between the two countries. Nothing can be done without the goodwill of the people of Kashmir.
>
> – Prime Minister Jawaharlal Nehru in the Lok Sabha, 31 March 1955
> (*Selected Works of Jawaharlal Nehru* [*SWJN*], Vol. 28: 318)

If, fifty-seven years later, the soul of Kashmir is in torment and cries for *azadi*, it is because, despite the profuse professions and pledges, Nehru cared little for the people of Kashmir; still less did Mohammad Ali Jinnah and, least of all, the British. The people have been in revolt, pelting stones rather than shooting bullets. Nobody alleges Pakistan's aid or complicity. The harsh truth which Nehru and his successors, as well as India's media and academia, suppressed for long is now out in the open. But the state of denial continues to hold the establishment in its firm grip.

This introduction is intended to serve neither as a summary of the articles in this book nor as a history of Kashmir's politics. Archival material and some milestones have been highlighted. The articles record the events in some detail.

The state of Jammu and Kashmir (J&K) was created by the British Raj for its own imperial ends. In this, it was aided by the treachery of the Dogra chieftain, Gulab Singh, to his masters in Lahore, the Sikh Darbar. When Ranjit Singh died in 1839, the Sikh empire began to come apart. The British were awaiting his death to annex Punjab, and Gulab Singh, to acquire Kashmir through them. While still in the service of the Sikh kingdom, he began ingratiating himself with the British.

On 13 December 1845, when the Governor-General, Sir Henry Hardinge, declared war on the Sikhs, the peace terms were negotiated by none other than Gulab Singh. Despite his loyalty to the Lahore Darbar, he withheld any help to his masters. Prem Nath Bazaz records in detail Gulab Singh's treachery which ensured Lahore's defeat in the first Anglo–Sikh war of 1845–46 (Bazaz 1954: 121).

By the Treaty of Lahore, dated 9 March 1846, the state was forced to cede all cis-Sutlej territories, the Beas–Sutlej Doab, and the provinces of Hazara and Kashmir to the East India Company, representing the British government. Article XII recorded Gulab Singh's treachery.

> In consideration of the services rendered by Rajah Gulab Singh of Jummoo to the Lahore State, towards procuring the restoration of the relation of amity between the Lahore and British Governments, the Maharaja hereby agrees to

> recognize the Independent Sovereignty of Rajah Gulab Singh, in such territories and districts in the hills as may be made over to the said Rajah Gulab Singh by separate Agreement between himself and the British Government.

That separate agreement was the infamous Treaty of Amritsar – a 'deed of sale' as Gandhi called it in 1947. It was signed a week later, on 16 March 1946.

Article III of the treaty said:

> In consideration of the transfer made to him and his heirs. . . . Maharaja Gulab Singh will pay to the British Government the sum of seventy-five lakhs of rupees (*Nanukshahee*), fifty lakhs to be paid on ratification of this treaty and twenty-five lakhs on or before the 1 October of the current year AD 1846.

The treaty was enforced with British arms. Sheikh Imamuddin, the Governor of Kashmir appointed by the Sikh rulers, refused to hand over the valley of Kashmir to Gulab Singh. A struggle ensued in which Gulab Singh's forces were defeated. British troops had to be sent to instal him as ruler of Kashmir (Lawrence 1895: 201). The 1929 edition of Aitchison's *Treaties* says: 'thus Gulab Singh owed not only his title to Kashmir, but his actual possession of it, wholly to the support of British power' (ibid.: 3).

Cunningham describes Gulab Singh's investiture as sovereign of his new territories on 15 March 1946. He 'stood up, and with joined hands, expressed his gratitude to the British Viceroy – adding without, however, any ironical meaning, that he was indeed Zurkharid, or gold-boughten slaves' (Cunningham, vide Hassnain 1974: 16). Captain Amrinder Singh's excellent research also establishes the perfidy most ably (Singh 2009).

Gulab Singh was not the founder of the state of Jammu and Kashmir, a legend popularized by K.M. Panikkar in his fawning 'Short Memoir', published first in 1930 under the title *Gulab Singh* by Martin Hopkins, and later in 1953 under the title *The Founding of the Kashmir State* (George Allen and Unwin).

Over his protest an Officer on Special Duty was sent to the state as early as in 1852 (Huttenback 2004: 46). He became the British Resident in 1885. So rife were oppression and corruption that the British even ruminated annexing the state. The Secretary of State, Lord Kimberley, wrote to the Viceroy, Lord Ripon, on 23 May 1884:

> As to the urgent need for reforms in the administration of the State of Jammu and Kashmir, there is unfortunately, no room for doubt. It may, indeed, be a question whether, having regard to the circumstances under which the sovereignty of the country was entrusted to the present Hindoo ruling family, the intervention of the British Government on behalf of the Mohammedan population has not already been too long delayed. (*Accounts and Papers, East India: Papers relating to Kashmir*)

Why the British created this state has been ably described by S.S. Bal in an article entitled 'British Interest in Creating the Dogra State of Jammu and Kashmir' (*Journal of the Indian History Congress*, XXX Session, 1967: 40–50). If Kimberley had gone ahead and taken back Kashmir in 1884, its fate would have been decided by a popular vote, as in the North West Frontier Province (NWFP). Kashmir was unique in that it had a choice. It could accede either to India or Pakistan. Only a plebiscite could have offered the means for exercising the choice. In Europe, with much less at stake, referenda were held on the treaty establishing the European Union in several countries.

In Kashmir a plebiscite was not a mere option or choice. It was a democratic necessity. Were it not for the highly controversial Radcliffe Award, India would not have had any access by land to Kashmir. It was not Pakistan alone which contested the award. Professor R.J. Moore, one of the foremost authorities on the partition, subjected it to close scrutiny and remarked:

> it seems inconceivable that Radcliffe would not have realized that a district-wise observance of the contiguous-majority principle in Gurdaspur, such as he followed to the expense of Muslim tehsils in the district of Amritsar (i.e. Jullunder Nakodar) would have closed off the Maharaja of Kashmir's option of adhering to India. (Moore 1987: 33)

Radcliffe gave India three of the tehsils of Gurdaspur: Pathankot, with a 61 per cent non-Muslim majority, which he rightly assigned to India, but along with the Muslim-majority tehsils of Gurdaspur (52 per cent) and Batala (55 per cent). Only the Sakargarh tehsil was given to Pakistan. The road to Kashmir lay through Pathankot, a tenuous route at the best of times. The only all-weather road which connected, and still connects, Srinagar to the rest of world is the old Rawalpindi road. The rivers flow into Pakistan. If the geographical factor cited apropos Junagadh and Hyderabad was overwhelmingly in favour of Pakistan, so was the democratic factor – largely but not decisively.

A plebiscite in Kashmir was a moral imperative, besides being a democratic necessity. A plebiscite was held in Junagadh on 20 February 1948 after the administration of the state was taken over by the Government of India on November 1947. It was called a 'referendum' (*White Paper on Indian State* 1950: 114), and was conducted by an ICS officer, C.B. Nagarkar. Out of an electorate of 20,1457, a total of 19,0870 cast their votes. Only 91 voted for Pakistan. Of the 31,434 votes cast in Junagadh's five princeling areas, only 39 voted for accession to Pakistan (Menon 1956: 142).

A referendum was also held in Sikkim. The Election Commission of India conducted it on 14 April 1975 'to confirm the resolution' passed in the Sikkim Assembly on the state's merger with India in 1973–74. Nari Rustomji, ICS, whose services were in 1954 placed with the Chogyal for appointment as his Prime Minister, opined that '*it would be injudicious to assess, however that the* resolution respecting Sikkim's merger with India . . . necessarily represented the wishes of the people'. He recorded the demand for a 'completely impartial authority' to conduct the poll, and added that 'the Army and the heavy Indian presence in Sikkim were also factors that inevitably weighed in influencing the vote' (Rustomji 1987: 146, 150).

To be sure, in both these cases in which the democratic principle was formally applied, the result was a foregone conclusion. *So it was in the case of Kashmir – which is why a plebiscite was never held.* Indira Gandhi warned Nehru in a letter from Srinagar on 14 May 1948, while the war was on, that 'they say that only Sheikh Saheb is confident of winning the plebiscite' (Gandhi, ed. 2005: 517).

The issue in 1947 was *who* was to exercise the choice, the ruler Hari Singh or the people? It came to the fore on 13 June 1947, just ten days after the Indian National Congress and the All India Muslim League had accepted the partition plan of 3 June 1947. On 12 May 1946, the Cabinet Mission to India had presented a memorandum on Indian states ruled by the princes. On 13 June, leaders of both parties met under the chairmanship of the Viceroy, Lord Mountbatten. 'Mr Jinnah said that in his view the States were fully entitled to say that they would join neither Constituent Assembly. Every Indian State was a sovereign State. Pandit Nehru said he differed altogether. He spoke as a lawyer. Mr Jinnah said that he spoke as a lawyer also' (*The Transfer of Power 1942–47*, Vol. XI: 320–26). It had come to that.

Jinnah's stand was utterly absurd and ruined the prospects of a conciliatory beginning in relations between the two countries. As Nehru correctly pointed out, there was no trace in the Cabinet Mission's memorandum of any state being allowed to claim 'independence'. Jinnah soon discovered that his stand was adverse to Pakistan's own interests (vide Saiyid 2004: 26–45). But not before he had inflicted irreparable harm on Pakistan, on the people of Kashmir and on Indo–Pak relations. In the hour of a historic triumph he emerged, not as a statesman or even as a wise patriot, like Mustafa Kemal of Turkey after the Treaty of Lausanne in 1922, but rather as a vindictive and petty tactician. That these traits were shared by Nehru and, even more so, by his deputy Vallabhbhai Patel, could be of small consolation. They had the superior might and more options. Jinnah wrecked his best option – an overall settlement proposed to him in writing in Lahore by Mountbatten on 1 November 1947. By then the Indian troops had occupied Junagadh, and were beating back the raiders who had entered Kashmir on 22 October with Jinnah's full knowledge and approval – a fact which few Pakistanis *care or dare* to acknowledge.

Truth to tell, India and Pakistan launched a cold war even while they were in the embryo of history. Restless to seize power, each leadership was out to do the other down. In the three cases of disputed accession – Junagadh, Hyderabad and Kashmir – each side adopted inconsistent stands on: (1) the irrelevance of the Instrument of Accession; (2) plebiscite; (3) territorial integrity or 'the geographical factor'; and (4) the religious factor. Both practised deception. Both used armed force as an instrument of policy.

Myths were spawned and still persist. Few know that it was India that first invoked the religious factor in a formal proposal on 1 November 1947, and spoke stridently of the religious principle underlying the partition. India's pain at the dismemberment of its territorial integrity was justified. But that very factor justified Pakistan's pain at Kashmir's accession to India, which only Cyril Radcliffe's controversial award of Gurdaspur in August 1947 made possible. Genuinely or otherwise, Mountbatten rued the award later in his talks with Dominique Lapierre and Larry Collins. The road and river communications were with Pakistan exclusively. 'I mean Radcliffe let us in for an awful lot of trouble by making it possible for them to accede to India. If he had not made that award, the Maharaja would really have had no option but to join Pakistan' (Mountbatten *et al.* 1984: 43).

The record is set out in my earlier book, *The Kashmir Question* (1964), while that of the bilateral negotiations on Kashmir (1947–2004) appeared in October 2006 in the magazine *Criterion*, published from Islamabad and edited by a veteran in diplomacy, S. Iftikhar Murshed. But new material continues to surface which compels a revision of opinion: for example, Kashmir's Prime Minister Ram Chandra Kak's paper deposited in the British Library, and M.O. Mathai's note to Indira Gandhi on her desire to visit Sheikh Abdullah in prison very shortly after he was put in jail on Nehru's order – a fact confirmed by a document in the *Selected Works of Jawaharlal Nehru*. The *Jinnah Papers*, published over the years in Pakistan, yield their own surprises.

Some of these are discussed here and some questions, long neglected, are raised. Did Sheikh Abdullah indeed wish to accede to India? How strong were his representative credentials on accession? What was the people's reaction to the accession to India, once the immediate menace of the tribal raid was over? How culpable was Jinnah in permitting that raid, organized though it was by the Chief Minister of the NWFP? What was the Indian leaders' immediate reaction to the raid? Was Kashmir's accession to India, while unquestionably valid, legally a 'provisional' one? How much or how little did the people matter to Nehru?

These are not academic questions. Kashmiris never forget their history. Their independence, they will tell you, was snuffed out by the Mughal emperor Akbar in 1586. Mughal rule was ended by the Afghans in 1752; Ranjit Singh occupied Kashmir in 1819. The British handed Kashmir over to the Dogra Gulab Singh in 1846 by the Treaty of Amritsar for Rs 75 lakhs – a tansaction that Gandhi called 'a deed of sale'.

The All India Congress Committee (AICC) emphatically declared on 15

June 1947 that 'the people of the States must have dominating voice in any decisions regarding them'. India's objection to Jinnah's attempt to secure Jodhpur's accession to Pakistan was valid. Only, it ran counter to the feverish attempts by Vallabhbhai Patel to secure Kashmir's accession to India regardless of the people's will, and Nehru's likewise, brandishing the fig-leaf of Sheikh Mohammed Abdullah's support, which, the record shows, was doubtful. What *was* the object of Sheikh Abdullah's two emissaries, first Bakshi Ghulam Mohammad and next G.M. Sadiq, to Pakistan in 1947? Why did he send them there at all? What offer did he authorize them to make to Pakistan's leaders?

Jinnah did worse than issue two statements, on 17 June and 30 July 1947, in support of the rulers' right to decide on accession. He acted on them by actively wooing the Maharaja of Jodhpur. As V.P. Menon revealed:

> The late Maharaja Hanwant Singh of Jodhpur continued to be intractable. Jinnah and the Muslim League leaders had a series of meetings with him. At the last of these interviews, Maharaja Hanwant Singh had taken then Maharajkumar of Jaisalmer with him, because the Maharaja of Bikaner would not accompany him and he shrank from going alone. Theirs were the three States geographically contiguous to Pakistan. Jinnah, I was told, signed a blank sheet of paper and gave it to Maharaja Hanwant Singh along with his own fountain pen, saying 'You can fill in all your conditions.' A discussion followed. The Maharaja was prepared to line up with Pakistan. He then turned to the Maharajkumar of Jaisalmer and asked him whether he would follow suit. The Maharajkumar said he would do so on one condition: If there was any trouble between the Hindus and Muslims, he would not side with the Muslims against the Hindus. This was a bombshell and took Maharaja Hanwant Singh completely surprise. Sir Mohammed Zafarullah, however made light of the whole affair and pressed Maharaja Hanwant Singh to sign the Instrument. But the Maharaja now felt unable to take a decision. He suggested to Jinnah that he would go to Jodhpur and return the next day. The Maharaja remained at Jodhpur for three days. The atmosphere in the State was hostile to the idea that Jodhpur should cast its lot with Pakistan. The Maharaja began to waver. When he returned to Delhi after three days I was informed that, unless I handled the Maharaja quickly, the chances were that he might accede to Pakistan. I went to the Hotel Imperial and told the Maharaja that Lord Mountbatten wanted to see him. We then drove to Government House and I kept the Maharaja in the visitors' room while I went in and explained the situation to Lord Mountbatten. The Maharaja was then called in. Lord Mountbatten made it clear that from a purely legal standpoint there was no objection to the ruler of Jodhpur acceding to Pakistan; but the Maharaja should, he stressed, consider seriously the consequences of his doing so, having regard to the fact that he himself was a Hindu; that his State was populated predominately by Hindus and that the same applied to the States

> surrounding Jodhpur. In the light of these considerations, if the Maharaja were to accede to Pakistan, his action would surely be in conflict *with the principles underlying the partition of India on the basis of Muslim and non-Muslim majority areas*; and serious communal trouble inside the State would be the inevitable consequence of such affiliation. The Maharaja started at once to ask for impossible concession. I told him plainly: 'If you want to sign on false hopes, I will agree to your demands', adding that most of the demands could not be conceded. He then told us that Jinnah had given him a blank paper in which he could put down all the concessions he wanted. I urged him not to be swayed by false promises. After a great deal of discussion, I gave him a letter conceding some of his demands. Thereafter he signed the Instrument of Accession. (Menon 1956: 112–13)

As we shall see, both Nehru and Abdullah had similar fears if Kashmir acceded to India.

The letters and the diary of George Cunningham, Governor of the NWFP, record the preparations for the tribal raid (Cunningham Collection, MSS. Eur. D 670). The researches of Professor R.J. Moore throw additional light on the matter (Moore 1987). Moore analyses the Cunningham papers and concludes: 'Cunningham's testimony establishes beyond reasonable doubt that the scheme of invasion originally emerged spontaneously among the tribes as a response to outrages against Muslims in East Punjab and the Maharaja's territories' (ibid.: 52). This was an allusion to the massacres in Jammu. Ian Stephens, editor of *The Statesman*, wrote that in autumn the 5,00,000 Muslims of Jammu 'were practically eliminated' and 2,00,000 of them 'just disappeared' (ibid.: 49). In a letter to Patel, dated 7 October 1948, Sheikh Abdullah provided the details (Das, ed. 1974, Vol. 1: 237).

Cunningham's diarized testimony shows how the anger was 'channelized' by the Chief Minister of the NWFP, Abdul Qaiyum Khan, and the central leadership concerned. Cunningham wrote to Jinnah, the Governor-General, on 15 October 1947: 'I am perturbed by the move which a lot of our people are making in the Kashmir direction. The talk now is not merely of defence against attacks by Sikhs from Kashmir, but of invasion into Kashmir.'

It was a risky adventure. On 2 October Prime Minister Liaquat Ali Khan talked of 'the weakness of the Pakistan Army . . . and the necessity, therefore, of preventing any clash between Pakistan and India' (Cunningham Collection). Earlier, on 20 September, the Commander-in-Chief of the Army, General Frank Messervy, had told the Governor that the Army was in 'a parlous state'. On 18 October the Governor confronted his Chief Minister with 'everything I knew' (ibid.). Qaiyum Khan 'was quite open with me. He confirmed his approval of the action while maintaining the "line" of official dissociation. He thought it would tend to "make the Maharaja join Pakistan"' (ibid.).

On that very day the States Minister, Agha Saiyid Bad Shah, met Cunningham and gave a contrary assessment which came true. He had been sent by Liaquat to persuade Kashmir's Prime Minister. Janak Singh, who had replaced Kak, to join Pakistan. He in turn was replaced by Meher Chand Mahajan, 'an Arya Samajist with all the mentality and fanaticism of that body', wrote Dalip Singh to Patel (Das 1974: 85). He was a colleague of Shah's father on the Lahore High Court Bench. Civilities over, he asked Shah to 'clear out' of Srinagar. Shah 'thinks that aggression *on Kashmir will make Hari Singh join India, and that might very probably lead on to war in the next three or four months*' (Cunningham Collection).

On 25 October Iskander Mirza, later Pakistan's President, came to Peshawar and gave Cunningham 'all the underground history of the present campaign against Kashmir'. He said:

> Liaquat had meant to come here last week and tell me about it personally but was prevented by his illness, which seems to be fairly serious heart trouble. Apparently Jinnah himself first heard of what was going on about fifteen days ago, but said, 'Don't tell me anything about it. My conscience must be clear.' Iskander is positive that Hari Singh means to join India as soon as his new road from Pathankot is made, which might be in 3 months. He had a lot of Sikhs and Dogras moved into Poonch and Jammu, and has been trying to shove Muslims into Pakistan in accordance with the general Indian strategy. (Moore 1987: 51)

On 18 October the States Minister Agha Saiyid Bad Shah had warned that 'aggression on Kashmir would provoke Hari Singh's accession to India, which might lead to war'. He had just returned from a failed mission to Srinagar at Liaquat's behest (ibid.: 50).

News of Kashmir's accession to India on 26 October took Pakistan's leaders by surprise. On 28 October the Governor was summoned to meet Jinnah at Lahore. The Supreme Commander, Field Marshal Sir Claude Auchinleck, was also there. The following is an account of the conversation:

> Yesterday, on hearing that Indian troops had been flown to SRINAGAR, after Hari Singh's accession to the Indian Union had been announced, the Pakistan Government wanted Pakistan troops to be sent there too. GRACEY had demurred strongly, as it would almost inevitably mean war. He asked me to support him in this.
>
> About 12 MUDIE and I went to LIAQUAT ALI's house, where L.A. is still in his bedroom. JINNAH explained his position at some length. He said AUCHINLECK had just told him that, in event of war between the 2 Dominions, all B.O.s [British Officials] in both armies would at once stand down (it seems odd he was never told this before; it is not a recent decision). He held that he had a good moral and constitutional case for intervening by force, just as INDIA had, and that the so-called 'accession' of HARI SINGH was fraudu-

lent and impossible to accept (I couldn't quite follow his reasoning here). KASHMIR had turned down every approach PAKISTAN had made to them, and the lives of MUSLIMS in all Kashmir were at stake. But he realized the Pakistan Army was weak at present; had we the power to intervene? JINNAH said he was not at all convinced that GRACEY was right in saying that we must not risk war, but I felt that in his own mind he had really ruled out the possibility of sending troops into fight. When talking even in a small intimate conference like this, JINNAH talks as if he were making a speech at the Bar. (Cunningham Collection)

The next day:

We then talked for 1 1/2 hours. He said he felt his hands were now free, legally as well as morally, to take any line he liked about Kashmir, as the accession of Kashmir to India was a 'fraudulent transaction'. I could not get him to define exactly where the 'fraud' came in, except that the method of acceding, combined with instant occupation by troops, was against the whole principles by which, it had been mutually agreed, accession would take place. He quoted GLADESTONE's intervention in regard to the Bulgarian atrocities.

He then said that it was essential for MUDIE and myself, and GRACEY as C-in-C too, to enter into the full spirit of this struggle for the safeguarding of the lives and rights of the Kashmir People. I was not quite sure whether he implied that hitherto I had not been playing up, so I pointed out that untill 4 or 5 days ago I did not even know whether the entry of my tribes into Kashmir was in accordance with his and LIAQUAT's policy or not; and that my last orders – on which I was still working – were the tribes were not wanted until PAKISTAN asked for them, that I had not yet been told they were wanted, and that I had told all my officers therefore not to assist – though they could not prevent – the movement. If this was his definite policy I was quite prepared to support it, provided I didn't have to do one thing and say another. But if I were to do this, JINNAH must face the risk that the co-operation of some of my officers with the tribesmen would become known and might be condemned by world opinion. JINNAH said he realized this and would take the risk; . . . I am not particularly happy, however, about the whole business, and I suspect JINNAH is conscious of having made a blunder (having assumed that tribal intervention would not at once – as seemed obvious to me – throw Kashmir into the arms of India) and is desperate to find a way out. Anyway, the harm has been done, and we have to make the best of the situation. It is full of snags, not the least being how we are to prevent our tribal contingents looting our own district on their homeward march.

By 9–10 February 1948 the results of his folly began to sink in Jinnah's mind.

> JINNAH says he has documentary proof that the [Radcliffe] Report was in MOUNTBATTEN's hands by 7 August, and could have been published then if M.B. had not held it up. JINNAH very bitter about the whole thing. . . . I dined with JINNAH and Miss JINNAH alone. Again JINNAH talked at the table for about an hour after dinner, mostly about the exchange of population, which he said, INDIA had forced on PAKISTAN. He was very rabid against PATEL and NEHRU, Miss JINNAH backing him up. It is a pity he nearly always talks as if he were making a speech at the Bar. It slows things down. I felt sometimes that he was talking in order to convince himself that he was not particularly to blame for what has happened in recent months. (Ibid.)

Jinnah learnt nothing from his mistake. He rejected this formula which Mountbatten had offered to him in Lahore on 1 November.

> The Governments of India and Pakistan agree that, where the ruler of a State does not belong to the community to which the majority of his subjects belong, and where the State has not acceded to that Dominion whose majority community is the same as the State's, the question of whether the State should finally accede to one or the other of the Dominions should in all cases be decided by an impartial reference to the will of people. (Das 1974: 73)

The formula was to be 'a basis for discussion' at the conference, as envisaged in 'Suggested Proposal to Pakistan Government to form the basis of discussion'. They covered the entire process from the ceasefire, withdrawal of the raiders and next of the Indian troops, followed by a UN-supervised plebiscite. India was 'prepared to agree that a joint India–Pakistan force should hold the ring while the plebiscite is being held' (ibid.: 84; also see Document 3 in this volume). The formula, including its basis, *the religious factor*, was offered by Nehru to Liaquat in a telegram on 8 November (*White Paper on Jammu and Kashmir* 1948: 62, paragraphs 14 and 15). *Omitted however was the offer of 'a joint India–Pakistan force'.*

Pakistan's negotiating strength was evaporating by the day. India's offer was made to a militarily weak Pakistan *after* its troops had occupied Junagadh and were beating back the raiders in Kashmir. Jinnah's objection to the inclusion of Hyderabad wrecked the best opportunity for peace. He could well have asked for some safeguards for Hyderabad as a part of the deal.

Pakistan could not have been established but for the tactical skills and tenacity of Mohammed Ali Jinnah. Pakistan could not have lost Kashmir but for the monumental arrogance and egregious folly of its Quaid-e-Azam. 'Kashmir will fall into our lap like a ripe fruit', he would say (Ali 1967: 297). This, despite its Hindu ruler and its popular hero, Sheikh Abdullah, whom he had estranged in 1939 and 1944, and rebuffed in 1947. 'I have great respect for Mr Abdullah', he said at Aligarh on 6 April 1939, but warned him against trusting the Congress. At Sholapur, on 7 May 1939, he declared a policy of 'non-intervention' (Ahmed, ed. 1992: 363, 374). Jinnah disapproved of the Sheikh's conversion of the Muslim Conference into the National Conference in 1939.

Sheikh Abdullah's speech at Lahore on 4 April 1939 provided warning enough.

> How can we tie ourselves to you? You are the people whose resolution at Patna threatened to create difficulties for the Congress if that organization of the masses interfered in the affairs of the States. While we are in great distress, the Congress came to our rescue. It was the Congress, which voiced our grievances and supported us. Maulana Zafar Ali has in a speech at Kapurthala declared that the Congress is an enemy of the prince and they in the League are their friends and protector. If that is right, let me say clearly that we cannot be with those who want the present state of affairs to continue. (*The Tribune*, 5 April 1939)

In Srinagar, in 1944, Jinnah was welcomed by Abdullah, but all he got was advice to wind up the National Conference (NC). In 1947 Jinnah refused to meet Abdullah's emissaries, Bakshi Ghulam Mohammad and G.M. Sadiq.

The November 1947 offer provided Jinnah an escape from the impasse. The tribal raid gave him a leverage – an inherently wasting asset. He squandered it. Both Messervy and Cunningham were firmly of the view that, 'if Pakistan had sat still and done nothing Kashmir would have simply drifted into the Indian Union'. In this they were right. Patel and Nehru plotted for Kashmir's accession to India even before the partition, while Jinnah waited for the ripe fruit to fall into his lap; Patel plotted as a Hindu nationalist and Nehru as an Indian nationalist.

Nehru reckoned with the people's views, albeit formally and only up to a point; Patel ignored these, and pinned his hopes on the ruler and his religious affiliation. A letter he wrote as early as 19 June 1946 reveals Patel in his true colours:

> The State being a Hindu State, situated in Muslim surroundings, finds itself in a very delicate and difficult position to take strong action against revolt or lawlessness, as such action at once disturbs the communal atmosphere outside, apart from its repercussions inside the State. The extreme poverty and illiteracy of the masses present an unpleasant picture to a foreign visitor and the State is generally represented outside as extremely irresponsible and unprogressive.
>
> Sheikh Abdullah is supposed to be [*sic*] very popular and his association with Pandit Nehru has been regarded as sufficient guarantee of his being against any separatist movement. (Das 1974: 4)

'Muslim surroundings' for a Muslim majority in the state was a giveaway. That was what Patel thought of them – a 'surrounding'. This, even before the establishment of Pakistan. He doubted Abdullah's intentions and his popular following (ibid.). One wonders if he would have accepted Hyderabad as 'a Muslim state' by his own perverse logic. In another letter on the same day he wrote of Nehru: 'After all, he is also a Hindu and that too a Kashmiri Hindu' (ibid.: 3). Nehru would not have approved of this. He relied on Sheikh Abdullah as an instrument of his policy – accession to India with the appearance of popular support. Patel relied on the autocratic Prime Minister Ramchandra Kak and Maharaja Hari Singh. He wrote to Kak on 3 July:

> You are aware that on 15 August, India, though divided, will be completely free, and you also know that by this time a vast majority of the States have joined the Constituent Assembly of India. I realize the peculiar difficulties of Kashmir, but looking to its History and its tradition, it has, in my opinion *no other choice.* (Ibid.: 32)

This was before the Radcliffe Report was even signed.

Nehru was as active before the partition, and as assertive that Kashmir had no other choice but accession to India. The idea of a plebiscite emerged later. He took up the matter with the Governor-General, Lord Mountbatten, as early as in May 1947 when the partition of India seemed inevitable, and even before the Partition Plan was announced on 3 June 1947. Mountbatten asked Nehru to send him a note on the subject, which he did on 17 June with population figures and a potted history. Jammu: Muslims 61 per cent, Hindus 39 per cent; Kashmir: Muslims 92 per cent, Hindus 7.8 per cent – total of 77 per cent Muslims and 21 per cent Hindus in a population of roughly 3.6 million in the entire state. There were then 1,205,675 Muslims in Jammu as against 772,760 Hindus, and 1,559,488 Muslims in Kashmir to 139,217 Hindus.

Nehru urged the removal of Ramchandra Kak from the premiership and the release of Sheikh Abdullah from prison, and warned against the state's accession to Pakistan. The National Conference was opposed to it and the Maharaja's position would also become very difficult. He concluded: 'The normal and obvious course appears to be for Kashmir to join the Constituent Assembly of India. This will satisfy both the popular demand and the Maharaja's wishes. It is absurd to think that Pakistan would create trouble if this happens.' He was wrong on all counts – 'the popular demand', which he identified singly with Abdullah, the ruler's wishes, and indeed the popular sentiment. It was not Pakistan but the people who might have created 'trouble' (*SWJN,* Vol. 3: 226–27).

On 4 July Nehru wooed the ruler Hari Singh, cautioning him, significantly, against independence (ibid.: 253). More revealing was his letter to Deputy Prime Minister Vallabhbhai Patel on 27 September 1947, a month before the tribal raid (*SWJN*, Vol. 4: 263–65). He wrote:

> The Muslim League in the Punjab and NWFP are making preparations to enter Kashmir in considerable numbers. The approach of winter is going to cut off Kashmir from the rest of India. The only normal route then is via the Jhelum Valley [the Rawalpindi road]. The Jammu route can hardly be used during winter and air traffic is also suspended. Therefore, it is important that something should be done before these winter conditions set in. This means practically by the end of October or, at the latest, the beginning of November. . . .
>
> It seems to me that there is no other course open to the Maharaja but this: to release Sheikh Abdullah and the National Conference leaders, to make a friendly approach to them, seek their cooperation and make them feel that this is really meant, and then to declare adhesion to the Indian Union. Once the State adheres to India, it will become very difficult for Pakistan to invade it officially or unofficially without coming into conflict with the Indian Union. If, however, there is delay in this accession, then Pakistan will go ahead without much fear of consequences, specially when the winter isolates Kashmir. It seems to me urgently necessary, therefore, that the accession to the Indian Union should take place early.

Nehru realized that Abdullah needed to take the people along. Only: 'He cannot carry his people with him unless he has something definite to place before them. What this can be in the circumstances, I cannot define precisely at the present moment' (ibid.).

To the state's Prime Minister, Mehr Chand Mahajan, Nehru defined what could be offered: 'a new interim government', followed by 'an ordinary election to the State Assembly at the suitable time'. Only then will the people 'develop some enthusiasm' which would assure success in 'a plebiscite or referendum'. His advice was significant. 'In view of all these circumstances, I feel it will probably be undesirable to make any declaration of adhesion to the Indian Union at this stage' (ibid.). The reason is not hard to discern. The Sheikh's support was no guarantee of popular support for accession.

Yet, accession was a firm policy. The first *White Paper on Indian States*, published by the Government of India in July 1948, stated: 'Standstill Agreement, *the acceptance of which was made by the Government of India conditional on accession by the States concerned*, were also entered into between the Dominion Government and the acceding State' (*White Paper on Indian States* 1948: 15, paragraph 59). Which is why India did not sign a standstill agreement with Kashmir, while Pakistan, which had made no such condition, did so. The state went along with this since its links lay with Pakistan. India, on the other hand, preferred not to freeze the situation.

The relevant documents have not been published, thanks to India's illiberal archives policy. Researchers have to repair to the files in the British Library in London. We get a fair picture, though, from tell-tale footnotes at page 226 of *SWJN*, Vol. 19. They read thus:

> The Prime Minister of Jammu and Kashmir in a telegram on *12 August 1947* expressed his desire of concluding *a Standstill Agreement with India and Pakistan*. The subject matter of the Standstill Agreement which was offered to India and Pakistan was *different*. While an offer was made to Pakistan only in regard to the State's communication, supplies, post office and telegraphic arrangement, the telegram which was sent to the Government of India extended to many other subjects such as *external affairs, control of fares* [forces?] *and defence*. The Government of Pakistan accepted the offer in its telegram of 16 August 1947. The Government of India replied that some authorized minister should come for negotiating the Standstill Agreement. Before this could happen Kashmir was invaded.

Even if the raiders had not come Nehru would have pressed for the accession. This exchange must now be published in full.

But, we know enough from the published record to discern that moves were afoot to stage Kashmir's accession to India *in the guise of a standstill agreement*; hence, New Delhi's invitation to 'some authorized minister' of the Maharaja. Note that this was in August 1947, when Sheikh Abdullah was still in prison; the accord was to be made with the Maharaja.

V.K. Krishna Menon spilled the beans in the United Nations Security Council at its 762nd meeting on 23 January 1957. The press could hardly report all that he said in his marathon speeches. Hardly anyone consults the official records; they are, however, indispensable for a study of the history of the Kashmir dispute.

Inebriated by the exuberance of his own verbosity, this is what Krishna Menon disclosed authoritatively. To begin with, the text of the telegram from the Prime Minister of Jammu and Kashmir to the Government of India on 12 August 1947, which he read out, belies totally the gloss which both he and the editor of the *Selected Works of Jawaharlal Nehru* put on it. It offered continuance of 'existing arrangements' and no more. Menon's gloss was that these words 'comprised the use of Indian forces if there was internal rebellion in one of the States' (United Nations Security Council 1957: 71). This could not possibly be true, for the texts of the telegrams to India and Pakistan were 'identical', as Menon admitted, thus belying the claim of different offers made by the editor of *SWJN* in that footnote. Pakistan accepted the offer; India sought to enlarge on it by negotiations with the ruler in order to include 'foreign affairs', and almost succeeded.

Menon went on to reveal: 'There had been no interruption by invasion, it is normal to conclude that a standstill agreement *would have been concluded* and that standstill agreement would *have included external affairs, control of State forces and other matters which spring from the sovereignty of a country*' (ibid.: 72).

The standard Instrument of Accession covered defence, foreign affairs and communications. What New Delhi sought to do was conclude a seemingly innocuous 'Standstill Agreement' which was, in effect, an Instrument of Accession. Sheikh Abdullah's release was not made a precondition to the conclusion of the agreement with the Maharaja. Menon also admitted that there was a 'difference between the Standstill Agreement of India and the Standstill Agreement of Pakistan'. Alone among all the states, Kashmir was the only one that did not, and could not, sign a Standstill Agreement with India in August 1947. Even Hyderabad accepted, in the interim, the existing arrangements.

Menon's disclosure explains the reason for the unique exception: India was after an accession in the guise of a standstill agreement. *The standard Indian draft Standstill Agreement included 'foreign affairs'* (item 7 in the Schedule) – a virtual accession (*White Paper on Indian States* 1948: 54). No such concession was made in the offer in Kashmir's identical telegrams to both countries. No state can possibly confer on two states, the authority over its 'external affairs'. Far more truthful is the statement made in the *White Paper on Indian States*, published in July 1948: the Government of India had made acceptance of the Standstill Agreement 'conditional on accession'. Since Kashmir would not, perhaps because it could not, sign the Instrument of Accession, the same result was planned to be achieved by a Standstill Agreement. It would have barred any accession to Pakistan and a plebiscite as well.

Clearly, Kashmir urgently *needed* a Standstill Agreement with Pakistan, given the existing situation. That it did not need one with India and could do without it for days, shows that the 'geographical factor' was heavily in Pakistan's favour. Details such as these were hardly relevant in 1957. It is doubtful whether they were appreciated by Menon's audience. By 1957, the hard line, based on a frozen state of denial, had come to stay.

Before long Nehru repeatedly denied that he had ever sought to push Kashmir to accede to India. He said at the Annual Session of the National Conference in Srinagar on 24 September 1949: 'We told him [Abdullah] that it did not matter if the whole thing continued unresolved for some time but there was no reason why a decision should be taken in a hurry.' His letters to the Governor-General and Patel had not been published then. Nehru's speech reveals that in September–October it was the Sheikh who asked India for time to decide, and Nehru concurred with him (*SWJN*, Vol. 13: 233). He claimed, though: 'in spite of my intense desire I maintained silence, except occasionally to express my views very lightly'. He repeated the claim on 5 and 24 July 1952 (*SWJN*, Vol. 18: 425 and Vol. 19: 222, respectively).

Little noticed was his Curzonian assertion, twice, that India was entitled to intervene *regardless of any accession*. 'There is a certain inherent paramountcy in the Government of India which cannot lapse – an inherent paramountcy in the dominant State in India. . . . Paramountcy must exist.' Accession to India was 'the only alternative' to it (*SWJN*, Vol. 3: 218).

This claim was made at the AICC on 15 June 1947, before the partition. It was repeated in Parliament on 7 August 1952. The princes had to

> acknowledge the suzerainty, the sovereign domain of the Republic of India . . . even if Kashmir did not decide whether to go to Pakistan or India . . . that did not make Kashmir independent and our responsibility even then continued as the continuing entity if anything happened to Kashmir whether Kashmir acceded to India or not. (*SWJN*, Vol. 19: 302)

Accordingly, when Junagadh acceded to Pakistan on 15 August, an egregious folly on the part of both, and Pakistan announced its acceptance on 13 September, the Indian Cabinet decided that 'military action was the only answer' (Hodson 1985: 431).

Mountbatten persuaded against it, but equally effective methods were adopted. India nearly went to war with Pakistan; first on Junagadh only a month after the partition, and next on Kashmir, in December 1947. In September, the only issue was when and how to move in. Governor-General Mountbatten, reported to the King: 'A Cabinet meeting to consider the Junagadh situation summoned for 5 p.m. on 17 September. I was informed that the members of the Cabinet had, prior to this meeting, decided among themselves that military action was the only answer.' Mountbatten sent for Nehru and Patel, and persuaded them 'to take no decision which the world could interpret as putting India in the wrong and Pakistan in the right, and that all the resources of negotiation should first be exhausted' (ibid.: 431).

A second track was set afoot with Patel's blessings. V.P. Menon, Secretary to the Ministry of States, and N.M. Buch, the government's Regional Commissioner at Rajkot, along with military officers, discussed the situation with local politicians. U.N. Dhebar, later Congress President, reported to Patel on 21 September, setting out the agreed strategy: a proclamation denouncing the Nawab of Junagadh and appointing a provisional government. 'The manifesto or proclamation will be drawn upon American lines.' The headquarters of the government 'will be on Indian soil. As we acquire Junagadh territories, Government will shift there. We shall receive moral and material support. We will hold the meeting in course of the next week in Bombay. We shall send draft proclamation tomorrow' (Nandurkar, ed. 1981, Vol. 2: 75–76).

In December 1947 there was 'every possibility' of India invading West Pakistan. On 25 December Mountbatten wrote a 2000-word letter to Nehru (Hodson 1985: 461), after reading the Cabinet minutes of 20 December on 'The Military Situation in Kashmir'. Relief of the garrisons of the state's forces at Poonch was one thing, but not so a campaign to seize territory in West Kashmir. That 'would mean war between India and Pakistan', he warned, adding that it would not 'be confined to the subcontinent'.

Mountbatten continued:

> I agree with you that it would be morally unjustifiable to try by force of arms to inflict our will on a predominantly Muslim population and I know that you feel that the plebiscite will ultimately settle the issue. But in the meanwhile how can we escape the charge of *using military force against people who do not want to link their fortune with India.*

With crass *impropriety* Mountbatten sent a copy of his letter, written as Governor-General of India, to the British government on 28 December, through its High Commission in New Delhi, while V.P. Menon kept him informed of the rifts in the Cabinet.

A crisis in the Cabinet erupted on 29 September, as Mountbatten recorded in his notes. Patel wanted military action and threatened to resign if it was not undertaken. By that time a Provisional Government of Junagadh (Arzi Hakumat), headed by Samaldas Gandhi, had been formed in Bombay. Mountbatten pleaded with Patel that:

> they should pin their hopes on the people's Provisional Government of Junagadh *which Mr Menon had so ably formed in Bombay under the leadership of Mr Gandhi's nephew, and which I understand had that day arrived at Rajkot in a beflagged special train.* . . . it was pointed out that funds, arms and volunteers were not likely to be lacking to help this rising in Junagadh.
>
> I urged the Prime Minister to inform the Prime Minister of Pakistan of the impending movement of these forces to Kathiawar and to explain that there was no aggressive intention in them. I also urged him to make a Statement of Policy that in cases of States whose accession was disputed by the people or who had not yet acceded, the Dominion of India would accept a clear indication of the will of the people. I pointed out that this clearly applied in particular to States where the great majority of the population was of the opposite community to the ruler, his Government, Police and Army. I told him that I thought such a declaration would help me in my negotiations with Hyderabad. But Pandit Nehru (revealing his well known emotional streak concerning Kashmir) said that he could not bring himself to frame a Statement of Policy in this form, since it might be taken to indicate that they were trying to discourage Kashmir from joining India. He told me that with the dismissal of the late Prime Minister of Kashmir, Pandit Kak, and the release of the previous day (28 September) of his friend Sheikh Abdullah, the leader of the Nationalist Party, there was every indication that Kashmir wanted to accede to India.
>
> I begged him not to consider accepting their accession unless it followed a really fair plebiscite referendum; for *I prophesied that there would be nothing but trouble in Kashmir* and incidentally the Dominion of India if we did a sort of Junagadh with Kashmir on Pakistan. (*Jinnah Papers* 1993, Vol. VIII: 313–14)

V.P. Menon, who drummed up that government 'ably' as Mountbatten noted, acted at Patel's behest. On 16 November, Samaldas Gandhi acknowledged Patel's help. Replying to an address presented to him in Junagadh in appreciation of his services, he said: 'All the honour goes to Sardar Patel who was kind enough to give me every possible guidance and cooperation. If there had been no Sardar Patel we could not have met today and could not have achieved such a brilliant success.'

In an article in *The Statesman* of 21 September 1997, Admiral Satyindra Singh recounted in detail 'the help of Indian Army and Navy'. These actions were undertaken *well before the tribal raid from Pakistan into Kashmir*. Samaldas and company's train journey from Bombay was well publicized and drew from a lawyer of high distinction a censure based strictly on the law, in a letter to *The Times of India* of 30 October 1947. Sir Chimanlal Setalvad wrote another on 3 November, in retort to Nehru's argument that Pakistan either connived at the tribal raid or was powerless to prevent it.

The Provisional Government of Junagadh's declaration of its formation was drafted by an eminent lawyer, K.M. Munshi, doubtless with the support if not at the instance of his mentor, Patel. A paragraph in the document read:

> And whereas the Dominion of Pakistan has accepted the said Instrument of Accession in disregard of such declared wishes and in defiance of all natural ties which bind the people of Junagadh (82% of whom are non-Muslims) to the people of Kathiawar and to the Dominion of India and in breach of the understanding on the basis of which certain parts of India were allowed to secede and form into a separate State of Pakistan; namely that only contiguous areas predominantly inhabited by Muslim were to be included into the Dominion of Pakistan with the free and willing consent of the people inhabiting those areas. (Munshi 1965: 68)

A letter by the Dewan of Junagadh, Sir Shah Nawaz Bhutto, to N.M. Buch, Regional Commissioner of Saurashtra, mentions his talks with Samaldas for surrender as early as on 1 October (vide Documents 1 to 3 in this volume).

What is more to the point, the terms India proposed to Pakistan on Junagadh were ones it would never have countenanced on Kashmir: a plebiscite 'under the joint supervision of the Dominion of India and Junagadh' (12 September), and 'reversion of Junagadh to the "*status quo*" preceding the accession of Junagadh to Pakistan'. (See my essay, 'The Kashmir Question', reproduced in Volume II of this book.)

Thus, both India and Pakistan adopted an inconsistent position on the sanctity of the rulers' Instrument of Accession; both resorted to the use of force and dissimulation. The tribal raid wrecked Hari Singh's ambitions completely. He would, like the Nizam of Hyderabad, bow readily before the British rulers of India and their Residents in the states. But, like the Nizam again, he nursed ambitions of sovereign monarchy. There was no assurance that would have accepted an Indian centre even if India had not been partitioned. The British Resident in Srinagar, Lieutenant-Colonel W.F. Webb, reported to the Political Department in New Delhi on 14 November 1946: 'I am inclined to think that the Maharaja and Kak are seriously considering the possibility of Kashmir not joining the Union if it is formed', in view of the 'the antagonism likely to be displayed by a Congress Central Government towards Kashmiris' (*The Transfer of Power 1942–47*, Vol. IX: 71).

Kak, arrogant towards Kashmiris, meekly sought the 'preliminary reaction of the Political Department' to a note he had penned. Its main theme was interference by Indians. British intervention he could live with. They gave him the throne after all.

> The State naturally does not feel happy about the future and unless satisfactory assurances are forthcoming that interference in its internal affairs in any shape or form will in future not to be made, may even decide to decline to join the Indian Union should it materialize. If such a contingency does arise, what would be the nature of this State's relations with the Crown be? Would necessary wherewithal be supplied to maintain the integrity of the State for such time as it may be able to stand on its own feet? (Ibid.)

The British could not have agreed to such links with the rulers they had propped up after they had served their imperial ends without incurring the lasting hostility of India, a greater interest. The note exposed fault lines more than one: between Nehru, who wanted replacement of Kak by the Sheikh, and, as we shall see, between Abdullah and his people. Mountbatten's meeting with Kak in Srinagar on 22 June is shrouded in mystery. Kak's paper (deposited in the British Library in London) has him all but counsel accession to Pakistan. Mountbatten's record of the interview tilts in that direction: decide

> in consideration of the factors of geography and probable attitude of the Congress and the Muslim League respectively on Kashmir. If Kashmir joined the Pakistan Constituent Assembly, presumably Mr Jinnah would protect them against pressure from the Congress. If they joined the Hindustan [*sic.*] Assembly, it would be inevitable that they should be treated with consideration by Hindustan. (*The Transfer of Power 1942–47*, Vol. XI)

Kak refused to commit himself:

> Pandit Kak replied that he was grateful for what His Excellency [H.E.] had said. His Highness's [H.H.] decision was that at present he could not commit himself. Clearly he must see what the set up was to be *in Pakistan*, and *until that was clear he would have to maintain his present non-committal position.* H.H. realized the various factors involved, but in any case was not now in any way alarmed by Pandit Nehru or disturbed by his threats. H.E. pointed out that Pandit Nehru felt very strongly about Kashmir, and it would be

> extremely difficult for him [H.E.] to do anything *to protect Kashmir* after the 15th August, when Pandit Nehru would become Prime Minister of Hindu India, and H.E. even if he remained, would become only a constitutional Governor General. The only protection for Kashmir after the 15 August was to join one or other of the Constituent Assemblies. (Ibid.: 555)

The entire trend was towards accession to Pakistan before India became independent with Nehru as its Prime Minister.

Two days before independence the British Resident at Kashmir reported by wire to the Viceroy's Principal Secretary, Sir George Abell. It is a most revealing document. Kak asked for permission to retire as he felt he had lost the confidence of the ruler, who, he found, had been corresponding with the Congress through other channels.

> I believe break came because of indecision of His Highness to make up his mind either to join one or other Dominion, or in peculiar circumstances for Kashmir to come into the open and ask for agreements with both. His Highness, Dogras and Hindu communities incline towards India but bulk of population are Muslim and if consulted would probably favour Pakistan especially Mirpur, Poonch and Muzaffarabad area. Kak although Hindu clearly saw implication and felt that if Kashmir joined either Dominion especially India it would mean serious trouble. . . . I saw new Prime Minister [General Janak Singh] yesterday, and he is aware of the situation and although inclining towards India as a Hindu, *realizes bulk of Muslims will not accept decision.* He therefore wishes for agreement for both. Kashmir Government issued Statement last night that they welcome Standstill agreements pending further negotiation with both Dominions. From this Press note it is apparent that they are likely to join neither Dominion at present. (*The Transfer of Power 1942–47*, Vol. XII: 696)

On the eve of independence, the Maharaja sought to resolve his dilemma by holding a referendum, as Mountbatten reported to London: 'The Maharaja has at last decided to sack his Dewan, Kak. He now talks of holding a referendum to decide whether to join Pakistan or India, provided that the Boundary Commission give him land communication between Kashmir and India' (ibid.: 769).

Interestingly, the first cry for secession was also heard from Hari Singh. In a letter to Patel on 31 January 1948, he warned:

> Sometimes I feel that I should withdraw the accession that I have made to the Indian Union. The Union only provisionally accepted the accession and if the Union cannot recover back our territory then there is no point in sticking to the accession of the State to the Indian Union. (Das 1974: 162)

His appreciation of the legal position was sound. The *White Paper on Jammu and Kashmir* published by the Government of India shortly after the accession said: 'in accepting the accession, the Government of India made it clear that they would regard it as *purely provisional* until such time as the will of the people of the State could be ascertained' (*White Paper on Jammu and Kashmir* 1948: 43).

In a letter to the Prime Minister of Pakistan, Liaquat Ali Khan, on 31 October 1947, Nehru assured him that Kashmir's accession to India 'was accepted *on the condition* that as soon as the invader has been driven from Kashmir soil, and law and order restored, the people of Kashmir would decide the question of accession. It is open to them to accede to either Dominion then' (ibid.: 51). This, incidentally, puts paid to the excuse he later trotted out, that Pakistan's aggression robbed her of a locus standi in the dispute or ruled out plebiscite.

Nehru's broadcast on 2 November 1947 repeated the words 'we made a condition', reiterated the basic policy of the people's decision on accession, and said, 'it was in accordance with this policy that *we added a proviso* to the Instrument of Accession of Kashmir' (ibid.: 41). In law, it matters not one bit whether a condition, stipulation or proviso is added in the principal document, or in a related, collateral document executed simultaneously. A letter granting the lessee right of way over the lessor's grounds to the leased land has the same force in law as the indenture of lease itself.

V.P. Menon revealed: 'Some rulers signed the Instrument of Accession and forwarded it with covering letters which laid down conditions subject to which the accession had been signed. They were told that the execution of the Instrument of Accession must be unconditional and subsequently complied' (Menon 1956: 115). Uniquely, on Kashmir the Governor-General himself imposed a precondition or proviso by his letter of 27 October 1947, written simultaneously with his acceptance of the Instrument of Accession. It set out the basic policy of popular arbitrament, and reiterated that 'as soon as law and order have been restored in Kashmir and her soil cleared of the invader, the question of the State's accession should be *settled* by a reference to the people' (*White Paper on Jammu and Kashmir* 1948: 47). The word 'settled' was aptly used apropos a disputed accession.

India's interim constitution then in force was the Government of India Act, 1935 as adapted by the Governor-General under Section 8(2) of the Indian Independence Act, 1947. Section 6 of the Government of India Act, 1935 did *not* prescribe any particular form of the Instrument of Accession. V.P. Menon simply borrowed the draft of 1935 for use in 1947. All that was required was a written offer to accede and its acceptance. So long as the terms specified in Section 6 were accepted, the accession, even if written on a scrap of paper, was valid. Section 6 did not rule out additional terms beyond the minimal it prescribed, still less any condition or proviso.

The Constituent Assembly debates on Article 370 of the Constitution; the Indo–Pak Agreement on plebiscite, embodied in the mutually agreed Resolutions of the United Nations Commission for India and Pakistan

(UNCIP) on 13 August 1948 and 6 January 1949; not to forget the proviso to Article 253 of the Constitution of India – all establish the provisional, conditional character of Kashmir's accession. The Government of India's definitive *White Paper on Indian States*, published in 1950 *after* the Constitution had come into force, said that the accession of Kashmir 'is subject to confirmation by the people of the State'. It added: 'This, however, does not detract from the legal fact of accession.' The fallacy springs from a confusion. The accession is legal and valid, but it is 'provisional' and 'conditional' with 'a proviso' added to it. It was open to cancellation if the plebiscite went against India, as Nehru declared in the Rajya Sabha on 5 August 1952: 'we would cancel it because we have given our word, but that did not lessen in any degree the total hundred per cent validity of the accession' (*SWJN*, Vol. 19: 271).

Nehru's initial reaction to the tribal raid moved him to look with favour on independence for the state, impliedly as part of an accord with Pakistan. However, a provisional accession was an immediate necessity. The minutes of the meeting of the Defence Committee of the Cabinet, held on 26 October 1947, recorded:

> It was agreed that when the accession was accepted this should be subject to the proviso that a plebiscite would be held in Kashmir when the law and order situation allowed this. The Governor-General suggested that this plebiscite should be on three questions – to join India – to join Pakistan – or to remain independent. He also suggested that before a plebiscite was held, the future defence of Kashmir might be discussed in the Joint Defence Council. The Prime Minister said the Government of India would not mind Kashmir remaining an independent country under India's sphere of influence. (Quoted in Jha 2003: 212)

The 'proviso' was thus added with full deliberation.

The Defence Committee's direction was explicit.

> The Committee directed the Ministry of States to prepare: (a) an Instrument of Accession to India by the Maharaja of Jammu of Kashmir; (b) a letter from the Government of India to the Maharaja, stating the *temporary* acceptance of this Instrument (with a view to assistance being rendered towards the restoration of law and order), but with the *proviso* that the will of the people of Kashmir on the question of final accession would be ascertained when conditions allowed this; (c) a Statement on the lines of (b), for issue to the Press. (Ibid.: 213)

Two days later, on 28 October, Nehru wrote to his sister Vijayalakshmi Pandit, then leader of the Indian delegation to the United Nations, without the 'sphere of influence' qualification: 'For my part, I do not mind if Kashmir becomes more or less independent, but it would have been a cruel blow if it had become just an exploited part of Pakistan' (*Vijayalakshmi Pandit*

Papers). One is reminded of the Persian saying, '*Na ba hubbe imam, Valey be zidde yazid*' ('Not for the love of Imam Hussain, but out of hatred for his assassin Yazid'). It is sad to recall how much antipathy towards Pakistan marked Nehru's policies even in those initial years. In a note to Patel on 18 November 1950, he wrote: 'the fact remains that our major possible enemy is Pakistan' (Das 1974: 344).

Kashmir's Prime Minister, Janak Singh's fears on 13 August 1947 that 'the bulk of Muslims will not accept [a] decision to accede' to India was shared by N. Gopalaswamy Ayyanger, Minister without Portfolio. He opined on 26 October, despite the tribal raid, that 'immediate accession might create further opposition' (Jha 2003: 212). This is why Nehru had advised Mahajan on 21 October not to 'make any declaration of adhesion to the Indian Union at this stage' (*SWJN*, Vol. 4: 274).

During the talks between V.P. Menon and Chaudhri Mohammad Ali in November 1947, the latter asked whether a plebiscite was really called for as Kashmir had a Muslim majority. Menon replied that 'he entirely agreed that Kashmir would go to Pakistan', but he 'emphasized in view of what has passed, a formal [*sic*] plebiscite was essential.' That V.P. Menon was honest in his remarks to Mohammad Ali is borne out by a record of his discussions in the same month with different interlocutors. On 3 November 1947 he met in his office in New Delhi, a delegation from Hyderabad led by the Nizam's Minister, Nawab Moin Nawaz Jung. The minutes read:

> MR MENON opened the discussions by making a reference to the Kashmir problem. He stated that the settled policy of the Government of India was that there should not be any further disintegration of the country after the partition and the States falling within the Dominion of India should join the Indian Union and those adjoining Pakistan should go with that Dominion. MR MENON further stated that the Government of India scrupulously followed this policy, but the Pakistan Government accepted the accession of Junagadh and this started the situation. As a matter of fact he believed that Kashmir should have joined the Pakistan Union and the Government of India never desired the accession of Kashmir to the Union of India. But it was impossible for the Government of Iniia to sit silently when Kashmir and Jammu were being raided and ruined by marauders and freebooters. In these circumstances, when the Maharaja applied for accession, Government of India readily agreed to the request, but as soon as peace was restored, they would leave Kashmir and ask the inhabitants to decide for themselves their future. (*Constitutional Discussions*, Vol 2: 193)

At another meeting with representatives of the Nizam's government, comprising Prime Minister Laik Ali, Sir Walter Monckton, K.C. and others, Menon said:

> If a plebiscite was considered a suitable long term solution, it had to be real-

> ized that, during the interval, that must necessarily elapse before a plebiscite scould be held, the present conditions cannot be allowed to continue. . . .
>
> The Government of India cannot subscribe to the view expressed by the delegation that the establishment of responsible government is purely an internal matter. In the ultimate analysis, sovereignty can only vest in the people and situated as Hyderabad was and the Ruler was a Muslim, the government of India cannot disclaim all interest in this matter. During the interim period, the Government should be reconstituted so as to reflect the composition of the population. (*White Paper on Hyderabad*, 1948: 50)

Menon was consistent in following the principle of popular opinion. However, Nehru's insistence on the continuation of Sheikh Abdullah's government in power during a plebiscite in Kashmir was directly opposite to his government's stand on an interim government in Hyderabad pending a plebiscite there.

Menon had seen through the game. In retirement, free from the constraints of the service, he unburdened himself to his predecessor as Reforms Commissioner, H.V. Hodson. In a tape-recorded interview to Hodson at his home in Bangalore in September 1964, Menon fully justified India's policy on Hyderabad and also on Kashmir; but, after the tribal raid in October 1947. He however, honestly and bluntly said: 'As for plebiscite, we were absolutely, absolutely dishonest' (quoted in Ahmad, ed. 1992: lxv).

An agreement was drafted, with Lord Ismay representing Mountbatten (Lamb 1994: 149). This accord was wrecked by both Nehru and Jinnah. The UNCIP's Resolution of 13 August 1948, which Nehru accepted, was based on this accord. Pakistan accepted the Resolution conditionally.

As well as the communal factor, two recent events had hardened feelings: the revolt against the Maharaja in Poonch and Hari Singh's responsibility for the massacre of Muslims in Jammu. Professor R.J. Moore writes:

> During the Second World War Kashmir had sent over 70,000 men to the Indian Army, some 60,000 of them were Muslims and they mostly returned to farm in Poonch or Mirpur, often retaining their arms. In late July they were called upon to deposit their arms with the police and the Maharaja strengthened his garrisons there with Sikhs and Hindu troops. The no-tax revolt that ensued was crushed ruthlessly. Arms were smuggled in from the village 'factories' of the frontier. In the second week of October they rose again and drove the State forces from the Poonch and Mirpur districts, save for Poonch town. Beginning somewhat later than the original revolt in Poonch, communal disturbances flared in Jammu. Sikh and Hindu refugees from west Punjab were arriving in force, apparently encouraged by the Dogra Governor, who, together with the militant RSSS, seems to have entertained ideas of establishing a non-Muslim-majority area. Muslims were driven from their villages and slaughtered en route to Pakistan. (Moore 1987: 48)

Sheikh Abdullah was later to imprison the Governor and to accuse the Maharaja for his part in the continuing massacre:

> As he moved over the tunnel [from Srinagar to Jammu] there was enacted in every village and town through which he passed an orgy of loot and murder of Muslims. In Jammu, the killing of Muslims all over the province continued unabated for weeks under his very nose, the town having been converted into a veritable hell. Innocent children and girls were not spared and the display of sadism to which they were subjected would render insignificant anything that happened on the two sides of the divided Punjab in its hour of madness. All this staggering tragedy on such a vast scale is alleged to have been accomplished by participation of high-ranking Hindu officials and Dogra military in Jammu as well as His Highness' own trusted relations and his then Prime Minister and Deputy Prime Minister. A widespread belief, certainly not without basis, was that the killing was carried on in pursuance of an organized plan of genocide under which free distribution of arms and ammunition was made to communalist organization like RSS through Hindu officials, high and low. (Letter to Patel, in Das 1974: 237)

Ian Stephens, editor of *The Statesman*, wrote that in autumn 1947 the 500,000 Muslims of Jammu 'were practically eliminated'; 200,000 of them 'just disappeared' (Stephens 1963: 200).

Putting aside his strong dislike for the man, Nehru pleaded with Hari Singh on 1 December 1947:

> If there is going to be a plebiscite, then obviously we have work in such away as to gain the goodwill of the majority of the population of the State, which means chiefly the Muslims. The policy recently pursued in Jammu province has alienated the Muslims there very greatly and has created a great deal of ill-feeling in certain parts of the country. . . . From our point of view, that is India's, it is of the most vital importance that Kashmir should remain within the Indian Union. . . . It cannot be done ultimately except through the goodwill of the mass of the population. Even if military forces held Kashmir for a while, a later consequence might be strong reaction against this. Essentially, therefore, this is a problem of psychological approach to the mass of the people and of making them feel that they will be benefited by being within the Indian Union. If the average Muslim feels that he has no safe or secure place in the union, then obviously he will look elsewhere. (Das 1974: 103)

Sheikh Abdullah also pleaded with Hari Singh when they met on 5 August 1948. Apparently sensing that he had not been able to swing the popular mood in favour of accession, he reminded the ruler angrily: 'I have got to turn the minds of Muslims of the State from Pakistan to the Indian Dominion' (ibid.: 215).

Nehru could have been in no doubt as to the state of popular feeling in Kashmir. His daughter Indira Gandhi had informed him in a letter from

Srinagar a few months earlier, on 14 May 1948: 'They say that only Sheikh Saheb is confident of winning the plebiscite.' These suspension marks are in the original. The editor or her advisers evidently preferred circumspection to candour (Gandhi, ed. 2005: 517).

Before long the Sheikh also lost hope. President Rajendra Prasad repeated to Nehru, in a letter on 14 July 1953, that Vice-President 'Radhakrishnan, on his return from a visit to Kashmir, came and told me that even Sheikh Saheb thought that we would lose in a plebiscite' (Choudhary, ed. 1984, Vol. 16: 91). The message could not have come as a surprise to the Prime Minister and would only have hardened him in his resolve to do away with the inconvenient messenger, Sheikh Abdullah. Nehru himself was none too confident of success. He frankly told the British High Commissioner, Sir Archibald Nye, on 6 September 1949: 'The result of a free and impartial plebiscite, if one could be held, would be for the Poonch area to go to Pakistan and for the Jammu area to go to India, whilst it was doubtful which way the valley would vote' (*SWJN*, Vol. 13: 225).

The agitation by the Jan Sangh's ally, the Praja Parishad, in Jammu confirmed Abdullah's fears and Nehru's as well. Nehru bared his thought to his close friend B.C. Roy, Chief Minister of West Bengal, on 29 June 1953:

> They [the people in the Valley] have become frightened of the communal elements in Jammu and in India and their previous wish to be attached to India has weakened. Indeed, at the moment, all the hostile forces against us are dominant in Kashmir. . . . The position now is that if there was a plebiscite, a great majority of Muslims in Kashmir would go against us. In fact there has been some petty violence also. So, this movement of the Praja Parishad, which aims at a closer integration of Kashmir State with India, has had the opposite effect. It is true that so far as Jammu Province is concerned, it has demonstrated that a majority of Hindus there want closer integration. Nobody ever doubted that and, whatever happens, Jammu cannot leave India. There need be no apprehension about that. The whole difficulty has been about the Valley of Kashmir and we are on the point of losing it because of the Praja Parishad movement. Psychologically we have lost it and it will be difficult to get back to the older position. . . .
>
> In the ultimate analysis, we gain Kashmir if we gain the goodwill of the people there. We cannot keep it at the point of the bayonet if it is clear that the people do not want us. For the first time public cries are raised in Kashmir that the Indian Army should get out. . . .
>
> It is true that if the Kashmir Government had implemented the rest of the provisions of our agreement with them, this would have helped considerably. But they were not given much of a chance. They started implementing it with the change in the Headship of the State. They would have followed with other provisions. But the first change itself was immediately followed by this agitation in Jammu and later outside. A new situation was thus created with which

> we have been struggling all this time and it become progressively more difficult to take any step in Kashmir of the kind we desired.
>
> It is easy to criticize Shaikh Abdullah and I think that he has acted unwisely in many matters during the past few months. But the point is that we have continuously lost ground there and have fought what might be called a rearguard action in regard to the main problem of the Kashmir State. All this because of this continuing Praja Parishad agitation, which had a cumulative effect on the people of the Kashmir Valley. . . . During the past few months, I have had no greater trouble or burden than this feeling of our losing grip in Kashmir. (*SWJN*, Vol. 22: 204–05)

He panicked and put in prison the only man who could have helped him, Abdullah, who, on Nehru's own admission, was not really responsible for the situation.

Instead, he decided to rely on stooges like Bakshi Ghulam Mohammad and G.M. Sadiq. The situation did not improve. It deteriorated and Nehru went into a prolonged self-induced state of denial, taking the country with him. The media and academia, no less than the political class, accepted the myths he had spread sedulously and for long.

A devoted and transparently sincere friend's warning was brushed aside. Jayaprakash Narayan's letter to Nehru on 1 May 1956 warned:

> From all the information I have, 95 per cent of Kashmir Muslims do not wish to be or remain Indian citizen. I doubt therefore the wisdom of trying to 'keep' people by force where they do not wish to stay. This cannot but have serious long-term political consequences, though immediately it may suit policy and please public opinion. From the point of view of the desirability of establishing a peaceful social order, it cannot but prove disastrous. I do earnestly wish that this question be considered more from a human; rather than a nationalist, point of view. (Prasad, ed. 1964, Vol. 7: 115)

But then, on Kashmir, Nehru's democratic credentials yielded to the claims of a short-sighted nationalism. In this he was not alone. Indira Gandhi's recipe for removing the Kashmiris' alienation won ready acceptance and that continues to this day in various forms of escapism. 'Personally,' she assured her father, 'I feel that all the political talk will count for nothing if the economic situation can be dealt with. Because after all the people are concerned with only (one) thing – they want to sell their goods and to have food and salt.' For her, they had no feelings, no opinions and no soul – a view no different from that of the Collector in colonial times. She had a sure and simple remedy, the like of which we hear still: 'But most important of all – and I feel the only thing that can save Kashmir for India and the Kashmiris – will be an influx of visitors this summer, preferably from Bombay and Ahmedabad, since those are ones (who) buy most' (Gandhi, ed. 2005: 517–18).

Her socialist father shared her wise prescription. He wrote to the Sheikh from Sonamarg on 25 August 1952:

> It must be remembered that the people of the Kashmir Valley and round about, though highly gifted in many ways – in intelligence, in artisanship, etc. – are not what are called a virile people. They are soft and addicted to easy being. . . . The common people are primarily interested in a few things – an honest administration and cheap and honest food. (*SWJN*, Vol. 19: 328–29)

It is beyond the purview of this essay to speculate whether Nehru's assessment of people in other parts of India was the same as he had for the people of Kashmir. What cannot be gainsaid is that no Kashmiri would utter those words for his own people. Nehru's outlook, moulded in the political climate of Uttar Pradesh, was exposed also to the Prime Minister of Pakistan, Mohammad Ali Bogra, when they met in New Delhi on 17 August 1953: 'Most people, of course, were hardly political and only cared for their economic betterment' (*SWJN*, Vol. 23: 332).

This was the big divide between Nehru and Abdullah, referred to earlier. Abdullah derived his power from the people. If their views on accession to India continued to diverge, without any hope of reconciliation, he could hardly act as India's stooge and lose everything. Nehru, in contrast, was happy with the façade of a 'popular' regime headed by the Sheikh, regardless of the depth or quality of its popular support.

One of the foremost scholars on princely India, Professor Ian Copland, wrote a definitive essay on the subject, titled 'The Abdullah Factor: Kashmiri Muslims and the Crisis of 1947' (Low, ed. 1991: 219–54). It was based on archival material including reports by British Residents at Srinagar in 1947. Apparently sensing the Maharaja's attitude, when the Muslim Conference leaders met Jinnah in New Delhi on 11 July 1947 to seek his advice, 'they were told to press for an independent Kashmir with the Maharaja as a constitutional figurehead'. Not till 29 July – sixteen days before the transfer of power – did the League give any public indication that it expected, or wanted, the state to join Pakistan (ibid.: 223).

As compared to the Congress, the Muslim League interfered little in Kashmir, presumably 'because of possible repercussion in Hyderabad', as noted by Francis Wylie of the Political Department in 1943. Despite this, 'many Kashmiri Muslims fully expected to be incorporated in Pakistan when it was formed' (ibid.: 229).

Unquestionably, in 1947, Abdullah's National Conference (NC) and not the Muslim Conference was 'the dominant political party in Kashmir'. But the intentions of the party leaders in 1947 were obscure and their representative credentials questionable. Many NC followers seem to have divided their allegiance, acknowledging Abdullah as their leader 'up to Kohala' – that is, locally – and Jinnah, beyond. Photographs of Abdullah and Jinnah hung side by side in the homes of supporters of the National Congress.

Copland sums up:

> Thus, despite its past connections with the Congress and Abdullah's friendship with the Indian Prime Minister, the NC's policy on accession remained, as late as September 1947, undecided. Indeed an English journalist who talked to Abdullah shortly after his release formed the impression that he 'was now in favour of Kashmir joining Pakistan', and for a while this seems to have been the preferred option of other party members as well – among them Begum Abdullah. At any rate, the NC took the idea seriously enough to hold protracted talks with a Punjabi Muslim League deputation led by Mian Iftikhar-ud-din and to send two of its senior WC [Working Committee] members, G.M. Sadiq and Bakshi Ghulam Mohammad, to Lahore to sound out the Pakistan Government on terms of accession. Moreover, though these particular negotiations fell through [largely as a result of the invasion of 21 October], the lines to Karachi and Muzaffarabad were never completely severed, and in 1953 Abdullah would be arrested and imprisoned by his former Congress friends for what were described as treasonous activities across the border.
>
> So what, then, did Sheikh Abdullah really want? Probably, like the MC [Muslim Conference] leaders, his first preference was for independence, qualified, perhaps, by a form of 'free association' with India and Pakistan. As he told Michael Davidson of the London Observer Foreign News Service in May 1949, 'independence would be best', for 'accession to either side cannot bring peace. We want to live in friendship with the Dominions.' (Ibid.: 241)

In his last report to the Government of India (on 13 August 1947), 'the British Resident advised that the bulk of the population, if consulted, would probably favour Pakistan, especially [those living in the] Mirpur, Poonch and Muzaffarabad areas (ibid.: 243).

Major W.P. Cranston, on the staff of the British High Commission in New Delhi, stayed in Srinagar from 10 to 14 October 1947 and wrote a report on 'The political situation in Kashmir' on 18 October, giving his assessment. He wrote:

> The future, however, is very uncertain and depends entirely on when the Maharaja makes his announcement as to whether Kashmir should remain independent or accede to either of the two Dominions. So far His Highness had given no indication whatsoever of his intentions but the general impression was that he would make an announcement either when he went to Jammu early in November or if and when he should go to Bombay a little later, and it was thought probable that he would then declare the accession of Kashmir State to the Dominion of India. This would cause an immediate reaction throughout the State by the Muslim population which numbers about 80 to 90 per cent and which is strongly opposed to any union with the Indian Government. If this happened it is also most probable that the tribes on the north and north western borders of Kashmir would invade the State. I was informed that at

> that time 20,000 Hazara tribesmen, 15,000 from Chitral and 10,000 from Hunza States were ready to invade Kashmir as soon as they considered the Maharaja was declaring for accession to India. The Mehtar of Chitral and the Nawab of Dhir have formally warned the Maharaja that if he accedes to the Indian Union they will invade his State. Sheikh Abdullah, the Muslim nationalist leader, is said to have favoured Kashmir remaining as an independent State. He is, however, believed to have made an agreement with the Maharaja that if the Maharaja should accede to the Indian Union he would support him. In such an event, however, it is extremely doubtful whether Sheikh Abdullah's Muslim followers would continue to support him. It is possible that if the Maharaja should announce his intention of acceding to the Indian Union whilst he is in Jammu, the State of Jammu which contains many Dogras would support him and join the Indian Union, but the remainder of Kashmir State would break away and join Pakistan. (Carter 2011: 523)

An invaluable work by a scholar of distinction. It bears mention that the postal service in Kashmir was run by Pakistan till the disruption in October 1947.

The state's ruler, Hari Singh, explained his calculations before the accession in a letter to President Rajendra Prasad in August 1952. It confirmed the well-known fact that both Nehru and Patel pressed him to accede to India. What was new was his disclosure that Mountbatten advised him to accede to Pakistan, and his confirmation that his own preference was for independence and so was Sheikh Abdullah's. Had he enrolled him as a partner in this, they might have pulled it off. That was beyond him. The tribal raid forced an uneasy partnership. The letter said:

> Then came the development of 1947 and the question of accession. The position of my State was very different, situated as it was in contiguity to India and Pakistan as also to Afghanistan, Tibet and Russia. The situation therefore required to be dealt with more tact and foresight than in the case of other states. Mahatma Gandhi and the Prime Minister were anxious that I should not make a declaration of Independence and the Prime Minister was anxious to secure the release from prison of Sheikh Abdullah. Having regard to what my Government had done when the Prime Minister visited the State in 1946, Lord Mountbatten chose to visit the State in June 1947 and we had several talks. Lord Mountbatten then urged me and my Prime Minister, Kak, not to make any declaration of Independence but to find out in one way or another, the will of the people of Kashmir as soon as possible and to announce our intention by the 14 August to send representatives accordingly to one Constituent assembly or the other. Lord Mountbatten further told us that the newly created States Department was prepared to give an assurance that if Kashmir went to Pakistan, it would not be regarded as an unfriendly act by the Government of India. Lord Mountbatten stressed the dangerous situation in which Kashmir would find itself if it lacked the support of one of the two Dominions

> by the date of the transfer of power. The impression which I gathered from my talks with Lord Mountbatten who explained the situation with plans and maps was that, in his opinion, it was advisable for me to accede to Pakistan.
> My difficulties were as follows:
>
> 1. The people of the State were divided in several groups, each group having its own idea about accession;
>
> 2. The Border Feudatory Territories such as Hunza, Nagar and Chitral and the District of Gilgit, where British influence was supreme were definitely for accession to Pakistan and pressing me to accede to Pakistan without delay and threatening me with dire consequences if I did not act according to their suggestion;
>
> 3. The Muslim population of the State was also divided into groups with divergent views. Muslims from parts of Jammu such as, Mirpur, Poonch, Muzaffarabad were for accession to Pakistan because of Pakistan propaganda inside the State. Muslims of Kashmir and some Muslims of Jammu who were led by Sheikh Abdullah and the leaders of the National Conference *did not want the question of accession to be decided at that stage but wanted me to part with power in their favour so that they could decide the question independently of me*. They made no secret of their views and obstructed me in deciding the question of accession *instead of helping me to accede to India*;
>
> 4. Hindus of Jammu and all the people of Ladakh were for affiliation with or accession to India;
>
> 5. A portion of the population of Kashmir was also for accession to Pakistan.
>
> Thus, there was a sharp division of opinion. The partition aggravated the situation and unhinged, and unbalanced the minds of the people with the result that the people of the State were not in a position to give any considered opinion if I chose to consult them. (Singh 2011: 297–99)

Hugh Stephenson, Deputy High Commissioner in Lahore – an old India hand, like most others – reported to his chief on 13 September:

> The Maharaja and Hindu ruling class would join India if they dared but in the present circumstances that will mean revolution. The State Army cannot possibly hold the whole border and could not meet the Muslim infiltration which would be inevitable if revolution occurred. In the meanwhile every effort is being made to push on the new road into India which might be ready for military traffic in three months' time. The alternatives are for Kashmir to join India, which the Ruler wants but which can only be accomplished by a *coup d'etat*, Indian troops being rushed to Kashmir and trusting to disorganization in Pakistan. Or, if that doesn't happen, Kashmir will fall eventually like a ripe plum to Pakistan.
>
> The impression is that the Maharaja and his advisers, who are completely undecided, will not have the courage to face a *coup d'etat* even if India agreed,

> which I think unlikely. In the meanwhile a decision will be put off as long as possible. (Carter 2011, Vol. 1: 214)

Pakistan's tribal raid launched on 22 October compelled a decision. It was an act of criminal folly.

Opinions differed even in 1947. What is clear beyond doubt is that Sheikh Abdullah could not be 'the sole spokesman' of Kashmiris on the future status of Kashmir. His support by no means represented 'the popular will', as Nehru conveniently argued. The Sheikh himself knew that. A plebiscite, the only sure and fair test, would have split his party leaders, the cadre and also his extended family. He did his best to avert the catastrophe. Till 1953 his interest in avoiding a plebiscite coincided with Nehru's. Even in 1953, it would seem that his heart was set on a compromise with Pakistan rather than accession to it where he had no place. He knew the fate of Khan Abdul Ghaffar Khan. Beneath Abdullah's changing attitudes towards Jinnah lay the realities of a fragmented party.

No one has explained his compulsions better than a devoted Kashmiri, Professor Chitralekha Zutshi, in her erudite work, *Languages of Belonging: Islam, Regional Identity and the Making of Kashmir* (2003). While the Muslim Conference 'reigned supreme in Poonch and Jammu in 1946 . . . the political loyalties of the Valley Kashmiris were divided in 1947' (Zutshi 2003: 298)

In April 1946 Abdullah proposed an all India federation in which the units would have the 'unfettered right to self-determination', and the option of joining or not joining the Indian Union (ibid.: 301). Zutshi agrees with Copland's assessment that 'even the National Conference followers in Srinagar accepted Jinnah's leadership beyond the Valley' (ibid.: 303). She notes that 'the Congress leadership, while expecting accession of Kashmir to India, was not willing to take any chances and had dispatched Acharya Kripalani [the Congress President] in May [1947] and Gandhi in August [1947] *to ensure Kashmir's accession to India*' (ibid.: 304).

In an article entitled 'Freedom before Accession', published in the party's organ, *Khidmat*, on 22 October 1947, the Sheikh urged India and Pakistan to come to terms with each other as two sovereign and independent states, and to try to evolve a common centre with defence, communication and foreign affairs – anything to rescue him from the dilemma. He was of course asking for the moon. What he sought was some modus vivendi. Other National Conference papers rejected both 'Indian Capitalists' and 'Pakistani Nawabs' (ibid.: 307).

The Sheikh's pro-Congress tilt was unmistakable. From Srinagar, on 4 October 1947, Dwarkanath Kachru assured Nehru: 'Sheikh Saheb and his associates have decided for the Indian Union. But this decision has not been announced yet and the impression is being given that so far the National Conference have taken no decision' (Das 1974: 54).

An explicit statement which Abdullah publicly made in New Delhi on 21 October was of a different tenor. He was reported by the Associated Press of India, ancestor of the Press Trust of India, as saying that:

> so far as Pakistan was concerned they were very keen on her accession. For, due to the strategic position that the State held, if the State joined the Indian Dominion, he thought Pakistan would be completely encircled.
>
> Explaining the difficulties with which the people were beset in making up their minds without responsible Government, Sheikh Abdullah said that the happening in certain States such as Patiala, Bharatpur, Kapurthala and elsewhere had naturally caused apprehension in the minds of the Muslims in Kashmir who formed the majority of the population. They were afraid that the States' accession to India portended danger to them. Similarly the Sikhs and Hindus of the States were apprehensive of Kashmir joining Pakistan.
>
> The Kashmir leader said that the problem could only be solved by the grant of complete responsible Government including the nationalization of the State Army which was now closed to the people of the Kashmir Valley.
>
> Sheikh Abdullah said that the present troubles in Poonch, a feudatory of Kashmir, were because of the unwise policy adopted by the State. The people of Poonch who suffered under their local ruler and again under the Kashmir durbar who was the overlord of the Poonch ruler, had started a people's movement for the redress of their grievances. It was not communal.
>
> The Kashmir State sent their troops and there was panic in Poonch. But most of the adult population of Poonch, he explained, were ex-servicemen in the Indian Army who had close connections with the people in Jhelum and Rawalpindi. They evacuated their women and children, crossed the frontier and returned with arms supplied to them by willing people. The present position was the Kashmir State forces were forced to withdraw in certain areas. Sheikh Abdullah deplored the course of events and suggested the only remedy was to trust the people and make them responsible for the governance of the States.

Kak's paper, deposited in the British Library in London, suggests that accession to India was farthest from his mind (see my article I.3, reproduced in Volume II of this book). To Phillips Talbot, a young American journalist who later rose to become Assistant Secretary of the United States for Near Eastern and South Asian affairs, Abdullah confided candidly. 'He told me that Kashmir would be "finished" if it had to join one Dominion and thereby incur the enmity of the other. What he sought, he said, was an arrangement by which Kashmir could have normal relations with both countries' (Talbot 2007: 378).

The Sheikh dispatched two trusted seniors, Bakshi Ghulam Mohammad and Ghulam Mohammed Sadiq, as his envoys to Pakistan soon after his release from prison on 29 September 1947. None but one writer has cared to explore this episode and ask what his aim was and what was their mandate.

That exception is Muhammad Yusuf Saraf, Chief Justice of the High Court at Muzaffarabad. He was born in Baramula and was associated with Sheikh Abdullah, from whom he parted company in 1945. His authoritative work, *Kashmir's Fight for Freedom* (1978), is critical of Abdullah. In it, he recalls the visit to Abdullah in Srinagar by Mian Iftikharuddin, Muhammad Din Taseer and Malik Tajuddin, who tried unsuccessfully to persuade him to accede to Pakistan.

> At long last, it seems to have been agreed that on their return, they should place these matters before the Pakistan Government for its consideration and that he would send Khwaja Ghulam Muhammad Sadiq to Lahore to continue the talks so that the ground was prepared for his visit to Karachi *to discuss the matter with the Qaid-e-Azam*. He told them that he had been invited by Pandit Nehru to visit him at Delhi and that after his visit to the Indian capital was completed, he would directly fly to Karachi. He also told them that so long as he did not come to Karachi, the situation should not be precipitated. Mr Justice Sheikh Anwar-ul-Haque, Chief Justice of the Supreme Court, who accompanied the delegation to Srinagar, confirmed to this writer on 28 July 1974, while on a visit to Muzaffarabad in the company of Mr Hamood-ur-Rehman, Chief Justice, that it had been agreed that Sheikh Abdullah would visit Karachi after his visit to Delhi for talks with the Pakistan Government. The three Pakistani leaders then returned to Lahore. (Saraf 1978, Vol. 2: 800)

Saraf also recalls Abdullah's speech in New Delhi on 21 October attacking the Maharaja's repression in Poonch. 'It is obvious that a man of Sheikh Abdullah's experience could not have taken such a line in Delhi as late as 21 October, 1947, if he were already committed to a pro-India and anti-Pakistan line. It not only represented a softening of his attitude but amounted to a discreet public assurance to Pakistan' (ibid.: 801). The highest official Ghulam Mohammad Sadiq could meet was the Nawab of Mamdot. Jinnah and Liaquat Ali Khan refused to meet him. Abdul Majid Qarshi of Jammu, one of the earliest political workers in the state, wrote in the weekly *Azad Kashmir* of 4 November 1959:

> On the 18 October 1947, I received a message from Maulvi Muhammad Saeed Masudi at Amira Kadal, Srinagar that Sh. Muhammad Abdullah had ordered me to leave for Lahore immediately in order to take part in the negotiations that were already going on there between Kh. Ghulam Muhammad Sadiq and the Muslim League Government. I was also told that Sh. Muhammad Abdullah wanted me to ensure that the talks *were not broken under any circumstances*. (Emphasis added.)

Qarshi reached Sialkot on 20 October 1947 to make arrangements for his family. He proceeds:

> I spent the 21 October in taking stock of the situation and on the 22 when I

> was preparing to leave for Lahore, news came that tribesmen were about to enter Muzaffarabad in aid of the Muslims of Kashmir. I reached Lahore on the 22 October but an hour before my arrival, Kh. Ghulam Muhammad Sadiq and his companions had, on hearing of the tribesmen's entry, flown to Delhi. (Ibid.)

Saraf remarks: 'One thing is now clearly established, that Sheikh Abdullah's representative was still holding negotiations with the Pakistan Government on the Pakistan soil and the idea was to pave the way for his leaders' visit to Karachi when tribesmen entered the State' (Saraf 1978, Vol. 2: 803). He also records the impact of the Sheikh's views on hordes of his followers who met him after his release and pleaded for accession to Pakistan. His dilemma was acute. Only an accord with both countries could have resolved it (ibid.: 800–03).

This remained the core of Abdullah's varying formulae in 1953, 1964 and 1968. The Sheikh would not accede to Pakistan because of his own predilections, and could not accede to India because of his people's predilections. The tribal raid imposed a decision on him, and facilitated Nehru and Patel's plans. Their embrace proved too tight for comfort. Before long he began to seek a way out. He made a bold attempt on 21 February 1948, when Britain's Commonwealth Secretary, Patrick Gordon-Walker, met Nehru at his house where the Sheikh was also staying. A wire from UK's High Commissioner reported Gordon-Walker's talks. The Sheikh's bold suggestion was made in Nehru's presence. It bears quotation *in extenso*:

> 7. At this point Nehru fetched in Sheikh Abdullah and said he would leave us to talk together. Just before Nehru left Sheikh Abdullah said he thought the solution was that Kashmir should accede to both Dominions. I had not time to get him to develop this idea before Nehru left the room but questioned him afterwards. He said Kashmir's trade was with India, that India was progressive and that Nehru was an Indian. On the other, Kashmir's trade passed through Pakistan and a hostile Pakistan would be a constant danger. The solution therefore was that Kashmir should have its autonomy jointly guaranteed by India and Pakistan and it would delegate its foreign policy and defence to them both jointly but would look after its own affairs. The two Dominions share a common interest in Kashmir and it would serve to unite and link them. I asked whether Nehru would agree to this solution and he said he thought so. He had discussed it with him. I will ask Nehru about this, this morning when I see him and shall hope to add a paragraph to the end of this telegram. Sheikh Abdullah had no idea whether Pakistan would agree to this solution, but he said it would avoid a Plebiscite which he did not really want. He thought India would win but the vote would be close, perhaps 60 to 40, and that either way the minority would be so large that it could never really accept the verdict. If Pakistan lost there would be constant trouble and no

> peace for Kashmir. The Muslim Conference would accept a joint accession and he could carry his own party.
> 8. He also said that the problems of the insurgents would solve itself when the raiders withdrew and that his own policy was to create four or five regions with full legal autonomy.
> 9. I then worked back to the idea of a joint guarantee and asked why this was not publicly put forward. He said it must be put forward by the UK backed by the US. This was an essential and we must tell Pakistan we thought it the only proper solution.
> 10. Since drafting the above I have seen Nehru again with reference to paragraph 7 above. He says that he would be prepared to accept a solution broadly on the lines of that proposed by Sheikh Abdullah.

When Sheikh Abdullah met President Ayub Khan in Rawalpindi on 26 May 1964, he complained that when 'he tried to contact the Pakistani representatives' to the UN Security Council in New York in 1948, during the debates on Kashmir, when he was a member of the Indian delegation, 'there was such arrogance and hostility toward him that the Pakistani representatives would not even talk to him'. Abdullah did meet Chaudhry Mohammed Ali in 1948 when he went there the second time, 'and told him that the only way to get the Indians out of Kashmir was to agree to the independence of the State' (Gauhar 2000: 264; Gauhar was close to Ayub Khan as his Information Secretary).

Abdullah was emphatic in his interview with Michael Davidson, published in *The Scotsman* of 14 April 1949: 'Accession to either side cannot bring peace' (Das 1974: 266–67). His talks in Srinagar with the US Ambassador Loy Henderson and with Adlai Stevenson were in the same vein (see my article I.3, reproduced in Volume II of this book).

Nehru had other plans. In private he had adamantly set his face against a plebiscite in 1947. In public, till 1954 he continued to make the most explicit – almost extravagant – and solemn pledges to hold a plebiscite. It was nearly fifty years later, in 1996, that the clue to Nehru's entire Kashmir policy emerged, with the publication of Volume 22 of the *Selected Works of Jawaharlal Nehru*. It contained a document as definitive as the famous US document NSC-68, which defined US policy in the Cold War. Nehru wrote a secret note to Sheikh Abdullah, dated 25 August 1952, while camping at Sonamarg in Kashmir (*SWJN*, Vol. 22: 322–30). It was one of the rare writings he authored – cogent, comprehensive, unemotional, yet destructive in the ruthless course it foreshadowed. Its thesis was: (1) the people did not matter; (2) the UN was powerless; (3) so was Pakistan, as 'we are superior to Pakistan in military and industrial power', which would acquiesce while India professed friendship all along; (4) the accession must be rendered non-provisional, it must be made final; (5) Kashmir's leaders must banish doubt for 'doubts in the minds of leaders percolate to their followers and to the people generally'. There must be no debate or argument in future; accession is an accomplished and final fact, and nothing is going unsettle it (vide Document 5).

Nehru arrogantly overlooked four factors: the people of Kashmir were not dumb-driven cattle; politicians who acted as their stooges would earn their contempt, rendering rigged polls necessary; Pakistan would not acquiesce for long either; and world opinion mattered despite India's growing strength. Of a piece with the candour of his prescription for a ruthless policy was the brazenness of his frank admission. 'Towards the end of 1948' he had decided against a plebiscite. This was inaccurate. He had so decided earlier, in 1947. He had written to Abdullah on 21 November 1947:

> Dwarkanath writes to me that there is strong feeling in the leadership of the National Conference against a referendum. I know this and quite understand it. In fact I share the feeling myself. But you will appreciate that it is not easy for us to back out of the stand we have taken before the world. That would create a very bad impression abroad and more specially in UN circles. I feel, however, that this question of referendum is rather an academic one at present. . . . If we said to the UNO that we no longer stand by a referendum in Kashmir, Pakistan would score a strong point and that would be harmful to our cause. On the other hand, if circumstances continue as they are and the referendum is out of the question during these next few months, then why worry about it now? . . . There is no difference between you and us on this issue. It is all a question of the best tactical approach. I would personally suggest to you not to say anything rejecting the idea of a referendum but to lay stress on the fact that the people of Kashmir, by their heroic resistance, are deciding the issue themselves; also that it is a little absurd for people to carry on a little war in Kashmir and, when defeated, to want a referendum. (*SWJN*, Vol. 4: 336–67)

If he arrived at an agreement with Pakistan on plebiscite in January 1949 and a cease-fire, it was only to buy time.

Indira Gandhi's warning on 14 May 1948 confirmed him in his stand, which is why, when he first met members of the UNCIP on 17 August 1948, Nehru deftly hinted at alternatives to plebiscite ('the general lines which a final solution would take'). Josef Korbel, father of Madeleine Albright, replied that 'a solution different from that envisaged in Security Council resolutions might be worked out' provided the parties agreed (UNCIP 1948: 107).

Nehru accepted the UNCIP's truce resolution of 13 August 1948 and the plebiscite resolution of 6 January 1949 with that reservation. In Paris, in October 1948, he had proposed partition of Kashmir to Liaquat Ali Khan. On 12 January 1949, only a week after the plebiscite resolution, Nehru wrote to Abdullah: 'You know well that this business of plebiscite is still far away and there is a possibility of plebiscite not taking place at all. I would suggest that this should not be said in public, as our *bonafides* will then be challenged' (*SWJN*, Vol. 9: 198). Comment is superfluous.

The cease-fire in Kashmir on New Year's Day 1949 was not intended as a preliminary to a plebiscite but to the freezing of a status quo arrived at by superior arms. In the process, myths were spawned which hold people in their thrall to this day, such as Pakistan had to 'vacate' its first aggression and to withdraw all its troops. This was a belated excuse. In 1947, as noted earlier, Nehru was prepared to and did discuss plebiscite, even after the tribal raid. The UNCIP's resolution of 13 August 1948 was unambiguous. Part B, paragraph 1 read:

> When the Commission shall have notified the Government of India that the tribesmen and Pakistani nationals *have* withdrawn . . . and further that the Pakistani forces are *being* withdrawn from the State of Jammu and Kashmir, the Government of India agrees *to begin* to withdraw the bulk of its forces from the State in stages to be agreed upon with the Commission. (UNCIP 1948)

In plain words, the tribesmen had to quit unconditionally and totally. Pakistan's forces also had to quit totally, but in a process in which India had begun to withdraw the bulk of its forces. For the tribesmen the UNCIP had to notify India that they '*have* withdrawn'. In total contrast, for Pakistan's forces it had to notify that they were '*being* withdrawn', whereupon India would '*begin*' its own withdrawals. At the end Pakistan's forces had to leave Kashmir totally, whereas India had only to withdraw 'the bulk' of its forces, leaving a minimum. There had to be a synchronization between the two processes, namely, Pakistan's continued withdrawal and the beginning of India's withdrawal. *India's withdrawal was not contingent on Pakistan's prior total withdrawal*, as later alleged. Nehru knew as much. The minutes of their meeting on 17 August 1948 record Korbel as telling him clearly enough: 'the requirement that Indian troops begin their withdrawal *before Pakistani forces had completed their withdrawal* from the State, he said, had been arrived at to meet Pakistan's fears of an attack by Indian forces' (ibid.: 106). The report contained this assurance to Pakistan: 'Synchronization of the withdrawal of the armed forces of the two Governments will be arranged between the respective High Commands and the Commission' (ibid.: 138).

Why, then, did Nehru agree to a 'fair and impartial' plebiscite in the joint communiqué with Mohammed Ali Bogra at New Delhi on 20 August 1953? Did he expect to win it with the Sheikh in prison since 9 August? The answer lies in his letter to Karan Singh the next day: 'But for some kind of an agreement between us and Pakistan, the matter would inevitably have been raised in the UN immediately and they might well have sent down their representative to Kashmir. All this again would have kept the agitation alive and made it grow.' The accord was not intended to be implemented. It was concluded to buy time (*SWJN*, Vol. 23: 347).

The UN's ablest mediator, Sir Owen Dixon, judge of Australia's High Court, foresaw this clearly in his Report to the Security Council on 15 September 1950 (Dixon 1950). He concluded:

> In the end I became convinced that India's agreement would never be obtained to demilitarization in any such form, or to provisions governing the period of the plebiscite of any such character as would in my opinion permit of the plebiscite being conducted in conditions sufficiently guarding against intimidation and other forms of influence and abuse by which the freedom and fairness of the plebiscite might be imperiled.

The US military aid to Pakistan, a foolish step on any reckoning, provided a good excuse. The truth emerged only in 1998, when Volume 23 of the *Selected Works of Jawaharlal Nehru* was published. It showed the hard-line approach of the Indian government on the question of the accord's implementation. This approach was executed in four stages from 1948–49 onwards: obstruction by tortuous interpretation of the UNCIP's resolution of 13 August 1948 and rejection of its truce proposals in 1949 signalling a refusal to withdraw the bulk of India's forces; rejection of mediation; pronouncement of closure; and denial of the existence of any dispute with Pakistan. The sole issue now was its handing over of west Kashmir (POK in Indian lingo) to join east Kashmir.

The hard line was pursued internationally as well as domestically. At the domestic level, the story of the wreckage of Article 370 of the Constitution, a guarantee of Kashmir's autonomy that was negotiated between Nehru and Abdullah over five months from May to October 1949, is by now well known. Nehru envisaged a closer integration of J&K with the Union of India (vide his note of 3 July 1952, *SWJN*, Vol. 18: 423). The Delhi agreement concluded that month was but one step in the direction. It created strains which were covered with humour. Nehru said at one stage: 'Sheikh Saheb, if you delay or avoid closeness with us, we will put chains of gold around your neck.' As meaningfully, the Sheikh retorted smilingly: 'Don't push things so far that you will have to wash your hands off Kashmir' (Abdullah 1982: 542).

Nehru's pressure for ratification of the accession was bad enough. His note of 25 August 1952 came as a bombshell to the Sheikh as he saw his own standing in public esteem dwindle. In public Nehru continued to chant about plebiscite. In private he increased the pressure on Abdullah just as the Sheikh's popularity was dwindling. The people took note of Nehru's speeches; their leader knew better. The people were oppressed by a sense of uncertainty which singled out their state in the entire sub-continent. Sheikh

Abdullah took his colleagues into confidence and placed the matter before the Working Committee of the National Conference which met in May 1953 under his presidentship. The Working Committee, after prolonged discussions, came to the conclusion that it was impossible to have internal stability so long as its future was uncertain. It accordingly appointed a committee consisting of the following eight members, to explore avenues of a settlement: Sheikh Abdullah, Maulana Mohammed Saeed Masoodi, Mirza Mohammad Afzal Beg, Bakshi Ghulam Mohammad, G.M. Sadiq, Sardar Budh Singh, Pandit Girdharilal Dogra and Pandit Shamlal Saraf.

Nehru, who had come to Kashmir when the Working Committee was in session, was informed about its deliberations. Here is an extract from the minutes of the Committee's final session, held as late as on 9 June 1953:

> As a result of the discussions held on the course of various meetings, the following proposals only emerge as possible alternatives for an honourable and peaceful solution of Kashmir dispute between India and Pakistan:
>
> a) Overall plebiscite with conditions as detailed in the minutes of the meeting dated 4 June 1953 [this apparently was a reference to Maulana Masoodi's suggestion that the choice of independence be offered in the plebiscite].
>
> b) Independence of the whole State.
>
> c) Independence of the whole State with joint control of foreign affairs.
>
> d) Dixon Plan with independence for the plebiscite area.
>
> Bakshi Sahib was emphatically of the opinion that the proposal (d) above should be put up as first and the only practicable, advantageous and honourable solution of the dispute. Maulana Saeed, however, opined that the order of preference as given above should be adhered to. (Vide Sarabhai, ed. 1956)

What G.M. Sadiq then said is worth recalling:

> If an agency consisting of India, Pakistan, Afganistan, Soviet Russia and China could be created to supervise and conduct the plebiscite, I would suggest that we should immediately ask for an overall plebiscite. Failing this, we may ask for a Supervision Commission representing all the members of the Security Council for ensuring free and fair plebiscite in the State. (Ibid.: 18)

In June 1953 Maulana Abul Kalam Azad, Union Minister for Education, visited Kashmir and was apprised of these developments. Early in July 1953, Nehru was informed about the decision. He was shortly going to have a meeting with the Prime Minister of Pakistan, Mohammed Ali Bogra, to discuss and find out an early solution of the Kashmir question.

In his talks Nehru disapproved of the independence idea, but apparently, not the deliberations themselves about the future of the state, for he met Mohammed Ali Bogra from 25 to 27 July 1953, to decide the future of the state. Early in August 1953 Sheikh Abdullah called a meeting of the Working Committee of the General Council in order to review the whole situation. On 9 August 1953, just two days before the scheduled meeting, Sheikh Abdullah was arrested at the dead of night, and so were a number his colleagues.

Apologists ascribed the shameful deed – then, as they do still – to the machinations of Rafi Ahmad Kidwai, Bakshi and the others. Only in 1998, forty-five years later, did 'the smoking gun' emerge from the wraps. It was Nehru's note of 31 July 1953. *Uniquely, he did not sign it.* Instead, it was recorded by his Private Secretary, M.O. Mathai (*SWJN*, Vol. 23: 303–05; vide Document 6 in this volume). It contained detailed instructions for Sheikh Abdullah's dismissal from the office of Prime Minister of J&K and his arrest, complete with the role of the Army and the rest (vide my articles II.2a and II.2b, reproduced in Volume II of this book). The scenario he sketched out boldly was followed to the letter. The note was not signed in order to facilitate deniability (see my article II.1, reproduced in Volume II).

In subsequent correspondence with Bakshi, Nehru sought deftly to hint that the initiative belonged to Srinagar. As the Bengali saying goes, '*Dhori mach, na chuin pani*' ('Catch the fish, but don't wet the hands'). The detailed prescription in Nehru's note reflected resolve. (1) Prepare a memorandum on 'the future of the State' and ask the Cabinet 'to support the policy laid down in its entirety'; it should be garnished with 'economic issues'. (2) Dissent there will be. The head of the state 'should ask for the resignation of Government because it cannot function as a team', but 'he should have an order ready for the dismissal of the Government' and appoint a new ministry speedily. (3) Prepare the ground with members of the party's executive. (4) 'All necessary steps should be taken for the preservation of law and order.' Assistance should be 'available', i.e. the Army should be alerted.

The note ended in good Nehruvian style with invocation of 'the good of the people and their wishes in the matter'. The documents were prepared in New Delhi. As early as on 10 July Nehru sent for Major-General Hiralal Atal from Srinagar. 'I do not want it to appear that he has been summoned to meet me', he wrote to Mahavir Tyagi (*SWJN*, Vol. 23: 288). Hatchet men proliferated, but it was Nehru who orchestrated their play.

The note highlighted an unflattering aspect. Nehru had systematically intrigued against his friend, the Sheikh, by tapping his colleagues – especially after the differences widened. D.P. Dhar was his own man anyway. Bakshi fell for the temptation. A letter he wrote to Nehru on 17 July shows how far the liaison had progressed. He complained that 'associates' of Abdullah and Beg were carrying on intrigues. Abdullah had resorted to a bitter campaign against India and the administration had collapsed. 'This has got to be arrested somewhere and that too very quickly' (ibid.: 290–91, footnotes 4 and 2 respectively). By now Nehru was in direct correspondence with Bakshi (ibid.: 293 and 300).

Apparently Bakshi had begun the game as far back as in 1950. Maniben Patel's *Diary* records his meeting with her father, Vallabhbhai Patel, on 11

July 1950, when he delivered a tirade against the Sheikh (Chopra and Chopra, ed. 2001: 376–77). It is unlikely that he neglected to woo the Prime Minister while wooing his Deputy, or that Nehru repulsed the overtures. Consistently opposed to the two-nation theory and to the set-up within the Muslim League, why would the Sheikh seek to accede to a Pakistan where Prime Minister Nazimuddin had been unconstitutionally sacked by Governor-General Ghulam Mohammed on 17 April 1953? Abdullah sought finality. Only a settlement with Pakistan could have ensured that. That remains true to this day.

In his letter of 26 September 1956 to G.M. Sadiq, Abdullah set out the minutes of the meeting on 9 June 1953. Sadiq did not contest their authenticity. In a letter to Maulana Masoodi on 6 August 1953, Abdullah recorded his meeting with Bakshi and Sadiq on 4 August, when he asked them

> why they had now retracted their previous agreement reached on various problems, in our last meeting, when the possible alternatives for solving Kashmir problem were agreed upon after months' discussions [and] when it was decided that members would not disclose the same. I told them that Bakshi Saheb's speech at Kulgam and Sadiq Saheb's speech at Ompora were in direct contravention of this decision. I showed them further newspaper reports and they said that it was correct. Bakshi Saheb said that he has not changed his views and that the stand taken by him in his Kulgam speech was the same as agreed to in the meeting. Sadiq Saheb said that Beg Saheb's and my speeches forced him to give expression to his views. I asked them to prove from the published reports if the stand taken by us was contrary to that agreed to in our meetings? They did not reply this question.
>
> I said that the reason for unrest, which has spread in the State, was that we were speaking in different languages and that it was necessary for us to publish a joint Statement on the present day problems of the State to check the growing unrest. Bakshi Saheb replied that that a joint Statement on any subject of the friends gathering would not be the decision of the National Conference, and so it would be necessary to call meetings of National Conference Working Committee and the General Council. It was decided therefore that a meeting of Working Committee should be held on 24 August and of the General Council on 29 August. (Sarabhai, ed. 1956: 49)

Little did he know that they were just leading him on and playing for time till their mentors in New Delhi were ready to strike and lull their chief into complacency. Meanwhile, this is what Bakshi said in his famous speech in Kulgam as late as on 29 July: 'Islam ordains that every Musalman must cherish faith in five cardinal principles, but I have a sixth principle as well. I have complete faith in the leadership of Sheikh Abdullah. If I have to go to the gallows for it, I am prepared' (Bazaz 1954: 669). This was twelve days after his letter to Nehru.

Zutshi is all too right when she writes that 'on Nehru's orders Abdullah was arrested and imprisoned in August 1953 for a period of eleven years until his release in 1964'. The Sheikh was, 'in favour of the settlement of the Kashmir issue through a plebiscite, an idea anathema to the Indian Government' (Zutshi 2003: 321).

Did Nehru mean to go the whole hog in that exercise or use it as a lever for an Indo–Pak settlement on Kashmir's dual status? For, he had declared emphatically on 25 July that 'so far as we are concerned we have full faith in secularism. We want justice for all alike. Why did the Kashmir Muslim set his face against Pakistan? . . . Pakistan wanted to enslave Kashmir by use of force.' He added: 'The communal happenings of the last year have shaken the foundation of our relationship. The responsibility for this does not lie at our door but at those sections in India who are attempting to force the State to merge with India' (Bazaz 1954: 667).

The aspect of intrigue is central to the episode and it has clear constitutional implications. Nehru first systematically undermined the Sheikh's authority as head of government, the office of the Prime Minister of J&K, and next, used this very situation as a ground for the Prime Minister's dismissal.

The Order made by the 22-year-old Karan Singh, Sadar-i-Riyasat, on 8 August 1953, obviously drafted in New Delhi, contained not a hint of Abdullah's intrigue with a foreign country, whether Pakistan or the United States; it contained no charge of subversion or corruption. Its *sole* ground for the dismissal of Prime Minister Abdullah was that 'the majority in the Cabinet has expressed [*sic.*] that . . . the present Cabinet has lost the confidence of the people'. This order has no precedent in the annals of the parliamentary system before or since. It deserves to be reproduced in full (Singh 1982: 161):

ORDER

Whereas for some months I have been noticing with growing concern that there have existed acute differences of opinion between members of the Government on basic issues – political, economic and administrative – affecting the vital interests of the States;

And whereas members of the Government have been publicly expressing sharply conflicting points of view regarding these matters;

And whereas on these fundamental issues the views of a majority of the members of the Cabinet are sharply opposed to the view held by the Prime Minister and one of his colleagues;

And whereas efforts to work in harmony and pull together as a team having failed, and the majority in the Cabinet has expressed that lacking as it does in unity of purpose and action, the present Cabinet has lost the confidence of the people;

And whereas the economic distress of the people has considerably increased which needs prompt and serious attention;

> And whereas a stage has reached in which the very process of honest and efficient administration has became impracticable;
>
> And whereas, finally, the functioning of the present Cabinet on the basis of joint responsibility has become impossible and the resultant conflicts have gravely jeopardized the unity, prosperity and stability of the State;
>
> I, Karan Singh, Sadar-i-Riyasat, functioning in the interests of the people of the State who have reposed the responsibility and authority of the Headship of the State in me, do hereby dismiss Sheikh Mohammad Abdullah from the Prime Ministership of the State of Jammu and Kashmir, and consequently the Council of Ministers headed by him is dissolved forthwith.
>
> Srinagar, SADAR-I-RIYASAT
> August 8, 1953. JAMMU AND KASHMIR

This is no ground for dismissal at all. The Order was brazenly unconstitutional. Legal advice was not considered necessary because Nehru had decided on the steps he took regardless of the law.

It was open to the dissenters, even if in a majority, to resign and move a vote of censure against their leader in the party or the legislature. But even the unconstitutionality of the dismissal from office appears trivial as compared to the Sheikh's arrest and long imprisonment. He was arrested right on the eve of the party meeting which was scheduled to be held on 24 August (for the Executive) and 29 August (for the General Council). Obviously, New Delhi dreaded the prospect of Sheikh Abdullah going to the people for their verdict. From October 1947 to August 1953 Nehru's Kashmir policy had rested on the support of Sheikh Abdullah. Now it was to rest on the continued imprisonment of this very man for eleven long years.

On 25 April 1952, Nehru wrote to Abdullah:

> The people of Kashmir must decide their own fate. For me the people of Kashmir were basically represented by you. If you feel as you do, then the link that has bound us together necessarily weakens and I have little heart to discuss these matters. You will do of course as you think right and I shall certainly not come in the way.

He was quick to add, 'My only difficulty is that I happen to hold a responsible position in fashioning our policy. For the moment, it is not clear to me what I shall do' (*SWJN*, Vol. 18: 388).

The Delhi agreement in July did not improve matters. On 28 June 1953 Nehru wrote to Sheikh Abdullah: 'it is always painful to part company' unless 'an overriding national interest so requires. . . . I am sending a copy of this letter to Bakshi' (ibid.: 199). Sheikh Abdullah was released on 8 January 1958 and rearrested on 29 April 1958. He was then released on 8 April 1964. His colleagues, Bakshi and Sadiq, were conspirators, not honest dissenters. That honour belonged exclusively to the General Secretary of the party, Maulana Mohammed Saeed Masoodi. Twenty-five years later, in October 1978, Abdullah said in an interview to this writer that if only he had stamped out indiscipline in the party in its early stages, the coup of 1953 would not have taken place (see my article II.8, reproduced in Volume II).

It was a coup executed with military precision and with the Army's help to suppress revolt. We have noted how, as early as on 10 July 1953, Nehru had sought the services of Major-General Hiralal Atal. Nearly two decades later Atal revealed the details of the operation in his memoirs (Atal 1972). He was Director of Personal Services in October 1947, when Nehru 'personally selected him for an assignment in Kashmir'. About the middle of July 1953 he was summoned by Nehru. He was then Commander of 21 Communication Zone, now known as XV Corps. When the Prime Minister asked him 'to be of all assistance that you can to the Government of the State', he could not have meant the Abdullah government (ibid.: 158).

Atal was well aware of what was afoot in Srinagar. He organized a 'tactical exercise' for the troops of all arms to be brought to Srinagar. Sheikh Abdullah was of course under close surveillance (ibid.: 162); a staff officer of the Adjutant General's Branch came to see Atal and met Karan Singh often in mufti.

> I was most curious to know how he, as Director of Organization, could have been selected by Army Headquarters for an assignment which militarily was not within his sphere. My suspicions about the motive of his visit to Srinagar were aroused on two counts. First, he mentioned that he was carrying with him a largish sum of money, and secondly his surprisingly secretive behaviour particularly when he normally confided in me to a great extent. I was left with the impression that he had been sent by a responsible political personage and that his mission was political and not military. (Ibid.: 164)

Personnel of the armed forces should not be used for such shady jobs. The 'political personage' must have been someone who could give such orders. It was a feudal political culture.

Atal 'had been visiting' Bakshi (ibid.: 165), apparently without Abdullah's knowledge. Atal 'discussed the political situation' with him and others. On 7 August he met Bakshi 'in company with my Divisional Commander to ascertain what his intentions were towards Sheikh Abdullah'. That was the day the Sheikh demanded Shamlal Saraf's resignation from the Cabinet, as he was perfectly entitled to – indeed even to ask the head of state to dismiss him. Instead, it was he who was dismissed. The Army's help was sought for Sheikh Abdullah and Mirza Afzal Beg to be transported to Udhampur, Headquarters of the Northern Command, and their detention in the guest house there.

When an angry mob threatened to break the fence around Bakshi's residence, Atal's advice to the Commandant of the Militia was to 'shoot the possible ring leader' if need be (ibid.: 179). Atal's mindset is revealed in his response to charges of excess.

> At about this time I was visited by the 'Secretary for Kashmir Affairs', Government of India. He was rather a meek and unimpressive looking individual who, in a very subdued voice, said that he had heard that about thirty to forty people had been either killed or wounded. He felt it was drastic action that resulted in such a casualty. I had many more important matters to attend to and could not be bothered with these trivialities. . . . I heard a message broadcast to the people of Kashmir from the Kashmir Radio Station, by Bakshi Ghulam Mohamed, in Hindustani and Kashmiri. It was evident from the intonation of his speech that he was halting, quivering and diddery. I went and saw him later in the morning. My impression of his nervous state was correct. He had a few kind words to say about the help and cooperation that was accorded to the State Government by the Army – I told him that that was our duty and our presence there was for that purpose. (Ibid.: 180–81)

Nehru also availed himself of the services of another favourite in the Army, B.M. Kaul, who was officiating as Adjutant General. In late July 1953 he said that Nehru 'called me in my private capacity' (Kaul 1967: 140). Kaul took ten days' leave from the Army Chief and went to Srinagar 'without an official status' and stayed with Atal. Characteristically, Kaul dressed up his account with tales of Abdullah's plans 'to meet [in Gulmarg] certain "friends" across the border' (ibid.: 143). Proprieties and professional discipline in the Army were obviously sidetracked. Kaul was to win 'high distinction' in the war with China in 1962.

The country naturally accepted, as it still does, the official version. This is what Nehru told President Rajendra Prasad on 9 August:

> Yesterday, late at night, we were informed of certain developments which indicated that *probably* the Sadar-i-Riyasat would dissolve the existing Government. This had not been actually done by the time. We did not wish to interfere in any way with these internal happenings, but we made it clear that our armed forces should be kept apart and not used in any way unless there was any grave threat to peace and order and the civil authority asked for their help. . . . The Sadar-i-Riyasat has acted on his own responsibility in this matter. In the course of the last day or so he informed us of the difficult situation he had to face. But he did not ask us for any intervention of any kind. We thought it best not to intervene as constitutionally the Central Government was not directly concerned. (*SWJN*, Vol. 23: 310)

Incredible as these words were even when they were uttered, the record that has appeared since reveals them to be completely untrue. Abdullah and Beg were arrested 'because of a fear of breaches of the peace' – a strange precaution on the dismissal. Nehru never explained why the detention lasted eleven years (ibid.). It had, as Mathai recorded, a deeper purpose.

On 10 August Nehru said in Parliament: 'Our advice was neither sought nor given. We have considered these recent developments in Kashmir as an internal matter with which we should interfere as little as possible. On the larger issues our policy remains what it was and we shall stand by the assurances we have given' (ibid.: 314 and 316).

Even his daughter, Indira Gandhi, was not spared. Nehru wrote to her on 9 August: 'The Cabinet there split up and . . . the Sadar-i-Riyasat dismissed his ministry.' As his policy on Kashmir evolved since 1948, Jawaharlal came increasingly to regard the truth as an inconvenience to be bypassed, only to discover, as his successors have, that it was an impediment which could not be surmounted. It was the policies that had to change. From Zurich Indira Gandhi wrote, in obvious pain: 'I got the Kashmir news in a Swiss paper . . . It is a heart-breaking thing to happen . . . like cutting a part of oneself' (ibid.: 311 and 3).

On her return to India, Indira Gandhi could not have failed to ascertain, from sources more than one and her father included, precisely what had happened. Nor could she have failed to see through the slanders spread about the Sheikh. They have persisted for long. Sarvepalli Gopal, Nehru's biographer who had access to all the records, unforgivably retailed them in his hagiography (Gopal, ed. Vol. 2: 131–32). Sample this: 'All the documents so far available indicate that Nehru did not interfere or even hint at his own preferences.' This was published in 1979; Atal's memoirs, in 1972. Nehru's papers were, of course, already available to Gopal.

That, soon after her return to India, Indira Gandhi desired to meet Sheikh Abdullah in detention, proves to the hilt that the charges of complicity with the US or Pakistan were false to the knowledge of those who made them. Nationalist to the core, she would not have sought to meet him if she had even a faint suspicion of such conduct. The facts are recorded in a confidential note by Nehru's Private Secretary, M.O. Mathai, dated 12 September 1953 (Document 7). Extracts were quoted by this writer earlier, in an article in *Frontline*. The full text is being published here for the first time.

Evidently, the daughter did not consult her father. It is unlikely that Mathai, who confided about it to Krishna Menon, kept it secret from his boss. Mathai's verbosity, in full display in his memoirs, exposes much.

> I do not believe that Sheikh Abdullah deliberately intended to switch on his band wagon to Pakistan. Any person accusing him of that is not only doing him an injustice but is also spoiling our own cause. However, it is a patent fact that the speeches and activities of Sheikh Abdullah during the past few months have had the effect, direct and indirect, of encouraging the pro-Pakistani elements among the Muslim population of the State (*M.O. Mathai Papers*).

That was the very charge made against him in the conspiracy case. The truth is that the secessionists, long suppressed by the Sheikh's brutal methods, now came to the surface – as they were bound to, sooner or later.

'It is being said in Parliament lobbies and elsewhere that Prime Minister recently told his Cabinet, "we have lost Kashmir". I felt very angry about it. Some Cabinet ministers also told me about it.' Mathai cited six grounds against Indira Gandhi's move. Embarrassment to the state government was one: 'Your action might even unnerve them' (ibid.). Mathai, however, made a valid point. What could she offer to the Sheikh?

> You should consult PM [Prime Minister] about your idea of meeting Abdullah secretly. If he agrees with your proposal, then in order to have any worthwhile talk with Sheikh Abdullah, you should have a very clear idea as to what the Government of India's intentions are in regard to Kashmir policy, in regard to both the immediate present and the long term one. (Ibid.)

There followed these revealing words:

> Is Sheikh Abdullah for us and with us an acquisition from the political point of view in Kashmir? I have no doubt about it. But the real question is – is Sheikh Abdullah big enough, after all that has happened, to be with us? I do not know. I also believe that in certain circumstances it is necessary for us to continue to support even a wrong action (once it has been taken) in public affairs. If for certain tactical reasons it is essential to buttress and prop up Bakshi, I would do so to the hilt unhesitatingly. We dare not vacillate and be soft. (Ibid.)

There was no doubt whatever in anyone's mind about the Sheikh's total and continuing rejection of accession to Pakistan. It was rejection of Nehru's diktat in the note of 25 August 1952 – close the chapter – which he did not accept because the people would have rejected him if he had.

Mathai knew Nehru's mind. These words reflect Nehru's grim resolve: 'It will be psychologically wrong for Sheikh Abdullah to be reinstated in Government until the Kashmir problem is finally solved in all its aspects – including the international aspect.' This was a dilemma of the leader's own creation. Nehru whipped up public opinion on the boundary dispute with China and found himself trammelled by its clamour. This happened on Kashmir as well. In both cases his own feelings also coincided with those of the public. What Mathai's note proves is that at the very outset, in August/September 1953, Nehru was determined to keep his erstwhile friend in prison 'until the Kashmir problem is finally solved in all its aspects – including the international aspects'. That explains the brutal detention for eleven years. That also explains why the conspiracy case was launched on a charge no one believed to be true: conspiracy to accede to Pakistan.

In parliament and to the President, Nehru minimized the Kashmiris' reaction to their leader's arrest. Two documents record it. One is a report by a Praja Socialist Party's (PSP) inquiry team, comprising Sadiq Ali, later Governor of Bombay, and Madhu Limaye. The other is a memoir by one who was, in 1953, a junior colleague of Bakshi and Sadiq: Mir Qasim (Qasim 1992).[1]

The PSP team went to Kashmir pursuant to a decision by its National Executive on 18 September 1953. The 37-page report on Kashmir by Sadiq Ali and Madhu Limaye deserves to be republished (Limaye and Ali 1954). Bakshi Ghulam Mohammad harped on 'Sheikh Abdullah's increasing association with Americans', and confused *The Scotsman* with the *Daily Express*. Only on 6 June he had said:

> It has become part of the faith of the workers of National Conference that Sher-e-Kashmir is their sole and greatest leader. This is no empty claim. We have shown by our action that we mean it. In future also we shall do the same. We may be hanged but like Majnoon our lips will utter just one word, Laila, Laila. (Ibid.)

The report quoted Abdullah's speech on 25 July. 'The honest truth is that last year's communal agitation has shaken the foundation of this connection. It is not we who wish to break this connection. India wants it. . . . On the Indian Army should be represented all communities. Compare the number of Muslims then and now!' Referring to the Post and Telegraph, he asked what exactly had been done to give encouragement to Muslims. The educated unemployed Muslims looked to Pakistan for employment. Why so? 'When I am myself not convinced how can I convince others? I feel that we cannot build the structure of our connection with India on weak and shaky foundation. *But let it not be understood that I want to get out of the ditch in order to fall into a well*' (ibid.).

When Abdullah drew Nehru's attention to the discrimination, he was called 'communal'. It was not a belatedly trumped-up charge. He had taken up the matter with Maulana Azad who wrote to Jagjivan Ram, the Minister concerned, in these scathing terms:

> We are questioned that Kashmir has acceded to India only on three subjects – defence, communications and foreign affairs. If such is the plight in the offices of the Ministries of Defence and Communications that there is no room for Kashmiri Muslims, what can we hope to gain by acceding on other subjects. What answer can we give them. 43 Kashmiris had applied for posts of clerks in Post and Telegraph; only one was selected. It is a pity that the effect of such treatment on Kashmiris and Kashmir accession has not dawned on the people in charge of recruitment (Perti, ed. 1990: 106).

Ironically, forty years later Professor Saifuddin Soz voiced these very grievances on the floor of the Lok Sabha.

Sadiq Ali and Limaye testified: 'The Indian Army was no unconcerned spectator of the whole disquieting development' (Limaye and Ali 1954: 10). The situation did not improve.

> If somebody who had heard of the events of August 9 visited the State in mid-September, nothing unusual would have assailed his senses. If per chance he

> experienced a sensation of something strained and unusual, it would have been dispelled by a look at the well-attended meetings which the new Prime Minister addressed everywhere with the sole exception of Srinagar. We were, however, not such ignorant visitors. We met Ministers, workers of the National Conference, representatives of minority organizations and others, but somehow we failed to get at the mind of that large section of the Muslims which had reacted so vigorously to Sheikh's arrest in the first fortnight but was now nowhere to be encountered. It soon appeared to us that this has been suppressed into silence. Its leaders were behind the bars and the police exercised constant vigilance. For a correct appraisal of the situation it would be necessary to bear this fact in mind. (Ibid.)

The lone honest dissenter, Maulana Masoodi, told them that

> the Sheikh was not in an irreconcilable mood, that the differences were due to come up for a frank and thorough discussion at a meeting of the Working Committee which Sheikh had already called and that the precipitate action of the 9th was not called for by circumstances as they then prevailed. (Ibid.)

The people's reaction was correctly reported:

> The demonstrations that followed the dismissal and arrest of Sheikh Abdullah were serious and widespread. The new common cries were 'Sher-e-Kashmir Zindabad, Pakistan Zindabad'. In the first one or two days, even workers of the National Conference joined the demonstrations, so sudden was the decision and so stunning its effect. But soon they withdrew and left the field to the pro-Pakistan elements and others who had no clear appreciation of the situation but who were very naturally affected by Sheikh's arrest. The police and the militia came out in full strength and did their job efficiently and fairly ruthlessly. The official estimate of the number of people killed by firing is between thirty-seven and forty. There is no reliable popular estimate. It varies from person to person according to his political sympathies. There was hartal in Srinagar for about fifteen days. The hartal was complete for the first seven or eight days. There were, according to official reports, some 500 arrests, which included some members of the Working Committee, the Legislature and the National Conference. There have been many releases since then. The exact number of those detained now was not available to us. The crowds do not appear to have been very violent. Stone-throwing was about the only serious charge brought against them. There was, on small scale in Srinagar, cutting of wires and pulling down of the telegraph poles. Firing could have been avoided in some places with a little more tactful handing of the situation. The police indulged in the violence; it did largely because it was a novel situation with unpredictable possibilities that they had to grapple with. (Ibid.)

In Kashmir, the tradition of stone-pelting goes back to the days of protests against the Maharaja by the National Conference.

> The new Government took little time to announce these and other measures. One wonders how within a few hours of the arrest of Sheikh Abdullah all these various reforms were conceived, elaborated and announced . . . in the procession or at the meeting we came across no visible sign of anger and resentment at the events of the 9th August, but there was one thing we could not help noticing, lack of honest and genuine fervour. Also it would have been a little cruel on our part to inquire too closely whether and to what extent the common people had contributed towards the expenses of the meeting which could not have been a very mean amount. (Ibid.)

Bakshi won a unanimous vote of confidence from the Assembly. 'Among those who spoke loud and clear in praise of the new Ministry were those who were released the very same day or the day before' (ibid.: 20). The report concluded:

> It was impossible for us not to feel that the Muslim population by and large has not reconciled itself to the new regime. It is not in a position to create trouble but if it has an opportunity for showing discontent it would fain do so. There is no free expression of opinion so far as this section is concerned. Happily the food and other necessaries of life have become cheaper. To that extent the sharp edge of their discontent is not allowed to get sharper. Their suppression and the constant vigilance of police is, however, not a safe foundation to build on. Sheikh Abdullah had lost a fair measure of his popularity in the closing days of his tenure of office. Now he wears the crown of martyrdom. He has reinstated himself in affection of the people. People are going about their work quietly and peacefully but they have not forgotten him. (Ibid.)

Further:

> We are, in this report, not much concerned with the part Government of India played in the crisis of August 8. That requires separate investigation. It is, however, plain that the Government of India's record in regard to Kashmir is not, to judge it by results, a very flattering one . . . the problem, however, must be solved both in the interest of the democracy in Kashmir and good relations between India and Pakistan. Human ingenuity need not be so resourceless as not to be able to devise acceptable alternatives to a plebiscite if fair conditions for the latter are wanting. (Ibid.: 30)

Mir Qasim noted that the Sheikh had begun complaining that 'the Centre was encouraging Bakshi' (Qasim 1992: 66). He regarded the Sheikh's dismissal from office unconstitutional. 'The Prime Minister [or, for that matter, a Chief Minister] does not survive on the support of his Cabinet, but on the confidence of the Legislative Assembly. No Chief Minister in any of the Indian States has ever been removed from his post because his Cabinet lost confidence in him' (ibid.: 67). He described the waves of protests over

Kashmir. 'Srinagar was in total chaos. Bakshi Saheb's own house, despite the police guard, was under attack. He was nervous and wanted to step down as Prime Minister in favour of Mr. Sadiq', who was President of the state's Constituent Assembly (ibid.: 70).

The Sheikh wrote to Sadiq from Udhampur jail on 30 September 1953, asking him to arrange for his presence before the House 'so that I could answer the charges that would have been brought against me by interested members of the House'. Sadiq's response reflected the condition to which the state had been reduced and, indeed, the identity of the man who had organized the coup. He did not take a decision on the request himself. Instead, he 'sent a copy of the telegram to the President and the Prime Minister of India, but Sheikh Saheb's request was not acceded to' (ibid.: 80). When Sadiq and Mir Qasim fell out with Bakshi, it was Bakshi whom Nehru supported (ibid.: 84), just as he supported another strong man, Partap Singh Kairon, to control the Akalis in Punjab. Maulana Azad, who favoured removal of Bakshi, lost all interest in Kashmir.

On his release from prison on 8 January 1958, 'the Sheikh received a massive enthusiastic reception wherever he went'. He wanted to meet Nehru and hosted a lunch for Vijayalakshmi Pandit (ibid.: 83). Pro-Pakistan sentiment was strong in Kashmir (ibid.). Bakshi had even to give up his morning walk. But Sheikh Abdullah was rearrested on 29 April 1958. A conciliatory letter he wrote addressed to 'My dear Panditji' on 11 April 1958 was ignored (vide Document 10 in this volume).

Nehru had realized that he had not been tamed and that the people supported him. He had received evidence of the Sheikh's firmness from his friend Dr P. Subbarayan, father of S. Mohan Kumaramangalam. He met Sheikh Abdullah in the sub-jail at Kud on 20 June 1956, obviously at Nehru's behest. His aim was two-fold: to size up the prisoner and his attitude, and to secure his consent to surrender terms, recant and repent. The Sheikh refused to commit political suicide. He recorded the conversation the next day in an eleven-page note which Mridula Sarabhai circulated over her signature. It is being published here for the first time (see Document 9).

Well before that, addressing a public meeting in New Delhi on 13 April 1956, Nehru declared: 'I am willing to accept that the question of the part of the Kashmir which is under you [Pakistan] should be settled by demarcation of the border on the basis of the present cease-fire line. We have no desire to take it by fighting' (*The Times of India*, 14 April 1956). This could not have come as a surprise to Pakistan. Nehru had made the offer to its Prime Minister Liaquat Ali Khan as far back as in 1948. Its public renewal was designed to tell Kashmiris that plebiscite was now dead. Dr Subbarayan began by drawing the prisoner's attention to this 'latest proposal'. The Sheikh did not treat it seriously.

The Doctor then suggested that in order to facilitate my release, I may issue a short statement to the effect that my heart is still with India and that if released, I will try to retrieve the position, though I still hold that the right of self-determination of the people of Kashmir must be respected. Such a Statement, added the Doctor, will in no way commit me. I may or may not succeed [in bringing round the people]. I expressed my surprise at this suggestion, coming as it did from a friend who knew me. I told him that one who has spent the best part of his life, nearly quarter of a century, in active politics cannot be expected to beg for his release. . . .

After the tragic partition of the country, if I advised my people to look towards India, it was not for her wealth or power but for the community of ideals. I sincerely felt that India was forging ahead as a real progressive democratic State with secularism as its goal. Though a veritable hell of communal massacre stood between Kashmir and India then, the people of Kashmir joined hands with India so as to be of some assistance to Gandhiji in his noble mission. The Musalmans of Kashmir bore with fortitude the mass killings of their co-religionists in the Jammu Province, the provocative and murderous behaviour of certain Indian Army units stationed in Srinagar in the early days of the raid and the hostile attitude of the local non-Muslim population, but did not falter to uphold the cause of secularism and human brotherhood. Light came to Gandhiji from Kashmir alone. (Document 9)

Abdullah proceeded to define his problem and tabulate his grievances.

I had to win and maintain the confidence of all sections of the population in the State, particularly Muslims and it was their vote which eventually counted, I had, therefore, to assure them that all their rights will not only be fully safeguarded but they will be treated generously by India . . . in the case of Muslim recruitment in various departments which came under the direct control of the Centre, such as Defence, Posts and Telegraphs, etc., the position became worse and the Muslims were being almost hunted out of employment.

Recruitment in the State Army has always been a tender sore with the Muslims as Kashmiris as a class had been scrupulously excluded. We had fought against this invidious class-composition since 1931. After the transfer of power, the Maharaja resisted handing over control of the State Forces to the Cabinet. The operational control had, however, been transferred to the Centre after the raid. The Government of India suggested temporary transfer of the administrative control also to the Centre on the definite assurance that the legitimate grievance of the Muslims will be looked into and redressed. We agreed but after a couple of years it became evident that instead of raising the representation, Muslims already in the State Forces – both high and low – were gradually squeezed out on some pretext or other. Surprisingly enough, Muslim units en bloc were sometimes forced out. This made the position grievously worse. I, therefore, asked for immediate clarification from the then Defence Minister of India, requesting him to furnish me with the statistics of the Muslim person-

> nel in the State Forces at the time of its taking over by the Centre and that obtaining now. This, I considered necessary in order to scrutinize the veracity of the allegation. My request fetched no reply and the conclusion was obvious. . . .
>
> I brought these cases of invidious discrimination to the notice of the Commander-in-Chief General Cariappa, and was shocked when the local station commander – Col. Kak – admitted in the presence of the General that the recruitment of Kargil Muslims in the Militia was intentionally avoided because of their pro-Pak tendencies. Similar reasons were advanced to justify the discriminatory treatment of the Muslims of the State Forces and the Ordnance Depots. . . .
>
> Fresh recruitment in Post Offices has the same sad tale to tell. In 1953, I pointed out a glaring case of injustice to the State Muslims to Maulana Azad who was then in Srinagar. Out of the nearly one hundred candidates who had offered to take the test for selection in the lower cadre of postal service from Kashmir, only 25 were Muslims and all of them were shown to have failed in the test whereas majority of non-Muslim candidates had been declared successful. I pointed out that though the number of employed Matriculates among State Muslims was quite large, only 25 had applied because the departmental notice was not properly advertised. The inexplicable failure of all the Muslim candidates added to the suspicion that the Muslims were being deliberately shut out.
>
> In All-India services a large number of non-Muslims from the State, particularly Kashmiri Pandits, secured employment since the provisional accession but unfortunately, however, the door remained closed for the Muslims. Naturally a strong feeling grew amongst the Muslim intelligentsia of the State that accession to Pakistan would have opened similar avenues to them as well. (Document 9)

Sheikh Abdullah revealed that as far back as early 1950 he had brought Nehru's attention to his Private Secretary D.N. Kachru's intrigues with Bakshi.

> Bakshi was encouraged and provided secretly with large funds to undermine my influence and position in the country. He took advantage and started amassing wealth and property by dubious means for himself and his kith and kin. Some of my other Cabinet colleagues took the cue from him and followed suit. The poison filtered down in the rank and file of the services and corruption became rampant. (Ibid.)

The Sheikh recalled the deliberations on Kashmir's future in May 1953, and Beg and Bakshi's visit to New Delhi to apprise the leaders of the proceedings. Beg returned to Srinagar but Bakshi stayed behind. To stop the drift, the Sheikh convened meetings of the party. A meeting with Shamlal

Saraf was fixed for 10 August at the instance of Karan Singh, whom he met at 5 pm on 8 August. He was dismissed from office and put under arrest less than twelve hours later.

Bakshi had begun to assert that

> an average Kashmiri is not interested in the political issue. His main interest is in being provided with cheap food. Therefore, a successful appeal can be made to his heart through his stomach. Accordingly, an old British example of distributing cheap rice to hungry Chinese was resorted to and Government of India made to foot the bill of nearly two crores of rupees per annum. . . . 'Yes India is spending colossal amounts in Kashmir', said the Doctor. He added further that if India had given even a part of this liberal aid and financial support to me, things would have been different. (Document 9)

Interestingly, Subbarayan sought the Sheikh's opinion of Mir Qasim.

> I observed that Mir Qasim was everything to everybody. To a Pakistani he dangles a certificate which he received from late Mr Liaquat Ali in appreciation of his work to help the League election campaign before partition. He was then a student at Aligarh. To a communist he is a Marxist, and to a Congressman an Indian first and last. He has, however, little influence in Kashmir and is not trusted. As regards Bakshi, the less said the better. He was bargaining with the League leaders in 1946 for the allotment of some factories in Lahore in his name when they wanted to enlist his support in favour of Kashmir's accession to Pakistan. (Ibid.)

As with the dismissal and imprisonment, so with the conspiracy case, apologists claim that it was all Bakshi's doing. We now have authentic documents which prove that Nehru was eager – impatient, rather – that the Sheikh be prosecuted. He was rearrested on 29 April 1958, though he had expressed a desire to meet Nehru. On 17 May, the Kashmir government ordered the prosecution of twenty-five persons for the offence of conspiracy to overthrow the state by use of force. Sheikh Abdullah was not cited as one of the accused. On 23 October 1958, however, a complaint was filed by the Inspector-General of Police in pursuance of these orders, and this time the Sheikh was included among the persons accused of conspiracy. The specific charge against Sheikh Abdullah and his colleagues was that they, 'between August 1953 to 29 April 1958, conspired to overawe by means of criminal force and show of criminal force the legally and constitutionally established Government of Jammu and Kashmir and facilitating the wrongful annexation of the Jammu and Kashmir State by Pakistan' (Court Papers). Later, in the Sessions Court, the charge of waging war was also added.

Committal proceedings began before Special Magistrate N.K. Hak in October 1958 and ended on 25 January 1962, when he committed the Sheikh and others for trial to the Sessions. The trial before the Sessions

Court began on 13 September 1962. There were 266 prosecution witnesses (listed 330) and the trial was expected to last for a few years at least.

On 29 June 1963, Senior Prosecution Counsel N.S. Pande announced his withdrawal from the case and said in open court:

> The accused are not ordinary people but big persons and the prosecution has a definite purpose behind this case. The prosecution is doing its very best to see that the trial is not delayed. But despite that, progress has not been very considerable. More than 200 witnesses are to be examined on either side. The way the trial is proceeding, it is not likely to conclude before five or seven years. (Chaudhari 1963)

He said that one of the considerations that had weighed with him in tendering resignation was the national emergency. 'I think the money that could be saved by going out will be spent for better purposes' (ibid.).

The expenditure on the case was not shown in the state budget. On 17 April 1963, Morarji Desai, the Union Finance Minister, said in the Lok Sabha:

> A question was asked about Jammu and Kashmir about the expenditure on the cases which are going on. The expenditure is certainly met by the Law Ministry, and, therefore, that cannot be shown in the Demands of the Jammu and Kashmir Government. . . . I have just got the figures of money which has been disbursed so far. It is about Rs twenty-seven lakhs. That is the amount of money that has been spent in this period. There is one lawyer, and he is the most senior lawyer, and senior lawyers have got these fees. He gets Rs 1665 out-of-pocket expenses all found.

Apart from the Kashmir conspiracy case, there was the Hazratbal riot and murder case in which 64 persons faced trial before the Sessions Judge, Srinagar. Maulana Mohammed Saeed Masoodi was one of the original accused, but he was discharged on grounds of health. Strangely enough, though the accused were committed to the Sessions on 20 October 1958, their trial there began properly only in 1963, and even then the proceedings were delayed by repeated adjournments. There were 101 prosecution witnesses.

Acharya Vinoba Bhave met Sheikh Abdullah in jail in 1959, and twice wrote to Nehru in the following year urging withdrawal of the conspiracy case and the release of the Sheikh and his colleagues. On 16 April 1958, before his rearrest on 29 April, Nehru wrote to Bakshi:

> I am much worried about one matter. Why is it that there is such delay in starting the conspiracy case about which there has so much talk for several months? This delay is having a bad effect on people who are beginning to say that we are in the habit of making vague charges without trying to establish

> them. If there is any further delay. I am afraid we shall suffer very much by it. As it is, the delay has not at all been to our advantage, and the psychological moment is rapidly passing. (*SWJN*, Vol. 42: 571)

The trial had a two-fold objective: silence criticism abroad, and silence and demoralize Abdullah and his supporters. On 19 April, Nehru wrote to the Commonwealth Secretary in the Ministry of External Affairs, N.N. Pillai:

> I have read the ten-page note at the end of these papers. It is for lawyers to assess the value of this evidence. Prima facie, there appears to be a good deal of documentary evidence to support the charge of conspiracy.
>
> 2. There has been talk about launching this Conspiracy Case for many months and some public reference has also been made to it. I have long felt that the delay in launching this Case was harmful to our interests. Some delay was perhaps inevitable in order to collect the evidence. But because of this delay an impression is now spreading that we have really no case and no substantial evidence. I have, therefore, recently written to Bakshi Ghulam Mohammad and spoken to Shri Vishnu Sahay urging them that the Case should be launched as early as possible.
>
> 3. As for Sheikh Abdullah being involved in this Case, I am inclined to agree with Commonwealth Secretary that it would probably be better to leave him out. If later on, it is considered important to proceed against him also, presumably there will be no bar to it. As a matter of fact, to proceed against Begum Abdullah would itself be a great blow to Sheikh Abdullah. (Ibid.: 574)

The object, clearly, was to strike 'a great blow' at his former friend.

With the Sheikh and his colleagues behind the bars, a basic Order was made by the President on 15 May 1954, extending several provisions of the Indian Constitution to Kashmir. The Constituent Assembly enacted the state's Constitution on 17 November 1956. More, it resolved that day formally to dissolve itself from 26 January 1957. Thus the sole ratificatory body for further extension of India's Constitution vanished. Central amassment of power thereafter is unconstitutional.

What of the Constitution itself that was enacted in such circumstances? The point was also made in respect of the 42nd Amendment to India's Constitution in 1976 during the Emergency. In a notable judgment on the habeas corpus petition of a veteran communist leader and trade unionist, Anandan Nambiar, Justice Somasundaram Mack of the Madras High Court observed:

> We readily concede the contention of Mr Kumaramangalam that if a party in power detains a political opponent or continues his detention with the mala fide object of stifling opposition and prejudicing the party to which he belongs in a forthcoming election, there would be an undermining of the basis of the Constitution. (*AIR* 1952, Madras 117: 119)

Five years later, on 27 November 1963, the Prime Minister told the Lok Sabha with obvious satisfaction:

> Article 370 as the House will remember is a part of certain transitional provisional arrangements. It is not a permanent part of the Constitution. It is a part so long as it remains so. As a matter of fact, as the Home Minister has pointed out, it has been eroded, if I may use the word, and many things have been done in the last few years which have made the relationship of Kashmir with the Union of India very close. There is no doubt that Kashmir is fully integrated. (*Lok Sabha Debates*, 27 November 1963, col. 1936).

Erosion was an inapt metaphor. It was a systematic abuse of Article 370, in violation of its terms, to increase central power. But, if it could be so used, where was the need to abrogate it, G.L. Nanda, the Home Minister asked in the Lok Sabha on 4 December 1964.

> The only avenue of taking the Constitution into Jammu and Kashmir is through the application of the provisions of Article 370. That is the only way of bringing back the Constitution to J&K. . . . May I submit to him and the other friends that Article 370 is neither a wall nor a mountain, but that it is a tunnel? It is through this tunnel that a good deal of traffic has already passed and more will. (*Lok Sabha Debates*, 4 December 1964, col. 3455)

He said: 'Article 370, whether you keep it or not, has been completely emptied of its contents. Nothing has been left in it.'

Eventually, 94 of the 97 entries in the Union List were extended to Kashmir, as were 260 of the 395 Articles of the Constitution of India – in each case with the 'concurrence' of the state government, which had no authority to accord the concurrence in the absence of the Constituent Assembly.

Moreover, the state government did not represent the people. B.K. Nehru, one of the ablest and most upright of our civil servants, was Governor of J&K from 1981 to 1984. He wrote in his memoirs published in 1997: 'From 1953 to 1975 [when Sheikh Abdullah returned to power] Chief Ministers of that State had been nominees of Delhi. Their appointment to that post was legitimized by the holding of farcical and totally rigged elections in which the Congress Party led by Delhi's nominee was elected by huge majorities' (Nehru 1997: 614–15).

Mir Qasim made the same point in his memoirs: 'Whenever New Delhi feels a leader in Kashmir is getting too big for his shoes, it employs Machiavellian tactics to cut him to size' (Qasim 1992: 119). Muzaffar Hussein Baig, Minister in the state government, disclosed on 2 May 2003 that during his party's – the People's Democratic Party's (PDP) – meeting with N.N. Vohra, then the centre's interlocutor, on 27 April, 'We told Vohra that the Government of India has always been purchasing the leaders of the State. That can be done even today.' The Jammu vote, the Congress's presence in the Valley, however small, help the security agencies to secure a few seats for the centre's favourite to install him as Chief Minister – as head of a coalition with the Congress. The present Chief Minister, Omar Abdullah, owes his post to those eight seats in Srinagar district (see my article II.29, reproduced in Volume II). In 2012, the failure of these tactics rudely stared New Delhi in the face.

Sheikh Abdullah's pronouncements after his release in 1964 belied the charges made against him. He came to New Delhi and stayed with Nehru as his guest. He said in a statement on 12 May 1964:

> Kashmir admittedly is the main irritant which has bedevilled the relations of the two countries for the last 17 years. Our first effort, therefore, must be to remove this irritant, and find an amicable solution for the problem. I need hardly say that such a solution must not give a sense of defeat to any country, *nor should it weaken India's secular basis*. The solution also satisfies the aspirations of the State so as to give them an honoured place. . . . Presently we are working on some formulae and in due time we hope we will be able to evolve an adequate framework of the possible solution. (*Kashmir Problem, Sarvodaya Topical* 1964, No. 1: 30–31)

It was a formula for a confederation, a non-starter; and President Ayub Khan of Pakistan, whom Abdullah met with Nehru's approval, rejected the very idea of a confederation. Nehru died on 17 May 1964 and none of his successors was strong enough even to strive for a settlement. Pakistan decided to settle Kashmir by recourse to war in 1965 and failed. Shortly before that, on 31 March 1965, the Sheikh had met China's Prime Minister, Zhou En-Lai, in Algiers. He was detained on his return to India on 8 May 1965, and was released from internment on 2 January 1968 from his residence at 3 Kotla Lane, New Delhi, where he had been shifted from Kodaikanal for reasons of health. He was again interned here on 9 January 1971 to prevent him from contesting the 1972 Assembly elections, and was released only on 19 June 1972.

If Pakistan's tribal raid of 1947 forced accession with India, its recourse to war in 1965 foreclosed many options. Jayaprakash Narayan, who was for plebiscite in 1964, rejected the idea after the war. Rightly so. Pakistan could not be permitted to acquire by plebiscite what it had lost at its own chosen forum, the battlefield.

While in detention at Kodaikanal the Sheikh told Jayaprakash Narayan's emissaries, K. Radhakrishna and Narayan Desai, on 6 and 7 October 1965 (vide Document 14 for minutes of the talks), that he would accept the pre-1953 status on honourable terms. In New Delhi, Foreign Secretary T.N. Kaul had long talks with Sheikh Abdullah. On 3 October 1967 Kaul sought a meeting with the Sheikh at his house in New Delhi. He was invited to tea on 10 October, again on 12 October for two hours, and then on 30 October for an equally long talk. After his release Kaul invited Abdullah to a quiet dinner on 6 January 1968, where P.N. Haksar, the Prime Minister's

Principal Secretary, was also present. At a Kashmiri lunch hosted by the Sheikh on 15 February, the issue was narrowed. Kaul insisted on accession first and then the details. Beg wanted the details to be settled before the accession was confirmed. Tragically, Indira Gandhi's advisers on Kashmir were hardline Kashmiri Pandits: D.P. Dhar, P.N. Haksar, T.N. Kaul and P.N. Dhar. The gap would, and could, have been bridged by a more conciliatory negotiator (vide Documents 12 and 13; *T.N. Kaul Papers*, Subject file no. 15).

By 1968 Sheikh Abdullah had accepted the state's accession to India, and Indira Gandhi and her advisers knew that. The accord of February 1975 was the worst he could have secured, a fig-leaf to cover abject surrender as the price for return to power – not least because of his own ineptness during the Bangladesh crisis when he supported Pakistan. The Shimla Accord of 3 July 1972 had frozen the status quo.

Constitutionally, the Sheikh lost all; but he aspired to retrieve what he could politically. He refused to merge his political party with either the Congress or, after 1977, the Janata Party. That Indira Gandhi was miffed by his revival of the National Conference was understandable. That Ashok Mehta struck similar postures in his brief days of glory, in the early days of the Janata Party in 1977, testifies to the potency of power as an intoxicant; in his case it was purely derivative power which did not last long.

The letters which Sheikh Abdullah wrote to Mirza Mohammed Afzal Beg, President of the Plebiscite Front, and to Mir Qasim, leader of the Congress Party in the Legislature, both on 23 May 1975, soon after the Accord, reveal the Sheikh's political aspirations. He derived power from the centre as well as the people, and sought to be his own man. Both Farooq and Omar Abdullah have been the centre's 'man in Kashmir'. Sheikh Abdullah even invited Mir Qasim to join the National Conference (vide Document 22 for the text of the letters). When, in April 1977, Ashok Mehta asked the Sheikh to merge his National Conference with the Janata Party, he was rebuffed (vide Document 23).

Abdullah won the 1977 election. His regime was riven with intrigue, and he proved to be as authoritarian and intolerant as before. This writer was an eye-witness to the break-up of Beg's public meeting by the police in 1978, which was his first in opposition to Abdullah. The Sheikh's popularity waxed and waned. He was put in power by the Government of India to resist the attack from Pakistan, a task he performed nobly, showing qualities of leadership. His government instituted land reforms, promoted education and did a lot for the people. But, as Chitralekha Zutshi recalls:

> the National Conference regime was without doubt an installation of the Indian Government, a fact made apparent by the presence of a vast number of Indian troops in the State. Not only had the National Conference lost its popular mandate with the Kashmiris – both Muslims and Hindus – but, as signifi-

> cantly, it had never commanded the support of Muslims, Hindus and Sikhs of the Jammu region, a region that now effectively came under its control. The regime was caught between preserving its own power in the face of multifarious challenges to its authority, pressure from the Indian Government to maintain the security of the newly-founded Indian State by suppressing dissident elements within the territory, and its own ideological platform that had promised far-reaching reforms in the political and economic structures of the State.
>
> Ironically, and perhaps predictably, the organization that had first demanded political and social rights on behalf of Kashmiris became their greatest repressor. The National Conference regime systematically suppressed papers and periodicals that did not agree with Sheikh Abdullah, particularly in the matter of Kashmir's accession to India. The State Government promulgated an ordinance entitled the Enemy Agents Ordinance, allowing for the arrest and summary trial of those suspected of pro-Pakistan leanings. (Zutshi 2003: 313)

He became an idol of the masses, especially in 1953, because he articulated their urges.

It is a fact that the events of 1953 robbed Kashmir of its autonomy, and Kashmiris of their pride and self-esteem. Abdullah did little to restore either. His main concern and achievement were to arrange for the succession. This he performed deftly. However, he took the final decision, preferring his son Farooq to son-in-law G.M. Shah, only 'three weeks before his death'. Governor B.K. Nehru, who knew both well, wrote that the Sheikh

> thought so poorly of Farooq as a possible successor that he was not at all sure that the future of the State would be safe in his hands. He regarded him as a spoilt play-boy, utterly irresponsible, not in the slightest interested either in politics or administration, not capable of handling either. *Not particularly attached to his father* and, on the whole unfit to be given the responsibility of governing a State of complexity of Jammu and Kashmir. . . . Till the very end, I was told, he doubted his son's capacity to run the State. (Nehru 1997: 600–03)

History has amply vindicated that astute and carefully written assessment. The grandson Omar has proved to be worse still.

The regimes of all three were riddled with corruption and repression. The Sheikh freely used the Enemy Agents Ordinance to throw dissenters across the cease-fire line. He was no democrat. He presided over a rigged election to the Constituent Assembly in 1951, was opposed strongly to a plebiscite from 1947–53, and abused political opponents and connived at acts of violence against them – for example, against Beg in 1978. But there was one fundamental difference between the patriarch and the progeny. *His heart lay with the Kashmiris and he had a vision. Their sights have ever been set on New Delhi, and on the loaves and fishes of office it can provide them.*

They set themselves up in business as the sole custodians of India's unity and engage with the people only the better to secure rewards for themselves from the centre. Sheikh Abdullah had many faults and flaws; but he was very much his people's man.

The PDP headed by Mufti Mohammed Sayeed is as Unionist as the Abdullahs' National Conference. The 'healing touch' promised by Mehbooba Mufti, who won popularity for the party, failed to heal. But it vastly improved the atmosphere. The PDP led the coalition from 2002 till 2005, when a Congress politician, Ghulam Nabi Azad, descended on a home state he had neglected for decades, to claim the pickings of power (2005–08). He had no sympathy for Kashmir's aspirations. But even he was not as repressive as Farooq and Omar have been. In a series of exposes on 12, 13, 19 and 20 July 2007, *The Kashmir Times* exposed Farooq's 'sordid record'. Founded by the veteran socialist Ved Bhasin, the paper earned universal respect for living up to the standards of independent, fearless and honest journalism even in the worst days of both the militancy and state repression. Another paper that deserves the same praise is the Urdu weekly *Chattan*, edited by Taher Mohiuddin. Its pages chronicled the sad course of history particularly since 1989. It became a daily recently.

On 11 August 1996, Farooq Abdullah publicly thanked the renegade militants for helping him to come to power in the rigged poll: '[The militants] had given us the privilege to go before the people. Now I am proud of them.' Earlier, on 14 July 1996, he had called the Lok Sabha polls 'a concocted and rigged exercise' (*Kashmir Times*). On 19 October 1996, shortly after he became Chief Minister on 9 October, Farooq said: 'Those who surrender will be welcomed into the mainstream and those who don't will have to die' (*Kashmir Times*). Reacting to his statement, Amnesty International issued a statement on 25 October in which it 'warned that a new wave of unlawful killings could be imminent in Jammu and Kashmir following an ultimatum issued by Chief Minister Farooq Abdullah to armed opposition groups'. The warning was proved true.

The All Parties Hurriyat Conference (APHC) was not spared. Farooq said on 8 October 1999, apropos its leaders: 'let them rot' in prison. 'I will ensure that they are detained in far off places wherefrom their return is very difficult' (*Kashmir Times*). He was so determined to be New Delhi's man that he said, 'in the negotiation on Kashmir, there is no role for Kashmiris' (ibid.). Small wonder that both the Congress and the Bharatiya Janata Party (BJP) so readily accepted him as an ally. Small wonder too that neither regime earned popularity in Kashmir. Those were not isolated utterances. Farooq said on 13 January 2001: 'I don't want to fill jails. My orders to the police are, wherever you find a militant, dispatch him' (*Kashmir Times*). On 12 December 1984, after the assassination of Indira Gandhi, he said: 'Those who used to call me communalist and anti-national and who used to fly in the aircraft are no more alive. God has taken revenge on my behalf.'

Omar Abdullah's record in power as Chief Minister so far, from 2009 to 2012, is no better – especially since 11 June 2010, when 17-year-old Tufail Mattoo was killed as he was returning from a tuition class. Stone-pelting protesters were shot at. The killings in 2010, the repeated and prolonged house arrests of Syed Ali Shah Geelani, Mir Waiz Umar Farooq, Shabbir Shah and others fall into a pattern of repression. Omar went so far as to defend the Central Reserve Police Force (CRPF), which is hated for its excesses: 'Too much of antagonism against the CRPF will be of no use as it will only disrupt the law and order situation in the State.' An article in *Outlook* of 12 July 2010 by Showkat A. Motta (Editor of an informative monthly, *Conveyor*) summed up Omar Abdullah's ways, the trips to Gulmarg and New Delhi, condonation of repression, and governance by proxy. 'The perception is that the Government is run by his political adviser, a business tycoon from Jammu, whose brother spearheaded the Amarnath Sangharsh Samiti that had called for the Kashmir blockade in 2008' (Motta 2010). That tycoon, one Devinder Rana, acquired hitherto unsuspected credentials as a 'political adviser' to Omar.

On 4 August 2010, Farooq Abdullah asked 'all parties to support him [Omar Abdullah] unequivocally. Otherwise, I fear, Kashmir would be a lost cause' (*The Indian Express*, 5 August 2010). The state's membership of the Union does not depend on this dynasty. But the two behave as if New Delhi owes them a living for keeping Kashmir in India.

This is what Omar said of Farooq on 21 June 2001, on the eve of the Assembly election:

> Whenever you [*sic.*] needed him to go and defend your human rights record, even when human rights were at their worst in the early 90s, he went to Geneva, Vienna and the UN and did the best he could. Even the human rights record was not worth the paper it was written on. To expect that man will accept anything you throw at him like some sort of a grateful dog waiting for some scrap is to add salt to the wounds *you* [the Centre] inflicted. (*The Indian Express*, 22 June 2002)

These remarks are as damning as they are revealing. They tell you as much about Omar as about Farooq. Rather than stand by his people, 'that man' went the world over to defend the wrongs inflicted on them. In return, he expected a reward – and Omar approves and adopts his style of politics. What can the people expect of men with such an outlook who support whoever is in power, the BJP or the Congress – the Bakshi Ghulam Mohammads of the twenty-first century.

The people resent the installation of an unrepresentative government with central help. On 10 July 2010 Omar admitted: 'The troubles erupted in areas where we got very low polling percentage in election, where voting was less than 20 per cent even in the 2008 election that was considered a major success' (*The Times of India*, 11 July 2010). This is a reference to the eight constituencies in Srinagar district, all won by his National Conference by 'external' aid. On the strength of these eight, he formed a coalition with the Congress. In a house of 85 seats, the National Conference won 28, Mehbooba Mufti's PDP 21 and the Congress 16. In the Valley itself, if the eight are excluded, the National Conference won 12 and the PDP won 19. Omar was nominated by the centre in preference to Farooq.

If the ploy has succeeded with very many in New Delhi, it is because of their ignorance of Kashmir's history and the psyche of its people. Why does the waiter in a Srinagar restaurant or a houseboat still hail the 'Indian' guest? That is why the history of Kashmir (1947–64), with all its tragic turns, bears recalling today. To Kashmiris history matters, as B.K. Nehru himself noted when

> a shoal of Congress politicians descended on the Valley from outside [in 1983, for the polls]. They did more harm than good; first, because the Kashmiris resented 'foreign' interference and second because they [Congressmen] were ignorant of Kashmiri sentiments. A favourite theme of their speeches was praise for Akbar the Great and his secularism. In Kashmir the name Akbar is hated as that of an arch-imperialist. He was the first outsider who destroyed in 1589 the independence of Kashmir. Nobody had succeeded in doing so before then. (Nehru 1997: 610)

The Kashmiri views the subcontinent's history differently from an Indian or a Pakistani, despite his links with both.

In 1988 Pakistan sought to promote its cause by launching a covert operation. The chairman of the Jammu and Kashmir Liberation Front (JKLF), Amanullah Khan, revealed in an interview to Zahid Hussain of the Karachi monthly *Newsline* of February 1990, how far back the planning had begun. In answer to a specific question – 'How did you mobilize the uprisings? Was it a long term plan?' – he replied: 'Yes, it was . . . it had to be well-prepared and well-planned. So we actually started political planning in 1986 and continued till the end of 1987. For one and a half years we were planning our strategy and it began in July 1988.' Asked, 'Was guerrilla training part of the preparations?', Amanullah mentioned precisely that 'it started on 31 July 1988 and it went on. There were bomb explosions' (Hussain 1990). In an interview to *Sunday*, in its issue of 18 March 1990, he repeated: 'Our armed struggle started on 31 July 1988, by blasting three buildings belonging to the Government of India in Srinagar.'

It was left to a responsible Pakistani journalist, M.A. Niazi, to reveal in the Lahore daily, *The Nation* (21 May 1990), that, in embarking on this course General Zia-ul-Haq had reckoned with the possibility of war with India. It was a cold-blooded decision. Reporting from Muzaffarabad, capital of west Kashmir, he wrote that its ruling party 'credits Zia with laying the foundation for the present uprising' in Kashmir. On 31 May 1990, Niazi reported that the 'operations mounted during the late President Zia-ul-Haq's time caused fierce debate in policy-making circles with opponents warnings that such activities would cause war'.

Two decades later the operation has all but petered out, exacting a toll of wrecked lives. In combating it, the Indian state has disgraced itself by the brutalities and humiliation its armed and para-military personnel inflicted on the people. The findings of the International Committee of the Red Cross, published recently, confirm those of Amnesty International, Human Rights Watch and Indian journalists.

It was an operation unrelated to a realistically achievable political goal. Not till President Pervez Musharraf hit upon his Four Points, after groping for months on end, did it become possible to achieve a goal. As late as on 16 July 2001, at Agra, the BJP regime wrecked a summit because it would not accept even this procedural formulation in Article 1 of the draft declaration, though its Foreign Minister, Jaswant Singh, had accepted it in writing jointly with Pakistan's Foreign Minister, Abdul Sattar. 'Progress towards settlement of J&K issue would be conducive towards normalization and will further the establishment of a co-operative relationship in a mutually reinforcing manner' (vide Sattar 2010: 368–69).

In sharp contrast, since 2004, for the first time in decades, Pakistan and India have been grappling with the substance, not mere procedures, of the Kashmir dispute. By 2007 they had reached the gates of an accord. Domestic developments in India had slowed the process somewhat, earlier. Similar developments in Pakistan, of a seismic character, brought it to a halt. Foreign Minister Shah Mehmood Qureshi declared in Islamabad, on 15 July 2010, that progress made in the talks in the past will not be set at naught.

Dr Manmohan Singh broke the mould set by the past. He decided consciously to break from it and proclaimed the resolve publicly before taking the oath of office. On 20 May 2004, *The Statesman* published his interview at breakfast given to a foreign correspondent, Jonathan Power, 'a few months ago'. Neither the guest nor the host imagined that the host would become India's Prime Minister before long. His remarks bear quotation *in extenso* for they reveal a sound blend of enlightened self-interest and idealism. 'Then, we have to find a way to stop talking of war with Pakistan. This is stopping us realizing our potential. Two nuclear-armed powers living in such close proximity is a big problem. We have an obligation to ourselves to solve this problem' (Power 2004).

Jonathan Power reported: 'I pushed him on how far he himself would accept compromise with Pakistan over Kashmir.' Dr Manmohan Singh's reply was candid and positive. 'Short of secession, short of redrawing boundaries, the Indian establishment can live with anything. Meanwhile, we need soft borders – then borders are not so important' (ibid.). A year later, he said they would become 'irrelevant'. What of a plebiscite? 'No Government in India could survive that. Autonomy we are prepared to consider. All these things are negotiable' (ibid.).

In the negotiations in the back channel India accepted grant of self-rule to both parts of Kashmir, demilitarization, redundance of the Line of Control (LoC) and a joint mechanism. No previous government had gone so far. The Mumbai blasts on 26 November 2008 stalled the peace process. India's grievance about Pakistan's inaction to secure punishment of the culprits of the Mumbai blasts remains unredressed. Clearly, some significant and effective steps were called for, without holding up the peace process. They were taken at Thimphu by the Foreign Secretaries of both governments, Nirupama Rao and Salman Bashir. It was announced on 10 February 2011 that there would be a 'quiet succession' of talks between Secretaries of various ministries on 'all outstanding issues'.

We have come a long way since 26 November 2008, through a route whose milestones testify to wasted time: the summits between President Zardari and Prime Minister Manmohan Singh at Yekaterinburg on 16 June 2009; between Prime Minister Manmohan Singh and Prime Minister Yousuf Raza Gilani at Sharm El Sheikh on 16 July 2009; the Foreign Secretaries' meeting in New Delhi on 25 February 2010; the two Prime Ministers' highly successful meeting again at Thimphu on 30 April 2010; the Foreign Secretaries' preparatory meeting in Islamabad on 24 June 2010 followed by the Home Ministers' meeting on 26 June, both at Islamabad.

Against this background, the failure of the Foreign Ministers' meeting on 15 July 2010 came as a rude shock. However, Foreign Minister Shah Mehmood Qureshi made a very helpful statement that day: 'We also feel that the progress made through a concerted effort in the last four years should not come to a naught and we should build on it.' Fortunately, the set-back was overcome. On 10 February 2011, Foreign Secretaries Nirupama Rao and Bashir put the dialogue process back on the rails. They agreed to hold wide-ranging talks on all outstanding issues, including Kashmir. This paved the way for a successful meeting between Foreign Ministers Hina Rabbani Khar and S.M. Krishna in New Delhi on 26–27 July 2011. The Prime Ministers also met twice in 2011: once on 30 March, during an Indo–Pak cricket match at Mohali, and next for more substantive talks on 10 November, in Addu City in the Maldives where both attended the SAARC Summit.

It has become a set tradition for the top leaders to meet on what are called 'the sidelines' of an international conference, or at the UN when the General Assembly convenes for its annual session. They do not meet in each other's capital. Manmohan Singh's planned trip to Islamabad in 2007 was aborted by President Musharraf's impetuous sack of the Chief Justice in May that year.

It is hard to imagine any progress on any of the pending issues – Kashmir, Siachen, Sir Creek and Wular Lake – unless the leaders meet, and meet with a resolve to settle. Time is running out as both countries gear up for general elections. Domestic political crises, like the one involving Hussein Haqqani, Mansoor Ijaz and, allegedly, President Zardari as well, do not make meetings any easier. Nor does a failure to come to grips with the aftermath of 26/11. But unless Prime Minister Manmohan Singh goes to Pakistan this year, talks between Foreign Ministers will go only thus far and no farther. His visit alone can revive the dormant Four Point formula.

During this entire phase the BJP has played a destructive role, especially after it lost power at the centre in New Delhi. On 4 July 2000, it brusquely rejected the plea of its own ally, Farooq Abdullah's government, for greater autonomy, which had been endorsed by the J&K Assembly on 26 June. In July 2001 it wrecked the Agra summit with Pakistan and massed troops along the LoC. Atal Behari Vajpayee pledged a lot in his 'Kumarakom Musings' – depart from the beaten path and '*insaniyat ke dairey mein*' ('within the bounds of humanity') – on 18 April 2003, which an obliging media interpreted as a generous offer. After its loss of power in 2004 the BJP began opposing the peace process at every turn, while at the same time asking Pakistan's representatives not to conclude a deal with the Congress-led United Progressive Alliance (UPA) – the BJP would offer better terms. On 14 March 2004, during the election campaign, L.K. Advani, then Deputy Prime Minister, communalized the issue: 'The BJP alone can find a solution to our problems with Pakistan because Hindus will never think whatever we have done is a sell-out' (*The Indian Express*, 15 March 2004).

While at home the refrain of 'sell-out' was kept up, Pakistan was asked not to settle with the UPA government. In New Delhi on 20 February 2007, Advani advised Pakistan Foreign Minister Khurshid Mehmood Kasuri against 'any haste' in the peace process. Atal Behari Vajpayee repeated the line the next day. *Sotto voce* Kasuri was told, 'wait till we return to power' – implying, 'you will get better terms from us'. The Opposition never censured the BJP regime for the zigzags in its policies: parleying with the Hizbul Mujahideen in August 2000 after its cease-fire on 24 July; inviting Pervez Musharraf for a summit in July 2001, which it wrecked wantonly; launching Operation Parakrama on 18 December 2001 and calling it off on 16 October 2002, all at a cost of Rs 8,000 crore; and complying with the Colin Powell–Jack Straw road map of 27 March 2003 to attend the Islamabad summit in January 2004.

On Kashmir, the Sangh Parivar has a lot to answer for. For half a century it has played with the national interest opportunistically and fecklessly. Sheikh Abdullah had sharply reminded Syama Prasad Mookerjee on 4 February 1953: 'This arrangement [Article 370] has not been arrived at now but as early as 1949 when you happened to be a part of the Government' (Bharatiya Jan Sangh 1953: 37). He was very much privy to the Constituent Assembly's enactment of Article 370 in October 1949. In his correspondence he espoused the trifurcation of the state. Mookerjee resigned from the Cabinet in April 1950 over the Nehru–Liaquat Pact on minorities, set up the Jan Sangh on 21 October 1951, and began looking around for an explosive issue to exploit. On 31 December 1952, at its first session in Kanpur the Jan Sangh voiced a demand for 'the complete integration of the State with India' (Graham 1992: 38). Mookerjee died suddenly on 23 June 1953, while in internment in a cottage near Srinagar (ibid.: 39). The Sheikh was falsely accused of neglect. By that time he himself was in trouble with Nehru who was pressing for an identical course: closer integration.

The outcry over Mookerjee's death had predictable repercussions in Kashmir. Nehru wrote to B.C. Roy, Chief Minister of West Bengal, on 29 July 1953 about the unrest in the Valley:

> Undoubtedly, a major reason for this has been the Praja Parishad and Jan Sangh agitation and its reaction in the valley of Kashmir. Whatever its justification might have been in Jammu itself, the reactions in the Valley of that agitation in Jammu and various parts of India had the most harmful results. The inhabitants of Kashmir, and they are 90 per cent Muslims, saw the communal face of India and were frightened by it. Their desire for remaining with India weakened and in fact many thought that they would be suppressed in many ways if they were completely merged with India. It was difficult to face this growing feeling in the minds and hearts of many people. One cannot deal easily with imponderable sentiments. . . . It is clear that we cannot, in the ultimate analysis, hold Kashmir or the Valley by force of arms alone. If it is patent that the people there do not want us to remain, then we have no case left and we cannot continue for long. (*SWJN*, Vol. 23: 296–97)

On the same day, he wrote to Jayaprakash Narayan:

> There has been a controversy about the measure of accession of the Kashmir State to India. That controversy has not ended. In the final analysis, we cannot hold any part of Kashmir by force of arms alone and without the wishes of the people concerned. If that is so, these reactions in the Kashmir Valley have weakened our position terribly and for the first time I feel very doubtful about the future. No amount of strong speeches or statements here on the subject help, because ultimately the decision will be made by the people of Kashmir; they have been frightened and angered by much that has been said here and is being said.
>
> When there is no such controversy about the measure of accession, for us to impose an enquiry from above, which is clearly outside the subjects of accession, would immediately raise not only constitutional issues of importance, but passionate resentment. It would become an example, in many people's eyes, of how we treat Kashmir as a subject country. It would, in fact, put an end to such case we have had in Kashmir based on the people's goodwill. (Ibid.: 300)

Nehru was woefully wrong in dismissing Abdullah's anxieties as 'imponderable sentiments'. In his letter to Nehru in July 1953, Abdullah brought attention to the fact that despite the Delhi Agreement, a senior Minister like N. Gopalaswamy Ayyangar had asserted in the Rajya Sabha on 5 August

1952, that Article 370 was not a permanent feature of the Constitution. The problem before the state now was 'not the character and shape of internal arrangement with India, but the larger question of solving the dispute between India, Pakistan and the people of Kashmir' (ibid.: 284–85, footnotes 2 and 7; Nehru's letters are available, albeit selected by the editors, but Abdullah's are not – the quotes are from the footnotes). Years later his colleague and later bitter opponent, Mir Qasim, testified that the Sheikh had begun to suspect that the Government of India would not abide by its pledges on autonomy in the future (*Chattan*, Srinagar edition, 26 July 1999). He was also alarmed at the rise of the Sangh Parivar.

The pity of it all is that Nehru himself was aware of the menace. His rift with Abdullah was not inevitable. He had foreseen the danger that the Sangh Parivar posed. At a rally in Calcutta on New Year's Day 1952, Nehru warned:

> If tomorrow Sheikh Abdullah wanted Kashmir to join Pakistan, neither I nor all the forces of India would be able to stop it because if the leader decides, it will happen. So what the Jan Sangh and the Swayamsewak Sangh are doing is to play into the hands of Pakistan . . . just imagine what would have happened in Kashmir if the Jan Sangh or any other communal party had been at the helm of affairs. The people of Kashmir say that they are fed up with this communalism. Why should they live in a country where the Jan Sangh and the Rashtriya Swayamsewak Sangh are constantly beleaguering them? They will go elsewhere and they will not stay with us. (*SWJN*, Vol. 17: 77–78)

American scholars on the Cold War attribute the United States' excesses to a flawed document of its National Security Council, NSC-68. Nehru's note to Abdullah of 25 August 1952 had the same baleful effect vis-à-vis the state of J&K as well as Pakistan. It shut the door to any compromise. Its inescapable consequence, which he did not reckon with, was to help the Sangh Parivar to build up a climate hostile to Pakistan – which itself needed little help in its hate campaign. In this, significant sections of the Congress Party sympathized with the Sangh Parivar – as they still do. Secularism suffered. The Report of the Commission of Inquiry on the Ranchi riots in 1967, headed by a former judge of the Supreme Court, Raghubar Dayal, said: 'the root cause of the breaking out of serious disturbances as a result of any minor incident has been found to be the mistrust existing between the two communities since 1947, when the partition of the country took place'. What was his recipe? 'Genuine improvement of the relations between the two countries – Pakistan and India – may go a ling way in allaying the apprehensions born out of mistrust and ultimately in removing the mistrust' (Ministry of Home Affairs 1968: 101)

Kashmir was prescribed as a loyalty oath to the Muslims of India by none other than its Deputy Prime Minister, Vallabhbhai Patel, who went so far as to impugn Maulana Azad's loyalty to the country. Azad had presided over the Indian Union Muslim conference at Lucknow on 27 December 1947, where he made a powerful appeal to the community to join the Indian National Congress. The conference was convened by pro-Congress Muslims. Less than a fortnight later, on 6 January 1948, Patel addressed a huge public meeting in the same city, Lucknow: 'I want to ask the Indian Muslims only one question. In the recent All India Muslim Conference why did you not open your mouth on the Kashmir issue? Why did you not condemn the action of Pakistan? These things create a doubt in the minds of the people' (Noorani 2004: 63–67). Asaf Ali's memoirs record that even before the partition, Patel never trusted the Muslims in the Congress.

The loyalty oath won adherents all round. To this day leading Muslims, especially the 'sarkari Muslims', vie with one another in supporting the official line on Kashmir, laced with fervid Pakistan-bashing. The sport is played at ridiculous lengths. In 1964, for example, Muslims in riot-torn Sambalpur met, not to ask for police protection but to send cables to the President and members of the UN's Security Council telling them that 'Kashmir's accession to India is irrevocable' (quoted in Noorani 1970: 362). The sport continues to this day.

Secularism had no champion more deeply committed and sincere than Jawaharlal Nehru. True, it was embedded in the ethos of the freedom movement. But he articulated it eloquently, gave precision to the concept and fought for it against all odds – including his deputy Vallabhbhai Patel and President Rajendra Prasad. His biographer, Sarvepalli Gopal, records Nehru's cry for 'a battle with our own selves', and adds:

> In performing this duty, his first as the leader of a free people, Nehru could not rely on the unqualified support of his Cabinet . . . the old stalwarts of the Congress, however, such as Patel and Rajendra Prasad, with the backing of the leader of the Hindu Mahasabha, Syama Prasad Mookerjee [a Cabinet member], believed not so much in a theocratic State as in a State which symbolized the interests of the Hindu majority.

To Patel, 'the Muslims of India were hostages to be held as security for the fair treatment of Hindus in Pakistan' (Gopal 1984, Vol. 2: 15–16). Nehru continued with the good fight. As the builder of the Indian state, history will rank him with Ashoka and Akbar.

For reasons not hard to appreciate, the Kashmir problem acquired communal overtones and affected the practice of secularism in India. It was a tragedy of colossal proportions and of baleful consequences that are still with us. Beyond a doubt, Sheikh Abdullah was the tallest leader Kashmir has produced. He had his flaws, some very grave. But he was the most consistent opponent of accession to Pakistan, having rejected the two-nation theory in 1939 when it was formulated by Jinnah. This was the man whom Nehru wronged, inflicting a wound on Kashmir's psyche which his successors had neither the capacity nor the will to heal.

Today, we have to grapple with the legacies bequeathed to us. A settlement of the Kashmir dispute must meet three tests and conform to four limits which time has imposed. It must be one that the Prime Ministers of India and Pakistan can get their Parliaments to ratify and their peoples to accept. It must also be acceptable to the people of Jammu and Kashmir, across the communities and regions of the state. This is the Red Fort, Mochi Gate and Lal Chowk test. To these must be added one moral imperative: the return of Kashmiri Pandits to the Valley so that they can resume their lives in their own homes with actively assured safety, dignity and respect.

There are, however, four *clear limits*, four bright red lines which cannot be crossed. No Government of India can possibly accept secession of the state of J&K. Likewise no Government of Pakistan can possibly accept the LoC as an international boundary. It is a revisionist power, India is a status quo power. Why would it accept in a deal, what it already has? That apart, it is a country which has a deep feeling of having been cheated on the unfulfilled pledges of plebiscite (1948–54) and nurses a sense of having been wronged by a militarily superior neighbour.

Kashmiris will not acquiesce in the partition of their land. They will not submit to denial of democratic self-rule either. Kashmiris resent the dominance of both the states. They resent India's persistent breaches of its pledges on plebiscite as well as autonomy. India ran a coach and four through the guarantee of autonomy. The least Kashmiris can now accept is the vital substance of self-rule within the Union of India with the indispensable safeguard of an elected head of state and cast-iron guarantees against repeat of the abuse. They seek reunification of the state and an Indo–Pak settlement which endorses the guarantee, facilitates the reunion and ensures self-rule.

This is not possible *de jure*, but it is pre-eminently attainable *de facto* by the Four Points which reduce the LoC to 'irrelevance' and just 'lines on a map', as Prime Minister Manmohan Singh put it. There will be a joint mechanism comprising the Chief Ministers of east and west Kashmir (the hideous words 'Indian-held Kashmir' and 'Pakistan-occupied Kashmir' must now be dropped). Additionally, there will be an agreed and equal devolution of self-rule on both parts, including the Northern Areas, now Gilgit-Baltistan, and disengagement of forces. The accord will itself be an international guarantee of self-rule. On the Indian side Kashmiris can devise a final draft of Article 370 to supersede all others, and embody the requisite safeguards and proclaim its demise as clause (3) provides. The 'tunnel' will be closed for good. That draft will fit the Four Points like a glove. There can be, besides, an All Jammu and Kashmir Consultative Assembly comprising legislators of both parts to discuss matters of common interest but without any legislative powers.

The three tests and four limits rest, however, on two harsh truths: Kashmiris do not want to stay in the Indian Union, and the Indian Union cannot possibly allow them to secede. The 'nationalist' rejects the first truth, fearing that it spells secession. The 'liberal' rejects the second truth. He fears that it spells denial of the first truth. However, *both truths are parts of the same coin*. Statesmanship lies in facing these complex realities and arriving at the best possible agreement which the circumstances permit. The perfectionist is a foe of the possible; he is an architect of ruin.

As mentioned earlier, a broad framework of precisely such an accord exists already. The parties have to finalize it and give it a legal shape. They have to make progress not only in the stalled dialogue, but also in getting their respective houses in order. Khurshid Mahmud Kasuri, former Foreign Minister of Pakistan, reaffirmed with yet greater detail in New Delhi on 20 January 2011, that an agreement on Kashmir was but a signature away. The leaders had only to tie the loose ends and sign the document. The Prime Minister of India was to go to Islamabad in 2007 when the crisis of the judiciary erupted in that city in March, triggering a chain of events that retarded the peace process.

Kasuri spelt out the basic elements of the accord in an article in *The Times of India* of 17 February 2011, entitled 'Peace within Our Grasp'. He wrote:

> The major features of the draft Kashmir agreement involved a gradual demilitarization as the situation improved, self-governance and a joint mechanism involving Kashmiris from both sides as well as the presence of Pakistani and Indian representatives in some form or other. The purpose was to improve the comfort level of Kashmiris. The joint mechanism envisaged cooperation in various fields including exploitation of water resources and hydroelectric power. Self-governance also provided the maximum possible powers to Kashmiris to manage their political, economic, financial and social matters, as well as those pertaining to economic development for enhanced travel and economic interaction on both sides of the LoC. For practical purposes, as far as the Kashmiris on both sides were concerned, the LoC would be made irrelevant for movement of goods and people and mitigate the misery of divided families.
>
> A related question that people sometimes ask is whether the agreement that we had arrived at had the support of the Pakistani Army. Of course, it had the support of all the stakeholders. Besides the presidency and the Foreign Office, the military was appropriately represented. The Pakistani Army high command understands clearly that national security is a very broad concept and military preparedness is only one – albeit, very important – component of it. The concept of national security includes economic and political stability, and a settlement with India on honourable terms strengthens Pakistan's national security.

In 2008 Kashmir was rocked by the controversy over grant of land for the Amarnath shrine which also split Jammu from the Valley, and in 2009, by the new Chief Minister Omar Abdullah's inept handling of the Shopian rapes. The less said about the set-up in west Kashmir the better (vide my articles in section III, reproduced in Volume II, on the constitutional force there). The Valley needs little provocation for its deeply aggrieved populace to rise in fury. The state government has provided it in ample measure. The most recent phase of the unrest began in April 2010 with the discovery of corpses of three civilians killed by the Army in a fake encounter in the Machil Sector near the LoC. In the Kalaroos graveyard of Kupwara, where they were buried as 'foreign militants', there were 65 unidentified graves. In the Pathribal fake encounter in 2000, the Army dragged the Central Bureau of Investigation (CBI) to the Supreme Court to prevent its officers from standing trial for murder.

The Army has served the nation nobly. But it has become a holy cow, exempt from any criticism and censure. Pandit Prem Nath Bazaz has referred to its excesses in Kashmir in his classic work. He wrote with 'personal knowledge' of 'acts of arson, rape, loot and murder' (Bazaz 1954: 337). It is also important to note the observation of T.C.A. Srinivasavaradan, a highly respected civil servant who spent most of his life in the Home Ministry after a tenure in Jammu. He wrote of the devastation wrought by Pakistan's Army in the 1965 war, but added:

> The devastation in Akhnoor and parts of Jammu, Ranbirsinghpura, Samba and Hiranagar tahsils was colossal but was to be expected in a war, as these areas were closest to the scenes of savage fighting. But the destruction in Rajouri, Mendhar and Poonch tahsils, extending to the remote interior of Buddhal, Mohor and Gulbargah, was unbelievable. I was rudely disillusioned for *our savagery was uncalled for, stupid and self-defeating*. Yet, no post-mortem could have helped. The consequences were identical in the two theatres: homes were destroyed, lakhs were uprooted and unprecedented human suffering followed. No one could however ignore a basic difference: nearer Jammu, there was an innate pride that the suffering was for the country, but farther away, the people were incredulous, deeply hurt, and afraid. (Srinivasavardan 1992: 18)

The Army has, for over twenty years, obstructed a settlement on Siachen and any withdrawal of troops from the area. Corps Commanders and even Army Chiefs think nothing of publicly opposing policies of the civilian government.

While there are a good many reports on violations of human rights, a well-documented 'blue book' on the events since 1990 remains to be compiled by scholars and activists who value objectivity over nationalist sentiment. Siddharth Varadarajan has documented the centre's refusal to accord sanction for the prosecution of soldiers indicted for murdering innocent civilians (Varadarajan 2010). The Army rewards soldiers monetarily for each 'terrorist' or 'infiltrator' killed. 'Informers' who lured three villagers in Machail for money and handed them over to the Army as 'infiltrators' to be killed were each paid Rs 50,000; each of the three armymen against whom an inquiry was instituted was paid Rs 1,50,000 (Joshi 2010; Das 2009).

No wonder that on 14 June, Lieutent-General B.S. Jaswal, Commander-in-Chief Northern Command, called the Armed Forces Special Powers Act (AFSPA), 1958, 'a pious book'. To him even political protest is 'agitational terrorism' (*Rising Kashmir*, 1 November 2010). It is a colonial mind-set. He conceded, though, that the AFSPA was 'despised by the people of Kashmir' (*Greater Kashmir*, 1 November 2010). The Army Chief, General V.K. Singh's plea on 25 June 2010 that its repeal would facilitate vexatious prosecution is spurious. New Delhi's sanction is necessary for prosecution. He however made a valid point, also made by his predecessors and Corps Commanders: 'I feel there is a great requirement for political initiatives which take all the people forward together. *Militarily we have brought the overall internal security situation in J&K firmly under control.* Now, the need is to handle things politically' (*The Times of India*, 30 June 2010).

Everyone concerned stresses that, but no one does anything about it. As Omar Abdullah said on 2 July 2010: 'The cure of the Kashmir issue lies in politics; it's not about jobs, roads, bridges and governance. The Centre has to find a solution through meaningful talks' (*The Times of India*, 3 July 2010). Earlier, on 28 October 2009, he had said at Anantnag in the presence of Prime Minister Manmohan Singh: 'The youth of Kashmir didn't pick up the gun twenty-one years ago for money [but for] political reasons' (*Greater Kashmir*, 29 October 2009).

A few months later the youth added a new dimension to the movement which assumed proportions reminiscent of 1990, this time forsaking the bullet for the stone. Nonetheless the police and the CRPF retaliated with the bullet, and 110 died by the time the upheaval subsided. It all began on 11 June 2010 after the Friday prayers when Tufail Mattoo, a 17-year-old schoolboy, was killed by a tear-gas shell from the police who had moved in to control a stone-pelting mob in downtown Srinagar. As Arati R. Jerath and M. Saleem Pandit put it, that was enough 'to burst the bubble of normalcy in Kashmir' (*The Times of India*, 3 July 2010).

It is little known that stone-pelting has a hallowed tradition in Kashmir, especially among the youth. The famous poet Zareef Ahmad Zareef traces its origin to the unpopular Mughal rule over Kashmir in the sixteenth century. Young men, known as 'Dilawar', would pelt stones at the patrolling Mughal soldiers. The hero of the 1931 uprising, Abdul Qadeer Khan, urged Kashmiris to fight the Dogra bullets with stones. More recently they have drawn inspiration also from the Palestinians (Ashraf 2010). Syed Ali Shah Geelani appealed to his 'supporters that nobody should resort to stone-pelting' (*The Indian Express*, 12 March 2010).

In the 2010 unrest, stone-pelting acquired a vogue few had imagined. It became a fashion to decry the stone pelters either as Pakistanis or paid performers. Photographs of middle-aged women, schoolboys and even double graduates braving bullets to fling stones at the police and CRPF caused little dent in the time-worn national shield of denial. The upheaval tested both the state and central governments. Predictably, both failed. Omar repeatedly urged the centre to initiate a political dialogue, disowning all responsibility. He did little to provide a healing touch, which is in his power to provide. He resorted instead to repression.

Home Minister P. Chidambaram proved himself to be spectacularly irrelevant and wide of the mark. A famous Lenin aphorism criticizes people who talk Left and act Right. Chidambaram talked often of a political remedy, but consistently harped on administrative measures and halting ones at that. He began by promising, on 11 June 2009 at Srinagar, 'small, baby steps one by one' – and lived up to it (*Hindustan Times*, 12 June 2009). By 14 October, at the same place, he announced: 'We'll hold a quiet diplomacy and dialogue with all the political groups in Kashmir and these would be held outside the glare of the media. We'll build a consensus which would then be made public.' He amplified: 'the Centre would engage all the groups in J&K, including the *smaller* groups that support secession' (*The Times of India*, 15 October 2009). Never short of confidence, he said, 'I am confident that within a short period of time we will be able to come up with some solution to the political problem of J&K' (*DNA*, 15 October 2009). Back in New Delhi on 30 October, he was more specific: 'I think, at least in the early stages, the talks should be held one-on-one or one with two or three people, so that we discover the contours of the proposals of each group.'

Obviously, he is unwilling to jettison the baggage he has acquired over the decades and, worse, is unwilling to learn. Even the National Conference and PDP do not consider the 'secessionists', whether of the Geelani or the Mir Waiz faction, to be 'the smaller groups'. Indeed, both Unionist Parties urge a dialogue with the Hurriyat leaders, who represent the people's 'secessionist' sentiment – which is why they have to be put under house arrest for days. The Kashmir question also has an external dimension, which the PDP's paper on self-rule emphasizes while the National Conference confines itself to its demand for autonomy. How could Chidambaram as Home Minister hope to solve the problem 'within a short period of time'? Secret diplomacy cannot go far if its initiation is proclaimed from house-tops. It bears recalling that he sought 'a *quiet* dialogue with all section of opinion, all groups, all political parties' (*The Times of India*, 30 July 2010).

Chidambaram was out to show results, and went about it as he did then and has since. The epitome of certitude, he reminds one of the county court judge who said 'this court might often be in error, but it is never in doubt'. Imagine for a moment the reaction in Kashmir if, in a formal announcement, Chidambaram had declared loud and clear: 'Total *azadi*, no government would be ready to say yes. Anything below *azadi*, we are open to negotiate on that. . . . We are ready to talk about anything.' This is precisely what P.V. Narasimha Rao said in 1995; what Manmohan Singh told Jonathan Power in May 2004; and what the Four Point formula ensures. Kasuri disclosed: 'we agreed on a point between complete independence and autonomy' (Roy 2010).

Those words were, however, also uttered by the Home Secretary, G.K. Pillai, on 5 April 2010 (*Rising Kashmir*, 6 April 2010). He said:

> We are telling everybody, please tell us what you feel is achievable. We have no fixed, closed mind. The Government of India is open. Total *azadi* (independence), no Government would be ready to say yes. Anything below *azadi*, we are open to negotiate on that. . . . We are ready to talk about anything.

Pillai was being very fair. While inviting the other side to state its terms, he also spelt out realistically the red lines within which he could act. New Delhi's besetting failing is never to state its terms but always ask the other side to state its – and then shoot them down.

Chidambaram told the Rajya Sabha on 6 August, 'The answer to the problem lies only through the political process' (*The Indian Express,* 7 August 2010). He said on 25 August:

> It is my hope that, in the next few days, we would be able to find that elusive 'starting point' from where we could reach out to the protesters, reassure them of their rights and dignity, restore peace and order, redeem the promises made, and restart the process of dialogue that will lead to a solution. (*Asian Age*, 26 August 2010)

That 'starting point' could not be the mere restart of a dialogue but a concrete basis for dialogue which other participants could find promising. His reference to pledges, as we shall see, did not include the ones of 1947–53, but illusory ones made later.

A good 'starting point' presented itself on 31 August 2010. It was studiously ignored. Syed Ali Shah Geelani gave the press a copy of his now famous 5 points – and declined to take questions. They had been prepared through wide consultations and had ample play at the joints; a promising initiative. At the very least, they could have been welcomed and Geelani invited to talks on the basis of his own document. His paper read thus:

> We, the people of Jammu Kashmir have been engaged in a struggle for our inalienable right of self-determination, for which we have been made to suffer immensely. Our right to self determination has been acknowledged by India herself in the United Nations Security Council and also in their repeated public pronouncements from 1947 to 1953. . . .
>
> Our resistance has always been met with violence from Indian State, resulting in the killing of 120,137 persons, disappearance of almost 10,000 people,

rapes and molestations of thousands of women, incarcerations, torture, extra-judicial murder, humiliation of our people and destruction of our property worth billions of dollars.

In response to the unabated brutality and the recent killings and violence from the Indian forces, people of Jammu Kashmir have for the last two and half months resorted to sustained peaceful mass protest. This non-violent up-rising has again been confronted with killings . . . amid this continued policy of oppression on ground, Indian leadership has spoken of its willingness to engage in a dialogue with Jammu Kashmir leadership . . . If India and the international community are serious in resolving the dispute its beginning is [*sic*] to be the end of Indian oppression which in itself will create conditions for resolution.

In this regard, we demand India and urge the international community to persuade India, for *creating conditions necessary for peace and resolution.*

The minimum necessary conditions that must be met without any delay are:

1) India must agree Jammu Kashmir is an international dispute.
2) India must announce and begin the process of complete demilitarization to be monitored by some credible agency.
3) Indian Prime Minister must commit publicly and ensure practically that henceforth no killings and no arrests shall take place. It should also discipline her troops and order them to stop humiliating people and destroying public and private property.
4) India should immediately and unconditionally release our children and the political prisoners. Withdraw cases against youth pending in courts for past 20 years.
5) The process of punishing the perpetrators of State violence has to begin with the conviction of troops responsible for recent 65 killings and has to be followed by convicting all those responsible for was crimes in Jammu Kashmir.

If implemented on ground in both letter and spirit, *these measures would facilitate in the creation of conductive atmosphere enabling Jammu Kashmir leadership to meet, consult and consolidate public opinion for the peaceful resolution of Kashmir dispute in accordance with the democratic principle of right to self-determination.*

The first condition can be met by drawing attention to the parleys with Pakistan. The second obviously hinges on an accord with it. The third is an admonition of the obvious. The rest are susceptible to a fair response. Muzamil Jaleel pointed out: 'If responded to constructively, this can open a new window on Kashmir – considering that Geelani currently enjoys far more confidence among Kashmiri people than any other leader.' Even the Unionists could have supported him (*The Indian Express*, 2 September 2010).

What emerged from the Cabinet Committee on Security on 25 September 2010 was the proverbial mouse from a mountain of labour. The 8 points which Chidambaram announced with fanfare belied hopes of a serious political dialogue. These extracts reveal the approach:

> (1) Appoint a Group of Interlocutors under the chairmanship of an eminent person to begin the process of a sustained dialogue with all sections of the people of Jammu and Kashmir, including political parties/groups, youth and student organizations, civil society organizations and other stakeholders; (2) Advise the State Government to immediately release all students and youth detained or arrested for stone pelting or similar violations of law and to withdraw the charges against such students and youth; (3) Advise the State Government to immediately review the cases of all Public Safety Act (PSA) detenus and withdraw the detention orders in appropriate cases; (4) Request the State Government to immediately convene a meeting of the Unified Command and to review the deployment of security forces in the Kashmir Valley, especially Srinagar, with particular reference to de-scaling the number of bunkers, checkpoints etc. in Srinagar and other towns, and to review the notification of areas as 'disturbed areas'; (5) Grant ex-gratia relief to the families of the deceased persons . . . (6) Appoint two Special Task Forces, one each for Jammu region and Ladakh region, to examine the developmental needs of the two regions . . .; (7) Request the State Government to take steps to immediately reopen all schools, colleges, universities and other educational institutions; . . . (8) Provide to the State Government a sum of Rs 100 crore as Additional Central Assistance (ACA) in order to make grants to schools and colleges for improvements and additions to the existing infrastructure such as class rooms, auditorium, laboratory, library, play ground, toilet complex etc.

The Omar Abdullah government has done little to implement points 2 to 8. Professor Angana Chatterjee of the California Institute of Integral Studies wrote a devastating critique of this plan. It

> made no commitment to investigate the killings of more than a hundred Kashmiris by the Indian forces in Summer 2010. . . . How do we take seriously that the Indian State is concerned about education in Kashmir and enabling academic freedom? School and University curricula in Kashmir largely cannot focus on issues pertinent to Kashmiri lives in global and historical context. Students seeking to study the conflict and issues of violence and militarization, in the arts, humanities, and the social sciences, are rarely permitted to do so. Faculty and student work is monitored. Institutions of higher learning in Kashmir are pre-empted from engaging in informed and empowered critique of the Indian State. Deliberate isolation of Kashmir from other worlds through the policies of the Indian State has endangered intellectual life. Innovative discourses and methodologies are infrequently accessible to Kashmiri

schoolteachers and faculty at universities. Kashmiri students who are related to former, even deceased, militants have not been permitted to travel abroad even when they have secured scholarships for further study.

The plan did not initiate a review into the conduct of Indian forces stationed at schools and colleges that psychologically degrade and physically harass girls/minors at institutions. Many young women have been traumatized by the conduct of Indian soldiers, and, at times, have been compelled to use the hijab or burkha to create a barrier to the unwanted advances of the Indian forces. . . .

Were the plan focused on demilitarization, it would have included a reduction in troops, and the elimination of electronic espionage and other monitoring mechanisms. The plan would promise to return land annexed from Kashmiris by the Indian Armed Forces. . . .

The Public Safety Act (PSA) of 1978 [which Sheikh Abdullah and Mirza Afzal Beg got enacted] has been systematically misused to contain civil disobedience, and detain persons characterized by the Indian forces as anti-national and agitational terrorists for up to two years on unconfirmed suspicion. . . . The plan outlined that the Unified Command would review the provisions of the Disturbed Areas Act of 1976. Headed by Chief Minister Omar Abdullah, the Unified Command is the supervisory organization for the Indian forces in Jammu and Kashmir. The apex body functions as a Government and military collective constituted of senior officers from the Army, CRPF, Border Security Force, Intelligence Bureau, Jammu and Kashmir Police, and civil administration personnel.

The powers of the Chief Minister have been subordinate to those of the military in Kashmir. Army officials have refuted changes proposed to impunity laws by the Chief Minister in the past. What is in place to allow different results now? Given the structure of governance in Kashmir, how is the Chief Minister in a position to compel the Unified Command to change impunity laws? Is New Delhi using the plan to implicate the Chief Minister in shifting liability from the Government of India?

Since 1990, over 70,000 people have died in Kashmir, over 8000 have been disappeared, and 2,50,000 have been displaced. More than 60,000 have been tortured. Approximately 6,71,000 troops administer Kashmir today, while official figures record the presence of approximately 800 militants. . . .

The 8-point plan is intended to disperse the resistance in Kashmir, not address injustices as a precursor to sincere dialogue. The Indian State's treatment of Kashmir betrays its state of mind. While the Indian State's discourse focused on how the Government of India was intent on ameliorating conditions in Kashmir, in practice, it regularized states of exception. . . .

New Delhi's strategy in Kashmir functions to control crises and maintain the status quo. The Government of India's promises are performative speech acts without follow-through, a national public relations campaign for local and international consumption that evades responsibility to address the concerns and hopes of Kashmiris. (Chatterjee 2010)

An all-party delegation of MPs visited Kashmir on 20 and 21 September 2010. Some of its members met Geelani, Mir Waiz and other separatists. They learnt a lot. On 13 October 2010, the Home Ministry made an order which read:

Keeping in view the immediate objectives to maintain peace and order and defuse the situation through confidence-building measures, Government of India took certain decisions and one of the decisions is to appoint a Group of Interlocutors under the chairmanship of an eminent person to hold a sustained dialogue with all sections of the people in Jammu and Kashmir.

Accordingly, the Government is pleased to appoint the following persons as Interlocutors. Shri Dileep Padgaonkar will chair the meetings of the Group of Interlocutors. (1) Dr Dileep Padgaonkar, Asia Pacific Communications Pvt. Ltd., Journalist, Editor, Author, (2) Professor M.M. Ansari, Central Information Commissioner, Economist, Professor, Author, (3) Professor Radha Kumar, Trustee, Delhi Policy Group, Professor, Author.

The detailed terms and conditions of appointment will be issued separately.

The terms and conditions were specified in another order on December 2010. They were:

(i) The appointment shall be effective from the date of joining of the Interlocutors until further orders. (ii) The Interlocutors shall be entitled for a fixed monthly remuneration of Rs 1.5 lakh. So far as Professor M.M. Ansari, Information Commissioner, CIC, is concerned, the remuneration would be minus existing lump sum pay/pension (after retirement). (iii) Each Interlocutor shall be permitted an Executive Assistant who will be appointed by the Interlocutor with an overall remuneration not exceeding Rs 40,000 p.m. Necessary office equipments and computers including furniture shall be lent by MHA. (iv) Interlocutors would be provided 3 rooms at the Vigyan Bhavan – one each for their common office, conference and staff respectively. Until the office accommodation is provided, they can meet at the India International Centre. The charges will be reimbursed by MHA. They will be provided secretarial assistance of one or two persons as per need from the Ministry. (v) Personal telephone charges of Interlocutors would be reimbursed upto Rs 2600 per month. However there shall be no ceiling on calls made for official purposes. (vi) The Interlocutors will be treated as State Guests during their travel and stay in Jammu and Kashmir. (vii) The cost of travel of Interlocutors outside Delhi in Executive Class would be reimbursed by MHA. The facility of travel for official purposes within Delhi would also be reimbursed by MHA. (viii) Expenditure on meetings etc. at Delhi and J&K State would be reimbursed as per actuals subject to a ceiling of Rs 200 per head.

According to Home Minister P. Chidambaram, the task of the Interlocutors was 'to understand their [Kashmiris'] problems and chart a course for the future'. The government 'hopes that after interacting with all shades of political opinion they will suggest a way forward that truly reflects the aspirations of Jammu and Kashmir, especially the youth'. Thus, their task was two-fold: (a) to ascertain what the people wanted; (b) to suggest a practicable solution. To a question that none of them had a political background, Chidambaram glibly replied that all had a political persona (*The Hindu*, 14 October 2010).

The *Concise Oxford Dictionary* provides instructive meanings of both words: 'persona' and 'interlocutor'. Persona is '(1) the aspect of a person's character that is presented to or perceived by others, (2) a role or character adopted by an author or actor.' To the people at large, none of the three had a political background or was a participant in politics. As we shall see, the Group readily and swiftly 'adopted' a political role for itself, and the members conducted themselves with an aim and ardour that squeezed out all traces of detachment and objectivity. They performed to a set script, living up to Dr Johnson's definition in his *Dictionary*: 'To personate: to represent by a fictitious or assumed character so as to pass for the person represented.' The *Concise Oxford Dictionary* says that an interlocutor is 'a person who takes part in a dialogue or conversation'. This is akin to the *informateur* in some European countries who takes soundings from political leaders in times of a constitutional deadlock. He listens and reports, thus initiating a process that holds promise.

Chidambaram's 8 points of 25 September 2010 envisaged a Group 'under the chairmanship of an eminent person to *begin* the process of a sustained dialogue'. The order of 13 October set out a limited mandate: 'to hold a sustained dialogue with all sections of the people' and to report. However, the Home Minsiter's statement on the same day expressed the hope that 'they will suggest a way forward *that truly reflects the aspirations of Jammu & Kashmir, especially the youth*' – not a way that reflected the Interlocutors' views but that of the people.

The Group's exertions reflected the aims and spirit of its origin, the sterile 8 points. It was a farce enacted at enormous waste of the tax-payers' money; a ploy to gain time. In Angana Chatterjee's words, the aim was 'to disperse the resistance movement'. Chidambaram was not one to handpick as Interlocutors persons who would touch the reality of the Kashmiri people's alienation; and those who accepted the assignment – solid establishment figures, all – were not the ones to dwell on the fundamental realities and speak the truth to power. The great constitutionalist lawyer A.V. Dicey has brilliantly described the delicacies of such a relationship in another context: 'People sometimes ask the idle question why the Pope does not introduce this or that reform. The true answer is that a revolutionist is not the kind of man who becomes a Pope, and that the man who becomes a Pope has no wish to be a revolutionist' (Dicey 1982: 80).

None of the three Interlocutors was known for empathy with Kashmiris. Padgaonkar was editor of *The Times of India* when militancy erupted in the state. His brand of nationalism, reflected in his writings, had no patience with Amnesty International as it gave one report after another exposing the wrongs perpetrated by the Indian state in Kashmir.

Far more disturbing is the record of Radha Kumar. In the wake of the disclosures in August 2011 about Padgaonkar's participation in a conference hosted by well-known Pakistani lobbyist in the US, Ghulam Nabi Fai, and similar indiscretion by Radha Kumar in 2004, she delivered herself of statements which condemned her of her own mouth. In a letter to Chidambaram, she openly admitted that in 2006 she had participated in a conference in Brussels convened by Abdul Majeed Tramboo, equally notorious as a lobbyist for Pakistan. She said that she went there at the behest of the Government of India, accompanied by G. Parthasarathi: 'We were both encouraged to go by the Government of India'; '[we] were *briefed* by the Ministry of External Affairs and were in touch with our Embassy in Brussels *before, during and after* the Conference'; 'I did not want to go to the Tramboo Conference but did so because government thought it might be useful' (*The Indian Express*, 8 August 2011; Chishti 2011). The newspaper published the entire text of her letter to Chidambaram on 10 August. On 16 August Radha Kumar boldly asserted: 'I was *asked* to go. And there is no question of that. *I did not go on my own*. So, I feel [this is] something I did for my country and the government' (*The Hindu*, 16 August 2011). A person who so readily lends herself to such services and, indeed, to a subterfuge, acting under the masquerade of an independent person while performing at the prodding of the government, brings into question her independence as an Interlocutor as well as her role in her previous forays into the Valley.

Chidambaram did not react to the disclosures, but Radha Kumar's claim was repudiated by the government. In replies received by the daily *DNA* under the Right to Information (RTI) Act, the Home Ministry and the Ministry of External Affairs denied giving permission to her or to Padgaonkar, respectively, to attend the Tramboo and Fai jamborees. 'Replies received by *DNA* to queries under the RTI Act show that Kumar neither sought permission *nor was she asked by the External Affairs Ministry or the Home Ministry* to attend the Conference . . . her travel expenses were picked up by Tramboo' (*DNA*, 11 October 2011). When contacted by *DNA*, she said: 'I do not have time to comment on this ridiculous matter. I did not need clearance. I said the government knew I was going and it was in the loop' (ibid.).

As for Dileep Padgaonkar, his wrath at being 'let down' and 'betrayed' by Fai is surprising. 'I did not know who he was or what are his links. In a way, he lied to us' (*Asian Age*, 9 December 2011). The question is, why did he accept expensive air tickets and hospitality from someone he 'did not know' and 'whose links' he was unaware of. By 2003 Fai's status as a lobbyist for Pakistan was known to all, bar those who kept their eyes shut.

In South Asia, the concepts of track II and back channel are little understood. Track II is conducted by persons who are knowledgeable and independent. Back channel is officially sponsored by governments to ensure speed and secrecy. The former civil servants, diplomats and intelligence officers let loose on Kashmir were neither. The country was not new to the institution of Interlocutors: they had served in Nagaland, Assam and in J&K as well. Some were men of grit and spine who gave up on their mandate: Swaraj Kaushal, for example. One of the main Interlocutors appointed by the Government of West Bengal to conduct a dialogue with the Maoists said, on 26 November 2011, after the killing of the CPI (Maoist) leader Kishenji: 'We are seriously considering our role as Interlocutors on this issue' (*The Hindu*, 27 November 2011; see Singh 2011).

The aptest parallel is a similar exercise set afoot by Chidambaram himself in the same year as the Group of Interlocutors was established. Pursuant to his meeting with eight recognized political parties of Andhra Pradesh on 5 January 2010, he constituted a Committee for consultations on the situation in Andhra Pradesh. Its members were Justice B.N. Srikrishna, retired judge, Supreme Court of India, as Chairman; Professor Ranbir Singh, Vice Chancellor, National Law University, Delhi; Dr Abusaleh Sharief, Senior Research Fellow, International Food Policy Research Institute, Delhi; Professor Ravinder Kaur, Professor, Department of Humanities and Social Sciences, IIT, Delhi; and V.K. Duggal, former Union Home Secretary, as Member Secretary.

The Chairman, Member Secretary and three members joined the Committee on 3 February 2010. The Chairman was accorded the status of a sitting Supreme Court judge and the Member Secretary, the rank of a Union Minister of State. The three members were appointed on a part-time basis. The Committee's terms of reference were :

1. To examine the situation in the State of Andhra Pradesh with reference to the demand for a separate State of Telengana as well as the demand for maintaining the present status of a united Andhra Pradesh;

2. To review the developments in the State since its formation and their impact on the progress and development of the different regions of the State;

3. To examine the impact of the recent developments in the State on the different sections of the people such as women, children, students, minorities, other backward classes, scheduled castes and scheduled tribes;

4. To identify the key issues that must be addressed while considering the matters mentioned in items (1), (2) and (3) above;

5. To consult all sections of the people, especially the political parties, on the aforesaid matters and elicit their views; *to seek from the political parties and other organizations a range of solutions that would resolve the present difficult situation* and promote the welfare of all sections of the people; to identify the optimal solutions for this purpose; and to recommend a plan of action and a road map;

6. To consult other organizations of civil society such as industry, trade, trade unions, farmers' organizations, women's organizations and students' organizations on the aforesaid matters and elicit their views with specific reference to the all round development of the different regions of the State;

7. To make any other suggestion or recommendation that the Committee may deem appropriate. (Government of India 2011)

The Committee commissioned studies by experts. Its members visited all the twenty-three districts of the state, met a large number of persons, and 'received utmost support and cooperation from the political parties'. Its report of 441 pages (Volume I) was promptly published on 30 December 2010 (Volume II has the Appendices and an Index). What is most noteworthy about this work is that it was conducted with perfect dignity and in earnest. There were no public spats between its members, nor did they conduct a running commentary on the issues before them.

Kashmir itself has had more than its fair share of Interlocutors – some public, some secretly sponsored by New Delhi. Two Interlocutors in the past – K.C. Pant in 2001 and N.N. Vora in April 2003 – failed conspicuously, but worked on the quiet. Incredibly, on 22 July 2002, the egregiously illiberal Arun Jaitley was nominated as 'Representative' of the Government of India for holding talks with the 'nominees' of the state government and others, on the issue of devolution of powers (Ministry of Home Affairs 2003: 20). His efforts can well be imagined.

We have a full record of Pant's failure in the correspondence he had with separatist leaders. On 14 April 2001, he wrote identical letters to the Chairman of the All Party Hurriyat Conference (APHC), Professor Abdul Ghani Bhat, to Shabir Ahmed Shah (formerly of the APHC and now President, J&K Democratic Freedom Party), and presumably to others as well. He enclosed the Government of India's Statement of 5 April 2001 which declared that 'the Government have decided to embark upon a *political* dialogue with all sections of the people'. No conditions were set; the APHC was asked not to set any either. The agenda was: 'Peace and how it may be attained in the troubled state'. The government was prepared for talks with Pakistan as well. Accordingly, Pant invited the leaders 'for a discussion', as a prelude to a political dialogue.

Shabir Shah replied on 1 May asking for 'a comprehensive dialogue' with all the three parties: India, Pakistan and 'the genuine representatives of the people' of the state. 'Redundant elements [must] be discarded', he said.

Pant met Shah's colleagues on 3 May and replied on 13 May. All must have a say, he insisted, and renewed his plea for a dialogue. Shabir Shah's letter of 29 May followed soon after Vajpayee's invitation to Pervez Musharraf, Chief Executive of Pakistan, to visit India for talks. Shah demanded an end to human rights violations and the creation of 'a congenial atmosphere in which a comprehensive dialogue . . . can thrive'.

This is the crux of the matter. New Delhi must first take a major policy decision on how far it is prepared to go to meet the Kashmiris' demands, and then select a negotiator who can win popular support for any settlement that may be reached. In all these years not one government at the centre has taken such a decision. Frustrated, the APHC has fragmented. The Unionists, the National Conference and the PDP, seek restructuring of centre–state relations and redressal of grievances. Jammuites and Ladakhis are content with the former, but have grievances. *The separatists seek a change in the present order itself, not mere redressal of grievances*. In this, they mirror public opinion.

None other than Omar Abdullah, the state's Chief Minister, said on 2 July 2010 that the crux of the Kashmir issue lies in politics. To quote him: 'It is not about jobs, roads and bridges and governance. The Centre has to find a solution through meaningful talks' (*The Times of India*, 3 July 2010) – he had said much the same in November 2009, when people had taken up the gun for political reasons. On 12 July he accepted that 'mainstream' parties do not have much influence in the areas that are disturbed: 'Even the moderate secessionists do not have much influence there' (*The Hindu*, 12 July 2010). In sum, what was needed was 'a political solution that addresses the alienation and emotional needs of the people' (*The Hindu*, 11 August 2010; Gupta 2010). Mainstream is a misnomer for the Unionists. In truth it is the separatists who are in the mainstream.

2010 was by far the worst year since the decline of militancy. Arun Joshi reported that:

> In the April 30 'encounter' in Machail in Kupwara district near the LoC, three villagers in search of work were lured by fellow Kashmiris looking for lucre and handed over to the Army as 'infiltrators'. They were promptly shot dead. The three 'informers' were paid Rs 50,000 each and the three armymen, against whom an enquiry has been instituted, were paid Rs 1,50,000 each, said a well placed official source who did not want to be named. (*The Hindustan Times*, 8 June 2010)

The Hindu had a scathing editorial in its issue of 14 June 2010, aptly entitled 'Murderers in Olive Green'.

Peaceful protest was not permitted because, Chidambaram said, this 'strategy' of the protestors was 'to convince the world about the so-called justice of Kashmiris' cause'. He went so far as to attribute the domestic upheaval to Pakistan's 'change in strategy' (*The Times of India*, 8 August 2010). He had unwittingly exposed New Delhi's problem – it simply cannot allow peaceful protest, or truly free and fair elections, in an atmosphere free from intimidation, press control, and the money power of the security and intelligence agencies. *For if it did, the people's rejection of the accession and of the Union will become manifest beyond denial, for all the world to see.*

It is, however, part of the same truth that India just cannot and will not allow Kashmir to secede. 2012 is not 1947. Equities have grown since 1947. The honest course is to accept both truths, and embark sincerely on a purposeful dialogue with Kashmiris and with Pakistan. This is beyond the ken of the Chidambarams of this world. The escapist course which he initiated and pursued, with great zeal and fanfare, was not designed to promote a settlement but to buy time. In the process, the Group of Interlocutors made a mess of an already hopeless situation. The separatists instantly and rightly refused to talk to the Group.

The Group's Report holds no secrets. Padgaonkar and Kumar had freely voiced their strong, preconceived notions ahead of their much-vaunted exploration. Here is a chart of the rake's progress:

13 October 2010: 'The Group hopes that after interacting with all shades of political opinion they will suggest a way forward that truly reflects the aspirations of the people of J&K' (*The Hindu*, 14 October 2010). Again, on 19 October, they hoped 'to arrive at a comprehensive political settlement of the Kashmir dispute' (*The Hindu*, 21 October 2010). Chidambaram endorsed that on the same day: 'The focus will be to seek a political outcome so that we put this dispute well and truly behind us' (*The Times of India*, 20 October 2010).

The team of Interlocutors arrived in Srinagar on 23 October. The next day, its leader Padgaonkar said: 'a dialogue with Pakistan is as essential as the dialogue with people in the State' (*The Asian Age*, 24 October 2010). On 27 October he expressed a desire to visit west Kashmir so as 'to talk to the leadership there' (*Hindustan Times*, 28 October 2010).

By 1 November Chidambaram was fully convinced that his nominees had managed to 'change the discourse', a claim he repeated two months later (*Hindustan Times*, 2 November 2010; *Greater Kashmir*, 5 January 2011). On December 9 he confidently assured the Consultative Committee of Parliament that 'contours of a political solution to the Kashmir problem are likely to emerge in the next few months' (PTI, *Greater Kashmir,* 10 December 2010). On 1 November, about a fortnight after the Group was set up, Chidambaram also cautioned that there should be no 'ball by ball commentary', even lecturing to the media: 'I think the media should not ask and the Interlocutors should not give a ball by ball commentary about their dialogue. This is interlocution' (*Hindustan Times*, 2 November 2010).

The Interlocutors trained their guns on the state government. On 28 November 2010, Radha Kumar said: 'Their [the people's] confidence and trust in the instruments of governance has been completely shaken' (*The*

Indian Express, 29 November 2010). The National Conference MP Mehboob Beg was provoked into telling them that they should address why the youth were shouting 'Go India, go' during the six months of agitation that year. Reacting to their comment of 23 December that there was a 'trust deficit between the rulers and the ruled', Beg said: 'Their efforts should have been directed at addressing the alienation instead of using the words "trust deficit"' (*Greater Kashmir*, 27 December 2010).

On 19 December 2010, ten months before submission of their report, Padgaonkar announced that the Group would indeed recommend Regional Councils for Rajauri and Poonch. In response, Mir Waiz Umar Farooq perceptively warned: 'A discourse is being run to project the freedom struggle in Kashmir as a Jammu versus Kashmir clash. It also tries to mislead people into believing that our movement is not supported by the Shia community, Gujjars or Paharis' (*Greater Kashmir*, 3 January 2011). Padgaonkar proved him right. He said on 21 January that only 'a small but vocal section of the people harped on UN resolutions, plebiscite and self-determination resulting in independence for the State as it existed before August 1947. However, most people we spoke to did not refer to these options' (*DNA*, 22 January 2011). As far back as on 14 October 2009 Chidambaram had sung the same tune without undertaking any elaborate tour of Kashmir, referring to 'the smaller groups that support secessionism'. Mir Waiz was proved right once again when Padgaonkar said, on 26 February 2011, that there were diverse opinions and aspirations among the people at the regional level. To be fair, the statement is true; but its motivation became evident when its suspected implications were fleshed out.

On 24 March 2011, in an interview to *Greater Kashmir,* Radha Kumar was surprisingly modest: 'The political contours report *was intended to stimulate a discussion, not make recommendations*, unlike our previous reports which recommended a slew of confidence building measures (CBMs) and improvements on the ground.' Further: '*We do not seek to recommend a solution*; we seek voices from Jammu and Kashmir on what a lasting solution could be. Our mandate was to hold a sustained political dialogue with all sections of public and political opinion in Jammu and Kashmir' – in short, furthering the dialogue process. She also revealed: 'I did some work for R.K. Mishra, who was doing a back channel [in 1999 with Niaz Naik of Pakistan], as well as during the Agra Summit [July 2011].' Come 16 June 2011, she said that a solution had to come from within. Her views on Kashmiris were odd. In an article to a newspaper, she criticized that 'suffering' was being 'couched in religious terms'. Jammu and Ladakh had become 'increasingly polarized distancing between their districts and/or communities' (*The Times of India*, 10 July 2011).

Dileep Padgaonkar declaimed, 'We are not Kashmir centric' (*Greater Kashmir*, 13 July 2011). To Sankarshan Thakur of *The Telegraph*, he spoke of 'a very strong and competitive victimhood' – a laboured formulation to equate the Valley's *rejection* of the Union with Jammu's grievances.

> Repeatedly during the interactions, the demand that Jammu deserves more seats in the Assembly than the Valley came up. Jammu sends 37 MLAs to the Assembly against the Valley's 46; Ladakh elects only four representatives. Jammu has a distinct population edge over the Valley and has been demanding greater representation. (*The Telegraph*, 4 August 2011)

Padgaonkar considered Jammu's demand 'absolutely fair'. Jammu, he said, not merely has 'a justifiable political case based on demography, it also feels "overpowered" by the Valley' (ibid.).

Against this background, the Final Report submitted by the Interlocutors on 12 October 2011 came as no surprise (Group of Interlocutors for J&K 2011). It fully vindicates the separatists' boycott of the Group, very much as the Simon Commission's Report vindicated the nationalists' boycott. The Report is worse than useless as a basis for a dialogue. To assess its worth and the competence of its authors one must read the Group's 'final interim document on the contours of a political settlement in Jammu and Kashmir', submitted to the Home Minister, P. Chidambaram, on 31 May 2011.

This 'final interim document' bristles with inconsistencies, disruptive formulations and crass ignorance. Sample the following passages.

> The Delhi Agreement was codified with minor changes in Article 370 and the Jammu and Kashmir Constitution, but subsequently a series of executive orders vitiated many of their provisions. Article 370 flowed from the Delhi Agreement of 1952, whose key features are . . .

Article 370 of the Constitution of India was enacted by the Constituent Assembly of India in October 1949. The Delhi Agreement was concluded between Prime Minister Jawaharlal Nehru and Prime Minister Sheikh Abdullah in July 1952. Article 370 could not possibly have 'flowed from the Delhi Agreement of 1952' – a document that came into being three years later.

> The sense of victimhood is articulated in the most intense, emotional terms in the Kashmir Valley. The reasons are all too compelling. Here, for over six decades, people have experienced what, in their eyes, constitutes a systematic denial of their democratic rights. They have been witness to rigged elections, the dismissal of elected governments and installation of pliant ones, the arrests of their tallest leaders, the choking of dissenting voices through harsh laws, the detention of political prisoners without the due process of law, the failure to bring to book those guilty of violating human rights (including the exodus of Kashmiri Pandits) and, not in the least, violence perpetrated by militants and, in retaliation, by the security forces.

> Add to this the widespread allegations of mis-governance, pervasive corruption among the political and bureaucratic elites, lack of quality education and public health services, poor physical infrastructure and woefully inadequate job opportunities, especially for skilled and educated youth. All these factors, taken together with what is seen as a mushroom growth of religious extremism of all hues, have brutalized Kashmiri society to such an extent that today it fears for the very survival of its religious and cultural identity.

The security forces perpetrate violence only 'in retaliation'. Kashmir's alienation from the Union and its yearning for a settlement with Pakistan are glossed over. Omar Abdullah is more realistic: 'The youth [of the Valley] did not take up the gun for *bijli, pani, sadak* [electricity, water, roads] but for resolution of the Kashmir issue' (*DNA*, 2 March 2011). In none of the profuse comments of the Group's members do we see even a glimpse of the grim reality known to all. They prefer to spin phrases and spread myths equating the Valley's alienation with the grievances of other regions, under the Group's umbrella of 'competitive victimhood'.

Professing support for the unity of J&K, the report fosters disruption.

> The concerns, interests and aspirations of Jammu and Ladakh are of another order. Both regions strongly believe that the Valley politicians have given them a raw deal. Significant sections of opinion prefer a closer integration of the State with the Indian Union. In fact they want Article 370 to be jettisoned root and branch.
>
> Within these regions, however, some communities have their own set of grievances. The five Muslim-majority districts of Jammu direct their ire at the Hindu and Muslim Dogra Jammuites, much like the Shia-dominated Kargil district in Ladakh nurses a grouse against Buddhist-dominated Leh. The people of these districts, especially the substantial non-Muslim minorities, rule out any attempt to divide the State along religious lines on the grounds that any such division – like granting Union Territory status to Ladakh or the creation of a separate state in Jammu – will force non-Kashmiri Muslims, much against their gain, to cast their lot with the Kashmir Valley.

Radha Kumar was more candid. Eschewing the cant in this passage, she said on 17 October 2011, after the finally Final Report: 'In Jammu there is a communal polarization when it comes to the status question. *The Muslims of Jammu feel a sense of solidarity with the Valley Muslims on the status of the State*' (*DNA*, 17 October 2011). That is no less true of Kargil, 'Shia-dominated' to Padgaonkar. Jammu Muslims will not be *forced* to cast their lot with the Valley 'much against their grain'. They long to do so. There is a hint of this in the Final Report (paragraph 28).

On 27 June 2000, at Leh, Union Home Minister L.K. Advani encouraged the idea of trifurcation of J&K. So did the Ladakh Buddhist Association's memorandum to the Prime Minister. Alarmed, Chief Minister Farooq

Abdullah warned in Srinagar on 2 October that in that event, the districts of Doda, Poonch and Rajouri will not live with Jammu, and that will trigger something worse than the Jammu massacres in 1947 (*Kashmir Times*, 3 October 2000).

Jammu will split evenly. Three of its six districts have a Muslim majority: Doda (63.59 per cent), Poonch (88.87 per cent) and Rajouri (60.97 per cent). The latter two abut the LoC. The other three are Udhampur, Jammu and Kathua. A tehsil in Udhampur, Gool Gulab Garh, and three in Rajouri will go to the Valley. Ladakh was split in 1979 into two districts: Muslim-majority Kargil and Buddhist-majority Leh. Having set the ball rolling himself and watched the Rashtriya Swayamsevak Sangh (RSS) take it up on 4 September, Advani mollified his ally Farooq Abdullah; he said in Srinagar on 22 October, 'we do not favour trifurcation'. Unlike Advani, the Chief Minister was alive to the implications: 'India will be left with two and a half districts while the so-called Greater Kashmir would go on a platter to Pakistan eventually' (*Greater Kashmir*, 11 December 2000).

The Press Trust of India reported from Leh on December 17 that, in the recently concluded polls to the Ladakh Autonomous Hill Development Council, 'votes were cast along communal lines'. In the 1996 elections to the State Assembly, Gool Gulab Garh and Gool Arns, another Muslim-majority constituency in Udhampur, returned Muslim MLAs; so did Darhal and Rajouri in Rajouri district. Bar the BJP, almost all put up Muslim candidates. Advani could not have been ignorant of this tragic communal polarization.

The Interlocutors' Final Report of October 2011 amplifies the themes and concepts constantly voiced by Padgaonkar earlier, shared by Radha Kumar and M.M. Ansari as signatories. The document is couched in the idiom of polemics; the bias is betrayed page after page. Who, pray, are in the 'mainstream', the Unionists or the separatists – called 'dissident political formations'? The latter are told that 'their commitment to democracy and pluralism must be above board'. Neither is the National Conference a shining example of such commitment, nor has New Delhi shown such commitment in its manipulation of the political process in the state, especially in the Valley.

On Article 370, the Final Report betrays the same paternalistic and patronizing approach that marked the Report of the Simon Commission. However, unlike the Chairman of the Simon Commission, Sir John Simon, who knew the successive Government of India Acts like the back of his hand, New Delhi's nominees could not read Article 370 properly, let alone understand its history and significance.

> A number of reports have been written on the political contours of a solution for Jammu and Kashmir, most of them dwelling on the history of agreements made and violated, both allegedly and in fact. We have not repeated these

> historical accounts because they already provide ready reference points, and because there are new realities to be factored in, which impact on the formulations of an earlier age. To this extent, *we have tried to get away from the baggage of history while dealing with its core issues, comprising the aspirations of the people of Jammu and Kashmir.*
>
> These aspirations are a complex mixture of desires for redressal of the past, including historical grievances, and anger at current daily life harassments, combined with the longing to envision a future that connects them to the opportunities of a globalizing world and a liberalizing India. . . . All of these, however, are tied in public perception to the larger political issue of Jammu and Kashmir's status and relationship to the Indian Union, with many, if not all, failures of the State administration being laid at New Delhi's door. (Group of Interlocutors 2011: 14)

The Group's solicitude for New Delhi is as touching as its attempt to dismiss the past and lump erosion of Article 370 with other grievances is laboured. Its perception of 'the aspirations' of the people reflects its perception of its real task.

It was New Delhi which propped up the regimes in Srinagar, as former Governor of J&K, B.K. Nehru, has testified. The 'aspirations' are for *azadi* or independence. Article 370 was crafted to ensure as much of it as possible within the Union. That explains why 'alienation runs very deep in the Valley, anger still bubbles on the surface'. Even trivial incidents trigger huge protests.

A report in *The Indian Express* of 8 November 2011 by Bashaarat Masood illustrates the realities: denial of the right to protest, total absence of any instigation to violence by any leader, police repression, and the traditional response of stone-pelting.

> Violent protests marred Eid celebrations in several parts of the Valley on Monday. In south Kashmir, seventeen police and paramilitary personnel, including seven officers, were injured when protesters threw stones at them. As the congregational Eid prayers ended, people took to the streets at Anantnag, Sopore and old Srinagar city, raising pro-freedom slogans. The biggest protest was held at Anantnag, where hundreds of people participated in a procession. When the police and CRPF personnel tried to stop them, the protesters pelted stones at them.
>
> Significantly, no separatist leader had called for protests today. Police had already put Hurriyat hardliner Syed Ali Shah Geelani under house arrest to prevent him from addressing an Eid congregation. However, Mirwaiz Umar Farooq was allowed to address the congregation at Srinagar's grand mosque.

The Interlocutors' Final Report 'calls, in the first place for upholding the distinctive status of Jammu and Kashmir – enshrined in Article 370 of the

Constitution of India – in letter and spirit'. It proceeds in the very next sentences to endorse its erosion, admitted by Nehru himself in 1963.

> The State must be at liberty to acquire such powers as it needs to promote the welfare of its people on its own terms. Political space must be provided to all stakeholders to finesse Jammu and Kashmir's constitutional bonds with the Indian Union that find mention in both the Constitution of India and the Jammu and Kashmir Constitution. It stands to reason that such an exercise would in no way compromise India's internal and external security requirements. (Group of Interlocutors for J&K 2011)

The Group of Interlocutors' prime task was to ascertain public opinion and recommend accordingly. Instead, the trio consistently impose their views, predetermined and rejectionist, on the people. Those who drafted Article 370 in 1949 had no such fears of security; the Group voices them in 2011. Article 370 will not be restored to what it was before it was wrecked systematically (vide Noorani 2011). Only the powers the state now 'needs' will be transferred. They ask: 'What powers does the State needs to assert its special status? And what is it [J&K] ready to surrender to the Centre to assert its constitutional bonds with the Indian Union?' (Group of Interlocutors for J&K 2011). After this gratuitous balancing they opine, 'we believe that retaining many of the Central laws made applicable to the State over the past six decades should not give rise to any strong objections' (ibid.). They, not the people, determine what is or is not objectionable. This recipe will satisfy none in Kashmir. But Kashmiris' opinion is irrelevant. Only the Group's edict matters.

On the Governor, the Final Report says: 'The State Government, after consultations with Opposition parties, shall submit a list of three names to the President. The President can ask for more suggestions if required. The Governor will be appointed by the President and hold office at the pleasure of the President' (ibid.). This makes a mockery of the Delhi Agreement. The recommendation reduces J&K to the level of other states. The Assembly will not elect the Governor, the Sadar-i-Riyasat, nor even elect a panel. The state government will 'do the needful', as the phrase goes.

A Constitutional Committee is proposed: 'to review all Central Acts and Articles of the Constitution of India' extended to the state after 1952. The review will therefore have to determine whether – and to what extent – the Central Acts and Articles of the Constitution of India, extended with or without amendment to the state, have dented Jammu and Kashmir's special status and abridged the state government's powers to cater to the welfare of its people (ibid.). All this, the Committee will 'determine'. Also, it

> should be future-oriented in that it should conduct its review solely on the basis of the powers that the State needs to address the political, economic,

> social and cultural interests, concerns, grievances and aspirations of the people in all the three regions of the State – Jammu, Kashmir and Ladakh – and all its sub-regions and communities. In this connection, the Committee will also need to reflect on the quantum of legislative, financial and administrative powers that the state Government should delegate to the three regions at all levels of governance – the regional, district and panchayat/municipality. (Ibid.)

Kashmir's grievance on Article 370 is deliberately ignored. It was the centre's amassment of power in breach of Article 370 which itself 'dented' the special status. It is not for others to determine what powers Kashmir 'needs'. What is demanded is restoration of usurped power – and fulfilment of pledges. The Final Report is emphatic in its denial of Kashmiris' rights.

The Interlocutors' confidence is not backed by competence. They propose a final order under Article 370: 'The order will need to be ratified by a Bill in both Houses of Parliament and by each House in the State Legislature by a margin of not less than two-thirds majority of the total membership present and voting in each House. It will then be presented to the President for assent' (ibid.). This is sheer nonsense. An order under Article 370 needs no such ratification.

> The Group of Interlocutors does not recommend a pure and simple return to the pre-1953 situation. This would create a dangerous constitutional vacuum in the Centre–State relationship. The clock cannot be set back. What it does recommend is a case-by-case review of all Central laws and Articles of the Constitution of India extended to the State after the July 1952 Delhi Agreement that takes into full account the following factors. (Ibid.)

These are listed. Interlocutors are supposed to learn from the dialogues they conduct. However, not one of the parties in Kashmir suggests these arrangements. They are designed to please not Srinagar but New Delhi.

If, on the limited but important issue of Article 370, the Group can be so insensitive to Kashmiris' rights, it only proclaims its ineptitude and irrelevance to the peace process. No Committee can determine a matter which is entirely for the people first to determine and, next, to negotiate with the Union.

In contrast, the Group is generous to Jammu and Ladakh. Just as it urges that Article 370 must be upheld 'in letter and spirit', and proceeds to rob it of worth, it pleads for upholding the unity of the state and goes on to prescribe the route for its disruption. 'Create three Regional Councils, one each for Jammu, Kashmir and Ladakh (the latter would no longer be a division of Kashmir but would be given provincial status). Devolve enabling *legislative* power, and executive and financial powers to them' (ibid.). A federation within a federation is proposed. It is unthinkable that Maharashtra, for example, would endow Vidharbha with *legislative* powers, a half-way house to its separation as a state proper. In J&K it is certain to have the same result, given the state of feelings in the regions.

There is a perfunctory and misleading reference in the Report to Sheikh Abdullah's proposals on regional autonomy. 'In a broadcast from Radio Kashmir on 17 August 1953, he remarked that such autonomy "would remove all fears of domination of one unit over the other and will make for the voluntary unity and consolidation of the people of the State".' Never mind the fact that the Sheikh had been arrested on 9 August 1953, the Report adds:

> In 1968, a Jammu and Kashmir Peoples' Convention, attended by leading personalities from within and outside the State, including Sheikh Abdullah and Jayaprakash Narayan, called for setting up elected Regional Councils with Executive Councilors. It defined the composition, powers and functions of institutions at the regional, district, block and panchayat levels.

Not surprisingly, Justice S. Saghir Ahmad's report is not quoted. He had completely rejected the proposal to create Regional Councils. This is what he said:

> The mere creation of Regional Councils may not be sufficient in dealing with the issue of sub-regional deprivation. Also no clarity could emerge from the discussions of the Working Group members on the composition of such Councils and the powers that should be devolved upon them. . . . It would not be possible to agree with the proposal to create Regional Assemblies, as this would go against the consensus of the Working Group that the State should continue as a single unit without any division into smaller legislative or administrative units. (Ahmad 2009, Vol. 2: 68–69)

The Ladakh Autonomous Hill Development Council Act, 1997, confers on the Council vast 'executive powers' in relation to twenty-eight matters (Section 23), as well as the power to levy and collect taxes on fifteen matters (Section 24). It is a model for emulation in Jammu, albeit with suitable adaptations.

It is, indeed, a recurring pattern: uphold the principle, deny it in practice. 'The house arrest of most of the Hurriyat and affiliated leaders on Eid was counter-productive *though understandable* given their stated objective of leading protests, and Mr Geelani's onslaught on Hazratbal.' The language belongs to journalism of the vulgar kind. 'Geelani's onslaught on Hazratbal' conveys precisely nothing. There is no discussion of his 5 points in the Report, nor any reference to his advice that the Kashmiris' struggle 'will be peaceful. There will be no use of gun, grenade, tear gas or any other weapon in it' (*The Telegraph*, 22 April 2011).

Sample this statement from the Report: 'Lift curbs on the media but also get them to observe a self-regulated code of conduct. Our Group had to cancel a couple of appointments because someone had tipped off the media to converge on the venues. The participants did not wish to be identified.' Will Padgaonkar, a veteran in journalism, prescribe this for the Indian media as well?

> Publishers have alleged that newspapers that do not toe the line are denied Government advertisements. On the other hand, the Government alleges that certain newspapers publish unsubstantiated stories and engage in a vilification campaign. Both these matters need to be investigated by a body like the Press Council of India or the Editors Guild of India.

This puts paid to the rulings of the Press Council.

Contrast the Group's views on press freedom with the unambiguous comment of Ambika Soni, Minister for Information and Broadcasting. She was asked, 'The government recently froze ads to some newspapers in Kashmir that are critical of the state. Are you trying to regulate the press this way?' She replied:

> I wasn't kept in the loop and was told it was an administrative decision to do so, taken by the Home Ministry at the highest level. I phoned Union Home Minister P. Chidamabaram and told him that while I can't interfere with an administrative decision arrived at out of security concerns, I must know about such decisions. We'll be discussing the issue soon and the decision will be reviewed. A freeze on ads should be the last resort; also, I must be kept in the loop. (*Outlook*, 14 November 2011)

Chairman of the Press Council, Justice Markandey Katju, wrote to the Chief Minister on 26 November 2011, apropos a protest demonstration in Srinagar the previous day when the police and CRPF personnel reportedly beat up four photo journalists and damaged their equipment. Omar Abdullah replied with characteristic insolence: 'It is easy for us, sitting far away from the scene of the action, to suggest that the police should look for cameras to ascertain whether a person is a press person or not . . . it is not good enough to just write to States and put the onus on them'. Their responsibility was admitted but it rests 'above all on the Press Council of India' (for the text of the letters, vide *Kashmir Life*, 4 December 2011). He took the cue from the Group of Interlocutors' Report.

Given the terms of the mandate, the Group's ventures into west Kashmir, under Pakistan's administration, and its ill-informed sallies on the Indus Treaty are hard to understand. No Committee, Commission or any such body has stooped to self-praise as the Group does repeatedly in its Report, with false claims of improving the situation. 'The bulk of the memoranda we have received (around 75 per cent) deal with confidence-building measures and/or issues of governance'. The rest were on political measures. Evidently, no one expected them to be able to deliver. Sops are offered and homilies delivered, but on the crucial issues that matter – Article 370, the

Governor, regional autonomy, the right to protest and the like – the Group speaks with a forked tongue.

It was a dubious character, D.D. Thakur, who shaped the Group's thinking and inspired its line on Article 370. Revisiting his role is important. The Indira Gandhi–Sheikh Abdullah Accord of 1975 was an abject surrender by the Sheikh. After Pakistan's invasion of Kashmir in 1965 and his own internment that year, prospects of recovery were bleak. In secret parleys with the emissaries of Jayaprakash Narayan and Indira Gandhi during his internment, Abdullah had accepted the accession. Its factum conceded, the issue was the quantum of the accession. None of this was known even to his closest followers except Mirza Afzal Beg (see Documents 17a to 17d). The noises he publicly made after his release, whether at the Convention in 1968 and 1970 and/or elsewhere, were for public consumption.

Indira Gandhi knew the truth and drove a hard bargain with a Sheikh avid for power. The concessions he won were limited. Para 4 of the Agreed Conclusions signed by Beg and Parthasarathi on 13 November 1974 envisaged the state's review of central laws extended after 1953. The centre promised that such proposals would be 'sympathetically considered', and that extension of provisions of the Constitution by abuse of Article 370 would be 'unalterable' (Noorani 2011: 404).

But Sheikh Abdullah sought nonetheless to do his best for his Kashmir. Once in power as Chief Minister, he got the Cabinet to appoint a sub-committee under the chairmanship of the co-author of the Accord, M.A. Beg. Other members of the sub-committee were D.D. Thakur, M.K. Tikoo, G.M. Shah, Ghulam Nabi Kochak, the Chief Secretary and the Law Secretary. In 1978 Abdullah expelled Beg from the Cabinet and the party, became chairman of the sub-committee, and came increasingly under the baleful influence of D.D. Thakur. On 2 January 1979 he ordered that Thakur should chair the meetings. The sub-committee *never* functioned. 'None of the members of the Sub-Committee however attended the meetings', as Justice Saghir Ahmad noted. Thakur took it upon himself to prepare his own report on 8 July 1981. Kochak was furious at its contents and drew up his report on 11 April 1982. Neither report was placed before the Assembly.

Thakur wrote: 'The comments offered and the conclusions drawn are my own.' They were couched in delightful prose as one might expect of a former judge of the state's High Court. 'The conclusions have been made self-speaking by assigning *all possible reasons* to sustain those conclusions so that the Hon'ble Chief Minister and other members of the Cabinet are not at a disadvantage in provoking their own thought process.' He noted that the Accord itself had 'abridged the scope' of the review (paragraph 13) and added:

> I feel that the Government or the Legislature of the State cannot by any unilateral action set at naught or render inapplicable any of the provisions of the

> Constitution of India or the laws made by the Parliament and extended to the State of Jammu and Kashmir. The only option which the State in the circumstances, would be left with, would be to again start a movement seeking a total reversal of all that has happened constitutionally since 1953. Such a course, it is obvious, would lead to a headlong collision, which the State can ill-afford to pursue. At the same time it might create a highly embarrassing situation for the State leadership in as much as the opposition in the State would perhaps launch a tirade of denigration against the leadership of the State on the ground that the Accord of 1975 was more of a hoax rather than a real Magna Carta for the preservation of the autonomy of the State. (Thakur 1981, paragraph 15)

In his memoirs, Thakur claimed: 'Sheikh Sahib appeared to have read my report and appreciated the findings recorded by me. At no time thereafter was the question of review raised in the Cabinet' (Thakur 2005: 289–90). It was clearly a political rather than a legal exercise. Even a review of the Governor's position was barred, he opined. Evidently Sheikh Saheb was not pleased with Thakur's 'report', and gave a copy to G.N. Kochak for a review.

One great merit of Kochak's effort was his survey of debates in the state's Constituent Assembly and the violation of its decisions prior to Abdullah's dismissal from office on 8 August 1953. Kochak was not for a review of 'all that has been done after 1953'. He knew the Sheikh's mind and the fragile nature of his power. The Sheikh did not desire a confrontation with Indira Gandhi. Kochak was strongly of the opinion that, 'what is more important is the *extent* of the legislative power of the State legislature rather than the good or bad content of the law' (Kochak 1982). That was to be considered 'when it is finally to be decided whether review is or is not to be sought'. The issue was legality, not benefit. The centre's usurpation of power 'cannot be lightly brushed aside'.

Altogether different, and vastly superior in quality, is the Report of the State Autonomy Committee. Its survey of constitutional developments since 1947 alone inspires respect. It heard evidence in New Delhi as well as in Srinagar, and was accepted by the State Assembly on 26 June 1990. For the Group of Interlocutors to lump up all three documents and dismiss them for offering conflicting views is to exhibit much more than intellectual sloth. There is a third report which escaped their notice. It is by G.M. Shah, who wrote:

> Many a million cusec of water which Brother Thakur finds having flown down the river Jhelum since 1953 is a dirty water polluted by corrupt political practices, moral turpitude, frauds, undue influence, bribery and deception which, if not ignored, will land one in fool's paradise. Let it be ignored once and for all. (Shah 1982)

Since the accession New Delhi has always had its man in Kashmir's Cabinet. Nehru had Bakshi and D.P. Dhar. From 1975–82, New Delhi's man was D.D. Thakur. Indira Gandhi, he wrote, had 'a soft corner for me' (Thakur: 305). Dropped from the Cabinet by Farooq Abdullah, he joined hands with G.M. Shah to topple him. He engineered Farooq Abdullah's ouster from the office of Chief Minister in July 1984. When Governor B.K. Nehru refused to fall in with his unconstitutional designs, Thakur wrote: 'I suggested to her [Indira Gandhi] that we needed a Governor in Kashmir who could appreciate the compulsions of the Central Government' (ibid.: 363). Thakur had courted and befriended B.K. Nehru, and this was treachery of a high order. In his memoirs, B.K. Nehru describes Thakur's many visits to him. 'He used to come at cocktail time.' Once he suggested a meeting 'late one night' to plot Farooq Abdullah's ouster. Nehru found him 'charming'; but he also found him 'altogether amoral'. Thakur once asked B.K. Nehru, 'what does morality have to do with politics' (ibid.: 622). He confessed to having lied to the Governor (ibid.: 604).

The money for bribing the MLAs was provided by Tirath Ram Amla, 'supplied to him in cash from Congress Party money in Delhi, transported in the mail pouches of the Intelligence Bureau' (ibid.: 627). The foul deed was perpetrated by his successor Jagmohan, of the Emergency fame. The Beg–Parthasarathi conclusions provided that the residuary powers of legislation shall remain with the state bar some exceptions. On 30 July 1986, with his own nominee Jagmohan's concurrence, the President made an Order under Article 370, extending to Kashmir Article 249 of the Indian Constitution. It empowers Parliament even to legislate on a matter in the State List if the Rajya Sabha so authorizes it by a two-thirds majority. But the Order was so worded as to rope in Article 248, the residuary power, as well.

The net result is that every solemn document concerning the state of Jammu and Kashmir has been systematically violated by successive Governments of India from Jawaharlal Nehru downwards – the Instrument of Accession (1947); Article 370 (1949); the Delhi Agreement (1952); and even the fig-leaf of the 1975 Accord.

This is the reality which the Group of Interlocutors seek to cap with a fiat of finality: 'the clock cannot be set back'. A wrong perpetrated over the decades becomes legitimized. They add: 'Parliament will make no laws applicable to the State unless it relates to the country's internal and external security and its vital economic interests, especially in the areas of energy and access to water resources.' Such vague concepts do not lend themselves to constitutional precision. Will the bar be a political act by way of a self-denying ordinance in a resolution open to rescission, or be engrafted as a constitutional limitation?

The Interlocutors have not the foggiest notion of constitutional values or, for that matter, the political realities. Their Report bears the title, 'A

New Compact with the People of Jammu and Kashmir'. Compacts are a product of *negotiation*, but this document is an edict handed from above. The Group set out to ascertain the popular will, conceding that the solution must come 'from within'. It ended up with a Report that prescribes its recipes to the people. That P. Chidambaram saw in it a 'practical road map' which suggested a way forward to find a solution to the political issues of the state is not surprising (*The Hindu*, 1 December 2011). Instinctively, he prefers the clever over the sensible course; the slick over the sound. And he falls into the mess into which the clever fall.

It was absurd of him to say, as he did on 30 December 2011, 'If they [the separatists] are ready for talks, we are ready for talks' (*Hindustan Times*, 31 December 2011). What will he offer them if they do come for talks? His Interlocutors' Report? It was published on 24 May 2012, seven months after its much-hyped submission to Chidambaram on 12 October 2011. Such delay for a document regarding which one of its authors, Padgaonkar, made tall claims, such as: 'The Report aims at a permanent political settlement of the Kashmir problem' (*The Hindu*, 13 October 2011); and it is 'an accurate and comprehensive reflection of the broadest possible spectrum of opinion' (*The Telegraph*, 13 October 2011). Radha Kumar was more modest: 'Had there been dialogue between us *or higher levels in Government* with the separatists, the Report would have been more inclusive and broad based' (*Greater Kashmir*, 19 October 2011).

The opaque language used in the Report cannot conceal why, despite those limits, it is so shoddy, nor how parleys between the government and the separatists could have improved the Interlocutors' performance. Their work was over in October but they could not bring themselves to shedding their job. Padgaonkar took it upon himself, on 19 January 2012, to explain why publication was delayed ('elections in U.P., Punjab'). He would meet Chidambaram and the Report would be published in April. 'We are planning to organize seminars throughout the country to make awareness of the Kashmir issue' (*Kashmir Times*, 20 January 2012). Even after the Report was published on 24 May, they clung on. The name of the new game was 'structured feedback for the Report'. Padgaonkar claimed, 'Say maximum of four months and then we will report back to the Government of the feedback that we get' (*Greater Kashmir*, 25 May 2012). That term and more elapsed without any sign of the promised document. The government, however, distanced itself from the Report. 'The views expressed in the Report are the views of the Interlocutors. The Government will welcome an informed debate on the contents of the Report' (ibid.).

Afraid of reaction in Kashmir, the Home Minister delayed publication of the Report till he could not avoid it any longer. Barren of any worthwhile proposal, he hoped to use it nonetheless for what it was worth – only to discover that it was regarded as utterly worthless in Kashmir. Whether it was Chidambaram's idea or Padgaonkar's, they decided to keep the team; this time as 'resource persons' in the debates to come, as Chidambaram put it on 31 May. 'At some point of time, we will have to call an all-party meeting to discuss the Report' (*The Indian Express*, 1 June 2012).

The government itself had no time for the Report. It was not considered by the Cabinet Committee of Security or by the Cabinet itself. On 8 August 2012, the Union Minister of State of Home, Jitendra Singh, informed the Rajya Sabha in a written reply: 'The Government has not taken any decision on the Interlocutors' Report on Jammu and Kashmir submitted last year and is *not planning any mechanism to implement the recommendations*' (*Greater Kashmir*, 9 August 2012). The italicized words are significant. Even months after the Report came into his hands Chidambaram took no view or decision on its recipes. The Minister of State said that a sum of Rs 63.20 lakhs had been spent on the enterprise (ibid.).

Chidambaram's transfer to the Finance Ministry brought a new face to the Home Ministry, Sushil Kumar Shinde. Padgaonkar and Radha Kumar briefed him on 27 August 2012 and secured his blessings for their continuance in the mission under a new umbrella, the Delhi Policy Group, of which Radha Kumar is Director (Ansari's omission went unexplained). The duo descended on Srinagar on 29 August. 'We are no longer Interlocutors; we are just resource persons and the Ministry can utilize our services at any point of time.' There were two instant reactions to this visit, conflicting and revealing. Belatedly, as if on a hint from New Delhi, Chief Minister Omar Abdullah descended from the fence and lent his support to the Report in unqualified terms, though its recommendations run counter to his own party's established stand on autonomy and to the Report on Autonomy endorsed by the State Assembly.

He said that the Interlocutor's Report should form the basis to initiate a dialogue between New Delhi and the state (*Rising Kashmir*, 30 August 2012). Who would represent the state in the dialogue, he did not explain. 'The Report can also pave the path of *meeting the aspirations of the people of the State* on the basis of a broader consensus that emerges from the process of the internal dialogue.' It had been 'formulated after consultation with different groups across the State and discussion with various shades of opinion, making it *one of the most exhaustive exercises of its kind in the last two decades*'. Radha Kumar, who met Omar Abdullah along with Padgaonkar, explained: 'We have come here on behalf of the Delhi Policy Group to get feedback from various shades of opinion' (ibid.).

The 'feedback' was prompt and deafening. Omar's uncle, Dr Mustafa Kamal, who is Additional General Secretary of the National Conference, said on the very same day, 29 August: 'There is no point in meeting them again. What for should we meet them.' Further: 'New Delhi should stop playing with the sentiments of Kashmiris by holding futile exercises. It is high time for New Delhi to realize that the wounds of Kashmiris need to be healed' (*Greater Kashmir*, 30 August 2012).

The disagreement reveals not only the divide between the party and the government, but also Omar Abdullah's disconnect from the people's aspirations. The PDP's spokesman, Naeem Akhtar, said: 'None of our top leaders are presently available this time in the Valley. It won't be possible to meet them' (ibid.). Far worse was store for the visitors the next day, 30 August, when they met members of the civil society. There was a 'heated exchange of words between the participants and the hosts', Javaid Malik reported. One of them tore to pieces the summary of recommendations. He had reason to feel betrayed. As independent MLA from Langate, Engineer Abdul Rasheed had organized a meeting for the Interlocutors to address, braving the displeasure of the alienated people, and all he had was that sorry document. He said: 'We are being killed, tortured and humiliated. . . . Check the records and see how many times Geelani Saheb has been allowed to offer Friday prayers in the past two years. It seems only stones wake up New Delhi.' Also, addressing the two directly: 'India has a history of breaking promises, but still we trusted you when you come here as Interlocutors' (*Greater Kashmir* and *Rising Kashmir*, 31 August 2012).

This was the end of a cruel farce that was enacted for over a year. In several respects it was a truly unique performance. The Interlocutors went about issuing contradictory statements at the very outset; squabbling and creating scenes in public; airing formulae which later found their way into their Report; making tall claims for themselves; and clinging to the job long after they had submitted their Report.

The whole world knows that at the heart of the problem is the secessionist sentiment of Kashmiris. This is deliberately evaded by the writers of the Report. A 'sense of victimhood . . . grips every region and every community'. Kashmiris' secessionist sentiment is thus put on a par with Jammu's grievances against the Valley, and those grievances are treated with an empathy that, like most Indian concerns, stops at the Pir Panjal Range. It does not enter the Valley.

'Kashmir's aspirations' receive a different hue from what is almost universally accepted. The language used in the Interlocutors' Report is unworthy of any State Paper. 'At the heart of all these dirges, however, is the sentiment that the woes of Kashmir are due to the emasculation of the substance of its distinctive status enshrined in Article 370 of the Constitution of India.' That 'emasculation' was part of a process that began in 1952 and picked up speed with Sheikh Abdullah's arrest and imprisonment in 1953 – a fact Kashmiris bitterly remember to this day.

It would be wrong to characterize it all as a wasted opportunity. It was an ill-conceived and ill-intentioned move to buy time and settle the problem on their mentor's terms. The Report partially succeeded on the first but failed on the second. It fouled up the atmosphere and added to the distrust. One must not flinch from asking just what were the qualities and achievements of the trio which emboldened New Delhi to handpick them for resolving a problem as complex and sensitive as Kashmir. Their attainments in other spheres did not qualify them for this task, especially in view of their lack of empathy and experience.

The fair course is for New Delhi to decide precisely what it can and will offer, and invite the separatists to talks on that basis. It should give a precise meaning to the vague offer that 'anything short of "*azadi*" will be acceptable'. The Hurriyat leaders have promptly retorted that 'the Government has been only talking about talks in a vacuum' (*Asian Age*, 2 January 2012). Chidambaram's role on Kashmir has been disastrous. In the entire discourse of his school of thought, the Pakistan factor has been wilfully ignored. Pakistan is not only a party to the Kashmir dispute but a party *within* Kashmir. The people empathize with it. The Indian state of denial of the depths and causes of the people's sentiments extends to this facet particularly. It cuts across the political divide.

As long as the Kashmir dispute continues to fester, India cannot attain the stature that is justly its due in the councils of the world. 'A source from the Russian delegation' told Interfax news agency on 15 June 2011 at Astana in Kazakhstan, that the unsolved Kashmir question was 'the major obstacle' to the accession of India and Pakistan to the Shanghai Cooperation Organization as its members (*Greater Kashmir*, 16 June 2011).

Realistically, the best route to an overall settlement lies in the pursuit of the 4 point formula. It provides for equal self-rule in both parts of the state. A restored Article 370 fits it like a glove. It can be coupled with a sound regional autonomy formula. In an interview to Barkha Dutt of NDTV on 10 October 2011, General (Retd) Pervez Musharraf, the co-author of the formula, revealed how close the parties had been to finalizing a settlement of the Kashmir dispute.

> Barkha: Let me ask you in the end to talk a little bit about India and Pakistan. Even till today, what has come to be known as the Musharraf four-point formula gets quoted all the time when we talk about Kashmir. Are you able to talk more openly today, about what stopped it from going through?
>
> General Musharraf: From going through? Yes, I thought it was, we were, moving forward all right. And I must give equal credit to Prime Minister Manmohan Singh for being very sincere, for being very flexible, in accommodating points of views from my side and me accommodating his points of view. But then time came, and I had been to India, and the back channel was operative and we were moving forward on both Sir Creek and Siachen. We had done everything. Sir Creek, where the survey of the points was carried out jointly by two Navies, so we knew exactly where is the problem area, how does it extend to the sea. Now the only decision is, okay, this is the problem area, this is the disputed area. Are we dividing it into half? Are we having it as a common area? Are we having it as a no-go area? I mean I was absolutely open to, okay, take a decision and let's sign it. Whatever it is. Also Siachen.

We had decided what are the troops to move behind which lines. So we were just stuck on some minor SD, in the military we call it SD issues, staff duty issues, which could very well just be resolved any time.

Barkha: And notes had been exchanged on both sides? Because the present government says there is nothing in writing.

General Musharraf: Yes, I think, that was on Kashmir mainly. On these two also. Yes, indeed, whatever we carried out is on paper. On Kashmir also, we were trying to move forward in drafting the deal. Now, in 2007, it was Prime Minister Manmohan Singh's turn to come to Pakistan to seal the deals.

Barkha: Including Kashmir?

General Musharraf: Possibly. I won't say certainly, because we hadn't reached that stage where the final pacer had been drafted. We were drafting. There were disagreements but we were trying to resolve them with an open mind. But the other two, and I had said that whenever you come, we have to sign some deal, otherwise it will be totally a failed visit.

Barkha: Ya.

General Musharraf: And he agreed that whenever we come, and it is his turn to come, we will sign some deal. Whether it is only Siachen and Sir Creek or Kashmir also. But unfortunately, he didn't come. You ask him why didn't he come. Did he think that I've got weaker because . . .

Barkha: Unrest had started within Pakistan?

General Musharraf: 2007 some unrest started. Is that why he didn't come? But I feel he should have come.

Barkha: And you believe if he had come in 2007, the history of our countries, in a sense, could have been different today?

General Musharraf: True. To quite an extent, yes. I was prepared to sign deals.

Barkha: So the Army was fully on board? Your Army was fully on board?

General Musharraf: Absolutely. This is another . . . misperception which must be corrected. This is an old misperception that the Army is the rogue which doesn't want a Kashmir solution, which doesn't want any solution, peace with India. This is . . . absolutely wrong. We have been carrying out assessments in Pakistan. Pakistan Army is for resolution of the Kashmir dispute, Siachen, Sir Creek, everything. We are all always, every general that I know, my predecessors, chiefs, have always been in favour of peace. But unfortunately, that is the misperception. And the rationale given by Pakistan's opponents, or whoever, is that Pakistan Army's importance will go. Negative. It will never go till the time that India has all its forces massed against Pakistan's borders. And we know that. Its Air Force's forward air bases are all on the Pakistan eastern border . . . All your offensive forces, the armoured division and mechanized division, all have locations against Pakistan. All infantry divisions, out of 31, 23 are arrayed against Pakistan. Your Navy is mostly on the west coast. So till such time that this does not go, Pakistan's military will always have to stay. So it's not the Kashmir dispute. This is a total misperception which everyone keeps spreading. And a lot of Indians keep saying this to malign the Pakistan Army. Pakistan Army is for peace.

Neither in India nor in Pakistan does the domestic political situation seem to permit any significant move towards finalization of that accord. It is, however, not an impossibility either. The impasse in India–Pakistan relations, absence of a united opposition in Kashmir and New Delhi's continuing support to the Chief Minister of Kashmir embolden Omar Abdullah to behave recklessly.

The question brooks no evasion: would the press and television have behaved as it did over the death of Haji Syed Mohammad Yousuf if the incident had occurred in any other state? Constitutionally, Kashmir's 'special status' in the Union is all but gone. Emotionally that status yet lurks in the minds of the Indian intelligentsia. It was the death of a man known to be close to both Farooq Abdullah and Omar. What happened to him on 29 September 2011 was set out accurately by a reliable correspondent, Muzamil Jaleel, in his report in *The Indian Express* of 1 October:

> A 61-year old retired teacher and National Conference (NC) 'sympathizer' who allegedly took money from two party leaders on the promise of getting them a ministership and a legislative council seat through Union Minister Farooq Abdullah, died in custody after he was handed over to the Crime Branch by Chief Minister Omar Abdullah. The family of the man, Haji Syed Mohammad Yousuf, has alleged he was killed by the police because he knew 'too many secrets'.
>
> The Chief Minister told the *Indian Express* that the police had told him that Haji Yousuf had died after 'a heart attack' this morning. The police told this paper that Haji had died in the police hospital where he was taken after he complained of 'nausea'.
>
> The Government today transferred three officers of the Special Security Group, including a longtime personal security officer (PSO) of the Chief Minister, DSP Shabir Ahmad, but said the transfers were not related to the incident. But it ordered a judicial inquiry by a sitting judge, and asked the Chief Justice of the Jammu and Kashmir High Court to nominate a colleague to carry out the probe.
>
> Haji Yousuf, of Laktipora village in Arwani in south Kashmir's Anantnag district, was close to Farooq Abdullah, said Haji's son, Syed Talib Hussain. 'He was very close to leaders of the National Conference. He was friends with Farooq Abdullah and would regularly go to Omar Abdullah and other leaders as well,' he said. 'He did not die, he was killed in custody.'
>
> He [Haji Yousuf] had been called by the Minister of State for Home Nasir Aslam Wani to his place, and I blame him [Wani] for this murder, Hussain said. Chief Minister Omar Abdullah said he had summoned Haji Yousuf to his residence yesterday after he received a complaint that Haji had taken over a crore of rupees from two party workers after promising them high posts. He

said Haji had 'admitted everything', following which he [Omar] had asked MoS Wani to call in the police. This is what the Chief Minister told *The Indian Express*:

'Two NC workers from Kokernag and Ganderbal came to meet me. One of them is our [NC] district president in Ganderbal and my constituency representative, Mohammad Yousuf. He told me that this Haji Yousuf has taken 71 lakh rupees from him as party fund and given it to Farooq Abdullah who has promised to make him Minister of State for R&B [Roads and Buildings]. The Kokernag guy [whose name is Abdul Salam Reshi] complained that Haji took 40 lakh rupees from him, saying he [Reshi] will be made a member of the Legislative Council. This Kokernag guy has contested an election as an independent candidate earlier.'

'Both of them told me that Haji is not returning the money. He had returned a part of the money to the Kokernag guy, but was refusing to even acknowledge that he had taken money from the Ganderbal guy. The guy [Yousuf] had even got an impersonator to call this Ganderbal guy mimicking Farooq Sahib's voice to assure him that the money was safe with him and his work will be done soon.'

The Chief Minister said he had asked MoS Wani to summon Haji to his [Omar's] residence so that the two men could confront him in his presence.

'When I asked Haji Yousuf about this issue, he first denied everything. Then he told me that he had taken a loan from the Kokernag guy. He told the Ganderbal guy that he had never taken any money from him. But when the Ganderbal guy said he has witnesses, he [Haji] admitted everything, and promised to return the money within a month and a half.'

'But I didn't agree,' the Chief Minister said. '*I told him that either he should give some property papers [as collateral] or nothing doing*. How could we believe him? I didn't know how many people he had duped. . . . The Kokernag guy told me there are around a dozen more that he knew. So I told Nasir [MoS Home] that this is a crime and I don't want to get involved in this. I asked him to call the IG Crime. He [Raja Ajaz] came and took all three of them away.'

Asked how Haji Yousuf had died, Omar said: 'The Crime Branch people told me that he complained of feeling dizzy and was taken to the police hospital where he had a heart attack this morning and died. It may be because of the shock that he has to cough up the money.' The Chief Minister rejected allegations by Haji Yousuf's family that he had been roughed up and strangled because he 'knew too much'. Asked why he had then decided to move out his PSO and two other officers of his personal security staff, Omar said, 'it has nothing to do with this issue. It is altogether a separate issue.' Apparently, Omar was prepared to hush up 'the crime' if the man had agreed to give him 'some property papers' as collateral.

Moozum Muhammad reported in *Greater Kashmir* of 1 October: 'One of the doctors at Police Control Room who performed autopsy on Yousuf confirmed torture marks on his face and neck.' His grandson Syed Wasiq had spoken to him on the phone, and 'I could make out that there was some argument going on at the other side of the line. Then suddenly the line got disconnected.' Apprehensive, the son contacted the SSF Srinagar, who informed him that Yousuf was in the custody of Crime Branch. Initially the Crime Branch feigned ignorance about him but said later that he had vomited around 8 pm and was shifted to a hospital. The meeting at Omar Abdullah's residence began around 4.30 pm and lasted till 6 pm. According to a government statement, also reported by the daily, Yousuf had 'reported uneasiness and nausea and as such he was asked to move to one of the escort vehicles of IGP Crime', moments after they had left the Chief Minister's residence. 'On reaching Police Headquarters, the Medical Officer examined him and he was declared to be alright.' This is flatly contradicted by Abdul Salim Reshi. He told *Greater Kashmir:* 'Syed Muhammad Yousuf went to the bathroom in the Crime Branch. When he came out, he fell down. He didn't talk even at that time as his health condition worsened . . . till 12 am two of us [Yousuf Bhat and Salim Reshi] were questioned by IG Crime.' The next morning Yousuf was dead. The government hand-out had another detail. On the morning of 30 September Yousuf complained of 'slight abdominal pain', whereafter the doctors advised an ultrasound test. However, Yousuf 'suffered a massive heart attack and expired'.

The government announced:

> in order to allay all apprehensions and in order to ensure an impartial investigation the State Government has decided to request the Chief Justice of the J&K High Court to nominate a sitting judge to conduct a judicial enquiry into the immediate [*sic*] circumstances leading to the death of Sayeed Muhammad Yousuf.

Mala fides are writ large all over this order. Public apprehension arose out of a reasonable suspicion of torture. The only way to allay it was to institute criminal investigations. That could not be conducted by the state police – only by the Central Bureau of Investigation (CBI) or a Special Investigation Team set up by the Supreme Court. The IG Crime, Raja Ajaz, was at the Chief Minister's residence and Yousuf died at the Crime Branch.

A Commission of Inquiry is a purely fact-finding body. It cannot give a binding order, let alone punish. It is for the government appointing it to accept or reject its 'recommendations'; in this case – Omar Abdullah himself. Crimes are investigated by the police and the culprits are tried by a court of law. Would the country have allowed the Government of India to set up a Commission of Inquiry in the 2G Spectrum scam with the ministers continuing in office meanwhile? There would have been a howl of protest. Have you ever heard of a case of crime being referred to a Commission of Inquiry rather than to a court of law after prompt police investigation?

Clearly, this quack remedy was designed to buy time and silence protest.

On 1 October, Justice (Retd) Bilal Nazki pointed out that neither the High Court nor the state government is competent to nominate a sitting judge. Only the President can, after following a time-consuming procedure. Furthermore, Commissions of Inquiry do not begin hearings immediately. A preliminary hearing is held, the procedure is outlined and then the police is asked to hold investigations to assist the Commission. There is a difference between 'investigations' and 'inquiry' in law. Mr Abdul Rahim Rather, the Finance Minister, rightly said on 2 October: 'It is a matter of investigation.' That is why the Commissions of Inquiry Act, 1952 empowers Commissions, via section 5A, to utilize the services of 'any investigation agency' of the government, i.e. the police, 'for the purpose of conducting any investigation pertaining to the inquiry'. But for this, the consent of the appointing government is necessary. So the Commission of Inquiry will depend on the state police itself.

Yousuf's son, Syed Tabik, alleged that he 'had told them that he will disclose all the frauds to the party President, Dr Farooq Abdullah' (*Kashmir Times*, 2 October). Abdul Salam Reshi, an eye-witness, spilled the beans to Azem Mohiuddin of *Greater Kashmir* (30 October 2011): he said that Syed Yousuf confessed to the Chief Minister that he did take Rs 85 lakhs from Bhat in March to help him secure a berth in the Legislative Council.

> Syed told Bhatt that he [had] talked to Farooq Abdullah and that the NC President had assured to help Bhat if only he was ready to pay Rs eighty-five lakhs. Syed told Bhat that Farooq had told him [that] if he wants a ministry he would need to give Rs one crore, for MLC berth Rs eighty-five lakhs. Syed assured Bhat that the MLC seat would be given to him on 17 April.

The promise was not kept. Mohiuddin reports: 'Reshi said that although Syed had earlier denied taking money from Bhat, he finally confessed and said he had handed it over to Farooq.' If true, this could not have failed to annoy Omar. Some allege that it caused him to panic. Reshi added, 'As we boarded the jeep we found Syed in bad condition already sitting there.' At the police headquarters, Reshi claimed, 'Syed wanted to go to the bathroom and he was accompanied by some policemen; but he never returned.'

A later report by Muzamil Jaleel established Yousuf's close proximity to the Abdullahs (*The Indian Express*, 5 October 2011). 'Omar Abdullah's home was his second home.' Reshi said that Yousuf was hale and hearty when he was taken to another room in the Chief Minister's residence. Yousuf repeated that he had handed over the money to Farooq and asked Omar to wait till his father's return.

> On hearing this, Omar threatened to hand him over to the Crime Branch. To this Haji [Yousuf] said if that was the case then he would reveal the truth there itself. Then Omar left in a huff and after 20 minutes, Yousuf was taken to

another room. He not only vomited but *was laced with blood*. (*DNA*, 7 October 2011)

Eventually, Justice Harjit Singh Bedi, a former judge of the Supreme Court, was appointed to head the Commission of Inquiry. He arrived in Srinagar on 28 November 2011, held a preliminary meeting on 29 November and returned to New Delhi on 1 December. He announced that he was putting the inquiry on hold till the disposal of a petition by the Supreme Court challenging the appointment of the Commission. Once again India's judicial system was on trial in Kashmir.

Even five months after Yousuf's death in mysterious circumstances, no probe into the deed had begun. Omar Abdullah adopted a diversionary tactic by raising the slogan of removal of AFSPA (Armed Forces Special Powers Act). Of course the same Omar Abdullah freely uses the draconian Public Safety Act, 1978, which is a state law, to silence dissent (Amnesty International 2011; Human Rights Watch 2006).

The word 'impunity', used in the title of the Human Rights Watch report of 2006 (*'Everyone Lives in Fear': Patterns of Impunity in Jammu and Kashmir*), is not a strong one to use in this context. It is singularly apt. On 23 January 2012, the Supreme Court strongly censured the Army for stalling the prosecution in the Pathribal encounter case in Kashmir in 2000. The CBI had registered a case against five Army officers and filed charge-sheets against them in court. But the Army would neither take action against them under the Army Act, nor allow the criminal courts to proceed against them. Seven innocent persons had been shot dead in cold blood and branded as militants. The Additional Solicitor-General, P.P. Malhotra, contended that in a place where AFSPA was in force, no inquiry could be initiated against armed forces personnel without the government's sanction. He claimed that 'they are protected under Section 6 of the AFSPA', and, 'We cannot take over the case. The Armed Forces are bound to protect their men' (*The Telegraph*, 24 January 2012; *The Hindu*, 24 January 2012). This is the culture of impunity under which the people of Kashmir have suffered for two decades and more.

Shocked at the counsel's assertion, Justice Swatantra Kumar told him: 'You [the Army] don't want to take over the case and initiate court martial proceedings against them. You can't allow the criminal justice system to go ahead.' This latter bit needs a qualification. As the Court observed: 'The Union of India has a dual responsibility. It has to ensure that the innocent are acquitted and the guilty punished.' The power to sanction prosecution vests in the Government of India. And successive governments have revealed their reluctance to go against the Army's wishes in such matters – indeed even on the Siachen question, on which the Army has successfully thwarted a settlement since 1989. As Praveen Swami reported in *The Hindu* of 7 February 2012:

> In the past four years alone, the Home Ministry has rejected at least 42 requests to sanction the prosecution of military personnel found by the police to have engaged in crimes such as murder, homicide and rape in Kashmir, data obtained by *The Hindu* reveal.
>
> Last week, two Supreme Court judges said the Armed Forces Special Powers Act (AFSPA) – which makes the Central government's sanction mandatory for prosecution – ought not to cover cases in which crimes such as murder or rape were commited. 'You go to a place in exercise of AFSPA, you commit rape, you commit murder, then where is the question of sanction?' Justices B.S. Chauhan and Swatantra Kumar said.
>
> Thirty-one of the cases in which sanction was denied relate to rape, culpable homicide or murder. The others involve a wide variety of crimes, ranging from criminal trespass to illegal confinement. In not a single case, *The Hindu* found, had sanction been granted.

This explains why the Army is dead set against the withdrawal of AFSPA from Kashmir or any amendment that affects the impunity from accountability it has enjoyed for decades.

Omar Abdullah's pleas for revocation, intended to divert attention from his grave lapses, fooled nobody. In response to an application filed under the Right to Information (RTI) Act by the Vice-President of the Baramula Bar Association, Irfan Hafiz Lone, a Deputy Secretary in the Union Home Ministry, revealed that from 2000 till 4 October 2011 it had received 'no such recommendation' from the state government for 'withdrawal/amendment/revocation [of AFPSA] from some particular areas of the State' (*Greater Kashmir*, 12 January 2012).

One disclosure after another, one event followed by another, added to the people's resentment. In the context of growing public discontent, the State Human Rights Commission (SHRC) has come forward to reopen cases of human rights violation by the armed forces. On 19 October 2011, the SHRC asked the government to reopen the case of the rapes at Kunanposhpura during the night of 23–24 February 1991 – the subject of a discredited report prepared by B.G. Verghese under the umbrella of the Press Council of India. This report has been received its just deserts from an upright civil servant, Wajahat Habibullah, who had served in Kashmir.

> The Verghese Committee, appointed in *an effort at damage control rather than because of any sincere interest in reaching the truth*, concluded that the complaint was 'invented'. *This ended any further pursuit of the investigation* and led to an abiding resentment among the villagers in the area, particularly women. The lack of an effective way to redress their grievances continued to blight the lives of the women of Kunan-Poshpura, well into the twenty-first century, with many failing to find husband. (Habibullah 2011: 131)

A police investigation team of the SHRC confirmed that 2,156 unidentified bodies lay in unmarked graves at thirty-eight locations in north Kashmir. The Association of Parents and Disappeared Persons (APOD) and the J&K Coalition of Civil Society (JKCCS) maintain that over 8,000 persons have disappeared over the years (Bukhari 2011; Manecksha 2011). Both these organizations have done noble work in the most trying circumstances.

Engineer Abdul Rashid, an Independent MLA from Langate, described the Army's behaviour in the rural areas in an interview to Tasavur Mushtaq of *Kashmir Life* on 20 November 2011. He said:

> I was myself subjected to about 350 to 400 days of forced labour. Army treated us as slaves. We were supposed to wash clothes of Army, patrol their roads, construct bunkers, any damn thing. In this, fifty villagers suffered and I was not an exception. It was also because of AFSPA and other draconian laws there was no accountability. That is why I protested last year when Prime Minister visited Kashmir and I had written an article in a local daily, 'Say Sorry Mr PM'. I was used as human shield at least on two occasions and I had a narrow escape. I was picked up and taken to the worst interrogation centre Cargo, then to central jail, CIK Humhama and Rajbagh. I had to pay bribe not less than Rs One lakh by selling land and few cattle to get myself released. It was these atrocities which forced me to come forward against them. I found no way better than participating in elections. So experiences are very bitter. I have seen hundreds of youth dying in front of me, getting handicapped, sisters turning widows. I have not come from the sky and unlike other politicians I had no dynasty background. I have seen things from grassroot level, right from the beginning since 1990. So, I think we have seen a lot of trouble. I have been tortured by Army twice or thrice during these years. I am one among many who tasted AFSPA.
>
> I have lost many of my close relatives in the ongoing struggle, so I think, like other Kashmiris, I have suffered the worst. The worst of all was that my own house was used as a temporary Army camp for about 4 months – the most barbaric thing which could ever happen – from November 1997 to February 1998. In the evening they used to come in the darkness and knock at the door, get inside; Major rank officer used to head them. They used to bundle all my family members and lock us up in one room. We were told that if this thing gets exposed you all will be dead. My house is at the outskirts of my village where they suspected militants move often on this road; and see the tragedy of Kashmir, we could not reveal it to anybody for 10 long years until I became MLA. I want to weep but who is listening. This is my question to the Hurriyat people. If you come and join hands, at least we can tell people what we have gone through. I have suffered, ask me how I have suffered. Neither was I an MLA nor any leader at that time, I was a common man. Answer me, what have you done to reduce my sufferings?

On a visit to Langate in November 2009, this writer saw armed soldiers standing on the roofs. According to the locals, in the evening they feel free to make themselves comfortable in those homes.

On 29 November 2011, a Srinagar court acquitted twelve men who had been charged with digging up the Srinagar cricket stadium pitch as a protest against the Indian team's presence in the city. That was on 13 October 1993 when a one-day innings was played against the West Indies, and *was thus six whole years before militancy began.* Muzaffar Raina of *The Telegraph* reported on 30 November 2011:

> From the pro-azaadi crowd's cheering it would have seemed that Kapil Dev's team was playing outside India. Every big hit by the West Indies batsmen was cheered as was every loss of an Indian wicket. Some in the crowd waved pictures of Pakistani players, and at least one report said that an apple was thrown at Dilip Vengsarkar. . . .
>
> The youths – some of whom became separatist leaders in later years – swarmed the pitch during the lunch break and tried to dig holes in the pitch. They were angry that India had hosted an international match in the 'disputed region'. Before they could do too much damage, they were taken away by the police. The separatists count the day as a milestone in their 'azaadi struggle'. At the time the pitch invasion happened, militancy was still six years away, and Jammu and Kashmir was largely a peaceful state.

Secessionist feelings preceded militancy and sustained it.

On Ashura (the tenth day of Muharram), which fell on 4 December 2011, an undeclared and therefore unlawful curfew was imposed 'in most parts of Srinagar city to prevent Muharram processions. And as people defied the restrictions, the police used force to disperse them resulting in injuries to several mourners' (Masood 2011).

This was the state of the fundamental right to freedom of assembly in Kashmir at the end of 2011. Hitherto the most quiescent of the three Interlocutors appointed in 2010, i.e. M.M. Ansari, became vocal towards the end of his work, especially after the submission of the Report. He loftily asserted: 'I don't agree that the Hurriyat has a substantial support based in the Valley' (Verma 2011). Why then did the Group try to meet its leaders? In an article in *The Indian Express* of 22 November 2011, Ansari delivered himself of this counsel: 'Draconian laws – namely the AFSPA and the PSA [Public Safety Act] – have no relevance in the contemporary situation of the State.' The AFSPA is a central Act. The PSA is a state Act. Omar Abdullah is eloquent on the former but quiet on the PSA which, Ansari wrote, 'has been grossly misused by the police to harass the youth and/or to collect bribe for letting them off'. As for Omar, he said: 'There is no reason why, on the present reckoning, the CM should not be encouraged to govern the State in a more civil way and be accountable to the electorate.' Censure of Omar Abdullah is not concealed. Nor that of New Delhi.

> Unfortunately, the Central agencies do not seem to have underscored the need to address people's concerns about human rights violations, including the circumstances in which recent custodial killings occurred. Despite various suggestions made from time to time by the State Government, there is no worthwhile monitoring mechanism to ensure effective implementation of recommendations for ameliorating the conditions of the people.
>
> In many districts, the Army and security forces are enjoying cohabitation in residential hubs, wherein the local people, including the separatist activists, are also concentrated. In the process of socio-cultural mobility and interaction, there are occasions when they develop friction, which at times leads to social disturbances and suddenly erupt in 'azaadi' slogans. Besides, the security forces' occupation of important buildings, commercial premises, educational institutions and sports complexes adversely affects the people's freedom to pursue the societal goals.
>
> Programmes like 'Operation Sadbhavna', designed, managed and financed by the security forces for providing education and health care facilities and for promoting sports and cultural activities, should be ideally left to the local elected bodies, as has been the practice in other states. (Ansari 2011)

All this is old hat. But it was exhibited by an Interlocutor appointed by the Government of India who had toured the state for nearly a year. Ansari's laments were belated; more so his astounding disclosure on 23 October 2011 to Namrata Biji Ahuja of *The Asian Age* where he said:

> It was untimely for anyone to discontinue the interlocution process. The interlocution process ended midway. It was because Mr Padgaonkar said that he would not be available because he has taken up a paid assignment in Pune. We must remember this was a group appointment and if one person decides to discontinue then the group fails apart. The whole action is undemocratic.

He added: 'had the group been given more time, it could have yielded more results as peace had just started descending on the Valley after decades'.

Padgaonkar, in contrast, said that 'all the three members of the Group had desired to complete the Report and submit it in a year. We were clear about it.' He also claimed there was no need for an extension. The contradiction apart, the question arises as to why Ansari signed the Report in such circumstances. However, Dileep Padgaonkar also seemed to be very eager to perform a role even after his mandate was exhausted. He told *Kashmir News Service* on 19 January 2012: 'We [*sic*] are planning to organize seminars throughout the country to make [*sic*] awareness about the Kashmir issue. We intend to invite separatists in these seminars. . . . We are in touch with them.' Very clearly the exercise was sponsored by the government.

It was not the government but Padgaonkar who announced that 'the Report would be made public in April', i.e. six months after it was submitted on 12 October 2011. He also provided an excuse for the delay which

Chidambaram himself had not made. 'The whole Government machinery is busy with elections in U.P., Punjab and other states'(*Kashmir Times*, 20 January 2012). Altogether, the trio have given a poor account of themselves – a classic case of ambition exceeding capacity.

Twenty-two years after the outbreak of militancy, which brought in its train a revival of self-assertion by Kashmiris, heightened mass consciousness amidst enormous outrages by the Indian state, continued denial of human rights and stripping away of the husk of the state's autonomy, the people had little to cheer about at the end of 2011. In the words of G.K. Pillai, a former Home Secretary:

> One of the biggest owners of land in J&K is the Army. Like in Delhi, it has a big cantonment. But here nobody is bothered because Delhi is expanding with Gurgaon etc. But if you go to the Srinagar cantonment area, you will ask why does the Army need so much land? Pillai said, Srinagar is an urban city. But if one goes to downtown Srinagar, it is crowded, congested. If someone requires 10 acres or 50 acres of land where will he go? But the Army has thousands of acres in the heart of the city. (*Kashmir Times*, 20 November 2011)

About the Pathribal case where the Army still has not given its sanction, Pillai noted: 'Then they should say we are not giving sanction because the Army personnel were innocent. In that case, the people can go to the court. But the Army will neither give this nor that' (ibid.). He said that despite the courts being 'a little bit pro-government when it comes to national security and it involves secession, Pakistan, J&K [etc.], courts have put down very clear-cut dos and don'ts which are not being followed'. People only protest when 'they feel that something unjust has taken place' (ibid.). Supporting Omar's campaign for partial revocation of AFSPA, Pillai said that the Army has not operated in Budgam for the past five years and militant activities are down.

> When they [militants] haven't fired at you with the Act, why should they fire at you without the Act? . . . When Omar Abdullah is saying lift the Disturbed Areas Act, he is taking a risk. The risk should be taken. If something happens, he can say that he was told the situation had improved, so he took the decision and lifted the Act. . . . I am sure the people will say that we would rather not have the Army there. In Kashmir, I think the presence of the Army is overbearing. We removed nearly 27 bunkers from Srinagar in the past one year. Has anything happened? (Ibid.)

New Delhi remains smug as ever, in a frozen state of denial, because it can afford to sort it out on the strength of overwhelming force – till another popular revolt breaks out. For, while militancy has abated, the sentiment of rejection of the Union (wrongly termed as 'alienation' – a word which implies prior affection) has not abated. Sheikh Abdullah did not ignore it in 1947. His hands were forced by the tribal raid. Nehru tried to suppress it; so did his successors in complicity with their men in Kashmir. It has not worked. The next revolt will be far worse than others. That would be a tragedy for, since 2004–07, the outlines of a fair solution, agreeable to all interests, has emerged in bold relief.

No effort will succeed unless and until the Government of India, the media and the intelligentsia grasp the stark reality that is central to the problem: the people's sentiments on the Union since 1947 – the heartbeat of the Kashmiris. Acceptance of this reality alone can pave the way towards a fair solution.

B.K. Nehru mentions a moving incident in his memoirs.

> At long last, after many farewell parties and the usual laudatory speeches and responses, there arrived the long awaited day of the departure of the Governor. One incident I recall with considerable pleasure. As I was getting into the plane, Begum Abdullah rushed up to the tarmac and said she was very sorry to see me go. *'Aap hi ek Governor hain jisne Kashmirion ke dil ki dharkan samjhee'* (You are the only Governor who has understood the heart-beat of the Kashmiris). (Nehru 1997)

B.K. Nehru was severely critical of the militancy which broke out later. But the man was honest to a fault. He was peerless in his understanding of the people's psyche: that they hated Akbar because he was the first outsider who destroyed in 1589 the independence of Kashmir (ibid.: 610); that rigged elections were held after the Sheikh's dismissal in 1953 and New Delhi ruled the state with its hand-picked Chief Ministers (ibid.: 614); and that the anti-India feeling which had gradually grown since 1953 existed *'probably since even earlier'* (ibid.: 635).

The time has come for India to understand the heartbeat of the Kashmiris. Conciliation must be based on this reality. Kashmiris must accept another reality as well – 2012 is not 1947. The Supreme Court of Canada has shown how secessionist sentiment in Quebec and the Union's claim can be reconciled. The Court's judgment was delivered on 20 August 1998. Unlike Kashmir, Quebec was never promised a plebiscite. Nonetheless, the Court ruled:

> A system of government cannot survive through adherence to the law alone. A political system must also possess legitimacy, and in our political culture, that requires an interaction between the rule of law and the democratic principle. The system must be capable of reflecting the aspirations of the people. But there is more. Our law's claim to legitimacy also rests on an appeal to moral values, many of which are imbedded in our constitutional structure. It would be a grave mistake to equate legitimacy with the 'sovereign will' or majority rule alone, to the exclusion of other constitutional values.

Secession is a legal as well as a political act. It entails amendment to the Constitution 'which perforce requires negotiation'. Referenda and negotiation go together. 'The democratic principle identified above would demand that considerable weight be given to a clear expression by the people of Quebec of their will to secede from Canada, even though a referendum, in itself and without more, has no direct legal effect, and could not in itself bring about unilateral secession.' To repeat, unlike Kashmir, Quebec was never promised a plebiscite. There was no Article 370 in the Canadian Constitution.

> We are equally unable to accept the reverse proposition, that a clear expression of self-determination by the people of Quebec would impose no obligations upon the other provinces or the federal government. The continued existence and operation of the Canadian constitutional order cannot remain indifferent to the clear expression of a clear majority of Quebecers that they no longer wish to remain in Canada. This would amount to the assertion that other constitutionally recognized principles necessarily trump the clearly expressed democratic will of the people of Quebec. Such a proposition fails to give sufficient weight to the underlying constitutional principles that must inform the amendment process, including the principles of democracy and federalism. The rights of other provinces and the federal government cannot deny the right of the government of Quebec to pursue secession, should clear majority of the people of Quebec choose that goal, so long as in doing so, Quebec respects the rights of others. *Negotiations would be necessary to address* the interests of the federal government, of Quebec and the other provinces, and other participants, as well as the rights of all Canadians both within and outside Quebec. . . .
>
> The continued existence and operation of the Canadian constitutional order cannot remain unaffected by the unambiguous expression of a clear majority of Quebecers that they no longer wish to remain in Canada. The primary means by which that expression is given effect is the constitutional duty to negotiate in accordance with the constitutional principles that we have described herein.

We face obstacles more than one, but none more serious than the spell of a false sense of nationalism – a chauvinism which would have shamed Nicolas Chauvin, known for his simple-minded devotion to Napoleon. There are three distinct mind-sets in this discourse. One is the communal nationalism of the Sangh Parivar, which stands out conspicuously like a sore thumb. The other is its softer variety: those who would be saddened by the Gujarat pogrom but extol V.D. Savarkar and L.K. Advani with a sneaking admiration for the RSS's 'discipline'. It is of such that the great secularist Nehru said on 5 January 1961: 'when the minority communities are communal, you can see that and understand it. But the communalism of a majority community is apt to be taken for nationalism' (*The Times of India)*. They abound; but unlike those in the first strand, are not impervious to reason. The last are the staunch secularists and staunch nationalists. Sadly, they view Kashmir through the prism of a fragile nationalism.

Fear binds all three; fear of the break-up of national unity. None of them is blessed with vision. The state of denial springs from fear and from a fragile nationalism. For decades myths were spawned – Kashmir has ratified its accession to India by free elections; never mind if they were rigged. For long, even the rigging was denied. There can be no self-determination of a part of the nation, though India pledged itself to a plebiscite right till the Nehru–Mohammed Ali Agreement on 21 August 1953. 'The Plebiscite Administrators should be appointed by the end of April 1954.' There was no talk of Pakistan having no locus standi as an 'aggressor' or vacating its aggression. Only Krishna Menon could have explained how a concept can be 'vacated'. Nor was there fear of its impact on Indian Muslims.

Outside the shores of India there were no takers for any of these pleas. Next came the disingenuous question to Kashmiris: 'what is the *azadi* you demand?' Another ploy was used: the majority of Kashmiris do not want *azadi*; indeed the Kashmiris are not in a majority in Kashmir itself. This writer was treated to this drivel in 2000 by none other than a Corps Commander, Lieutenant General J.R. Mukherjee, with slides and 'statistics'. We heard this refrain from the Magi (the Interlocutors) even before they submitted their predictable and predicted Report.

None so blind as those who refuse to see. Not for them the women who rush to their windows to wail as funeral processions of slain militants pass by their homes. On such issues, whether Kashmir or the boundary question with China, mainstream media never hesitates to bat for the state. It is of such that Edmund Burke said: reason is fatigued; invention is exhausted; experience has given judgment; but obstinacy is not conquered.

The academia is no better. Contrast this with Israeli academics like Ilan Pappe who question the very legitimacy of the birth of their state and explode the myths about Palestinians leaving their hearth and home voluntarily in 1948 to welcome the Jewish terrorists. Tom Segev, a columnist in the leading Israeli daily, *Haaretz*, has written a remarkably objective history of Palestine from 1917 to 1948, *One Palestine Complete* (Segev 2000), which prizes the values of scholarship and the historical truth over the claims of nationalist apologias. But you cannot ask the Kashmiri to forget history. Discussing the demand for independence in Kashmir, I asked Tahir Mohiuddin, when we met in Srinagar in November 2009, when it began and indeed who inspired it. Pat came the answer: when we lost our independence to Akbar. In his work *The History of Struggle for Freedom in Kashmir*, Prem Nath Bazaz lavishes praise on Zainul Abideen or Bud Shah as the people affectionately called him. He was a student of Sanskrit and of Hindu philosophy (ibid.: 57), and a devout Muslim who invited scholars of Islam (ibid.: 58). He died in 1470. Lesser men followed him. Akbar's armies marched into Kashmir on 28 June 1586. Mughal rule lasted for 166 years till 1752 when a brutal reign of the Afghans began. In 1814 Maharaja Ranjit Singh invaded Kashmir. The Lahore Darbar was betrayed by its Dogra feudatory, Gulab Singh of Jammu, who was in league with the British. He acquired Kashmir by the infamous Treaty of Amritsar signed on 16 March 1846 for Rs 75 lakhs. Gandhi aptly called it 'a deed of sale' during his stay in Srinagar from 1 to 3 August 1947. 'He supposed it would be dead on the 15th August' (Tendulkar 1963, Vol. 8: 79). If so, what could be the worth of the ruler's signature on the Instrument of Accession? To resume, Sheikh Imamuddin, the Governor of Kashmir who was appointed by the Sikhs, refused to hand over Kashmir. He revolted. Gulab Singh's forces were defeated. British troops crushed the revolt.

Exactly a century later Sheikh Abdullah launched his 'Quit Kashmir' movement against Maharaja Hari Singh precisely with that Treaty as the gravamen of his charge. He also drew inspiration from Imamuddin's revolt. At his trial for sedition, the prosecution cited his speeches on 14 and 16 May 1946, in which he denounced the Treaty of Amritsar and therefore the legitimacy of Hari Singh's rule (Noorani 2006: 285–310). In 1946 the Urdu poet Hafiz Jalandhari wrote a long and fiery poem on the *Pachattar Lakh ka Sauda* ('The Rs 75 Lakh Deal'). These lines provide a flavour of the whole.

Mulk par qabza hamara hai pachattar lakh men
Maal yeh sab humne mara hai pachattar lakh men

Yeh moeshi hon ke adamzad, sab hai zarkhareed
Inke bachey, bachiyan, aulad sab hain zarkhareed

Ho nahi sakte kabhi azaad sab hain zarkhareed
Ta qayamat khanmal, barbad, sab hain zarkhareed

Loot li insaan ki qismat pachattar lakh men
Bik gai Kashmir ki jannat pachattar lakh men

Mard ka sarmayae mehnat pachattar lakh men
Auraton ka jauhare ismat pachattar lakh men

Mulk, millat, qaum, maal-o-jahan pachattar lakh men
Haan pachatar lakh men, haan, haan, pachattar lakh men

We possess the country, we paid seventy-five lakhs for it
We acquire the entire booty for seventy-five lakhs.

Be they cattle, be they humans, all belong to us
Their sons, daughters and progeny, all are our slaves.

They can never be free, these slaves of ours
Till doomsday, ruined and homeless, all are our slaves.

Man's destiny has been looted for seventy-five lakhs
Kashmir's paradise was sold for seventy-five lakhs.

The fruits of man's labour, bought for seventy-five lakhs
The jewel of woman's virtue for seventy-five lakhs.

The country, the nation, the community, life and its possessions, all for seventy-five lakhs
Yes for seventy-five lakhs; yes, yes, for seventy-five lakhs.

If history matters to Kashmiris, it is because it was repeated after 1947. History always drives a people who feel that they had been wronged and betrayed by their own leaders, as well as the leaders of India and Pakistan; men at the very apex of power who were of high quality. None of the high offices and institutions helped Kashmir – the President, Prime Minister, Parliament or their Chief Minister; least of all the Supreme Court of India. It delivered a promising judgment on Kashmir's autonomy one day in 1959 and washed it away another day, nearly a decade later, without referring to the earlier case (Prem Nath Kaul v. State of J&K, *AIR* 1959; Sampat Prakash v. State of J&K, *AIR* 1969). Justice M. Hidayatullah was a member of the Bench which decided both cases.

The 1996 elections to the State Assembly were practically forced on a reluctant Election Commission by the Supreme Court. In 1995 Pakistan had sent the 'guest' (foreign) militants across the LoC. India sponsored armed surrendered militants with a license to kill their former colleagues, emulating the tactics of Latin American dictators.

The Assembly was dissolved early in 1990. Elections seemed the best device to create a façade of normalcy. Articles II.19 and II.21 of Volume 2 record 'the electoral crackdown', that is, a poll forced on an alienated people amidst denial of civil liberties and absence of a political process. Farooq Abdullah denounced the parliamentary elections in the state earlier in the year, terming it 'a concocted and rigged exercise' (*The Indian Express*, 15 July 1996). He demanded that the surrendered militants be disarmed before he could participate in the Assembly polls. They were not; he participated all the same, assured of certain victory and return to power.

President's Rule in Kashmir was to expire on 17 January 1996. On 10 November 1995 the Election Commission, headed by T.N. Seshan, stated that, in view of the situation in the state, it could not recommend that elections be held there. In almost identical circumstances in Assam, the then Chief Election Commissioner R.K. Trivedi was prepared to certify, under clause (5) of Article 356 of the Constitution, that continuance of President's Rule 'is necessary on account of difficulties in holding the elections' to the Assam Assembly. Such a certificate is requisite under Article 356 (5).

A Constitution Bench of five judges of the Supreme Court had ruled in 1984 that 'the ultimate decision as to whether it is possible and expedient to hold the elections at any given point of time must rest with the Election Commission' (Election Commission of India vs. State of Haryana, *AIR* 1984). This was the settled law when the Supreme Court heard a petition on 22

November 1995 challenging the Election Commission's decision. The Court cited a far-fetched possibility which it knew was unreal. 'Suppose the Commission does not recommend the dates, what should the Governor do?' The Court raised afresh the issue decided in 1984 – namely, whether the 'volatile conditions' permitted a poll. It decided to rule on the Election Commission's powers (*The Times of India*, 23 November 1995). The Election Commission decided to beat a retreat, to fight another day in calmer times.

What drove the Supreme Court to such lengths can only be guessed. But we have in Governor K.V. Krishna Rao's memoirs a good account of the pressures to hold the election. His account of the Supreme Court's proceedings reveals a lot. During the hearing Justice J.S. Verma asserted that the attitude of Chief Election Commissioner T.N. Seshan – that he was the only person who was right and all others were wrong – must change. He also observed that a decision by the Court in the matter may have the effect of *reducing the powers of the Commission*. However, later, as the Attorney-General had stated that 'there has been an agreement for the time being between the Government of India and the Election Commission of India regarding the timing of the Assembly election in the State of Jammu and Kashmir', the Supreme Court disposed of the petition saying that 'there is no occasion for us now to decide the controversy raised in this writ petition' (Rao 2001: 495–96). The American Ambassador, Frank G. Wisner, also threw his weight in support of the polls (ibid.: 550). Rao enjoyed Wisner's pat on his back (ibid.: 536).

The Union Home Ministry, as ever, took a cynical view of ascertaining the people's choice. It preferred to make its own choices. Rao writes that before the polls 'it came to [*sic*] notice that the Home Ministry was continuing efforts to develop alternative leadership and this had upset the National Conference' (ibid.: 516). Farooq Abdullah got wind of it. 'Farooq met me a couple of times and reiterated his concern that the Home Ministry, by propping up certain militant leaders, was trying to develop an alternative leadership. I told him not to bother about it, but to continue with his political activities, in preparation for the elections' (ibid.: 531).

Even while the election was under way Farooq Abdullah acknowledged his debt to the surrendered militants whose disarming he had demanded. He said at Srinagar on 11 August 1996, 'If the National Conference is before you [journalists] today, the counter-insurgents are also the ones who have given us this privilege. I am proud of them.' (*The Times of India*, 12 August 1996)

Statistics provided by the visiting Election Commissioner, M.S. Gill, showed that not a single polling station was deemed normal; 1,342 were declared sensitive, while 1,996 others were declared hyper-sensitive (*Kashmir Times*, 18 August 1996). It was such a farce that the Supreme Court compelled the Election Commission to enact.

Farooq was gifted 'an unprecedented majority' – 57 seats in a House of

87, bagging 43 out of 46 seats in the Valley. Krishna Rao was jubilant. 'We assessed that in about six to nine months of return to democracy [*sic*] any residual militancy would be eliminated.' This reveals in a flash the establishment's assessment of: (a) the causes of the militancy; (b) the depth of popular alienation; and (c) the quality of 'democracy' offered to Kashmir. It is on assessments such as these that India's Kashmir policy has been shaped since 1948 to this day.

Whom, then, can the Kashmiris look up to for redress and succour, given a sustained record of broken pledges by the Centre, and the corrupt and incompetent governments it installed in the state. As Ghalib asked, '*Kya kiya Khizr ne Sikander se? / Ab kise rahnuma kare koi?*' ('What was it that Khizr did to Alexander? / Whom can we now accept as a guide?'). It will simply not do to dismiss the entire record as irrelevant. The UNCIP's resolutions of 13 August 1948 and 6 January 1949 on plebiscite are, doubtless, obsolete. The UN's mediator, Gunnar V. Jarring, noted in his Report how 'agreements of an ad hoc character' may become difficult to implement because 'the situation with which they were to cope has tended to change' (Gunnar 1957, para 21). Half a century has elapsed since.

But no change of circumstances can dilute UN Resolutions – or India's pledges – of a fundamental rather than 'ad hoc' character. On 30 March 1951, the Security Council affirmed (Resolution 91 of 1951) that any decision by the proposed Constituent Assembly of Kashmir on accession 'would not constitute a disposition of the State in accordance with the above principle'; a disposition 'made in accordance with the will of the people' and expressed through a plebiscite. That procedure and mechanism are obsolete. Not so the fundamentals of the democratic principle. As Nehru said in the Lok Sabha on 25 February 1955: 'A question like this cannot be solved unilaterally.' A proviso to Article 253 of the Constitution of India itself envisages a 'decision affecting the disposition of the State' by the Government of India, for which the proviso requires 'the consent' of the state government.

In 2012 the challenge that faces us is to abide by the fundamentals and the pledges in the light of the conditions of today – not deny their very worth or relevance altogether. Indrajit Hazra and Samar Halankar of *Hindustan Times* asked Chidambaram: 'Do you think it is time for India to redeem its promises to the people of Kashmir? If so, what promises?' It was a very intelligent and pointed question that touched the heart of the matter. Chidambaram did not evade it; only, he showed scant familiarity with the record. He replied: 'Yes, over the years, several promises have been made to the people of J&K *and we should act on those promises*. Based on the agreements and accords of 1952 [Delhi Agreement], 1975 [Sheikh–Indira Accord], 1986 [Rajiv–Farooq Accord], we must address these promises' (*Hindustan Times*, 19 September 2010).

The Delhi Agreement was wrecked twice over. The elected head of state it envisaged was removed. The 1975 Accord was a fig-leaf for the Sheikh's surrender. The 'promises' it made were a cruel joke. It was a political accord broken by Indira Gandhi in 1977 when she withdrew the Congress support to Chief Minister Abdullah and toppled his government which she had put up in 1975. The 1986 one was a shotgun marriage so that the Congress could piggy-back on the National Conference. The 1975 and 1986 Accords are hated today. *The pledges which Kashmiris cite are the ones which were made from 1947 to 1953.* Chidambaram ignored them. Here is a list. It is illustrative of the solemnity and scope of the pledges. An exhaustive list should be prepared if only to educate people. History is witness to pledges broken over the centuries. Its annals provide few precedents for breaches as willful, sustained and harmful in consequences as the ones India publicly made, despite the fact that, as the record shows, Prime Minister Nehru had privately decided, at least in 1948, not to fulfil them.

The Pledges

1. The Prime Minister of India, Jawaharlal Nehru's telegram to the Prime Minister of Britain, Clement Attlee, on 25 October 1947, *before* Kashmir's accession to India, which was repeated to the Prime Minister of Pakistan, Liaquat Ali Khan, on 26 October 1947:

> I should like to make it clear that the question of aiding Kashmir in this emergency is not designed in any way to influence the State to accede to India. Our views which we have repeatedly made public is that the question of accession in any disputed territory or State must be decided in accordance with the wishes of the people and we adhere to this view. (*White Paper on Jammu and Kashmir* 1948: 46)

2. Governor-General Mountbatten's letter to the ruler of Jammu and Kashmir, Hari Singh, on 27 October 1947, in reply to his 26 October letter offering Kashmir's accession to India:

> in the special circumstances mentioned by your Highness, my Government have decided to accept the accession of Kashmir State to the Dominion of India. Consistently with their policy that, in the case of any State where the issue of the accession has been the *subject of dispute*, the question of accession should be decided in accordance with the wishes of the people of the State, it is my Government's wish that as soon as law and order have been restored in Kashmir and her soil cleared of the invader, the question of the State's accession should be settled by a reference to the people. (Ibid.)

He accepted the appeal for military aid and said: 'action has been taken today to send troops of the Indian Army to Kashmir to help your own forces to defend your territory and to protect the lives, property and honour of your people' (ibid.: 47–48). This letter mentions 'action' taken today (27

October). There is some controversy on precisely when the Instrument of Accession was signed and when Indian troops landed in Srinagar. This subject is, however, beyond the purview of this essay.

3. The accession was legally made by the Maharaja of Kashmir, and this step was taken on the advice of Sheikh Abdullah, leader of the All Jammu and Kashmir National conference, the political party commanding the widest popular support in the State. Nevertheless in accepting the accession the Government of India made it clear that they would regard it as *purely provisional* until such time as the will of the people could be ascertained. (Ibid., Part I: 3)

4. This formulation was repeated in the same document, with yet greater emphasis in Part IV defining 'India's Objectives'. It said:

> In Kashmir as in other similar cases, the view of the Government of India has been that in the matter of disputed accession the will of the people must prevail. It was for this reason that they accepted *only on a provisional basis* the offer of the ruler to accede to India, backed though it was by the most important political organization in the State. The question of accession is to be *decided finally* in a free plebiscite; on this point there is no dispute. It is, however, impossible to hold a plebiscite so long as the State is infested by freebooters from outside. The only purpose for which the Indian troops are operating in Kashmir is to ensure that the vote of the people will not be subject to coercion by tribesmen and others from across the border who have no right to be in Kashmir. (Ibid., Part IV: 45).

5. Nehru's telegram to Liaquat Ali Khan, on 28 October 1947:

> In regard to accession also it has been made clear that this is subject to reference to people of the State and their decision. Government of India have no desire to impose any decision and will abide by people's wishes. But these cannot be ascertained until peace and law and order prevail. (Ibid.: 45)

6. Nehru's telegram to Liaquat Ali Khan on the same day, 28 October 1947: 'I earnestly hope that there will be cooperation between Pakistan and India in stopping raids and putting down disorder and then leaving choice about future to people of Kashmir' (ibid.: 48).

7. Statement issued by Government of India on 30 October 1947: 'It is desirable to draw attention to the *conditions* on which the Government if India have accepted Kashmir's accession.' It proceeded to mention that 'the people of the State should *decide* the question of accession' (*The Times of India*, 31 October 1947).

8. Nehru's telegram to Liaquat Ali Khan on 31 October 1947:

> Kashmir's accession to India was accepted by us at the request of Maharaja's Government and the most numerous representative popular organization in the State which is predominantly Muslim. Even then it was accepted *on the condition* that as soon as the invader has been driven from Kashmir soil, and law and order restored, the people of Kashmir would decide the question of accession. It is open them to accede to either Dominion then. (*White Paper on Jammu and Kashmir* 1948: 51)

Further:

> Our assurance that we shall withdraw our troops from Kashmir as soon as peace and order are restored and leave the decision about the future of the State to the people of the State is not merely a pledge to your Government but also to the people of Kashmir *and to the world.* (Ibid.: 51, paragraphs 5 and 7)

9. Nehru's broadcast to the nation on 2 November 1947:

> We decided to accept this accession and to send troops by air, but we made a *condition* that accession would have to be *considered by the people of Kashmir* later when peace and order established. We were anxious not to finalize anything in a moment of crisis, and without the fullest opportunity to the people of Kashmir to have their say: *it was for them ultimately to decide.*
>
> Let me make it clear that it has been our policy all along that where there is a dispute about the accession of a state to either Dominion, the decision must be made by the people of the state. It was in accordance with this policy that we *added a proviso to the Instrument of Accession of Kashmir.* . . . We have declared that the fate of Kashmir has ultimately to be decided by the people. That pledge we have given, and the Maharaja had supported it, not only to the people of Kashmir *but to the world.* We will not, and cannot, back out of it. We are prepared, when peace and law and order have been established, to have a referendum held under international auspices like the UN. We want to be a fair and just reference to the people, and we shall accept their verdict. (Ibid.: 53 and 55; emphases added)

The next day, on 3 November, Nehru drew Liaquat Ali Khan's attention to his broadcast:

> I wish to draw your attention to the broadcast on Kashmir which I made last evening. I have stated our Government's policy and made it clear that we have no desire to impose our will on Kashmir but to leave final decision to people of Kashmir. I further stated that we have agreed on impartial international agency like UN supervising any referendum. (Ibid.)

10. Nehru's telegram to Liaquat Ali Khan on 21 November 1947:

> I have repeatedly stated that as soon as the raiders have been driven out of Kashmir or have withdrawn and peace and order have been established, the

> people of Kashmir should decide the question of accession by plebiscite or referendum under international auspices such as those of the United Nations. (Ibid.: 67)

11. Nehru's statement on Kashmir in the Constituent Assembly (Legislative) on 25 November 1947: 'Kashmir and India have been bound together in many ways from ages past. *These last few weeks* have forged *a new link which none can surrender*' (ibid.: 71). An ominous declaration.

12. India's complaint to the UN Security Council on 31 December 1947:

> But in order to avoid any possible suggestion that India had taken advantage of the state's immediate peril for her own political advantage, the Dominion Government made it clear that once the soil of the state had been cleared of the invader and normal conditions were restored, the people would be free to decide their future by the recognized democratic method of plebiscite or referendum, which, in order to ensure complete impartiality, may be held under international auspices. (Ibid.: 77, paragraph 6).

The complaint was made under Article 35 of the UN Charter in Chapter VI.

13. India's delegation to the United Nations Security Council, N. Gopalaswamy Ayyangar's opening speech on 15 January 1948:

> The question of the future status of Kashmir vis-à-vis her neighbours and the world at large, and a further question, namely, whether she should withdraw from her accession to India, and either accede to Pakistan *or remain independent, with a right claim admission as a Member of the UN* – all this we have recognized to be a matter for unfettered decision by the people of Kashmir, after normal life is restored to them. (227th Meeting, UN Security Council 1948: 32)

14. Gopalaswamy Ayyangar's statement at the United Nations Security Council on 3 February 1948:

> Before I proceed I might say that, apart from the stoppage of fighting, the *two parties interested in the Jammu and Kashmir question* – each for its own reason – are the insurgents, who want responsible government , and Pakistan, which wants the question of accession to be finally settled. As far as the insurgents are concerned. I have indicated what the Maharaja is prepared to have announced in his name as his decision. As the Security Council is aware, the Government of India is fully committed to the view that, after peace is restored and all people belonging to the state have returned there, a free plebiscite should be taken and the people should decide whether they wish to remain with India, to go over to Pakistan *or to remain independent*, if they choose to do so. (239th Meeting, UN Security Council 1948: 302)

15. Gopalaswamy Ayyanger's statement at the United Nations Security Council on 6 February 1948:

> We accepted Kashmir's offer of accession at a time when she was in peril, in order to be able to effectively to save her from extinction. We will not, in the circumstances, hold her to this accession *as an unalterable decision on her part*. When the emergency has passed and normal conditions are restored, she will be free, by means of a plebiscite, either to ratify her accession to India or to change her mind and accede to Pakistan *or remain independent*. We shall not stand in the way if she elects to change her mind. That, I think, is the proper description of India's attitude. (242nd meeting, UN Security Council 1948: 37)

16. M.C. Setalvad, member of the Indian delegation to the United Nations Security Council, said on 23 January 1948:

> But I make bold to say that the conduct of my Government has been entirely above board in this matter. It was not until the Ruler of Kashmir and the popular leader of Kashmir approached the Indian Government for assistance in the extremity which I have described, that the Indian Government stated – and, I submit, rightly stated – that it could not interfere in the matter of Kashmir unless the State was a part of Indian territory, which could come about only if Kashmir acceded to the Indian Union. On that understanding, in the peril in which it found itself, Kashmir offered to accede to the Indian Union – not only the ruler but also the popular leader. The Indian Government was careful, even though the request came from both, *to stipulate* that it was accepting the accession *only on the condition* that later, when peace had been restored, the expression of the popular should be ascertained in a proper manner. *It was on that condition, and that condition alone, that the Indian Government accepted accession.* (234th Meeting, UN Security Council 1948: 208)

17. Nehru's speech at Jammu on 15 February 1948:

> We have not come here to rule; we have been called here by the people and by the National Conference leaders and the Maharaja to save the beautiful country and the people from the invaders; we have not come here as aggressors or to forcibly rule over Kashmir. . . . We are here at Kashmir's request to help the people of Kashmir from the enemy. (*The Times of India*, 17 February 1948).

18. Nehru's speech in the Constituent Assembly (Legislative) on 5 March 1948:

> Even at the moment of accession, we went out of our way to make a unilateral declaration that we would abide by the will of the people of Kashmir as declared in a plebiscite or referendum. We insisted further that the Govern-

> ment of Kashmir must immediately become a popular Government. We have adhered to that position throughout and we are prepared to have a plebiscite, with every protection for fair voting, and to abide by the decision of the people of Kashmir. (*Selected Works of Jawaharlal Nehru*, Vol. 5: 249)

19. Deputy Prime Minister Vallabhbhai Patel's speech at a public meeting in Bombay on 30 October 1948:

> Some people consider that a Muslim majority area must necessarily belong to Pakistan. They wonder why we are in Kashmir. The answer is plain and simple. We are in Kashmir because the people of Kashmir want us to be there. The moment we realize that the people of Kashmir do not want us to be there, we shall not be there even for a minute. . . . We are asked why we are in Kashmir. The reply is clear. If the Muslims in Kashmir tell us to go away, we will get out. We shall not let the Kashmiris down. (*The Hindustan Times*, 31 October 1948)

20. Resolution of the UN Commission for India and Pakistan, dated 5 January 1949, which both sides accepted: 'The question of the accession of the State of Jammu and Kashmir to India or Pakistan will be decided through the democratic method of a free and impartial plebiscite' (UN Security Council 1949: 23–25).

21. Sir B.N. Rau's speech in the United Nations Security Council on 7 February 1951: 'Kashmir has the right of representation [in India's Constituent Assembly] ever since April 1947; it acceded *tentatively* in October 1947' (463rd Meeting, UN Security Council 1951: 21). Here Rau's use of the word 'tentatively' is significant and must be noted. He was a judge of the Calcutta High Court, Constitutional Adviser to the Constituent Assembly of India, and judge of the International Court of Justice.

22. Nehru's speech at a public meeting in Srinagar on 4 June 1951:

> First of all, I would like to remind you of the fateful days of 1947 when I came to Srinagar and gave the solemn assurance that the people of India would stand by Kashmir in her struggle. On that assurance, I shook Sheikh Abdullah's hand before the vast multitude that had gathered there. I want to repeat that the Government of India will stand by that pledge, whatever happens. That pledge itself stated that it is for the people of Kashmir to decide their fate without external interference. That assurance also remains and will continue. Indian troops came to Kashmir in the hour of great peril at the invitation of the constitutional authorities of the state as well as representatives of the people. They will not remain here a single day if they are unwanted for the purpose for which they came or if the people of Kashmir feel that they do not desire them any longer here. (*The Hindu*, 5 June 1951)

23. Nehru's speech at Calcutta on 1 January 1952:

He [Syama Prasad Mookerjee] wants to know what we are going to do about the one-third of Kashmir which is under Pakistani control. Let me explain first of all, Kashmir is not the property of either Pakistan or India. Kashmir belongs to its people. The people of Kashmir have acceded to India of their own free will and we accepted gladly. Even then we have made it clear that once the war was over, we would hold a plebiscite to allow the people of Kashmir the right to express their views about the accession. If then, the people of Kashmir tell us to get out, we will do so. We will not stay there by force. We did not conquer the territory . . .

There is no doubt about it that he is the leader of the people of Kashmir, a very great leader. If tomorrow Sheikh Abdullah wanted Kashmir to join Pakistan, neither I nor all the forces of India would be able to stop it because if the leader decides, it will happen. . . . Since the matter has been referred to the UN, *we have given our word of honour that we shall abide by their decision.* India's pledge is no small matter and we shall stick by it in the eyes of the world. (*Selected Works of Jawaharlal Nehru*, Vol. 17: 76–78).

24. Nehru in Parliament on 26 June 1952:

And I say with all respect to our Constitution that it just does not matter what your Constitution says, if the people of Kashmir do not want it, it will not go there. . . . Let us suppose there was a proper plebiscite there – and the people of Kashmir said, 'We do not want to be with India', well we are committed to it, we would accept it. It might pain us but we would not send an Army against them; we might accept that, however much hurt we might feel . . . and we would change our constitution about it. (Ibid., Vol. 18: 418)

25. Nehru in Parliament on 7 August 1952:

So, while the accession was complete in law and in fact, the other fact, which has nothing to do with law, also remains, namely our pledge to the people of Kashmir, if you like, to the people of the world, that this matter can be reaffirmed or cancelled or cut out by the people of Kashmir, if they so wish.

We do not want to win people against their will and with the help of armed forces, and if the people of Jammu and Kashmir state so wish it, to part company from us, they can go their way and we shall go our way. We want no forced marriages, no forced unions like this. I hope this great Republic of India is a free, voluntary, friendly and affectionate union of the States of India . . . *ultimately – I say with all deference to this Parliament – the decision will be made in the hearts and minds of the men and women of Kashmir, neither in this Parliament, nor in the United Nations, nor by anybody else.* (Ibid., Vol. 18: 293–96)

26. Even after Sheikh Abdullah was dismissed from the office of Prime Minister of Kashmir and arrested on 9 August 1953, Nehru said on 15 August 1953:

> I want to repeat: it was not today but five and a half years ago that we gave a pledge that only the people of Kashmir can decide their future, we said this and later repeated it. Today also it is our firm opinion that the Kashmir issue can ultimately be decided only by the people of Kashmir. This issue cannot be settled by force. (*The Statesman*, 16 August 1953)

27. Indo–Pak Prime Ministers' Joint Communique issued at New Delhi on 21 August 1953:

> Kashmir dispute was especially discussed at some length. It was their firm opinion that this should be settled in accordance with the wishes of the people of the State, with a view to promoting their well-being and causing the least disturbance to the life of the people of the State. The most feasible method of ascertaining the wishes of the people was by fair and impartial plebiscite. Such a plebiscite had been proposed and agreed to some years ago. Progress, however, could not be made because of the lack of agreement in regard to certain preliminary issues.

It was even decided that 'the Plebiscite Administrator should be appointed by the end of April 1954'. However, following all these claims and assurances, Nehru soon changed tack.

28. Nehru, on 19 July 1961: 'There is no question of any plebiscite in Kashmir, now or later . . . I am sick of the talk about plebiscite, which does not interest anybody' (*Times of India*, 20 July 1961).

29. Nehru's statement in the Constituent Assembly (Legislative) on 7 September 1948: 'the moral aspect of this question [Kashmir] has always troubled me'.

As Milton wrote, ease recants vows said in pain as unsaid and void. Nehru's own admission in his note to Abdullah on 25 August 1952 traces his recantation to 1948, a fact confirmed by his secret offer of partition of the state to Liaquat Ali Khan at Paris on 27 October 1948, and his secret assurance to Abdullah on 11 January 1949. The question arises, why did he make these pledges repeatedly and in terms so earnest and unqualified, dripping with political morality, from 1948 to 1953? Indeed, on 27 October 1950 he wrote to Girija Shanker Bajpai, 'We cannot now be asked to confine ourselves to the plebiscite issue' (*Selected Works of Jawaharlal Nehru*, Vol. 15, Part II: 261).

Regardless, it is *these* pledges which Kashmiris recall today and it is these pledges P. Chidambaram will have to reckon with in his exertions, to fulfil them in the light of the realities of 2012. Plebiscite is ruled out; not so a decision in accordance with the will of the people. That is where the judicial statesmanship and creativity shown by the Supreme Court of Canada in the Quebec case helps (see article VI.5, reproduced in Volume 2). The Centre cannot crush the people or the secessionist sentiment by force. The secessionists cannot declare independence unilaterally. In keeping with its pledges, India must *negotiate* – and so must the advocates of *azadi*. To repeat, the self-rule element in the agreed Indo–Pak Four Points fits a revised Article 370, with cast-iron guarantees, like a glove. The issue is not redressal of 'grievances'. It is rejection of the present political and constitutional order based on force and fraud, and its replacement by one that rests on consent and sincerity. To win the allegiance of a people as creative as the Kashmiris will be a gain for the Union. India's diplomacy and aspirations will receive a boost.

Incidentally, arrogance of power was not absent in the councils of the Janata Party in 1977 either. However, the world was not, and indeed is not, blind. In September 1964, Ambassador B.K. Nehru recounted to this writer an episode in the Security Council when the Soviet Union vetoed a resolution on Kashmir. Krishna Menon turned to the Ambassador, 'pale in the face', and asked if the United States would move for reference of the issue to the UN General Assembly under the Assembly's 'Uniting for Peace' Resolution (i.e. 6A Resolution 377(V) of 3 November 1950). B.K. Nehru remarked that had the matter been referred to the Assembly, India would have been in the same predicament as South Africa and Portugal were then.

B.K. Nehru wrote to the Commonwealth Secretary Y.D. Gundevia, a man as honest as himself, on 24 September 1963, in these sharp terms:

> Thank you for preparing and circulating to us the *Report on the Conference of the Heads of Missions in South East Asia*. It is a document which I have read with much interest and profit. . . .
> 2. On page 27 of this booklet is the statement that the United States 'did not bother about the rights or wrongs of the case in regard to Kashmir, nor did they believe that Pakistan had a good case on Kashmir; they only support Pakistan as an ally'.
> 3. It is my duty to point out, as I have done before, that this Embassy does not accept this assessment of the American view on Kashmir as correct. The Americans do believe that Pakistan has a good case on Kashmir – though the Administration is very careful not to say so – and the sympathy with Pakistan is not only because Pakistan is an ally but because it is regarded as the wronged party. (*Y.D. Gundevia Papers*)

On a visit to Kashmir in 2002, what Jean Dreze – a committed friend of India, especially its poor – saw was an alert people living in the midst of intimidatingly huge Army camps. He hired a bicycle in Srinagar, and spent a few days riding around the Valley and talking with local residents.

> My initial purpose was to study the schooling situation, but it turned out to be difficult not to focus on people's overwhelming concern: the endless *zulm* (repression) unleashed by the security forces.
>
> The security forces were rarely out of sight, even in remote villages. As far as the local population is concerned, Kashmir is 'occupied' by a foreign Army. Everywhere I went, there were sobering tales of harassment at the hands of the Indian Army and paramilitary forces: curfews, searches, interrogations, killings of suspected militants, and accidental as well as intentional killings of innocent civilians, to name a few complaints. In one village, I was told that a father and son had recently been shot in the knee before being pushed into a house in flames. In several villages, shops and houses had recently been burnt in retaliation against recent killings of Army personnel – a prime example of 'collective punishment', proscribed by international conventions. Physical hardships are compounded by constant humiliation. 'Imagine how we feel when a Bihari or a Madrasi asks us for our identity card in our own country, when we should be asking them for their papers', said one. In a similar vein, a middle-class woman in Srinagar complained that her house had recently been searched by a *'Chambal ka daku'* in uniform. . . . There is no simple solution to the Kashmir impasse. What seems clear is that the present stand of the Indian Government is a trifle contradictory. In international fora, mediation is rejected on the grounds that Pakistan and India have agreed to resolve the Kashmir dispute bilaterally. When Pakistan approaches India for talks, it is told that Kashmir is an internal matter (despite India's own claim to 'Pakistan-Occupied Kashmir'). Within India, however, Kashmir is treated like a colony, unworthy of democratic rights. It is no wonder that the Indian Government's attempt to entice the State into the national fold has failed to strike a chord with the Kashmiri people. (*The Hindu*, 29 March 2002)

All UN maps, over the years, consistently show Kashmir as a territory in dispute between India and Pakistan. The exact words are: 'The final status of Jammu and Kashmir has not yet been agreed upon by the parties.' The word 'yet' suggests a lot. Not only the United States, even Russia makes no secret of its reservations on India's stand. As recently as on 11 June 2009, the US Under Secretary of State for Political Affairs, William Burns, said in New Delhi: 'Any resolution of Kashmir has to take into account the wishes of the Kashmiri people' (*The Times of India*, 12 June 2009). How the United States feels itself free to intervene, with the United Kingdom formally in tow, becomes clear in their Joint Statement of 27 March 2003; it prescribed a road map which India and Pakistan followed. It said: 'Both sides should consider immediately implementing a ceasefire and taking other active steps to reduce tension including by moves within the SAARC context. The dif-

UN Map of South Asia, 2004

Note: The legend to this UN map clearly states: 'The final status of Jammu and Kashmir has not yet been agreed upon by the parties.'

Source: UN Cartographic Section, http://www.un.org/Dept/Cartographic/map/profile/seasia.pdf

ferences between India and Pakistan can only be resolved through peaceful means and engagement. The United States and the United Kingdom stand ready to help both countries to start a process aimed at building confidence, normalizing bilateral relations and resolving outstanding differences, including Kashmir' (UK High Commission 2003).

The Statement envisaged a ceasefire and talks 'within the SAARC context'. Both followed. The contrived appearance of spontaneity could not conceal the orchestration. Soon thereafter, on 18 April 2003, Prime Minister Atal Behari Vajpayee addressed a public rally in Srinagar where he said: 'The issue of home and outside issues, all need to be resolved through dialogue. The dialogue should take place on the basis of justice and in the framework (*daira*) of *insaniyat* (humanity)' (*The Indian Express*, 19 April 2003). In the Lok Sabha, Vajpayee amplified on 23 April 2003: 'I assured the people of Jammu and Kashmir that we wish to resolve all issues, both domestic and external, through talks. I stressed that the gun can solve no problem, brotherhood can. Issues can be resolved if we move forward guided by three principles of *insaniyat*, *jamhooriyat* (democracy) and Kashmiriat.'

Not a few put the spin that '*insaniyat*' went beyond Article 370. The text and the context of this famous talk of '*insaniyat*' reveal it to be mere rhetoric. Vajpayee was offering a ceasefire and talks to reinforce it. 'I am willing to talk on any issue including Jammu and Kashmir. And I hope to get a favourable response from Pakistan' (*The Indian Express*, 20 April 2003). Sure enough, on 28 April, Pakistan's Prime Minister, Mir Zafarulla Khan Jamali, called Vajpayee to discuss how a dialogue could begin. On 23 November Pakistan announced a ceasefire. Two days later both sides agreed to a ceasefire along the International Border, the LoC and the Actual Ground Position Line in the Siachen area. Vajpayee duly went to Islamabad to attend the SAARC summit. A Joint Statement he issued with President Musharraf on 6 January 2004 initiated the dialogue process. It was interrupted by the Mumbai blasts on 26 November 2008.

Meanwhile, on 22 January and 27 March 2004, Deputy Prime Minister L.K. Advani met a delegation of the Hurriyat. It was a cynical charade, for successive Annual Reports of the Home Ministry during the BJP regime poured scorn on the Hurriyat – the 2003–04 Annual Report stated that 'None of the factions enjoys popular support' (Ministry of Home Affairs 2004: 17) – and asserted that 'the State of J&K already enjoys autonomy' (ibid.: 20). The Report for the year 2002–03 was even more strident.

The BJP regime had nothing to offer to the people of Kashmir; still less to Pakistan. The peace process began in earnest only after the UPA government, led by Dr Manmohan Singh, came to power in May 2004. Together, he and President Musharraf inched forward towards an accord on the basics of Kashmir. The Prime Minister was due to visit Pakistan in 2007 to finalize it. That was not to be. On 9 March 2007, Musharraf dismissed from office the Chief Justice of the Supreme Court, Iftikhar Muhammed Chaudhry, setting in motion a train of events that led to Musharraf leaving the office of Chief of Army on 28 November and the Presidency on 18 August 2008 (Khan 2001: 689–720).

It is to the credit of India and Pakistan that they owe nothing to the busy bodies in the United States who are raring to have a go in mediation between the two. The progress made since 2004 is exclusively an Indo–Pak achievement. However, if these efforts are to succeed India must face the grim reality that Kashmiris seek not the redress of 'grievances' but replacement of the present order which they never accepted, and which was imposed by force of arms after the tribal raid from Pakistan. It, therefore, makes no sense to fling the Indian Constitution at them and ask which items in the Union List and which of its provisions they want omitted. Acquiescence is not acceptance. Kashmiris never accepted the Union, as Indira Gandhi's letter of 1948 reveals. Given this reality the Valley will erupt again and again ostensibly for small reasons; in reality, to express a deeper rejection. Suppression never establishes peace, only desolation. As Tacitus, the historian of ancient Rome said, 'They create desolation and call it peace'.

India is faced with a clear choice – purchase the purchasable, institute cosmetic reforms and play for time, hoping that it will provide a cure. Or, it can settle realistically and in earnest. Time has proved the sagacity of the caution which Bazaz administered in 1954:

> If Kashmir remains with India against the will of the State's people it will always find itself in political turmoil. One puppet will succeed another but no Government will be stable . . .
>
> It is tragic that, of all people in India, the Congress leaders should be instrumental in subjugating Kashmiris by might of armed military. For more than thirty years the Congress waged a titanic war against British Imperialism under the leadership of Mahatma Gandhi. All patriotic Indians in general and the Congress leaders in particular know how enraged one feels at the loss of civil liberties and human rights; how galling it is for a self-respecting citizen to know that his country is occupied by foreign forces which defend an irresponsible, unpopular and fascist Government in his motherland. . . . Did not the British appoint Indian rulers under them some of whom were renegade Congressman? Did that meet with the approval of India? The question is not if Kashmir is ruled by local Muslims, however boosted; it is if the rulers are the true representatives of the State's people. So long as the freely chosen leaders are not placed at the helm of affairs Kashmir will remain sullen and disturbed. (Bazaz 1954: 707–08)

When militancy erupted in 1990, Professor Hiren Mukherjee was quick to perceive what it signified and lamented, on 25 February 1994: 'Even today, perhaps the best of us do not quite realize the depth of Kashmiri alienation and are unready to ponder ways and means of overcoming it' (*The Hindu*, 25 January 1994).

The astute D.P. Mishra grasped the truth years ago. His parting words to Srinivasavaradan in 1964 as he was about to leave Bhopal for a posting in Jammu, were: 'Hindustan was still to Kashmir an alien country and it can only be the conduct and behavior of Hindustanis, particularly in Kashmir, that would induce the Kashmiris to become Indians willingly' (Srinivasa-varadan 1992: 14–15).

Mir Qasim, who had opposed Abdullah in 1953, put it bluntly when asked, 'What do the people of Kashmir demand?' He replied: 'They clearly say that they would not like to remain in India. They would like to go out of India. They ask for a plebiscite so that they will be allowed to answer whether they want to remain in India or go out of India' (Qasim 1992: 298).

That is *azadi* for you, a concept which eludes the understanding of Chidambaram's 'Interlocutors' as well as some bright sparks in the electronic media. All ask, 'What do they mean by *azadi*?' Omar Abdullah knows better than to fall for their gimmicks. 'Whoever said the *azadi* sentiment went away? Just because people came out to vote in 2008 doesn't mean the issue has been resolved. They voted because of their day-to-day concerns' (Jerath and Pandit 2010). *Azadi* means, first and foremost, secession from India. Nothing else.

It was left to one of India's foremost public intellectuals, Ashok Mitra, former Finance Minister of West Bengal, to rip apart the veil of falsehood and expose the havoc India's policies have wreaked.

> Behind the facade of the constitutional apparatus rests the nitty-gritty of rude fact: the Valley is an occupied territory; remove for a day India's Army and security forces and it is impossible to gauge what might transpire at the next instant. Some of the stone-pelters may nurse illusions about Pakistan, some may think in terms of a sovereign, self-governing Kashmir, but they certainly do not want to be any part of India . . . the great Indian nation, with its load of civilization stretching 5000 years, is extraordinarily mum.
>
> The media can afford to be full of narratives of sickeningly shady deals linked to the preparatory arrangements for the impending Commonwealth Games. But the debauching of civilization in Kashmir, no matter what its underlying reason, creates no ripples. One is suddenly hit by a fearsome realization: Indians by and large do not perhaps feel at all, this way or that, about the Valley's people. In other words, the Indian nation is alienated from Kashmir. (*The Telegraph*, 27 August 2010)

Reckoning with these truths, how do we go about devising a solution? In 1968 Jayaprakash Narayan preferred a two-stage approach: settle with Abdullah and confront Pakistan with a fait accompli. So did Indira Gandhi's Principal Secretary, P.N. Dhar, in 1972 (Dhar 2000: 212).

A bad advice was badly executed. From 3 July 1972, when the Shimla Agreement was signed, till the end of the year, Z.A. Bhutto and even Aziz Ahmad begged of Indira Gandhi to visit Pakistan. She could have firmed up the oral understanding at Shimla and allowed the 90,000 prisoners of war to return with assurances of recognition of Bangladesh. She did not. By the time the Accord with the Sheikh was concluded in 1975, Bhutto had strengthened his position. The oral understanding evaporated.

In 2012, the best course is to pursue the Four Point blueprint with Pakistan, and to negotiate with Kashmiris on the self-rule it envisages plus the safeguards they need to ensure against a repeat of the abuses since 1954.

The Hurriyat is split. Its leaders are barely on speaking terms with each other. The constitution of the United All Parties Hurriyat Conference itself envisaged alternatives to plebiscite which Clause 2(i) preferred but sub-clause (ii) added:

> to make endeavours for *an alternative negotiated settlement of the Kashmir dispute amongst all the three parties to the dispute* viz., (a) INDIA (b) PAKISTAN (c) PEOPLE OF THE STATE OF JAMMU AND KASHMIR, under the auspices of United Nations or any other friendly countries. Provided that such settlement reflects the will and aspirations of the people of the State. . . . EXPLANATION: for the removal of doubts, it is hereby declared that in this Article, negotiated statement shall not be deemed to include any settlement within the framework of the Constitution of India.

The Indo–Pak Accord renders the Explanation of 1993 irrelevant. Kashmir's leaders too have given a poor account of themselves. The Mir Waiz, Umar Farooq, acknowledged on 2 January 2011 that 'ups and downs come in every struggle, but the need is to introspect why we were not able to give right direction to three successive years of uprising in Kashmir. We should introspect on our weak points' (*Greater Kashmir*, 3 January 2011). He was alluding to the upheavals of 2008, 2009 and 2010. Given the clash of personalities, it is unlikely that matters will improve. A tripartite process is neither possible nor necessary after the consensus on the Four Points.

The peace dividend they will yield will be enormous. In this regard, we have a lot to glean from the repercussions of the Cold War. In the United States, thoughtful scholars have been analysing the origins and course of the Cold War within the Soviet Union and the harm the conflict inflicted on American society. American Ambassadors are not known for thoughtfulness, judging by their conduct in recent years. Thomas W. Simons Sr., Ambassador to Pakistan, was a rare exception. In a speech to the United Service Institution in New Delhi, he preached little to his guests and reflected more on the impact of the Cold War on American society.

> We preserved our liberties, but we paid for the Cold War with a serious degradation of many of our basic national structures: our schools, our roads, our cities, and our civil courtesies. If we now seem absorbed as a nation with our domestic affairs, it is partly because we need to repair and revitalize those structures. We earnestly hope our friends and partners in the new international community will have the wisdom and good fortune to bypass this painful series of steps, which is such a drain on human and economic resour-

ces better applied to the normal activities of free societies. (American Centre, Mumbai, press release, 1996)

It was obvious even in late 1947 that the manner in which the Kashmir dispute was managed would shape the future of the entire subcontinent. The way it was tackled affected for the worse the domestic as well as the foreign policies of both its units. An early solution would have brought home to many Pakistanis the folly of the partition. The common cultural heritage with India would not have been sidelined as was done consciously later (for a collection of poignant memoirs by Pakistanis and Indians, see Siddiqi and Ikramulla 1997). Pakistanis, even the most liberal of them, acquired a sense of having been cheated and wronged. They were, and still are, oblivious to the mistakes of their leaders – a trait Indians share fully.

The Jamaate-e-Islami, headed by Abul Ala Maududi who had opposed Pakistan, exploited the sentiment and campaigned for an Islamic state. The secularists were virtually side-lined. In this climate the left suffered the most, a fact which Indians and Pakistanis alike overlook (Zaheer 1998: 208). As Hasan Zaheer wrote: 'The Communist Party might have become a significant element in the mainstream politics in both wings of Pakistan.' A siege mentality developed. Democracy suffered and Army rule became the norm. In India it strengthened the Sangh Parivar and the chauvinistic impulse in its campaign of hate. Even in some secular parties like the Congress, its cries found a welcoming response.

As in a clash of arms, the truth became the first casualty. Pakistanis still celebrate 6 September as Defence Day though it had itself launched the war of 1965 on 5 August and with armour on 1 September. In Indian mythology Pakistan launched the war of 1971 on 3 December. In truth Indian armour had entered East Pakistan on 21 November. B.K. Nehru, then Governor of Assam, was informed by the local Army commander, Major-General Gurbax Singh, 'that D-Day was the 4 of December . . . Yahya Khan saved us from the charge of starting the war by himself bombing (wholly ineffectively) airfield on the afternoon of 3 December' (Nehru 1997: 491). The UN's maps show the status of the state of J&K as territory in dispute. But the D word makes Indian diplomats foam at the mouth.

From 1947 to 1951 the foreign policies of both countries were broadly similar as their voting record in the UN General Assembly shows. We owe to Professor M.S. Venkataramani's research in the United States archives the discovery that in 1948 Nehru sought arms from the United States, and expressed 'the interest of the Government of India in a long-term military collaboration between the US and India'. The approach was made through his favourite, Colonel B.M. Kaul, then Military Attache at the Indian Embassy, bypassing Ambassador Asaf Ali. On 2 April 1948, the Secretary-General of the Ministry of External Affairs, Girja Shankar Bajpai, met officials in the State Department and assured them that:

> India would under no circumstances align itself with the Soviet Union in a war between the latter and the US . . . with the knowledge and full authority of Prime Minister Nehru he would like to propose the sending of an Indian Military Mission to the US at an early date to explore the possibilities of obtaining military equipment in this country. (Venkataramani 1999)

In later exchanges the Indian government sought to know 'where it stood' with the United States government 'in the overall evaluation of what contribution might be made by India in the event of further deterioration in international relations in general'. This question was asked on 30 July 1948 by the Embassy on Nehru's orders. As he wrote to Bajpai on 14 February 1949: 'We are now much closer to the USA and UK group than to the USSR' ('An Elusive Military Relationship', *Frontline*, 9–23 April and 7–21 May 1999).

In Pakistan men like Sir Muhammad Zafrullah Khan, Ghulam Mohammed and leading bureaucrats did not share Prime Minister Liaquat Ali Khan's preference for non-alignment. They were all for ties with the US. Non-alignment can subsist only if there is no major dispute between the neighbours. If there is one, generally, the weaker of the two, it seeks external support, driving the other to the rival bloc.

With its strong democratic institutions, India forged far ahead of Pakistan economically and in the esteem of the world. It knows, however, that not a single power endorses its claim on Kashmir – bar the Cold War interlude when the Soviet veto was handy. Kashmir was a noisy skeleton in a cupboard that was not soundproof. Prime Minister Manmohan Singh freely admitted to Jonathan Power in May 2004, 'This is stopping us from realizing our potential.' A World Bank Policy Research Working Paper on 'The Peace Dividend' states: 'our empirical estimates clearly indicate that high levels of military expenditure detract from economic growth both because they reduce productive fixed capital formation and because they act more generally to distort resource allocation' (Knight *et al.* 1996: 40).

An entente will have a great effect on Kashmiris' outlook. Self-rule as an integral component of the Four Points will go a very long way towards satisfying their aspirations and their views on India and Pakistan. Once the LoC becomes irrelevant, the grass 'on the other side' will look less green. Ghulam Rasool Kar is a veteran Congress leader in Kashmir. In 2010 he made a passionate plea for improvement in India's relations with Pakistan and acceptance of this 'harsh' reality of Kashmiri sentiment. Addressing a convention of Congressmen in Sopore, he said: 'Every Kashmiri is emotionally attached to Pakistan whether they [*sic*] are in Congress or National Conference. . . . I am an Indian but I am pained to see Pakistan in trouble' (*Kashmir Life*, 22 May 2010).

Right from the time of the partition, Kashmiris have viewed Pakistan altogether differently from their fellow-citizens in the rest of India. On Kargil their censure of Musharraf was different from that of other Indians. Their criticism was in terms of Mao's censure of Khruschev after the Cuban missile crisis: adventurism was followed by capitulation.

In 2007 again the Kashmiris' reaction to the upheaval in Pakistan was in total contrast to that in the rest of India. But the phenomenon was little noticed and aroused no reflection. The jehadis and the extremist fringe, having rejected President Pervez Musharraf's concessions on Kashmir, spoke with an air of vindication. All others felt despondent. Right across the political divide, both the Unionists and the separatists saw him as one who could clinch a settlement on Kashmir. On 30 November 2007, none other than Chief Minister Ghulam Nabi Azad praised him to the skies as a unique conciliator.

On 4 November 2007, the People's Democratic Party (PDP) president, Mehbooba Mufti, said on a local TV channel, Take One: 'Naturally we are concerned. We have a sentimental and geographical affinity with Pakistan.' She defended the Provisional Constitution Order by Musharraf on 3 November 2007, a day after he had proclaimed an Emergency. She said: 'In Pakistan, the generals have imposed martial law during normal times, but Musharraf's decision comes at an abnormal time. For the past seven months, things had turned ugly. And the judges had not played their role as the people would have expected them to. The General had no option.'

The former chairman of the Hurriyat's moderate faction, Abdul Ghani Bhat, spoke in the same vein. 'Pakistan is not the only country where Emergency has been imposed. Sri Lanka, too, has imposed Emergency because of disturbed situation' (*Greater Kashmir*, *Rising Kashmir*). He also criticized the judges. 'There has to be harmony among the three pillars of the State – the executive, the legislature and the judiciary. And when there are problems in this harmony, it endangers stability' (ibid.). On the same day (November 5) Shabbir Shah, a separatist, said that the Emergency was a 'necessary step for Pakistan's stability'.

There were jubilant celebrations on Musharraf's re-election as President. Activists burst firecrackers and danced on the streets of Srinagar. This was not the first time Kashmiris responded to events in Pakistan altogether differently from other Indians. They made little secret of their support for Pakistan despite its brutal crackdown in the then East Pakistan. When Z.A. Bhutto was executed in 1979, activists went on a rampage attacking the Jamaat-e-Islami's men and property.

How do we explain this? Sumeet Kaul's report in *The Hindustan Times* on 4 September 2007 helps us to understand it.

> I had read somewhere that your preconceived notions of nationalism, of Indian nationalism, are severely tested in the Valley. They were and that,

> perhaps, was more difficult to come to terms with than even the guns. Wherever we went, we were almost invariably referred to as the 'guests from India', not with malice, but casually, incidentally.

Three times in as many weeks – on 19 and 23 November and 5 December 2007 – a Unionist, Farooq Abdullah, leader of the National Conference, warned that if violations of human rights continued, 'the people might be forced to rethink about the accession [of J&K to India in 1947]'. He knew that this would please his listeners in Kashmir.

Frustration has mounted as the peace process with Pakistan came to a halt in 2007. Added to it is the increase in repression since Omar Abdullah became Chief Minister. He says one thing and does the opposite. On the one hand, Omar Abdullah said in Srinagar on 28 February 2011: 'The youth [of the Valley] did not take up guns for *bijli*, *pani*, *sadak* (electricity, water, roads), but for resolution of the Kashmir issue' (*DNA*, 2 March 2011). But in 2010 when, in sheer despair, the youth pelted stones, not fire bullets, he began a campaign of repression – which was ably documented by a journalist who has for long observed the Kashmir scene and viewed Omar's assumption of office of Chief Minister favourably and with hope. Prem Shankar Jha's critique is devastating, alike of the government's repression and the media's suppression of its abuse of power. It bears quotation *in extenso*:

> Not a whisper about this campaign of repression has found its way into the national media. Not a single television channel has reported what the State Government is doing. Instead, all have swallowed the official line that Kashmir has calmed down; that Omar's popularity is once more rising; that Kashmiris are sick of violence, they have rejected the stone-pelters, and are longing for peace and good governance.
>
> But this state of denial is only for public consumption. Behind its facade, New Delhi has quietly given the State Government a *carte blanche* to do whatever is needed to prevent a 'repeat of last summer'.
>
> Since the 'Durbar' moved to Jammu in November [2009], hundreds have been arrested in midnight swoops that hark back to the worst days of the insurgency of the 90s. The goal of the police is to arrest stone-pelters and send the message: 'We know you. You cannot hide from us. We will come and get you.' It is also to remove potential leaders of future stone-pelting.
>
> All this is being done surreptitiously. Officially, the Government claims to have fulfilled the Centre's promise, made on 25 September, to release all stone-pelters. As a result, there are only 195 of them left in jails, booked under the Public Safety Act. In reality, however, the total number of stone-pelters imprisoned has more than doubled, from 1800 at the end of September to 4294 on 20 February. The arrest of 614 of these carried out this year has been hidden from the Interlocutors.
>
> Stone-pelters are not the only ones being targeted. All the local cable tele-

> vision channels have been shut down. An estimated four million prepaid SIM cards are being withdrawn. SMS remains banned and newspapers that are deemed to be pro-separatist of anti-Abdullah have had their advertising cut off. Among the newspapers that have suffered are *Greater Kashmir*, *Rising Kashmir*, *Kashmir Monitor* and the Urdu newspaper *Ikhlaq*. The last is owned by Shia leader Maulvi Iftikhar Ansari, who is a PDP member. *Kashmir Monitor* and *Ikhlaq* have lost both State Government advertisements and those from the Centre's Directorate of Audio Visual Publicity. . . .
>
> The single most self-defeating action has been taken by the Delhi Government almost certainly at the behest of the Home Ministry. This is to prevent the return of Syed Ali Shah Geelani to the Valley by detaining him in connection with a series of the hawala cases. Geelani is the undisputed leader of the Valley's extremist youth. As he has shown before, he is also the only person in that camp who does not want Kashmir to sink into an abyss of violence, and has sufficient control over the youth to prevent it.
>
> The Government's purpose is clear: with Geelani's principal lieutenants, Masarat Alam, Asiya Andrabi and her husband Mohammed Kais Faktoo, already in jail, they only have to remove him to render the stone-pelters leaderless. But history should have taught it that if such action is not accompanied with measures to address the root cause of alienation, removing one set of leaders only creates space for the emergence of more hardline leaders.
>
> Bottling up the rage of the youth over last summer's killing would have led to an explosion in any case. But the timetable for the explosion has been moved up by the popular revolts in Egypt, Tunisia and Libya. (Jha, *Tehelka*, 12 March 2011).

The national media behaves as it does partly under tacit constraints and partly under a mistaken notion of 'nationalism'. What a 'senior police officer' in Srinagar confided to *The Indian Express* on 17 February 2011 is true of most of the media: 'At times one has to close his [*sic*] eyes in the national interest.'

A refreshing change in an otherwise dismal situation is a significant shift in the left's position on Kashmir – specifically, that of the Communist Party of India (Marxist). Till 1953 the left and Sheikh Abdullah were 'natural allies'. The Adlai Stevenson scare and Krishna Menon's politics creat-ed a rift. It is to the credit of the late Harkishen Singh Surjeet that he rose to the occasion and began to empathise with the people. His successor in office as general secretary of the CPI(M), Prakash Karat, pursued the same course. He went to Kashmir on 22 and 23 August 2010. The statement he issued at the end of the trip reflected deep anguish:

> The way forward is by recognizing the special status of the State and the need to assure the Kashmiri people of their identity. These require a new political framework in which the bedrock is maximum autonomy. . . .
>
> In the meantime, the Central Government should pursue the Confidence

> Building Measures with Pakistan which can widen the canvas of ties and relations across the LoC.
>
> This is the time all democratic-minded persons, organizations and groups should appeal and work for restoration of peace and normalcy so that people can express their views and *maintain their right to protest peacefully*.

This is the nub of the matter – the right to peaceful protest.

An all-party meeting on Kashmir, convened by Prime Minister Manmohan Singh on 15 September 2010, decided to send a delegation of Members of Parliament to the state, led by Home Minister P. Chidambaram. It was boycotted by the separatists. However, MPs like Sitaram Yechury of the CPI(M), Gurudas Dasgupta of the CPI and Asaduddin Owaisi of the Ittehad-ul-Muslimeen pierced through the reserve and met separatist leaders on 20 September. The trip was an eye-opener. Gurudas Dasgupta said on 22 September, after his return, that the situation in Kashmir was 'much graver' than they had thought.

> I have no hesitation in saying that the rest of India does not know what is happening in Kashmir and the people of the Valley feel that Indians do not show concern. There is a critical degree of alienation and if we do not realize that we all need to do something, Kashmir may be lost to India. (*The Hindu*, 23 September 2010)

He remarked: 'The special position of the State has been gradually diluted. We have allowed the situation to deteriorate' (ibid.).

Sitaram Yechury spoke in the same vein. 'The gravity and depth of alienation is much deeper than we thought. People speak of *azadi* passionately even in hospitals' (*The Times of India*, 26 September 2010). There are some, however, who profess not to understand what *azadi* means and ask Kashmiris to define it.

Brinda Karat, MP and member of the Central Committee of the CPI(M), was a member of the women's delegation who met the Centre's three Interlocutors, behind closed doors, in Srinagar on 12 March 2011. Speaking to Shujaat Bukhari, she said:

> It was painful to hear about the gross violations of human and democratic rights in Kashmir. Since 2009, and particularly in 2010, the assurances made by the Government to deliver justice have not been fulfilled and the utter failure in punishing the guilty has led to lack of confidence in the system. You cannot talk about calm because without justice it is fragile. (*The Hindu*, 13 March 2011)

Advocating quick delivery of justice, she said: 'The beginnings of the justice process have to be in punishing those who were killing children, maiming them and throwing them in jails. After meeting the victims' families I could feel that wounds are fresh because of lack of justice' (ibid.).

In the Rajya Sabha, on 15 March 2011, an outraged Brinda Karat was scathing in her censure: 117 people were killed in the summer but not even a single constable was punished though 37 FIRs had been registered. She condemned the 'militarization of the entire Valley' and asked the government to 'stop behaving like an occupying power' – a description which comes to the mind of most who care to see (*Greater Kashmir*, 16 March 2011).

Even such a parlous state of affairs has not bestirred Kashmir's leaders to forge a united front. The Unionists, the National Conference and the PDP, make no effort to evolve an agreed draft of a new Article 370 to replace the old, with guarantees of self-rule within the Union and cast-iron safeguards against a repeat of the past. Nor do they pursue their election manifestos in between elections.

The separatists are torn apart, less by differences on policy and more by clashes of the monumental egos of their leaders. Suffering from a total incapacity for creativity, they cling to the forms of struggle which only earn criticism for the leaders and inflict hardships on the people – strikes, hartals, boycotts, etc. Syed Salahuddin, chief of the Hizbul Mujahideen and the militants' umbrella group, the United Jehad Council, which is based in west Kashmir, said: 'I have good advice to my friends; but they did not listen to me. No nation can remain dependent on constant strikes' (*Conveyor* newsmagazine, Srinagar, January–February 2011).

If only they had come together on just one issue, the right to peaceful protest – the fundamental right 'to assemble peaceably and without arms' which is guaranteed by Article 19(1)(b) of the Constitution of India. Involved here are two distinct issues: the form of the agitation and protest, and their content. Militancy has lived on borrowed time since 1995 when 'guest fighters' entered Kashmir. The state armed surrendered militants. After 9/11 armed militancy came under a cloud. Pakistan never related its covert operation to an achievable diplomatic solution. Since it provided the guns, the reins of militancy were in *its* hands, not those of Hurriyat – not even when it was united. As Geelani said, the Hurriyat had no control over the militants.

The separatists face a challenge as well as an opportunity. Pakistan remains a party to the Kashmir dispute. But the self-assertion of the separatists will make its solution easier and also add to their own self-esteem. They must not rock the boat of the Four Points. They ought, instead, to enrich its content with sensible contributions. New Delhi will not be able to deny for long the demand to respect the right to peaceful protest if it is made by a united front of all separatists – supported possibly by the PDP.

No two situations are alike, but analogies are helpful. David D. Kirkpatrick and David E. Sanger of *The New York Times* reported from Cairo how Ahmed Maher, a 30-year-old civil engineer and a leading organizer of the April 6 Youth Movement, which helped to organize the 25 January protests, learnt from protest movements in other countries. Maher and his colleagues began reading about non-violent struggles. They were especially drawn to a Serbian youth movement called Otpor, which had helped topple the dictator Slobodan Milosevic by drawing on the ideas of Gene Sharp, a US political thinker. The hallmark of Sharp's work was well-tailored to Hosni Mubarak's Egypt. He argues that *non-violence is a singularly effective sway to undermine police states that might cite violent resistance to justify repression in the name of stability.*

'Another influence, several said, was a group of Egyptian expatriates in their 30s who set up an organization in Qatar called the Academy of Change, which promotes ideas drawn in part on Mr Sharp's about non-violent democracy movement' (*International Herald Tribune*, 15 February 2011). Gene Sharp's 'writings on non-violent revolution – most notably *From Dictatorship to Democracy*, a 93-page guide to toppling autocrats, available for download in 24 languages – have inspired dissidents around the would, including in Bosnia, Estonia, Myanmar and Zimbabwe and now in Tunisia and Egypt' (ibid.).

The International Centre on Nonviolent Conflict, which slipped into Cairo several years ago to conduct a workshop, distributed Sharp's paper, '198 Methods of Nonviolent Action', among others. Sheryl Gay Stolberg of *The New York Times* reported:

> Based on studies of revolutionaries like Gandhi, non-violent uprisings, civil rights struggles, economic boycotts and the like, Mr Sharp has concluded that advancing freedom takes careful strategy and meticulous planning, advice that Ms Zelda said had resonated among youth leaders in Egypt. Peaceful protest is best, he says – not for any moral reason, but because violence provokes autocrats to crack down. 'If you fight with violence', Mr Sharp said, 'you are fighting with your enemy's best weapon, and you may be a brave but dead hero.' He has just finished work on a new book, '*Sharp's Dictionary of Power and Struggle*'. He holds, 'If people are not afraid of the dictatorship, that dictatorship is in big trouble' (*International Herald Tribune*, 18 February 2011).

Sharp's analysis was fully confirmed in Srinagar by a top government source requesting not to be named. He told Randeep Singh Mandal: 'Militancy we can handle. After 9/11 [we've seen[it backfires on its promoters. People here are sick of violence. But our greatest fear is 50,000 people landing up at Lal Chowk for a dharna. How do you handle that?' (*The Times of India*, 25 February 2011). The correspondent remarked: 'Post-Egypt uprising, things look different. A similar test would put the Centre and the State Government in a spot. The police believe that for such a mass upsurge, all that the separatists need is a spark. This is where stone-pelters come in. One death could ignite a fire' (ibid.).

In 1989, when armed militancy erupted, the militants were encouraged by the fall of the Ceaucescu regime in Romania. The gun failed to deliver – except to infuse life into dormant issues whose death certificate many had written. In 2011, Tunisia and Egypt inspired the protest movement and guided it into an effective non-violent course. So much for the *form* of protest; now for its content. The Indian National Congress and the All India Muslim League did not consider it demeaning to raise issues of immediate concern besides propagating their respective goals. The cry of *azadi* will not become weaker if issues like *roti, kapda, makan* (bread, clothing, housing) and those of *bijli, sadak* and *pani* are also raised continuously by the rank and file in the rural areas, and the top leadership at appropriate moments.

Astonishingly, neither the Unionists nor the separatists seriously raise questions like the Kashmiri Muslims' representation in the Central Services as strenuously as Sheikh Abdullah and Maulana Azad did sixty years ago. The situation has not improved since, as a detailed report by Naseer A. Ganai in *Greater Kashmir* of 7 May 2007 establishes. He wrote:

> Official sources said out of 63 IAS officers – both direct and indirect – 30 are Muslims, 28 Hindus, three Sikhs and two Buddhists. Muslim representation in the present top bureaucratic line up is zero. Most of the Financial Commissioners and Principal Secretaries of the State happen to be non-Muslim. No Muslim bureaucrat heads important departments like Home, Finance and Planning, Health, Industry and Works. The only senior-most Muslim IAS officers are Iqbal Khandey and Khurshid Ahmed Ganai. While Ladakh region has had its first Chief Secretary in the shape of incumbent Phunsong, only eight of the 23 CSs since 1947 were Muslims. The situation in the Police department is worse.

The masses support the separatists; but their leaders have wasted the asset by their ineptness and indolence. Separatism has not been organized into a strong non-violent mass movement which can negotiate with New Delhi for a realistic settlement.

At the end of 2011, Kashmir was more peaceful than at any time since 1989. In 2009 there were less than 500 militancy-related incidents and there was a drop of 30 per cent in 'violent incidents' that year (*Rising Kashmir*, 16 June and 12 October 2009). The progress was maintained. Even the DG of Police, Kuldeep Khoda, noted that 'militancy is on decline' (*Rising Kashmir*, 30 April 2011). On 19 May 2011, *Greater Kashmir* reported that 'for the first time since eruption of militancy, no infiltration bid was reported from any part of the state between March and May'. The newspaper recalled the GOC-in-C of Northern Command, Lieutenant General K.T. Parmariki's recent remark: 'As far as our information is concerned they [militants] have not succeeded in infiltrating into our side yet'. Major General Revri Thodge, GOC Kilo Force, confirmed this.

The IG of the Border Security Force, Siddarth Chattopadhyay, said on 24

May: 'For 300 odd militants we can't blame entire Pakistan or its Army.' A day earlier the GOC-in-C 15 Corps, Lieutenant General Syed Atta Hasnain, had denied media reports about infiltration. 'There was no incident of infiltration and neither was there any gunfight on the LoC. These reports are concocted and baseless. This kind of baseless stuff appears in the media in May and June every year' (*Greater Kashmir*, 24 and 25 May 2011).

This did not suit Omar Abdullah's book. How could he justify repression in a Kashmir that was at peace. On 25 May he claimed that 'anything between 30–40 militants' had crossed the LoC in 2011. The precision was as remarkable as his confidence. However, the Army would have none of his falsehood. The very next day its spokesman, Lieutenant Colonel J.S. Brar, told *Greater Kashmir*: Our stand on the issue of infiltration is clear. Two days back our Corps Commander Lt. Gen. Syed Atta Hasnain made a statement on infiltration. We stand by our Commander's comments on the issue.' It was 'the first time in the past 20 years that no infiltration attempt was made between March and May' (*Greater Kashmir*, 27 May 2011). Lieutenant General Atta Hasnain emphatically reiterated his stand on 2 June (*Greater Kashmir*, 3 June 2011). Within the state there were 325 militants of whom only 119 were active, 'the lowest figure ever since militancy erupted in the State in 1990'. Of the 325, 168 were locals, 134 foreign nationals (Basharat Masood, *The Indian Express*, 6 June 2011). This report was based on 'data compiled by the J&K Police Criminal Investigation Department'.

Despite this, there was no let up in repression by the state government and no attempt to reach out to the people. Processions and meetings remained under a ban. Way back, on 11 July 2010, India's Army Chief, General V.K. Singh, had said: 'Over the past two years after the Army was pulled out of the cities, the State Administration should have reached out; but instead *frittered the opportunity away*' (*The Indian Express*, 12 July 2010). The same point was made by Lieutenant General Atta Hasnain on 3 April 2011. The Army's role was to provide an environment for a 'political solution of the longstanding issue' (*Greater Kashsmir*, 4 April 2011). The point has been made by almost every head of the Northern Command and of the 15 Corps since the outbreak of the militancy.

Both features of the situation continued in 2012 as well: a steep decline in the militancy and rising severity of the regime's repression. New Delhi continued to ignore the separatists whose internal squabbling continued unabated. Only one leader has repeatedly raised his voice to denounce wrongs by his own people, Syed Ali Shah Geelani. On 3 June 2011, he said, 'I want to make it clear that tourists arriving in Kashmir are our guests. We welcome and respect them.' He appealed to the people to treat the tourists 'with the utmost respect' (*Greater Kashmir*, 4 June 2011). On 7 July he warned against 'stone throwing' (*The Indian Express*, 8 July 2011). He criticized the self-styled Sharia court in Srinagar which 'expelled' four Christian priests charged with conversions, and praised schools run by Christian missionaries in Kashmir such as Burn Hall Tyndale Biscoe and Presentation Convent (*The Times of India,* 29 January 2012). On 15 September 2012, Geeelani denounced the killing of panchayat representatives. 'No person should be killed for his political ideology' (*Greater Kashmir*, 16 September 2012). On a political dialogue with the Centre, he said on 19 October 2011: 'If and when there is an invitation for talks we will discuss it in the Advisory Council.' His Tehreek-e-Hurriyat and the Hurriyat Conference, of which it is a part, each has its advisory council (*The Indian Express*, 20 October 2011). The offer, like his famous Five Points, was ignored. Worse still, he was put under house arrest and prevented from offering the congregational Friday prayers.

The Indian government's calculations are clear. With the virtual end of militancy, and rifts among separatists and between the National Conference and PDP, it can afford to keep up a facade of conciliation, leaving the NC–Congress coalition headed by Omar Abdullah to enjoy the fruits of office. Omar has admitted that they differ fundamentally on the crucial issue of Kashmir's autonomy: 'The National Conference stands by its commitment to restoration of autonomy, but I am a part of a coalition. My coalition partners feel it starts with the Indira–Sheikh accord of the mid-1970s' (*Hindustan Times*, 7 June 2012). The ideological divide cannot bother him. He had accepted a post in the BJP-led coalition at the Centre of which NC was a member. His statement on the Interlocutors' Report puts his own commitment to autonomy in question.

There can be no doubt that it is the Congress which is the dominant partner in Omar's coalition. On two occasions and in rapid succession, the president of the State Congress, Professor Saifuddin Soz, confidently predicted: 'The situation is such that no political party in J&K State can form the Government in *future* without the support of Congress' (interview to *Greater Kashmir*, 11 September 2012). He repeated this at Jammu on 22 September 2012: 'It is impossible to form government in the State under the prevailing circumstances without the Congress' support' (*Greater Kashmir*, 23 September 2012).

Soz is absolutely right. The NC and the PDP can fight it out in a free vote. Rigging of just a few seats in the Valley in favour of the Congress can decisively tip the balance. The Jammu seats will do the rest. As a young man, Soz was picked by Sheikh Abdullah to join the National Conference. In the 1990s he valiantly spoke for the people in the Lok Sabha. In 1999 he rejected Abdullah's pressure to vote for the BJP regime in the Lok Sabha to ensure its survival. This erstwhile champion of Kashmir's unity is now a champion of the Centre's political control which his Congress ensures.

It undermines autonomy in diverse ways. One glaring example will suffice: the Peerzada case. School Education Minister Peerzada Mohammed Sayeed's foster son, Imam Sauban, was alleged to have used 'unfair means' to pass the Senior Secondary Examination in 2009, in connivance with officials of the J&K Board of School Education. The state police's Crime Branch found the charge to be valid. Omar Abdullah said: 'Peerzada heads the department about which allegations have been levelled and that fact is inescapable.' He divested Peerzada of the portfolio of School Education. But the Chief Minister lacked the power to sack him – not constitutionally, but politically – if he was to preserve his own job. Peerzada sent his resignation, not to the Chief Minister but to Sonia Gandhi, the Congress President. 'She is my leader and not Chief Minister Omar Abdullah.' Peerzada continued in office as Minister for Public Enterprises; he claimed that Mrs Gandhi did not accept his resignation (*Asian Age*, 12 February 2012). Farooq Abdullah saw nothing wrong in the procedure. He disclosed that, 'when the coalition government was formed, the President of the Congress cleared the list of Ministers' (*Greater Kashmir*, 19 February 2012). He might have added that it was she who decided, not he, that Omar would be Chief Minister.

This is more than a subversion of the Cabinet system and of the rules of public morality. It is subversion of Article 370 itself and will be so even if it is restored to its pristine purity. Of what avail the most stringent *constitutional* guarantees of a state's autonomy if *politically* the Centre can ask its Chief Minister to do as he is told. This is exactly what coalition with the Congress entails.

Mufti Mohammed Sayeed, patron of the PDP and former Chief Minister, said at Pahalgam on 10 September 2012 that New Dehli cannot decide the destiny of Kashmiris, nor rule the state by remote control (*Greater Kashmir*, 11 September 2012). But how is that to be accomplished in the present political set-up? His anguish is deep and universally shared. 'India and Pakistan got independence in 1947 but Jammu and Kashmir was turned into a virtual jail', he said on 29 January 2012 (*Greater Kashmir*, 30 January 2012).

It is not an inapt description for a state whose government throws minors into prison on petty charges (vide the harrowing exposé by Rahul Pandita in the weekly, *Open*, 8 October 2012). Indian activists and NGOs take little interest in the fate of disappeared persons, rampant arrests, imprisonments without trial, stifling of protests, denial of the right to march in procession, to hold rallies and much else besides.

For years a string of persons – former foreign secretaries, bureaucrats and chiefs of intelligence – have tried a hand each at persuading the separatists to accept the Union and thus claim their rewards from New Delhi. Even Rahul Gandhi, general secretary of the Congress, took his turn at the game. He went to Kashmir on 4 October 2012 with some of India's topmost industrialists – doubtless with support from the government. 'My family is from Kashmir' – true, though the Nehrus left it two centuries ago. He wished to establish the same equation with Omar Abdullah as Nehru had with the Sheikh (whom he put in prison) and that Rajiv Gandhi had with Farooq Abdullah (whom he ousted from power 1984). It bids fair to be a repeat of the Rajiv–Farooq Pact of 1986 ahead of the polls. Rahul Gandhi wished to meet the young, and so the audience in Kashmir University was carefully selected.

The recipe is the same as Indira Gandhi's on 14 May 1948 and Nehru's on 25 August 1952 – give the Kashmiris bread and they will keep quiet. Only a year earlier Omar Abdullah had said at Sumbal, on 7 July, that Kashmir is not an issue of money or gun but a political one. In November 2009 he had said much the same thing in Prime Minister Manmohan Singh's presence, in Srinagar. The investments which the industrialists promised are welcome. But they provide no cure to the ailment. Rahul Gandhi betrayed no sign of understanding what drives the youth to wrath.

The gun is gone. But alienation remains. The people are not bereft of souls. They have aspirations, feelings and memories of wrongs. 2012 is not 1986. It takes but a small incident that hurts the people's feelings and revives memories of wrongs to set Kashmir aflame. It happened in 2009 and 2010, and can happen any time. Only a political settlement will satisfy the people.

Indian democracy and norms, such as they are, stop at the Pir Panjal range. Pakistan-administered Kashmir is in a far worse situation. Both countries and their civil societies, writers and artists, covet the land. In neither country is there much concern for the people, and their rights and well-being. In the words of the historian of ancient Rome, Tacitus: 'They created desolation and call it peace.' The status quo will prevail, until disturbed rudely for some reason or the other by an alienated and inflamed populace.

2012 saw a glimmer of hope in some movement in the Indo–Pak dialogue on Kashmir. The Pakistan People's Party (PPP) government no longer regards the Four Point proposal, agreed between former President Pervez Musharraf and Prime Minister Manmohan Singh, as something the cat had brought inside. The remarks which Pakistan's Foreign Minister, Hina Rabbani Khar, made in an interview to Iftikhar Gilani of the *DNA* (8 September 2012) are significant. She said:

> Jammu and Kashmir for us remains a core and central issue. What we have to see is that have our efforts and our way we adopted in the past led us to the resolution of the dispute. Now the question is, has the attitude and formulation we adopted over past 60 years, if we continue sticking to it, will it give us a resolution even in the next 65 years? The answer to that is a resounding no. Simple reason is we did not succeed in that. When I say both countries, I mean India also. Now without compromising on the centrality of the issue, we need to move forward. Let me first clarify, movements on other issues should not be misinterpreted. The issue has centrality, it concerns the rights of Kashmiri people. . . . [We] need a relook. Not at the nature of dispute, but the nature of strategies. If it has to be resolved on the dialogue table, we need to do some homework for that.

She was alluding clearly to the 'homework' that remains to be done on the

Indo–Pak consensus reached so far, so that a draft agreement can be prepared for signature by the leaders. That consensus is represented in the famous Four Points.

The former Prime Minister of Pakistan, Yousuf Raza Gilani, specifically referred to it in an interview to Barkha Dutt of NDTV.

> There had been some formula earlier which was decided between General Musharraf and the Indian Government. But there had been some loopholes which we wanted to tighten, *aur uspe hum kaam kar rahe the*, when there was a change of the government here in Pakistan.

Tightening the loose ends would be a more accurate description of that constructive exercise than filling the 'loopholes'.

It will be 'a non-territorial solution', Dr Manmohan Singh pointed out on 2 May 2008; an *ad hoc* arrangement reviewable after ten or fifteen years. Without undermining the agreed basic structure of the Four Point formula, some improvements can be considered. For instance, an all Jammu and Kashmir Consultative Assembly comprising elected legislatures from all regions of the state, meeting alternately in Muzaffarabad and Srinagar. It will have no legislative powers but the very existence of such a forum will fortify the sense of *Kashmiriyat*.

Settlement of the Kashmir dispute will enable those in exile for twenty years and more to return home – and jump into the election battle. Very many of the 'leaders' of today will become irrelevant once the LoC is reduced to irrelevance. Only the serious and dedicated ones will survive. These are not in abundance. The shine began to wear off in 2008. What remains, impresses few. To whom, then, can the masses turn when faced with a repressive regime, an insensitive Centre and an inept leadership? In sheer desperation, Kashmiris ask: '*aisi bhi koi shab hai jis ka sahar na ho?*' (can there ever be a night which does not yield to a dawn?)

Only those who have borne the torments of the darkness that descended on them since 9 August 1953 can cry thus. Sheikh Abdullah's dismissal from office and his imprisonment were a political holocaust the Kashmiris refuse to forgive and forget. It not only stripped the state of autonomy, but robbed its people of their pride and self-esteem. Both need to be restored if there is to be peace. And both can be restored today without the slightest detriment to the national interests of India or Pakistan.

Despite their desperation and anger, Kashmiris yearn for that dawn. No one can express their thoughts and emotions better than that pride of Lucknow, Asrar-ul-Haq Majaz, in his celebrated poem, '*Khwab-e-Sahar*' (The Dream of Dawn). It reflects both the pain and the torment of the dark night, and the yearning for a dawn.

> *Yeh musalsil aafaten, yeh shorishen, yeh qatlaam*
> *Aadmi kab tak rahe auham batil ka ghulam.*

Zahne insaani ne ub auham ke zulmaat men
Zindagi ki sakht toofani andheri raat me.
Kuch nahi to kum se khwabe sahr dekha to hai
Jis taraf dekha na tha ab tak udhar dekha to hai.

These endless misfortunes, these tumults, these massacres
How long can man remain enslaved to arbitrariness and deceit
Now the mind of man, amidst the tyranny of arbitrariness
In the dark severe stormy night of life
Has dreamed at last of a new dawn, if nothing else
Has looked towards a vista it had never seen before.

References

Abdullah, Sheikh (1982), *Aatish-e-Chinar: Autobiography,* Srinagar: Ali Mohammed & Sons.

Accounts and Papers, East India: Papers Relating to Kashmir (1890), C.6072, LIV f.233, New Delhi: National Archives of India.

Ahmad, Justice Saghir (2009), *Report of Working Group V on Strengthening Relations between the State and the Centre,* 2 volumes, New Delhi: Government of India Press.

Ahmed, Waheed, ed. (1992), *The Nation's Voice, Towards Consolidation: Speeches and Statements, March 1935–March 1940*, Karachi: Quaid-i-Azan Academy.

All India Reporter (AIR) (1952), 117: 119, Madras.

American Centre (1996), 'Press Release', 27 November, Bombay.

Amnesty International (2011), *A Lawless Law: Detentions under the Jammu and Kashmir Public Safety Act*, London: Amnesty International.

Ansari, M.M. (2011), 'Time to Act Is Now', *The Indian Express*, 22 November.

Ashraf, Hamid (2010), 'Stone Pelting Diary', *Conveyor,* Srinagar, January.

Atal, Major-General Hiralal (1972), *Nehru's Emissary to Kashmir,* New Delhi: Army Educational Stores.

Bal, S.S. (1967), 'British Interest in Creating the Dogra State of Jammu and Kashmir', *Proceedings of the Indian History Congress*, XXX Session, Patiala, December.

Bazaz, Prem Nath (1954), *The History of the Struggle for Freedom in Kashmir*, New Delhi: Pamposh Publications.

Bharatiya Jan Sangh (1953), *Mukherjee, Nehru and Abdullah Correspondence*, New Delhi: Bharitya Jan Sangh.

Bukhari, Shujaat (2011), *Frontline*, 7 October.

Chari, Chandra, ed. (1992), *The Federal Concept: The Indian Experience*, New Delhi: Allied Publishers.

Chatterjee, Angana P. (2010), 'Kashmir: A "No-Peace" Political Initiative', *Conveyor*, Srinagar, September–October.

Chaudhari, Nabakrushna (1963), 'Note on the Kashmir Trial', circulated by Mridula Sarabhai.

Chaudhary, Valmiki, ed. (1984), *Dr Rajendra Prasad: Correspondence and Select Documents*, New Delhi: Allied Publishers.

Chisti, Seema (2011), *The Indian Express*, 8 August.

Chopra, P.N. and Prabha Chopra, eds (2001), *Inside Story of Sardar Patel: The Diary of Maniben Patel 1936–50*, New Delhi: Vision Books.

Conveyor, Srinagar, January–Febuary 2011.

Copland, Ian (1991), 'The Abdullah Factor: Kashmiri Muslims and the Crisis of 1947', in D.A. Low, ed., *The Political Inheritance of Pakistan*, London: Oxford University Press.

Cranston, Major W.P. (2011), 'The Political Situation in Kashmir', in Lionel Carter, ed., *Partition Observed: British Official Reports from South Asia, 16 October–31 December 1947,*

Vol. II, New Delhi: Manohar Publications.
Cunningham Collection, MSS. Eur. D670, British Library, London.
Cunningham, J.D. (1955), *History of the Sikhs: From the Origin of the Nation to the Battles of the Sutlej*, New Delhi: S. Chand and Sons.
Das, Durga, ed. (1971–74), *Sardar Patel's Correspondence, 1945–50*, 10 volumes, Ahmedabad: Navjivan Publishing House.
Das, Soumitro (2009), *The Hindustan Times*, 19 March.
Dhar, P.N. (2000), *Indira Gandhi, the "Emergency" and Indian Democracy*, New Delhi: Oxford University Press.
Dicey, A.V. (1982), *An Introduction to the Study of the Law of the Constitution*, 8th revised edition, London: Liberty Fund Inc.
Dixon, Sir Owen (1950), 'Document S/1791, Report to the UN Security Council', in *Official Records of the Security Council: Supplement for September through December 1950*, 15 September, New York: United Nations Security Council.
DNA, 15 October 2009.
———, 2 March 2010.
———, 22 January 2011.
———, 2 March 2011.
———, 11 October 2011.
———, 17 October 2011.
Durrani, Mahmud Ali (2001), *India and Pakistan: The Cost of Conflict and the Benefits of Peace*, New York: Oxford University Press.
Election Commission of India v. State of Haryana (1984), S.C. 1406, SCC 104, 110, *All India Reporter*.
External Affairs Secretariat (1948), *Constitutional Discussions*, Vol. 2, Pt. VII–XII, Andhra Pradesh Archives, Hyderabad.
Ganai, Naseer A. (2007), 'Muslims a minority in JK service', *Greater Kashmir*, 7 May.
Gandhi, Sonia, ed. (2005), *Two Alone, Two Together*, New Delhi: Penguin.
Gauhar, Altaf (2000), *Ayub Khan*, Lahore: Sang-e-Meel.
Gopal, Sarvepalli (2012), *Jawaharlal Nehru: A Biography*, 3 volumes, New Delhi: Oxford University Press.
Government of India (1948), *White Paper on Hyderabad, Supplement*, New Delhi: Government of India Press.
——— (1948), *White Paper on Indian States*, New Delhi: Government of India Press.
——— (1948), *White Paper on Jammu and Kashmir*, New Delhi: Government of India Press.
——— (1950), *White Paper on Indian States*, New Delhi: Government of India Press.
——— (1963), *Lok Sabha Debates*, col. 1936, New Delhi: Government of India Press, 27 November.
——— (1963), *Lok Sabha Debates*, col. 3455, New Delhi: Government of India Press, 4 December.
——— (2011), *Report of the Committee for Consultations on the Situation in Andhra Pradesh 2010*, New Delhi: Government of India Press.
Graham, Bruce (1990), *Hindu Nationalism and Indian Politics: The Origins and Development of the Bharatiya Jana Sangh*, New York: Cambridge University Press.
Greater Kashmir, various issues.
Group of Interlocutors for Jammu and Kashmir (2011), *Final Report: A New Compact with the People of Jammu and Kashmir*, 12 October.
Gupta, Smitha (2010), 'Give peace a chance, Manmohan tells Kashmiris', *The Hindu*, 11 August.
Habibullah, Wajahat (2011), *My Kashmir: The Dying of the Light*, New Delhi: Penguin Books.

Hassnain, F.M. (1974), *British Policy towards Kashmir, 1846–1921*, New Delhi: Sterling Publishers.
Her Majesty's Stationery Office (HMSO), *The Transfer of Power 1942–47*, London: HMSO.
Hodson, H.V. (1985), *The Great Divide: Britain, India, Pakistan*, Karachi and New York: Oxford University Press.
Human Rights Watch (2006), *'Everyone Lives in Fear': Patterns of Impunity in Jammu and Kashmir*, New York: Human Rights Watch).
Huttenback, Robert A. (2004), *Kashmir and the British Raj, 1847–1947*, Karachi: Oxford University Press.
International Herald Tribune, 15 Februay 2011.
———, 18 February 2011.
Jarring, Gunnar V. (1957), *Document S/3821: Report on the Indo–Pakistan Question*, New York: United Nations Security Council, 24 April.
Jerath, Arati and Muzamil Jaleel (2002), 'Omar puts in father's Delhi job application: a tirade against Government', *The Indian Express*, Srinagar, 22 June.
Jerath, Arati and M. Salim Pandit (2010), *The Times of India*, 3 July.
Jha, Prem Shankar (2003), *Kashmir 1947: The Origins of a Dispute*, New Delhi: Oxford University Press.
———, (2011), 'Omar has failed Kashmiris. So, the stones will speak again', *Tehelka Magazine*, Vol. 8, Issue 10, 12 March.
Jinnah Papers (1993), edited by Z.H. Zaidi, First Series, Vol. III, Karachi: Government of Pakistan.
Joshi, Arun (2010), *The Hindustan Times*, 7 June.
Kashmir Problem (1964), *Sarvodaya Topical*, No. 1, Varanasi: Sarva Seva Sangh Prakashan.
Kashmir News Service, 20 January 2012.
Kashmir Times, various issues.
Kasuri, Khurshid Mahmud (2011), 'Peace Within Our Grasp', *The Times of India*, 17 February.
Kaul, B.M. (1967), *The Untold Story*, New Delhi: Allied Publishers.
Kaul, Sumeet (2007), 'A Passage to Kashmir', *Hindustan Times*, 4 September.
Khan, Hamid (2001), *Constitutional and Political History of Pakistan*, Karachi: Oxford University Press.
Knight, Malcolm, Norman Layaze and Delano Vilanueva (1996), 'The Peace Dividend', Policy Research Working Paper No. 1577, World Bank Policy Research Department and International Monetary Fund, February.
Kochak, Ghulam Nabi (1982), *Report*, 11 April.
Krishna, K.V. (2001), *In the Service of the Nation: Reminiscences*, New Delhi: Viking.
Lamb, Alastair (1994), *Birth of a Tragedy: Kashmir 1947*, London: Roxford Books.
Lawrence, Walter R. (1895), *The Valley of Kashmir*, London: Oxford University Press.
Limaye, Madhu and Sadiq Ali (1954), *Report on Kashmir*, Bombay: Praja Socialist Party.
Manecksha, Freny (2011), *The Times of India*, 3 December.
Masood, Basharat (2011), *The Indian Express*, 5 December.
Menon, V.P. (1956), *The Story of Integration of Indian States*, New Delhi: Orient Longman.
Ministry of Home Affairs (1968), *Report of the Commission of Inquiry on Communal Disturbances: Ranchi-–1967*, New Delhi: Government of India Press.
Ministry of Home Affairs (2003), *Annual Report 2002–03*, New Delhi: Government of India.
Ministry of Home Affairs (2004), *Annual Report 2003–04*, New Delhi: Government of India.
M.O. Mathai Papers, Nehru Memorial Museum and Library, Delhi.
Moore, R.J. (1987), *Making the New Commonwealth*, Oxford: Claredon Press.
Motta, Showkat A. (2010), 'Stone Sepulchre', *Outlook*, 12 July.
Mountabatten, Louis, Larry Collins and Dominique Lapierre (1984), *Mountbatten and Independent India, 16 August 1947 – 18 June 1948*, New Delhi: Vikas Publishing House.

Muhammad Ali, Chaudhari (1967), *The Emergence of Pakistan*, New York: Columbia University Press.
Munshi, K.M. (1965), *Somanath: The Shrine Eternal*, Bombay: Bharatiya Vidya Bhavan.
Nandurkar, G.M., ed. (1981), *Sardar's Letters – Mostly Unknown: Post-Centenary*, 2 volumes, Ahmedabad: Sardar Vallabhbhai Patel Smarak Bhavan.
Nehru, B.K. (1997), *Nice Guys Finish Second*, New Delhi: Viking.
Niazi, M.A. (1990), *The Nation*, 21 May.
——— (1990), *The Nation*, 31 May.
Noorani, A.G. (1970), *India's Constitution and Politics*, Bombay: Jaico.
——— (2004), *The Muslims of India: A Documentary Record*, New Delhi: Oxford University Press.
——— (2006), *Indian Political Trials 1775–1947*, New Delhi: Oxford University Press.
——— (2011), *Article 370: A Constitutional History of Jammu and Kashmir 1947–2010*, New Delhi: Oxford University Press.
Outlook, 14 November 2011.
Pandita, Rahul (2012), *Open*, 8 October .
Perti, R.K. (1990), *Asar-e-Azad*, New Delhi: National Archives of India.
Power, Jonathan (2004), 'Interview', *The Statesman*, 20 May.
Prasad, Bimal, ed. (1964), *Jayaprakash Narayan: Selected Works*, New Delhi: Manohar Publications.
Prem Nath Kaul v. State of J&K (1959), S.C. 749, *All India Reporter*.
Qasim, Sayyid Mir (1992), *My Life and Times*, New Delhi: Allied Publishers.
Rising Kashmir, various issues.
Roy, Ranjan (2010), 'Kashmir pact was just a signature away', *The Times of India*, 24 April.
Rustomji, Nari (1987), *Sikkim: The Himalayan Tragedy*, New Delhi: Allied Publishers.
Saiyid, Dushka H. (2004), *The Accession of Kalat: Myth and Reality*, Islamabad: Institute of Strategic Studies.
Sampat Prakash v. State of J&K (1969), S.C. 1153, *All India Reporter*.
Sarabhai, Mridula, ed. (1956), *Sheikh–Sadiq Correspondence*, New Delhi, privately published.
Saraf, Muhammad Yusuf (1978), *Kashmir's Fight for Freedom*, 2 volumes, Lahore: Ferozsons.
Sattar, Abdul (2010), *Pakistan's Foreign Policy: 1947–2009*, Karachi: Oxford University Press.
Segev, Tom (2000), *One Palestine Complete*, New York: Little Brown and Co.
Selected Works of Jawaharlal Nehru, General Editor: Sarvepalli Gopal, Second Series, 43 volumes, New Delhi: Jawaharlal Nehru Memorial Fund, distributed by Oxford University Press.
Shah, G.M. (1982), *Report*.
Siddiqi, Muhammad Ali and Shaista Suhrawardy Ikramulla (1997), *Common Heritage: The Jubilee Series: 1947–1997, 50 Years of Pakistan*, Karachi: Oxford University Press.
Singh, Amrinder (2009), *The Last Sunset: The Rise and Fall of the Lahore Durbar*, New Delhi: Roli Books.
Singh, Harbans (2011), *Maharaja Hari Singh*, New Delhi: Brahaspati Publications.
Singh, Karan (1982), *Heir Apparent: An Autobiography*, Vol. I, New Delhi: Oxford University Press.
——— (1985), *Sadar-i-Riyasat: An Autobiography*, Vol. II, New Delhi: Oxford University Press.
Singh, Shiv Sahay (2011), *The Hindu*, 27 November.
Srinivasavaradan, T.C.A. (1992), 'Federal Concept', in Chandra Chari, ed., *The Federal Concept: The Indian Experience*, New Delhi: Allied Publishers.
Staff Reporter (2004), 'Hindus won't trust Congress on Indo–Pak dialogue', *The Indian Express*, 15 March.
Stephens, Ian (1963), *Pakistan*, London: Ernest Benn Limited.

Sunday (1990), Calcutta, 18 March.
Swami, Praveen (2012), *The Hindu*, 7 February.
Talbot, Philips (2007), *An American Witness to India's Partition*, New Delhi: Sage Publications.
Tendulkar, D.G. (1963), *Mahatma: Life of Mohandas Karamchand Gandhi*, Vol. 8, New Delhi: Ministry of Information and Broadcasting, Government of India.
Thakur, D.D. (2005), *My Life and Years in Kashmir Politics*, New Delhi: Konark Publishers.
——— (1981), *Report*, 8 July.
T.N. Kaul Papers, File No. 15, Nehru Memorial Museum and Library, New Delhi.
The Asian Age, various issues.
The Hindu, various issues.
The Hindustan Times, various issues.
The Indian Express, various issues.
The Statesman, 16 August 1953.
The Telegraph, various issues.
The Times of India, various issues.
United Nations Commission for India and Pakistan (UNCIP) (1948), *Document S/1100: Interim Report of the UN Security Council, Supplement for November 1948*, New York: United Nations Security Council, 9 November.
United Kingdom High Commission (2003), 'Press Release', 27 March, New Delhi.
United Nations Security Council (UNSC) (1948), *Official Records*, Third Year, 227th Meeting, 15 January.
——— (1948), *Official Records*, 234th Meeting, 23 January.
——— (1948), *Official Records*, 239th Meeting, 3 February.
——— (1948), *Official Records*, 242nd Meeting, 6 February.
——— (1949), *Official Records*, *Supplement*, 5 January.
——— (1951), *Official Records*, 463rd Meeting, 7 February.
——— (1951), 'Resolution 91', *Document S/2017/Rev. 1*, 30th March
——— (1957), *S/PV762*, *Official Records*, 762nd Meeting, 23 January.
Varadarajan, Siddharth (2010), 'This is not zero tolerance, Mr Prime Minister', *The Hindu*, 4 June.
Venkataramani, M.S. (1999), 'An Elusive Military Relationship', *Frontline*, Part 1: 9 April, Part 2: 23 April, Part 3: 7 May.
——— (1999), 'A Mission Without Success', *Frontline*, 21 May.
Verma, Gyan (2011), *Business Standard*, 26 January.
Vijayalakshmi Pandit Papers, Nehru Memorial Museum and Library, New Delhi.
Y.D. Gundevia Papers, Nehru Memorial Museum and Library, New Delhi.
Zaheer, Hasan (1998), *The Times Trial of the Rawalpindi Conspiracy 1951*, Karachi: Oxford University Press.
Zahid, Hussain (1990), *Newsline*, Karachi, February.
Zutshi, Chitralekha (2003), *Languages of Belonging: Islam, Regional Identity and the Making of Kashmir*, New Delhi: Permanent Black.

Abbreviations

AFSPA	Armed Forces Special Powers Act
AICC	All India Congress Committee
APHC	All Party Hurriyat Conference
APOD	Association of Parents and Disappeared Persons
BJP	Bharatiya Janata Party
BSF	Border Security Force
CBI	Central Bureau of Investigation
CBMs	Confidence-Building Measures

CM	Chief Minister
CPI	Communist Party of India
CPI(M)	Communist Party of India (Marxist)
CRPF	Central Reserve Police Force
CS	Chief Secretary
DSP	Deputy Superintendent of Police
EC	Election Commission
IAS	Indian Administrative Service
IB	Intelligence Bureau
IG	Inspector General
J&K	Jammu and Kashmir
JKCCS	Jammu and Kashmir Coalition of Civil Society
JKLF	Jammu and Kashmir Liberation Front
JP	Janata Party
LoC	Line of Control
MLA	Member of Legislative Assembly
MLC	Member of Legislative Council
MP	Member of Parliament
NC	National Conference
NWFP	North-West Frontier Province
PDP	People's Democratic Party
PM	Prime Minister
POK	Pakistan Occupied Kahmir
PPP	Praja Parishad Party
PSA	Public Safety Act
PSO	Personal Security Officer
RSS	Rashtriya Swayamsevak Sangh
RTI	Right to Information Act
SWJN	*Selected Works of Jawaharlal Nehru*
UN	United Nations
UNCIP	United Nations Commission for India and Pakistan
UNSC	United Nations Security Council

Portrait of the Dogra chieftain, Raja Gulab Singh

Reproduced from *Recollections of India, drawn on stone by J.D. Harding, from the original drawings by the Honourable Charles Stewart Hardinge, Part II: Kashmir and the Alpine Punjab*, London, 1847. The author is extremely grateful to Mr. Hameed Haroon, CEO, Dawn Media Group, Pakistan, for providing him with this reproduction.

Jayaprakash Narayan's letter to Nehru, dated 1 May 1956

Permanent Address:
C/o, Mahila Charkha Samiti
Kadam Kuan, Patna

Camp Chaibasa
1-5-56

Dear Bhai,

May I make a complaint? It is rarely that I have asked you for anything. One such occasion was when I met you last in New Delhi. I asked you for Narendra Deva's seat in the Council of States to be left for the P.S.P. Pantji was also present when I had made this request. I was asked who would be the likely P.S.P. candidate & I had said that the choice was between Farid Ansari and Shakuntala Devi (widow of the late Harinath ji). This little request however went unheeded, it seems. I believe Sampurnanand had also been approached in this matter. I do not think that had the Congress let the seat go, it would have lost in any manner. For those of us who look forward to a modification of the party system, this attitude of the Congress party of wanting to have everything for itself is most discouraging. However, my complaint is entirely on a personal basis & has nothing to do with any political consideration.

May I also take this opportunity of saying

a word about Kashmir – merely to put my views before you, without in the least wanting to criticise or influence. From all the information that I have, 95% per of Kashmir Muslims do not wish to be or remain Indian citizens. I doubt therefore the wisdom of trying to keep people by force where they do not wish to stay. This cannot but have serious long-term political consequences, though immediately it may suit policy & please public opinion. From the point of view of the desirability of establishing a peaceful social order, it cannot but prove disastrous. I do earnestly wish that this question be considered more from a human, rather than a nationalist point of view. All men have to live upon this earth as brothers, irrespective of what national frontiers divide them. World peace is possible upon no other hypotheses.

yours affectionately,
Jayaprakash

P.S. I am not expecting a reply to this letter.
J.P.

See Document 8, p. 186 of this volume, for the typed version of this letter.

Final Draft of Agreement on Bilateral Relations between Government of India and Government of Pakistan, 2 July 1972

Final Indian Draft (2/7/1972)

Agreement on Bilateral Relations between the Government of India and the Government of Pakistan

.....

1. The Government of India and the Government of Pakistan are resolved that the two countries put an end to the conflict and confrontation that have hitherto marred their relations and work for the promotion of a friendly and harmonious relationship and the establishment of durable peace in the sub-continent, so that both countries may henceforth devote their resources and energies to the pressing task of advancing the welfare of their peoples.

In order to achieve this objective, the Government of India and the Government of Pakistan have agreed as follows :-

(i) That the principles and purposes of the Charter of the United Nations shall govern the relations between the two countries;

(ii) That the two countries are resolved to settle their differences by peaceful means through bilateral negotiations or by any other peaceful means mutually agreed upon between them. Pending the final settlement of any of the problems between the two countries, neither side shall unilaterally alter the situation and both shall prevent the organization, assistance or encouragement of any acts detrimental to the maintenance of peaceful and harmonious relations;

(iii) That the pre-requisite for reconciliation, good neighbourliness and durable peace between them is a commitment by both the countries to peaceful co-existence, respect for each other's territorial integrity and sovereignty and non-interference in each other's internal affairs, on the basis of equality and mutual benefit.

(iv) That the basic issues and causes of conflict which have bedevilled the relations between the two countries for the last 25 years shall be resolved by peaceful means.

(v) That they shall always respect each other's national unity, territorial integrity, political independence and sovereign equality.

(vi) That they will refrain from the threat or use of force against the territorial integrity or political independence of each other.

2. Both Governments will take all steps within their power to prevent hostile propaganda directed against each other, shall cease. Both countries will encourage the dissemination of such information as would promote the development of friendly relations between them.

3. In order progressively to restore and normalise relations between the two countries step by step, it was agreed that:

contd. ...

(i) Steps shall be taken to resume communications, postal, telegraphic, sea, land including border posts, and air links including overflights.

(ii) Appropriate steps shall be taken to promote travel facilities to the nationals of the other country.

(iii) Trade and co-operation in economic and other agreed fields will be resumed as far as possible.

(iv) Exchange in the fields of science and culture will be promoted.

In this connection delegations from the two countries will meet from time to time to work out the necessary details.

4. In order to initiate the process of the establishment of durable peace, both the Governments agree that :

(i) Indian and Pakistani forces shall be withdrawn to their side of the international border

(ii) In Jammu and Kashmir, the line of control resulting from the cease-fire of December 17, 1971 shall ~~henceforth~~ be respected by both sides, ~~as a Line of Peace~~. Neither side shall seek to alter it unilaterally, irrespective of mutual differences and legal interpretations. Both sides further undertake to refrain from the threat or the use of force in violation of this Line.

(iii) Minor adjustments to the Line of Peace in Jammu and Kashmir or the rest of the international border considered necessary by both sides to make the border more rational and viable, may be made by mutual agreement.

(iv) A joint body composed of an equal number of representatives, nominated by each Government, shall be appointed to establish ground rules and to supervise the effective observance of the Line of Peace and the rest of the border between the two countries.

(iii) The withdrawals shall commence upon entry into force of this Agreement in accordance with the ground rules evolved by the above-mentioned joint body and shall be completed within a period of 30 days thereof.

5. This Agreement will be subject to ratification by both countries in accordance with their respective constitutional procedures, and will come into force with effect from the date on which the Instruments of Ratif_ication are exchanged.

6. Both Governments agree that their respective Heads will meet again at a mutually convenient time in the future and that, in the meanwhile, the representatives of the two sides will meet to discuss further the modalities and arrangements for the establishment of durable peace and normalisation of relations, including the questions of repatriation of prisoners of war and

and civilian internees, a final settlement of Jammu and Kashmir and the resumption of diplomatic relations.

(Indira Gandhi)
Prime Minister
Republic of India

(Zulfikar Ali Bhutto)
President
Islamic Republic of Pakistan

Simla, the July, 1972.

Note: The writing at the bottom of page 2 of the draft agreement is in Bhutto's hand, as confirmed by a high source familiar with his handwriting. The rest are either in Aziz Ahmed's or Rafi Raza's hand. Bhutto apparently wanted a 'Declaration' and also instructed his aides to add the words 'pending further consideration'. For further details, see Article I.13 in Volume 2.

- Progress on addressing outstanding issues, including Jammu & Kashmir, and the establishment of a cooperative relationship will be mutually reinforcing.

Progress towards settlement of J&K issue, would be conducive towards normalisation and ~~the fostering of relations~~ will further the establishment of a cooperative relationship in a mutually reinforcing manner/

Jaswant Singh's reformulation of Clause 1 of the declaration, which he brought along and showed to Abdul Sattar at 6 p.m. (see the printed text above). It presumably had the approval of the Indian Cabinet. Abdul Sattar and Jaswant Singh jointly revised this printed text in their own respective handwritings. The first part is in Abdul Sattar's handwriting. From the word "and" the rest is in Jaswant Singh's own handwriting. He thus endorsed the entire jointly reformulated clause and, with it, the entire draft declaration. The handwritten part reads: "Progress towards settlement of J&K issue would be conducive towards normalisation and will further the establishment of a cooperative relationship in a mutually reinforcing manner."

Note: For details of the Agra Summit, see Article I.31 in Volume 2.

Agreement Between the Jammu and Kashmir Liberation Front and Hizbul Mujahideen

AGREEMENT

We the following signatories belonging to Hizbul-Mujahideen Jammu Kashmir (HM) and Jammu Kashmir Liberation Front (JKLF) agree on behalf of their respective organisations on the points detailed below subject to approval by respective highest policy making bodies of the two organisations:-

1. that Hizbul-Mujahideen Jammu Kashmir recognises JKLF's right to preach and project its ideology of independence of the whole state. Similarly JKLF does not have any objection to HM preaching and projecting its ideology of State's accession to Pakistan. Nevertheless both the organisations agree that while preaching their ideology or otherwise, neither organisation will, directly or indirectly, have any negative criticism of the ideology, leadership or the programme of the other organisation.

2. that both JKLF and HM agree on the point of view that the right of self-determination of Kashmiri people can neither be limited nor conditioned and that Kashmiri people have full right to determine the future of the State according to their free will. If in free exercise of their right of self-determination the majority of the people of the State vote for State's accession to Pakistan, JKLF will accept this popular verdict and if the majority votes in favour of complete independence of the State, HM will accept this popular verdict.

3. During freedom struggle, both organisations will cooperate with each other in their fight against their common enemy, Indian colonialism. They also agree that, if and when needed, both organisations will extend moral, military and political support to each other.

4. That in case of any difference arising between the two organisations, a committee consisting of the nominees of the two parties will settle the dispute.

Signed this Friday, the 2nd April, 1993 at Islamabad (Pakistan)

FOR & ON BEHALF JAMMU KASHMIR LIBERATION FRONT		FOR & ON BEHALF OF HIZBUL-MUJAHIDEEN JAMMU KASHMIR	
Name & Designation	Signature	Name & Designation	Signature
1. Raja Mohammad Muzaffar, Sr. Vice Chairman JKLF	[signature]	1. [illegible] Majid Dar, Advisor General HM.	[signature]
2. DR. HAIDER HIJAZI, Central Press and Publicity Secretary.	[signature]	2. Shams-ul-Haq, [illegible] Supreme Command Council	[signature]
3. DR. [illegible] HAIDER, Senior Leader	[signature]	3. Prof. [illegible], Representative of Jamaat-e-[illegible] [illegible] Kashmir.	[signature]

From the agreement signed between the Hizbul Mujahideen and the JKLF in Islamabad on April 2, 1993.

Note: For further details, see Article I.15 of Volume 2.

DOCUMENTS

1. Letter by Sir H. Chimanlal H. Setalvad to the Editor, *Times of India*, 30 October 1947, on the Provisional Government of Junagadh

Many of those who are enthusing over the activities of the so-called 'Provisional Government' of Junagadh do not seem to realize the dangerous consequences that are likely to follow from what is happening. The Junagadh Government has acted unwisely in acceding to Pakistan, ignoring geographical considerations and the wishes of its subjects, but that affords no justification for what is being done.

The 'Provisional Government' was formed and functioned for some days in Bombay with the avowed object of overthrowing by force the established Government in Junagadh. The Government of Bombay was, I venture to say, bound not to allow the 'Provisional Government' to start its hostile activities against a State which is at peace with the Government of Bombay and with the Government of India, who are at peace with Pakistan to which Junagadh had acceded. Their permitting this to be done amounts to an unfriendly and hostile act against Junagadh and amounts to an unfriendly and hostile act against Junagadh and Pakistan.

The Government of India should not have allowed passage over its railways to a body proceeding to Rajkot with the proclaimed object of raising a volunteer army to overthrow the establishment of Junagadh.

The Government of Rajkot should not have given asylum to a body that was raising an army to overthrow the Junagadh Government.

It is most surprising that the Government of Rajkot should have tolerated the seizure by force of Junagadh State property within its territory.

Legally and constitutionally, the Governments of Bombay and India and those of the Kathiawar States are bound to stop and prohibit all activities within their territories of the 'Provisional Government'. The consequences of their inaction would be very serious.

2. Declaration on the formation of the Provisional Government of Junagadh, drafted by K.M. Munshi, September 1947

WHEREAS the Nawab of Junagadh has, against the declared wishes of an overwhelming majority of his subjects and under the influence of the agents of the Dominion of Pakistan, executed on 15th September 1947 an Instrument of Accession whereby the State is declared to have acceded to the Dominion of Pakistan;

AND WHEREAS the Dominion of Pakistan has accepted the said Instrument of Accession in disregard of such declared wishes and in defiance of all natural ties which bind the people of Junagadh (82 per cent of whom are non-Muslims) to the people of Kathiawar and to the Dominion of India and in breach of the understanding on the basis of which certain parts of India were allowed to accede and form into a separate State of Pakistan; namely that only contiguous areas predominantly inhabited by Muslims were to be included into the Dominion of Pakistan with the free and willing consent of the people inhabiting those areas;

AND WHEREAS by his said act of executing the Instrument of Accession, the Nawab has purported to transfer the allegiance of the subjects of the State against their will to the Dominion of Pakistan so as to compel them to be nationals of Pakistan which is a state foreign to them and formed with the object of providing a national home for Muslims;

AND WHEREAS before and after the said purported Accession, the authorities of the State under the guidance of Pakistan, and in the name of the Nawab, armed a section of the Muslims of the state with a view to terrorize the subjects of the State and to prevent them from claiming self-determination and voicing their antagonism to the Accession with the result that more than a hundred thousand of the subjects have already left and many more are leaving the State every day and the state authorities are infiltrating the State territories with Muslim refugees;

WE, THE SUBJECTS OF JUNAGADH STATE, HEREBY DECLARE that by transferring the allegiance of his subjects against their will to Pakistan and preparing for a reign of terror to coerce them to acquiesce in such transfer, the Nawab has forfeited his claim to allegiance of his subjects;

WE HEREBY FURTHER DECLARE that the Dominion of Pakistan in accepting the said Instrument of Accession of the Nawab has violated the principle of self-determination as also the aforestated understanding on which Pakistan was agreed to be formed and that therefore the said Instrument of Accession is null and void and not binding on the subjects of the state or the territories thereof;

WE FURTHER DECLARE in exercise of our inherent right of self-determination our decision to accede to the Dominion of India and to join the territories of Junagadh State with the contiguous territories of the Dominion of India;

WE FURTHER DECLARE our firm and solemn resolve to adopt all such means and to take all such steps as may be necessary or incidental to the State of Junagadh formally acceding to the Dominion of India and forming and remaining an integral part thereof.

In furtherance of our said solemn declaration and resolve we hereby appoint a Provisional Government consisting of

1. Samaldas Laxmidas Gandhi (President),
2. Durlabhji Keshavji Khetani,

3. Bhavanishanker A. Oza,
4. Suragbhai Kalubhai Varu,
5. Manilal Sunderji Doshi,
6. Narendra Pragji Nathwani,

with all power, authority and jurisdiction heretofore vested in and exercised by the Nawab of Junagadh prior to 15 September 1947, over/and in relation to the said State of Junagadh and all territories thereof and WE HEREBY AUTHORIZE our said Provisional Government to take immediate steps for implementing and carrying out our said declaration and resolve and to exercise all power, authority and jurisdiction hereby conferred upon them.

AND WE HEREBY SOLEMNLY pledge our allegiance to the said Provisional Government and through it to the Dominion of India and call upon all the subjects of Junagadh State wherever resident to carry out loyally the orders and directions of the said Provisional Government.

The Provisional Government of Junagadh moved to Saurashtra and took possession of the Junagadh House at Rajkot. Young men from all over Saurashtra flocked to its banner of freedom. Large sums of money flowed in, volunteers were *armed* and trained. On the Dussehra Day, the 'Day of Victory' – 24 October 1947 – the volunteers of the Provisional Government began their operation. . . .

[The Dewan] S.N. Bhutto . . . wrote a letter to . . . Buch, the Regional Commissioner of Saurashtra in the Government of India:

> Dear Mr Buch,
>
> After discussion with Mr Samaldas Gandhi at Rajkot on October 1, Capt. Harvey Jones, senior member of Junagadh State Council, brought certain proposals for the consideration of the Council. The Council were prepared to accept them under protest but before a final decision could be communicated to Mr Samaldas Gandhi it was thought necessary to ascertain the opinion of the leading members of the public. A meeting was therefore held this evening and the view of the leaders was unanimously expressed that instead of handing over the administration to the Indian Union through the so-called Provisional Government, it should be directly given over to the Indian Union, through the Regional Commissioner at Rajkot.
>
> The Junagadh Government, therefore, has requested that in order to avoid bloodshed, hardship, loss of life and property and to preserve the dynasty, you should be approached to give your assistance to the administration particularly with a view to preserve law and order, which is threatened by aggressive elements from outside. This arrangement is sought pending an honourable settlement of the several issues involved in Junagadh's accession. We have already wired His Excellency Lord Mountbatten, Mahatmaji, Prime and Deputy

Prime Ministers of India, Hon'ble Abul Kalam Azad and the Governor-General and Prime Minister of Pakistan.

I hope you will kindly respond to this request.

Yours sincerely,
Sd/ S.N. Bhutto
Dewan, Junagadh

From K.M. Munshi, *Somanatha: The Shrine Eternal*, Delhi: Bharatiya Vidya Bhavan, 1951: 68–71. The Declaration was drafted by Munshi, he wrote (p. 67).

3. Mountbatten's offer to Jinnah in Lahore on 1 November 1947

This was the formula:
The Governments of India and Pakistan agree that, where the ruler of a State does not belong to the community to which the majority of his subjects belong, and where the State has not acceded to that Dominion whose majority community is the same as the State's, the question of whether the State should finally accede to one or the other of the Dominions should in all cases be decided by an impartial reference to the will of the people.

SUGGESTED PROPOSALS TO PAKISTAN GOVERNMENT
TO FORM THE BASIS OF DISCUSSION

1. It is of paramount importance, not only to the Government of India, Pakistan and Kashmir, but also to the cause of world peace, that the fighting in Kashmir should cease at the earliest possible moment.
2. The best, if not the only, hope of achieving this object is a very early meeting between accredited representatives of the two countries.
3. The Government of India, for their part, have no desire to maintain troops in Kashmir, once the Valley is safe from attack and law and order have been restored. They are therefore prepared to give an undertaking to withdraw their troops immediately the raiders have left the country and returned to their homes.
4. It is the sincere desire of the Government of India that a plebiscite should be held in Kashmir at the earliest possible date and in the fairest possible way. They suggest that UNO might be asked to provide supervisors for this plebiscite, and they are prepared to agree that a joint India–Pakistan force should hold the ring while the plebiscite is being held.
5. The Government of India suggest that both Governments should agree on the form of the public announcement to be made in regard to the procedure for accession of those States in which this matter is in dispute. A draft is attached as a basis of discussion.

6. They suggest that the above proposals should be the subject of a round-table discussion at the earliest possible date.

From *Sardar Patel's Correspondence 1945–1950*, edited by Durga Das, Vol. 1, Ahmedabad: Navajivan Publishing House, 1971: 77 and 81.

4. Letter by Sir Chimanlal H. Setalvad to the Editor, *Times of India*, 3 November 1947, on Kashmir and Junagadh

The appeal made by you in your leader this morning for reason and common-sense is very opportune. Recent unfortunate events have so frayed the nerves of those in the Governments of the two Dominions that indulgence in charges and counter-charges and attributing motives has become the order of the day and has widened the gulf between the two Dominions.

It is hoped for the welfare of the whole country that reason and common-sense will take the place of the present temper on both sides. Pandit Nehru in his broadcast has rightly asked the Pakistan Government how and why the invaders of Kashmir came across the Frontier Province or West Punjab, and how they came to be fully armed. He charges the Pakistan Government with violation of international law and an unfriendly act towards India. He alleges that the Pakistan Government was either too weak to prevent the invaders of Kashmir from marching across its territory or that it was willing that this should happen.

Exactly the same poser can be put to the Indian Dominion with regard to Junagadh. The so-called 'Provisional Government' of Junagadh was openly formed in Bombay, and for days it proclaimed its intention of marching to Junagadh to overthrow the Junagadh as by law established; the leaders of the 'Provisional Government' have openly raised a volunteer army and have captured several villages in Junagadh territory. Junagadh House in Rajkot was forcibly seized by the 'Provisional Government'. And Rajkot State, which has acceded to India, and the Indian Government themselves have remained passive spectators of all unfriendly and hostile acts against a State which is, together with the Dominion to which it has acceded, at peace with India.

Undoubtedly, Junagadh's action in acceding to Pakistan is unwise from all points of view and deserves condemnation, but that cannot justify the action that has been taken against it. The Indian Dominion may well be asked the self-same questions that Pandit Nehru has put to Pakistan. Was the Government of India too weak to prevent the armies of the 'Provisional Government' from invading Junagadh territory, or was it willing that this should happen?

5. Nehru's note to Sheikh Abdullah to finalize Kashmir's accession, Camp Sonamarg, 25 August 1952

I am writing this note to convey to you my own basic views about the situation in Kashmir. During the last five years or so, I have naturally given a great deal of thought to the various factors governing this situation – military, political, economic and others. I have tried to make my approach as objective as possible. Naturally, to some extent, I am influenced by my own personal feelings and attachment to Kashmir. Thus it may be said that I have two approaches – that of the Prime Minister of India and the personal one. As a matter of fact, however, I have not found any conflict between those two. Some difficulties have arisen occasionally in my mind, because I was not sure if my approach, personal of official, was completely in line with your approach. So far as I was concerned, you represented to me what the people of Kashmir wanted to be done, and as that was paramount consideration for me, in the ultimate analysis I would accept that in preference to my own views. As a rule, there was no such conflict or difficulty.

2. My own view has been clear for the last four years or so and, in spite of changing circumstances, I have found no reason to alter it basically. Because of this, I have not been worried much on account of new developments. Being clear in my mind as to what should be done, it did not matter much to me what Pakistan did or what the UN might do. I was, however, sometimes a little surprised, and somewhat worried, to find that the leaders of Kashmir were not so clear in their minds about the present or the future and were, therefore, worrying a great deal. To give an instance, the present talks with Dr Graham in Geneva do not appear to me have any great importance.

They do not alter my appraisal of the situation, or what we should do about it. I find, however, that much greater importance is attached to these Graham talks in Geneva, here in Kashmir, and there is some apprehension also about their result. . . .

4. After some experience of the UN, I came to the conclusion that nothing substantial could be expected from it. It was clear that we would not give in on any basic point, whatever the UN might say. It seemed also clear that Pakistan would not simply walk out and revert to the *status quo ante-war*. Thus, towards the end of 1948 it seemed to me that there were only two possibilities open to us: 1) continuation of the war in a limited way; 2) some kind of a settlement on the basis of the then existing military situation.

5. I have not mentioned the plebiscite, because it became clear to me then that we would never get the conditions which were necessary for a plebiscite. Neither side would give in on this vital issue, and so I ruled out the plebiscite for all practical purposes.

6. So far as continuing the war was concerned, it was clear to me that

while gradual success would come to us, no quick or effective decision was likely. We might carry on the war in Kashmir itself for a considerable time, gaining some successes and advancing our fronts, but this would be a long drawn-out affair, and would not put an end to the conflict or the problem. There was a possibility of the war extending beyond Kashmir State, i.e. becoming an all-out war between India and Pakistan. That was not a prospect to be welcomed, and it was much more likely at that stage that there might be foreign intervention in such a war. Even that war, apart from foreign intervention, would not be a very easy or quick one. We had definite superiority . . .

7. The result of all this thought, and my own powerful inclination to avoid war on a big scale which brought disaster in its train, whatever the result, led me to certain definite conclusions towards the end of 1948. These conclusions were that the only possible way of putting an end to this conflict was by accepting, more or less, the *status quo* then existing. We were not prepared to give up any territory we possessed to Pakistan. But we might, for the sake of peace and a settlement, agree to their holding what they then had. I was doubtful if Pakistan would accept this. If not, then we continued where we were.

8. This conclusion was not a very pleasant one to me, but logically I could not help arriving at it. When I met Attlee and Bevin and Liaquat Ali Khan in London in the last quarter of 1948, I mentioned this briefly to them saying that it was entirely a personal suggestion because of my desire to end this conflict. I was not at all sure how far my own government, or the Kashmir Government, would agree to it, because they felt strongly on this question of Pakistan aggression. Liaquat Ali Khan refused to consider this matter on this basis and there it ended. . . .

13. As Prime Minister of India, I have to look ahead and consider the basic national interest of India. It is my duty to guard that interest. That interest fits in with ideas of world peace and the avoidance of war whether in the world or with Pakistan. But, of course, that does not mean that we should not be prepared for any contingency. That interest itself demands full preparation for war or peaceful effort. Fortunately, we have no troubles with any of our neighbours, or, for the matter of that, with any country in the world. Nor are we afraid of any country, however big it may be, invading India or compelling us by force to do something that we do not want to do. There is one present exception and that is Pakistan. We are superior to Pakistan in military and industrial power. But that superiority is not so great as to produce results quickly either in war or by fear of war. Therefore, our national interest demands that we should adopt a peaceful policy towards Pakistan and, at the same time, add to our strength. Strength ultimately comes not from the defence forces, but the industrial and economic background behind them. As we grow in strength, and we are likely to do so, Pakistan will feel less and less inclined to threaten or harass us, and a

time will come when, through sheer force of circumstances, it will be in a mood to accept a settlement which we consider fair, whether in Kashmir or elsewhere. The only danger is that the Government of Pakistan, or some military clique there, might, in sheer desperation, launch on an adventure. That danger has to be faced and prepared for. Otherwise, our national interest demands that we should adopt a farm but non-provocative attitude towards Pakistan, and build up our economic strength, keeping our defence forces in good condition for any possibility. The world situation also demands that we should follow this policy.

14. What is the position of Jammu and Kashmir State *vis-à-vis* India? Looking at it objectively, this State is of importance, both from the strategic and other points of view, to both India and Pakistan. Hence, the conflict between the two. We are not prepared to give in to Pakistan on that issue, even though it means war. The utmost we can do is to give in so far as that area is concerned which is occupied by Pakistan. That itself, strategically, is a disadvantage to us. But we are prepared to accept that disadvantage for the sake of peace, if the whole of the State went to Pakistan, it would be a danger to the north of India, and there would be continuous tension between us and the party controlling the State. Thus, purely from the point of view of India's national interest, we cannot agree, unless circumstances force us, to see this part of Kashmir State go to Pakistan. There are no circumstances visible that can force us to do this. Pakistan cannot. The UN cannot override our wishes in this matter.

15. This is an objective statement from the point of view of India's national interest. There is another aspect which we have stressed, and which is important. This is the wishes of the people of Kashmir. If the people of Kashmir clearly and definitely wish to part company from India, there the matter ends, however we may dislike it or however disadvantageous it may be to India. But, as I have stated above, I see no chance or whatever of any proper plebiscite determining this question, because the plebiscite itself raises highly controversial issues in regard to the conditions governing it and all that, So, ruling out the plebiscite we have to accept the present leadership of Kashmir and the Constituent Assembly there as representing the will of the people of Kashmir. If the Constituent Assembly told India to get out of Kashmir, we would get out, because under no circumstances can we remain here against the expressed will of the people. As far as I know, the Constituent Assembly will not do such a thing and therefore, the question does not arise for me.

16. Speaking now for a moment purely as a Kashmiri, I think that it would be the ruin of Kashmir if Pakistan took possession of it. I need not dilate on this issue, but I am convinced of it. . . .

19. In fact, Jammu and Kashmir have to hold together. If Jammu is separated, Kashmir goes. If Kashmir goes, Jammu's position becomes precarious and the conflict does not end. Statesmanship therefore requires that Jammu

and Kashmir should hold together. The people of Jammu, therefore, should be made to feel the advantages of this union and the dangers of breaking. They should be won over and not irritated, because the safety and freedom of Kashmir is linked up with the retention of Jammu. . . .

23. It must be remembered that the people of the Kashmir Valley and roundabout, though highly gifted in many ways – in intelligence, in artisanship, etc. – are not what are called a virile people. They are soft and addicted to easy living. They are surrounded by hardy tribes in the north-west of Pakistan and even in the northern areas of the State. It will be difficult, and indeed hardly possible, for the people of Kashmir to survive by themselves, if left to their own resources. It was all very well when there was a strong suzerain power like that of England which could prevent harassment and raids. But if a strong suzerain power is absent, then Kashmir is likely to fall an easy prey to these depredations.

24. The result of all these considerations is that the only desirable future for the State is with a close association with India, retaining her autonomy in most ways; that Kashmir and Jammu should hold together; that we should consolidate our position in these areas and not care very much for what happens in the 'Azad Kashmir' areas. Most important of all is that we should have no doubts in our minds about these matters. Doubts in the minds of leaders percolate to their followers and to the people generally. The weakness of the situation in Kashmir is the constant discussions which go on between people holding different views. I do not know how many such groups there are, but obviously some people talk about a close association with India, others talk about a loose association with India, yet others think, if not talk, of an association with Pakistan, and yet others talk about independence. All this confusion in ideas and constant debate weakens the basic position. What is required is a firm and clear outlook, and no debate about basic issues. If we have that outlook, it just does not matter what the UN thinks or what Pakistan does.

25. Personally, I have that clear outlook and have had it for these years and it has surprised me that there should be so much discussion about obvious matters.

26. We have to consolidate the position in Kashmir, firstly, on the political plane by having this clear-cut idea about the future, and no nonsense tolerated, and, secondly, by improving the lot of the people, i.e., economic and other issues. Personally, I think that more important even than economic issues is an efficient administration. The common people are primarily interested in a few things – an honest administration and cheap and adequate food. If they get this, then they are more or less content. That is not enough, of course, and we have to go ahead. But there is far too much talk of going ahead, when we do not pay enough attention to basic things like administration and food policy. Slogans are good in their day, but slogans are dangerous companions when these basic problems have to be faced. It is

dangerous to make promises which cannot be fulfilled, or to talk tall just to gain the goodwill of the people for the moment. Facts cannot be ignored and have to be faced. The most important thing today in Kashmir is efficiency in administration and in food policy. . . .

27. Finally, I would repeat that there must be a clear-cut idea about what we want in Kashmir and about Kashmir, and that idea must be adhered to without debate or argument in future. I have indicated that the only possible course for Kashmir is for the State to be closely associated with India, that association not interfering with its autonomy in most respects. If that is so, then it is not wise to say or so things which imperil that association. Again, Jammu and Kashmir have to hold together for the sake of each other. They cannot be separated. If that is so, then every effort should be made to encourage that idea, and not to say or do anything which irritates people or makes them think of parting company.

28. Our general outlook should be such as to make people think that the association of Kashmir State with India is an accomplished and final fact, and nothing is going to undo it. I am not talking of speeches repeating this, but rather of other facts being mentioned which tend to make people believe it. For instance, I should stress the fact that a tunnel is going to be built under the Banihal or that trade etc. is developing with and through India or that development schemes are being undertaken.

29. . . . I would repeat that I have held these views concisely and precisely for the last four years, and nothing has happened during this period which has made me change them in the slightest. It is for this reason that meetings with Dr Graham or anyone else, or any developments in Pakistan, do not worry me in the least, in so far as Kashmir in concerned. What has sometimes worried me is what happens in Kashmir, because I have found doubt and hesitation there, and not clarity of vision or firmness of outlook.

From *Selected Works of Jawaharlal Nehru*, Second Series, Vol. 23, New Delhi: Jawaharlal Nehru Memorial Fund, 1999: 322–30.

6. Nehru's instruction for Sheikh Abdullah's dismissal and arrest, recorded by M.O. Mathai, Private Secretary to Prime Minister, 31 July 1953

The present drift and the resulting confusion cannot be allowed to go on. The policy of Government must be clearly stated to the public. The members of Government should not speak in different voices. In order to remove doubt about this policy, a brief memorandum might be prepared and placed before the Cabinet. In this Government's policy should be precisely stated.

Apart from other major issues, there might be some reference in it to certain economic issues also; or, if it is preferred, the economic issues con be stated in a separate note. Among these economic issues might be mentioned the raising of the price of procurement of rice, the removal of the customs barrier, etc., the object of all this being to lessen the burden on the common man

The main point clarified in the memorandum should be the future of the State which has given rise to so much argument in public recently. Members of Government should be asked to support the policy laid down in its entirety.

If, as is probable, some members of Government do not agree with this policy and this statement, the majority should nevertheless accept that policy. If the minority refuse to abide by it, the continuation of the present Government becomes impossible. The Head of the State should be informed accordingly. He should ask for the resignation of the Government because it cannot function as a team and pursue its contradictory policies. If the resignation is offered, then the Head of the State should call upon another person representing the majority view to form a new Government.

It will be desirable not to allow any marked lapse of time between the demand for resignation and the formation of the new Government. The Head of the State should send for all members of Government and inform them of his decision and ask for their resignations. If the resignations are not forthcoming, he should have an order ready for the dismissal of the Government because it cannot fulfill its functions properly. Immediately he should entrust the formation of the new Government to the other person.

It will be desirable to prepare the ground for this, insofar as considered feasible, with prominent members of the Executive of the Party.

Immediately after the formation of the new Government, the Executive of the Party should meet. Both, the new Government and the Party should issue statements to the public stating the facts and indicating their policy, including their economic policy.

Some persons who are notorious for their corrupt activities should be apprehended and steps taken for an inquiry into those activities.

It may be desirable to arrest one or two such persons, who are known to be corrupt, even before the steps indicated above are taken. But this is a matter of judgment.

All necessary steps should be taken for the preservation of law and order. Any persons taking a lead in creating any disturbance should be apprehended. Such assistance as may be considered necessary for the maintenance of law and order should be available. Any action taken should be carefully calculated so as not to exceed the necessities of the situation, and the changeover should be as peaceful as possible.

Immediate first steps afterwards should be the removal of certain well-known corrupt officers, etc., suspension of others whose loyalty is doubted, and an appeal to the people for maintenance of peaceful conditions. The broad outlines of the programme of the new Government should be given and it should be stated that it would be for the people to decide ultimately what political or economic policy has to be adopted – the sole test will be the good of the people and their wishes in the matter.

From *Selected Works of Jawaharlal Nehru*, Second Series, Vol. 23, New Delhi: Jawaharlal Nehru Memorial Fund, 1999: 303–05.

7. M.O. Mathai's note to Indira Gandhi regarding her desire to visit Sheikh Abdullah in prison, 12 September 1953

I have given considerable thought to your proposal to meet Sheikh Abdullah. I have also taken the liberty of discussing it with Krishna Menon informally because I myself was not quite clear in my mind.

You know that I largely agree with your analysis and assessment of the Kashmir situation and the basic issues involved in it. Two days ago I asked you a direct question purposely and I was happy to note that in your judgment of the problem the personal attachment to Kashmir as an ancestral place and as a beautiful valley did not play an important part. To me that attitude is very important because sometimes supremacy of the head over the heart is essential. I know you don't like my quoting Napoleon; but he once said to Countess Walewska as she pleaded for Poland, 'Politics has no heart; it has only a head.'

You said that in whatever you talk to Sheikh Abdullah, he will trust you. That, of course, is of basic importance. However from the psychological point of view it implies that you trust him too because only trust begets trust. Where trust is lacking, it is smelt instinctively in human dealings.

I do not believe that Sheikh Abdullah deliberately intended to switch on his band-wagon to Pakistan. Any person accusing him of that is not only doing him an injustice but is also spoiling our own cause. However it is a patent fact that the speeches and activities of Sheikh Abdullah during the past few months have had the effect, direct and indirect, of encouraging the pro-Pakistani elements among the Muslim population of the State. It was Sheikh Abdullah's activities, assisted by those of Afzal Beg, that made the dormant pro-Pakistani elements highly vocal and encouraged them to function in the open freely. It has also been reported by our Intelligence Service and Army that quite a large number of undesirable people from Pakistan-held territory infiltrated into the Valley in recent months. The matter was reported by responsible people to Sheikh Abdullah and Afzal Beg; but they prevented Bakshi from taking any action either to prevent further infiltration or to apprehend some of the worst characters who had already infiltrated.

I think in certain circumstances it is immaterial in public affairs what the motive of a leader is. It is by the effect he produces that he is to be judged. In this I think Sheikh Abdullah failed in leadership. I find it difficult to agree with you entirely about how PM was influenced by the reports of wrong kind of people including Yunus etc. I am convinced that PM took a realistic view of the situation.

Even an unrefined person like me was shocked when Sheikh Abdullah replied to the Prime Minister (who built up this man to the point of his being somewhat inflated) that no useful purpose would be served by his coming to Delhi for talks. This was in reply to a pleading letter from PM. No other Chief Minister in India (including Sardar Gian Singh Rarewala – Akali) would have dared to do any such thing. It is only because Jawaharlal Nehru is a rare individual that he was not affected by this discourtesy and insult. I think it was shameful behaviour on the part of the 'Sher-e-Kashmir'. I don't claim to understand the meaning of words such as 'courtesy' and 'manners' as is understood in the drawing rooms and parlours of Delhi. But I claim to understand the import of the word 'loyalty'. Sheikh Abdullah's refusal to come to Delhi and the reasons he advanced for such refusal were, in my judgment, deliberate acts of disloyalty. It was a symptom of what has been happening during the past few months in Kashmir.

Also in the past two or three months or more there was no government, in the generally accepted sense of the word, functioning in Kashmir. Therefore, I entirely agree with Sadiq that 'the action taken was timely and correct'. I agree with you fully, however, that if we had been alert all the time and exercised firmness on appropriate occasions we could have averted the situation developing into an unfortunate crisis as happened early in August. But we have now to function in the present and do all we can to save the future on which so much depends – even the stability of this country. I do believe what happens finally in regard to the Kashmir problem will affect the temper and course of events of this country for many years to come.

It is being said in parliament lobbies and elsewhere that PM recently told his Cabinet 'we have lost Kashmir'. I felt very angry about it. Some Cabinet Ministers also told me about it. I don't believe in giving way to despondency. I should like to hold on to my faith and fight to the last. If we give way to despondency, then it is better to give up straight away and not tinker with the problem.

It is in the context of sheer self-interest and self-preservation which are bound up with certain basic principles we have proclaimed that we have to view and deal with the Kashmir question. We are playing for high stakes and not to acquire the mere territory of Kashmir which is beautiful no doubt. I dismiss the beauty and territory aspects of it summarily.

In regard to your proposal to have a talk with Sheikh Abdullah, we must consider a few points:

1. Possible embarrassment to the present regime in Kashmir. Your action might even unnerve them.

2. Is it possible to do it without the press smelling it? I have my doubts. With a great deal of care perhaps it might be possible to keep it a secret.

3. Possible hostile attitude on the part of Sheikh Abdullah. Perhaps it is not very important. After all you know you are taking a risk.

4. Attitude of Begum Abdullah. I would not brush aside her reaction lightly.

5. Krishna, who is on the whole against your proposal, agreed with me that if you finally decide to meet Sheikh Abdullah, secretly, then someone else possessing some judgment might pave the way for you.

6. Obviously you are not going to meet Sheikh Abdullah purely in your personal capacity. This personal capacity business is anyhow a difficult thing for people in certain positions. That, of course, does not mean that you are going on anyone's behalf or that you are being sent as an emissary to effect a rapproachment. In the first place you should consult PM about your idea of meeting Sheikh Abdullah secretly. If he agrees with your proposal, then in order to have any worth-while talk with Sheikh Abdullah, you should have a very clear idea as to what the Government of India's intentions are in regard to Kashmir policy, in regard to both the immediate present and the long-term one. In order to be clear about this policy you should have a talk with PM (it is no use being talked at). It would also be essential for you to have talks with others who have something to do with the shaping of our Kashmir policy – Maulana Azad, Dr Katju and Rafi particularly. Whether you like them or not, you cannot dismiss them for they are in the picture. Thereafter you should have a further talk with PM.

I asked Krishna what he thought of Sheikh Abdullah. Krishna told me that from such talks as he had with him on various occasions in Delhi, Kashmir and London, he appeared to be extremely muddle-headed. Krishna added that otherwise also he did not form a good impression of the man. Krishna did not get a sensation that Sheikh Abdullah would be a reliable person in a crisis where his personal position was involved. In short Krishna did not consider him to be a man of real substance. However Krishna made much of Sheikh Abdullah in London because he thought that it was in our interest to do so and also because he considered him to be Panditji's man.

However I look at it from an entirely different point of view – i.e., is Sheikh Abdulla for us and with us an acquisition from the political point of view in Kashmir? I have no doubt about it. But the real question is – is Sheikh Abdullah big enough, after all that has happened, to be with us? I do not know.

I also believe that in certain circumstances it is necessary for us to continue to support even a wrong action (once it has been taken) in public affairs.

If for certain tactical reasons it is essential to buttress and prop up Bakshi, I would do so to the hilt unhesitatingly. We dare not vacillate and be soft.

Suppose Sheikh Abdullah is released; will he function in the open swearing by secularism and all the rest he has proclaimed publicly in the past and refrain from attempting to overthrow the present Government, and indeed will he support that Government? That is the real test of statesmanship. Now the idea of independence is finally buried. The two alternatives before us and the people of Kashmir are accession to India or Pakistan.

It will be psychologically wrong for Sheikh Abdullah to be reinstated in Government until the Kashmir problem is finally solved in all its aspects – including the international aspect. Any other step will have far-reaching consequences in India and may even affect PM's personal position. Will Sheikh Abdullah have enough detachment and wisdom to function on the public stage outside of Government and take the correct stand in conformity with his past declarations? That is the most important question. On how it is answered depends his usefulness for us.

Personally I have always felt that Sheikh Abdullah failed on the whole as Prime Minister of Jammu and Kashmir State. I shall not go into the personal aspects of the question. He had no constitution fettering him in any way. He was a virtual dictator with a completely free hand. His performance as Prime Minister has not impressed me. I think he was not very competent. I never got the impression that Sheikh Abdullah was a man of his word. His sense of honour was certainly different from my conception of it.

You know the story of Trotsky whom I admired for a long time. Krishna told me that Trotsky was for Trotsky – always. Stalin, who was at one time nothing compared to Trotsky, became truly the builder of his country and the Father of his Nation. There is difference between a demagogue and a statesman. I am not suggesting that the analogy applies to Sheikh Abdullah and Bakshi Ghulam Mohd completely.

To sum up, in regard to your proposal I do not wish either to encourage you or to discourage you. I suggest that you think hard and follow the dictates of your conscience and be guided by your instinct. I am making this suggestion because I know you are not unrealistic and you are gifted with discernment and judgment. Even when I find I cannot agree with you, I shall certainly give you such personal support as you may need and as I am capable of.

(M.O. Mathai)
12 September 1953

Indiraji
(Note: I have typed this myself.)

From M.O. *Mathai Papers*, Nehru Memorial Museum and Library, New Delhi.

8. Jayaprakash Narayan's letter to Nehru, 1 May 1956

Dear Bhai,
May I make a complaint? It is rarely that I have asked you for anything. One such occasion was when I met you last in New Delhi. I asked you for Narendra Deva's seat in the Council of States to be left for the PSP. Pantji was also present when I had made this request. I was asked who would be the likely PSP candidate and I had said that the choice was between Farid Ansari and Shakuntalaji (widow of the late Hariharnathji). This little request went unheeded, it seems. I believe Sampurnanandji had also been approached in this matter. I do not think that had the Congress let one seat go, it would have lost in any manner. For those of us who look forward to a modification of the party system, this attitude of the Congress party of wanting to have everything for itself is most discouraging. However, my complaint is entirely on a personal basis and has nothing to do with any political consideration.

May I also take this opportunity of saying word about Kashmir – merely to put my views before you, without in the least wanting to criticize or influence. From all the information that I have, 95 per cent of Kashmiri Muslims do not wish to be or remain Indian citizens. I doubt therefore the wisdom of trying to 'keep' people by force where they do not wish to stay. This cannot but have serious long-term political consequences, though immediately it may suit policy and please public opinion. From the point of view of the desirability of establishing a peaceful social order, it cannot but prove disastrous. I do earnestly wish that this question be considered more from a human, rather than a nationalist, point of view. All men have to live upon this earth as brothers, irrespective of what national frontiers divide them. World peace is possible upon no other hypotheses.

Yours affectionately,
Jayaprakash

P.S.: I am not expecting a reply to this letter.

From *Selected Works of Jayaprakash Narayan*, edited by Bimal Prasad, Vol. 7, Delhi: Manohar Publications, 1964: 115.

9. Dr P. Subbarayan's meeting with Sheikh Abdullah in jail, 20 June 1956: record of the conversation

Dr Subbarayan, former Minister of Madras and ex-ambassador to Indonesia, paid a surprise call on me on the 20 June 1956 at 8.30 p.m. He had gone to Srinagar with the Language Commission. He stated that he had expressed a desire to Panditji at Delhi to see me as an old friend and the latter had gladly agreed and written to Bakshi to provide the necessary facilities. Mr Bakshi gave him the permission to see me, providing him with a State car for the journey. The interview lasted till 12 p.m..

The Doctor told me that he was on no mission here and had called only as an old friend. (He asked me if I had any solution for resolving the Kashmir dispute now that I had had enough time to ponder upon the question. He also wanted to know my views on plebiscite. I replied that I could not offer any alternative solution. I further stated that once I had attempted to do so and conveyed my feelings and those of my colleagues to Panditji in regard to the final settlement of the dispute and that contributed to the present situation. Having been under detention now for nearly three years and completely cut off from the political trends in the country, it was difficult for me to suggest a solution.) Doctor Saheb referred to my contact with outside world through press and radio and commented that I could not be completely out of touch. I replied that the press and radio usually flash out prejudiced versions of the situation, generally lacking in objectivity. As for interviews with me, they are almost exclusively confined to my wife and children who are not interested in politics. Doctor Saheb agreed and added that my wife has absolutely confined herself to the education of her children. I said that under the circumstances it was for the Prime Minister of India to find a way out which will be acceptable to all. Then Doctor Saheb referred to the latest proposal of Panditji ruling out plebiscite and suggesting partition of the State on the basis of the present cease-fire line. I remarked that the proposal has not, in my opinion, been made in all seriousness and other parties have rejected it.

With regard to my views on plebiscite, I said that 'sovereignty vests in the people' has been the sheet-anchor of the whole Kashmir movement since its very inception. We opposed the Cripps' proposals, giving to the Indian Princes the right to decide the future of their respective States on this basis, and that led to QUIT KASHMIR agitation. Congress leaders fully supported our stand. In fact my whole defence in the QUIT KASHMIR prosecution case was initiated and conducted by the late Mr Asaf Ali on this ground with the full knowledge and approval of Panditji himself. Again, when Pakistan wanted to take possession of the State by force in 1947, India came to our rescue only to defend this right. Panditji fought back the raiders on the basis of this fundamental right of Kashmiris. He has made innumerable commitments both in public and Parliament, holding out solemn promises to the people of Kashmir that they alone shall have the right to decide the future of their country in a free and democratic manner.

In due course Pakistan also subscribed to this basic principles and the UNCIP resolutions of 13 August 1948 and 5 June 1949 were the result. According to these resolutions both India and Pakistan agreed that the final disposition of the State must be in accordance with the wishes of the people expressed through an impartial plebiscite to be conducted under the U.N.

auspices. These resolutions were subsequently endorsed by the Security Council. Unfortunately, however, the dead-lock arose on settling details.

When Pakistan raised an objection before the Security Council to the convening of the Consembly in the Indian-held part of Kashmir, accusing India of trying to by-pass the decision of the Security Council, Sir B.N. Rao assured the members of the Council that India had no such intention and while the Consembly may express its opinion on accession, 'it could take no decision on it'. He added that India will not be bound by its pronouncement but will stand faithfully by her international commitments.

Gopalaswamy once suggested in a conference that the accession to India may be got approved by the *Consembly* but Panditji disagreed and in excited voice said that he was not prepared to back out and thus compromise India's international reputation. I said to Doctor Saheb that my own commitments to the people of Kashmir are not less numerous or less emphatic. It was not, therefore, possible for me to go back now only because Panditji has changed his mind.

Doctor Saheb asked if Mr Beg had my blessings in organizing the 'Plebiscite Front'. He further told me that Beg is considered by many as my evil genius and a Pakistani at heart. I replied that Beg's only 'crime' is that he holds views similar to those of mine on the Kashmir situation. If because of that he is considered a Pakistani then I can hardly escape the charge. I added that Beg, after his release from detention, was pressed by his opponents to restate his political stand vis-à-vis accession. He, therefore, made it clear that he continued to stand by the fundamental objective of the National Conference that the right of self-determination is the *inalienable* and the most sacred right of the people and any decision affecting their future taken by a party or a group behind their back, will be resisted. This led to the formation of *the Plebiscite Front*. No one who believes in democracy can question his stand.

Doctor suggested that in view of the recent facilities provided to me by the Kashmir authorities in regard to my correspondence with the Prime Minister of India, I should avail of this opportunity and write a letter to Panditji, asking for a meeting with him. He would either come to Kud or call me to Delhi and we can have heart-to-heart talk on the present situation. I replied that I see no objection in writing to him although an answer to my last letter to Panditji, sent in reply to his, was still due. The point worth consideration, however, is whether such a meeting will serve any purpose if conditions in Kashmir continue to remain as they are now. The first and foremost question for decision before any such meeting takes place is the *vindication of my position*. Three years is enough time for Panditji to come to his own conclusion. Many new facts must have come to his knowledge since 9 August 1958 of which he may not have been aware then. Bakshi and his colleagues have not proved a single charge against me. Let even Panditji himself act as a judge. If he is convinced that the charges were fabricated and maliciously false, then they should be duly punished and a new atmosphere created in the State in which the people can breathe freely. On the contrary, if Panditji still nourishes the feeling that Bakshi and his colleagues were justified in their 9 August action, then I will continue to suffer till time vindicates me. In that case, obviously, no useful purpose will be served by the proposed meeting.

The Doctor then suggested that in order to facilitate my release, I may issue a short statement to the effect that my heart is still with India and that if released, I will try to retrieve the position, though I still hold that the right of self-determination of the people of Kashmir must be respected. 'Such a statement' added the Doctor, 'will in no way commit me. I may or may not succeed (in bringing round the people)'. I expressed my surprise at this suggestion, coming as it did from a friend who knew me. I told him that one who has spent the best part of his life, nearly quarter of a century, in active politics cannot be expected to beg for his release. No one, said I, can accuse me as a reactionary, believing in communal or sectarian politics. My whole political career is there for any one to judge. I valiantly fought communalism at a time when even leading Congressmen surrendered to it.

After the tragic partition of the country, if I advised my people to look towards India, it was not for her wealth or power but for the community of ideals. I sincerely felt that India was forging ahead as a real progressive democratic state with secularism as its goal. Though a veritable hell of communal massacre stood between Kashmir and India then, the people of Kashmir joined hands with India so as to be of some assistance to Gandhiji in his noble mission. The Musalmans of Kashmir bore with fortitude the mass killings of their co-religionists in the Jammu Province, the provocative and murderous behaviour of certain Indian Army units stationed in Srinagar in the early days of the raid and the hostile attitude of the local non-Muslim population, but did not falter to uphold the cause of secularism and human brotherhood. Light came to Gandhiji from Kashmir alone.

In spite of the grave misdeeds of the Maharaja, I cooperated with him and accepted office under him in order to maintain law and order and communal peace and harmony in the State. Unfortunately, however, when I realized that the Maharaja was not amenable to reason and continued to sabotage, I was compelled to demand his removal. This led to a misunderstanding between me and Sardar Patel who supported the Maharaja. Though the Sardar acquiesced in the end, this gave rise to a campaign of vilification against me in his circles and a move began to build up an alternative leadership in the State.

An assembly was convened for the purpose of giving the administration in the State a constitutional form. The first task facing the Assembly was about the Headship of the State. The National Conference had all along fought for the removal of the personal rule of the Maharaja and to replace it by an elected Constitutional head. The Government of India considered it a suitable opportunity to ask for more powers to the Centre than was envisaged under Article 370 of the Constitution of India. They maintained that the accession had certain concomitants which we should settle with them before the Centre could give its recognition to the change of the Headship in State. This led to the Delhi Agreement.

The ink was hardly dry on this agreement when a violent agitation was started by the Praja Parishad in Jammu Province for the complete merger of the State in the Indian Union. This agitation was aided and abetted by all Hindu communal organizations in India, particularly the Jana Sangh. Many in the Congress organization, including some Congress Ministers, secretly sympathized with it. Surprisingly enough, even the nationalist press of India, by and large, supported the objective of the agitation. This was indeed *a serious shock that I received*, giving rise to doubts in my mind as regards the reliance that could be put on India's word.

Meanwhile, the Consembly approved the Delhi Agreement and it was left to the appropriate Committees of the House to give it legal shape and form. This naturally required time. My enemies seized the opportunity to cast doubts on my intentions and alleged that I was deliberately postponing the implementation of the agreement.

In addition to the Supreme Court's full jurisdiction over the three acceded subjects, viz. Defence, Communications and Foreign Affairs, we had also agreed in the Delhi Agreement to further surrender the State's jurisdiction in certain other matters, but as regards complete application of jurisdiction of the Supreme Court, the matter had been left for our further consideration and examination. There was difference on this point amongst my colleagues. One group, led by Beg, thought that any further extension of the powers of the Supreme Court will lead to curtailment of the State's autonomy, while the other group headed by D.P. Dhar was of the view that such a course would be advantageous to the state. Not being a lawyer myself, I could not clearly understand the legal implications involved and so asked the leaders of either group to prepare draft memoranda detailing therein their respective viewpoints so that an expert opinion of an eminent jurist may be obtained for the guidance of the Working Committee of the National Conference. Mr Beg handed me his memorandum after some time but D.P. Dhar failed to do so. The matter, therefore, could not be proceeded with further.

I was assigned a difficult and complicated job in Kashmir which for its successful execution called for unreserved and fullest co-operation from all quarters concerned. I had to win and maintain the confidence of all sections of the population in the State, particularly Muslims, and it was their vote which eventually counted. I had, therefore, to assure them that all their rights will not only be fully safeguarded but they will be treated generously by India. It was vital that these assurances were backed by action from India. This alone could counteract the anti-Indian propaganda of the interested parties. Unfortunately, however, things moved in the reverse direction.

In the case of Muslim recruitment in various departments which came under the direct control of the Centre, such as Defence, Posts and Telegraphs, etc., the position became worse and the Muslims were being almost hunted out of employment.

Recruitment in the State Army has always been a tender sore with the Muslims as Kashmiris as a class had been scrupulously excluded; we had fought against this invidious class-composition since 1931. After the transfer of power, the Maharaja resisted handing over control of the State Forces to the Cabinet. The operational control had, however, been transferred to the Centre after the raid. The Government of India suggested temporary transfer of the administrative control also to the Centre on the definite assurance that the legitimate grievance of the Muslims will be looked into and redressed. We agreed but after a couple of years it became evident that instead of raising the representation, Muslims already in the State Forces – both high and low, were gradually squeezed out on some pretext or other. Surprisingly enough, Muslim units en bloc were sometimes forced out. This made the position grievously worse. I, therefore, asked for immediate clarification from the then Defence Minister of India, requesting him to furnish me with the statistics of the Muslim personnel in the State Forces at the time of its taking over by the Centre and that obtaining now. This, I considered necessary in order to scrutinize the veracity of the allegation. My request fetched no reply and the conclusion was obvious.

In the J&K Militia, which is a post-independence organization, the position is no better. This organization, though under nominal administrative control of the State, is mainly officered by the Centre and is also under the operational control of the Union Army. As a new organization, it was quite easy to give adequate representation to the Muslims of the State. The actual position is that out of approximately ten thousand total strength, the number of Muslims hardly exceeds two thousand. A battalion of the Militia was raised in Leh by the Indian Army which is almost exclusively Buddhist in composition, although the population ratio of Budhists and Muslims is fifty–fifty.

Complaints of similar nature were received by me from a Hindu member of the Assembly regarding the employment of Muslim labour in various Ordnance Depots in the Valley. It was alleged that the local Muslims were being suspected of pro-Pakistan leanings and refused employment in spite of the fact that an attestation from the local District Magistrate was invariably produced by them. It was further alleged that non-Muslims from far-off areas were being employed instead.

I brought these cases of invidious discrimination to the notice of the C-in-C General Cariappa, and was shocked when the local Station Commander – Col. Kak – admitted in the presence of the General that recruitment of Kargil Muslims in the Militia was intentionally avoided because of their pro-Pak tendencies. Similar reasons were advanced to justify the discriminatory treatment of the Muslims of the State Force and the Ordinance depots.

I explained at length to Dr Subbarayan the case of Muslim employees of the Kashmir Postal department who had opted for Pakistan at the time of Partition, but had subsequently changed their mind. Under the Standstill Agreement with Pakistan, the Kashmir Postal department came under her temporary control in early 1947 and it was therefore natural for the employees of the department to be influenced by the change. With the subsequent change leading to the State's provisional accession to India, the Muslim employees who had opted for Pakistan were thrown out despite the fact that they changed their previous decision and offered to remain in India. This right was given to all the employees of undivided India under an Inter-Dominion Agreement. I had to fight hard against this injustice but succeeded only partially.

Fresh recruitment in post offices has the same sad tale to tell. In 1953, I pointed out a glaring case of injustice to the State Muslims to Maulana Azad who was then in Srinagar. Out of nearly one hundred candidates who had offered to take the test for selection in the lower cadre of postal service from Kashmir, only twenty-five were Muslims and all of them were shown to have failed in the test, whereas majority of non-Muslims candidates had been declared successful. I pointed out that though the number of unemployed Matriculates among State Muslims was quite large, only twenty-five had applied because the departmental notice was not properly advertised. The inexplicable failure of all the Muslim candidates added to the suspicion that Muslims were being deliberately shut out.

In all-India services a large number of non-Muslims from the State, particularly Kashmiri Pandits, secured employment since the provisional accession, but unfortunately, however, the door remained closed for the Muslims. Naturally a strong feeling grew amongst the Muslim intelligentsia of the State that accession to Pakistan would have opened similar avenues to them as well. It was difficult to remove this feeling particularly in view of the fact that I failed to get the position rectified by the Centre. Instead of understanding and appreciating my difficulties and the disastrous effect such a course of action was having upon the Muslim population in the State, the Indian authorities began to feel suspicious about me and efforts were redoubled to replace the leadership in Kashmir.

Panditji's Private Secretary, the late Shri D.N. Kachru, started a whispering campaign amongst certain friends of mine against me as early as 1950. He advised them to boost up Bakshi as he alone was enjoying the confidence of Government of India. I brought this fact to the notice of Panditji and offered to step down voluntarily in case he felt the same about me. He however wrote back expressing complete ignorance of the move made by his Private Secretary and assuring me his full support and confidence, and I left the matter at that.

The campaign, however, continued. Unabated and all manner of difficulties were created in my way to make my administration a failure. Indian Central Intelligence men were posted to spy upon my movements and even many State employees were engaged to communicate information to the Centre. Thus the administration deteriorated considerably. Bakshi was encouraged and provided secretly with large funds to undermine my influence and position in the country. He took advantage and started amassing wealth and property by dubious means for himself and his kith and kin. Some of my other Cabinet colleagues took the cue from him and followed suit. The poison filtered down in the rank and file of the services and corruption became rampant.

In his last meeting with me at Srinagar in 1953, I hinted to Panditji this sad state of affairs confronting me but there was no response. I could not take action myself as the guilty would take immediate shelter under feigned loyalty to India and none in the Central Government would have supported my action. I, however, made several attempts to persuade Bakshi to the correct path but that resulted in more estrangement.

I called a meeting of the Working Committee of the National Conference to review the situation. Some prominent members of the organization were also specially invited to attend. I explained to the Committee at length the internal, external and the administrative situation confronting me then and long discussion followed. Finally the Committee came to the unanimous conclusion that internal stability was not possible unless the external political uncertainty ended. An 8-man high-level committee was therefore nominated to explore possible methods of resolving the political dead-lock. This committee, besides myself, comprised of Bakshi, Beg, Sadiq, Saraf, Dogra, Budh Singh and Maulana Sayeed. The committee deliberated upon the task assigned to it nearly for a month, and considered and examined thoroughly all possible solutions suggested from time to time for resolving the Kashmir dispute. At the end, three or four alternative solutions were agreed upon, the first being holding of an immediate plebiscite of the whole State as agreed to by all the parties to the dispute, including the UN. *The choice of independence was, however, added to the alternative of accession to India or Pakistan.* Another solution proposed by Bakshi as 'the only honourable and practical one' was to carve out a buffer autonomous State comprising of the Valley with its adjacent Muslim areas, leaving the Jammu Hindu districts and 'Azad' Kashmir the option to merge direct with India and Pakistan respectively. Bakshi gave detailed arguments in favour of this proposal and the committee, *with the only exception of Sadiq*, agreed. One or two other alternative proposals were also agreed to, the details of which I cannot recollect.

On Panditji's return from London, I deputed Bakshi and Beg to Delhi, in early July, to place the conclusions of the committee before him and to ascertain his reaction. As reported back to me, Panditji's reaction to the proposals was not favourable. He had expressed surprise when told by Bakshi that the committee was unanimous and desired to have a personal talk with me in Delhi. Beg, however, suggested his going on a short trip to Srinagar and having talks there because of the tense atmosphere throughout India on account of the recent demise of Dr S.P. Mukerjee. Panditji, I am told, agreed to this suggestion.

Beg returned to Srinagar but Bakshi remained behind. D.P. Dhar was also in Delhi at the time without my knowledge. Both carried out secret talks with Jana Sangh and Praja Parishad leaders. These talks, I am told, were arranged by the late Mr Kidwai. An understanding was arrived at between the parties followed by the mysterious and sudden withdrawal of the Jana Sangh and Praja Parishad agitation. A Praja Parishad poster later revealed that the decision about my dismissal and arrest was taken in the presence of Dr Katju, the then Home Minister.

Thus the plans of the conspiracy having been completed, Bakshi returned to Srinagar. He did not care to apprise me of the talks he had had in Delhi with Panditji and other Central Ministers or the leaders of Jana Sangh and Praja Parishad, but plunged himself straight into a campaign of vilification. A virulent disruptive propaganda against me and some of my colleagues was carried on throughout the Valley by him and Sadiq and I made a final effort to stop the rot and convened a special meeting of some of my prominent colleagues at my residence but to no effect. I, however, pressed for an immediate meeting of the Working Committee and the General Council of the National Conference in order to discuss the whole situation and come to some decision. This was agreed and accordingly the meetings were fixed for the last week of August 1953.

Meanwhile there was some exchange of letters between me and Panditji. I was perturbed by the language used by Panditji in these letters, expressing doubts in my fundamental beliefs. In one of his letters he added at the end that he was sending a copy to Bakshi 'as he was also interested in the matter'. This letter was marked secret and personal. I felt naturally upset as it indicated lack of confidence in me. Under these circumstances and in this background my visit to Delhi was rendered still more difficult.

I informed Dr Subbarayan that the detention and unfortunate demise of Dr Mukerjee in Srinagar had created bitterness against me in India although I was not responsible for it. When Bakshi, as Home Minister, suggested his arrest to me, I advised him to consult Panditji and act accordingly. Dr Mukerjee was, however, arrested and brought up to Srinagar for detention. Bakshi and Saraf as Ministers in charge of Law and Order and Jails respectively remained in contact with him throughout his detention. My idea of visiting him was not liked and I was not kept properly informed about his deteriorating health. It was in these circumstances that Bakshi informed me one morning that Mukerjee had died in the hospital. I could do nothing now and had to keep my mouth shut because of the joint responsibility of the Cabinet. I requested Dr B.C. Roy to conduct an enquiry but he did not accept it.

Conditions deteriorated further. Certain grave charges of administrative nature were brought to my notice against Pandit Saraf. In a Cabinet meeting held on 7 August 1953, these charges were discussed and when no satisfactory explanation was offered, I called upon Saraf to tender his resignation to me by the evening, to which he agreed. Bakshi, suspecting the next turn may be his, quickly joined hands with Saraf and Girdhari Lal Dogra and advised Saraf not to resign. He thought it dangerous to his interests to wait any longer, as the plans for the coup had been finalized both at Delhi and in Srinagar; only the button had to be pressed.

I met the Sadar-i-Riyasat at his residence at 5 p.m. on 8 August 1953 and apprised him of the circumstances that compelled me to demand resignation from Saraf. The Sadar-i-Riyasat suggested holding a special Cabinet meeting which he would also attend, to patch up differences, if any, amongst us. I said that though we had no disagreement on major questions of policy, yet I see no objection to the course suggested. Accordingly, Monday the 10th August was fixed for the meeting. I left for Gulmarg the same evening. Strangely enough, an order of dissolution of my Cabinet by Sadar-i-Riyasat was delivered to me in the early hours of the following day (at 4.20 a.m. to be exact) by one of his ADCs at Gulmarg. The sealed cover contained, besides the order, a forwarding letter by the Sadar-i-Riyasat, a letter from Saraf in reply to one of mine addressed to him the previous day asking for his resignation, and a memorandum signed by Bakshi, Dogra and Saraf expressing their lack of confidence in me. A Superintendent of Police also accompanied the ADC with a posse of Militia and a warrant of arrest and detention issued under the signature of DIG Police, for me and some other Government officers who had accompanied me to Gulmarg, and we were taken to various detention camps.

A reign of terror was immediately let loose in the whole Valley. Central Reserve Police (CRP) had already been called in from Jammu and they, along with Militia and Special Police, etc., were detailed to various places and given a free hand to shoot and commit other atrocities in order to suppress peaceful demonstrations of the masses against this unwarranted and uncalled for action of the Sadar-i-Riyasat. Even the Indian Army lent a helping hand. Simultaneously, a campaign of slanderous propaganda was unleashed against me in full blast, and the All India Radio and the entire Indian press helped in carrying the fabricated stories and completely suppressed the true facts of the situation from the public. A virtual iron curtain was drawn upon the Valley. I was charged with having conspired with the USA to gain independence for the State. I was also accused of having begun a life of luxury and comfort at the cost of the poor tax-payer with dozens of costly cars and scores of riding horses at my disposal. In fact no effort was spared to paint me in the blackest possible colours in the public eye. The Government of India not only connived but in a way supported this malicious propaganda. If, perchance, any solitary newspaper dared to question the veracity of the charges, all possible pressure was brought to silence it.

Attempt is being made to explain away the arbitrary and unconstitutional action of the Sadar-i-Risayat in dissolving my Cabinet and thus removing me from office on the plea that I had lost the confidence of the majority of my colleagues in the Cabinet. Two months later, post facto ratification of this act was sought from the Assembly. The procedure is unique and novel in the history of democracy. Even if some of my colleagues had any difference of policy with me, the established procedure was to resign from office and approach the House by a formal no confidence motion against me. If the motion was carried I would have tendered my resignation. This established practice and procedure of parliamentary democracy was thrown to the winds and the Sadar-i-Riyasat took the initiative without any legal powers vested in him under the State Constitution. His subsequent appointment of Bakshi Ghulam Mohammed as Prime Minister is also arbitrary and unconstitutional. At that moment of crisis on 9 August 1953, the party position being unknown, the Sadar-i-Riyasat could have had no idea about Bakshi's backing in the House. His action, therefore, clearly indicates that he was acting not as an independent Constitutional Head of the State but as a mere partisan.

Two months later, a session of the Assembly was called at Srinagar in order to cover up this highly arbitrary and unconstitutional act of the Sadar-i-Riyasat. I have already referred to the atmosphere of brutal repression created in Kashmir after 9 August 1953. In this holocaust a large number of MLAs were jailed or put under house arrest, and the rest, though nominally free, were under the constant threat of arrest and persecution. Gradually, only those MLAs were released who gave an unequivocal assurance of supporting Bakshi and approving the 9 August action. It was in these circumstances that the vote of confidence in Bakshi was secured.

From Udampore Jail, I sent telegrams to the President and Prime Minister of India and also to the Speaker of the State Assembly, to make it possible for me to appear in the House and face the motion of no-confidence. This was my fundamental and minimum right under any democracy, but even this was summarily refused and a colossal farce in the name of democracy was staged.

Having thus explained the whole background and history of the developments, I put it to Dr Subbarayan if it would be fair to ask me to issue the suggested statement. If it is intended to facilitate my release, I am sorry that I am not prepared to pay the price. What have I done to deserve it now that you know all the facts, I asked. Any statement from me on the present political situation is besides the point in view of being totally cut off from my people for the last three years. Before expressing myself on the situation it is necessary that I should freely mix with my people, feel their pulse and have an unfettered opportunity to consult my colleagues and take stock of the situation. A meeting with Panditji also will only then serve any purpose.

On the contrary if I now issue a statement as suggested, it will be gravely misconstrued and will seriously damage my position. The Doctor appreciated my point and said that in view of what I had stated he will reconsider. By the way, I told the Doctor that why should anybody be particular about a statement from me, now that according to my opponents, I had lost all influence. Doctor Saheb replied that unfortunately I was not aware of my power. I said, on the contrary, Bakshi and his friends tell a different tale to Government of India and make them believe that they have succeeded in completely eliminating me from the Kashmir scene. They assert that an average Kashmiri is not interested in the political issue. His main interest is in being provided with cheap food. Therefore, a successful appeal can be made to his heart through his stomach. Accordingly, an old British example of distributing cheap rice to hungry Chinese was resorted to and Government of India made to foot the bill of nearly 2 crores of rupees per annum. Besides this, many other measures were taken in hand to purchase the conscience of the people, and Government of India is advancing huge sums on interest to Kashmir government apparently for developmental purposes but actually with an eye to gain this objective. The Kashmiris are not so credulous as not to understand the game. The result is, therefore, zero. Kashmir has drifted and is drifting away from India. 'Yes, India is spending colossal amounts on Kashmir', said the Doctor. He added further that if India had given even a part of this liberal aid and financial support to me, things would have been different.

Referring to the resolutions that emanate from time to time in the name of the National Conference, Doctor Saheb enquired if this organization really exists. I replied that it does but in name only. The resolutions are passed by a small coterie which controls the Government as well as the organization. They have a few henchmen also who are provided with regular jobs in the administration.

The Doctor remarked that there are people in India who still believe that the charge of having conspired with the USA has some substance and the material is being collected by Bakshi. I asked, why does he not publish the letters which he claimed on the floor of the Assembly to contain all the proof needed to establish the charge? At least he could show them to you in private. Doctor Saheb replied that he was not so intimate with Bakshi to ask for the privilege. I told the Doctor that let an impartial judge be appointed to investigate into the allegations and if I am found guilty I shall have no grouse to continue to suffer. On the contrary, if the charge is not proved against me then those responsible for having falsely implicated me should be brought to book. Nothing can be fairer. I made it clear that so long my position is not vindicated, it is difficult to talk of rapproachment.

Doctor Saheb wanted to know the facts about the Cadillac car. I informed him that the car was imported from USA for ceremonial purposes for VIPs from India, with the approval of the Cabinet and with the full knowledge of the Central Government. It was not meant for my personal use.

Referring to the opposition group in the Assembly, the Doctor said that he was told that their number is hardly six. I corrected his information and told him that the exact number so far is eleven, including myself. Majority of others were either coerced or heavily bribed to support Bakshi. Some, it is being alleged, were paid Rs 7000 each or even more for their continued support to the present regime. They also receive other monetary advantages from the Government in the form of big employment of relations in Government service, irrespective of qualifications, and are given a free hand to share the loot. Those who resisted such temptation are under detention since August 1953. Recently three have been released on short parole and only four are left free to deceive the world opinion that an opposition party is allowed to function within the Assembly. Even these four members are kept under constant watch and are harassed and persecuted. The Assembly has during the last three years taken some major policy decisions and we are expected to ditto them. Nothing can be more unfair and undemocratic.

Doctor Saheb wanted to know the number of my old colleagues in the present Cabinet. I told him that their number was four: Bakshi, Sadiq, Saraf and Dogra. He, however, seemed interested to know about Mir Qasim and said that he was young, educated and intelligent. I observed that Mir Qasim was everything to everybody. To a Pakistani he dangles a certificate which he received from late Mr Liaqat Ali in appreciation of his work to help the League election campaign before Partition. He was then a student at Aligarh. To a Communist he is a Marxist, and to a Congressman an Indian first and last. He has, however, little influence in Kashmir and is not trusted. As regards Bakshi, the less said the better. He was bargaining with League leaders in 1946 for the allotment of some factories in Lahore in his name when they wanted to enlist his support in favour of Kashmir's accession to Pakistan. Sadiq is an avowed Communist and both Panditji and Maulana Azad are aware of it. He toes the Party-line. I said that my difference with Indian Communists is on their extra-territorial loyalty. The Doctor shared this view. I added that the Communists felt that so long I remained at the helm of affairs there was no chance for them to spread their tentacles far and wide in Kashmir. The 9 August coup d'état was therefore a welcome opportunity for them and they are taking full advantage of it.

I informed Doctor Saheb that on 9 August, even high Government officers – both Hindu and Muslim – were jailed on the mere suspicion that they were either sympathetic or related to me. No charge was ever brought against them and some are still under detention. Doctor Saheb wanted to know as to how I was treated in jail and if my wife and children are allowed to stay with me. I replied in the affirmative but added that for whatever liberal treatment I receive in jail, the credit must go to Panditji. The Doctor remarked that Panditji had the same regard and affection for me as before. I replied that it could not be otherwise. Panditji always considered me as one of the family. Doctor Saheb asked if I believed that Panditji was in any way associated with the events of 9 August 1953. I replied that it could not have been possible for Sadar-i-Riyasat to take action without previous approval or instruction from the Centre. Panditji's subsequent conduct lends support to it. One can at best say that pressure of circumstances forced Panditji to agree to such a step. When some of my own erstwhile colleagues turned against me and carried tales, perhaps he could not help it. My only grievance, however, is that he ought to have confronted them with me before believing in them, which he did not do.

Doctor Saheb asked if the Sadar-i-Riyasat had acted on his own initiative or on instructions from the Centre. I replied that having no personal knowledge I could not say anything definitely, but my feeling is that he could not dare to take such a step without the previous approval and support of the Centre, and subsequent events fully substantiate this.

While recapitulating, I asked Doctor Saheb what his advice to me should be as a friend now that I had frankly explained the whole position. His reply was that he would report about it to Panditji. When pressed to give me his own reaction, his only answer was that he will reconsider the position in the light of what he had heard. Reverting to my release he said again that he thought that my issuing a short statement as suggested by him and meeting Panditji would facilitate matters. I replied that if after the lapse of nearly three years, Panditji does not feel the urgency of doing away with the corrupt and most oppressive regime in Kashmir and the monstrous laws enacted by it to suppress the civil liberties of the people, my mere release will not serve any purpose.

Finally, Doctorr Saheb said that he was moved by the extreme poverty of Kashmiris and in spite of the fact that India was advancing large sums on their welfare, they 'looked sullen'. This he considered a bad sign (for India). I said that 'approach to heart through stomach' is an exploded colonial policy and the sooner India realizes it, the better it would be for her.

While bidding good-bye, Doctor Saheb remarked that Pakistan is threatening India with an armed attack over Kashmir though he would personally desire that conditions be so created as would make it possible for both the countries to have a joint defence and common foreign policy. This would enable them to play an effective role in the comity of nations, particularly of Asia. I said that the key to such a desire is to find an immediate solution of the Kashmir dispute which should be acceptable to all the parties concerned.

S.M. Abdullah

Sub-Jail, Kud
21 June 1956

Letter circulated by Mridula Sarabai.

10. Letter from Sheikh Abdullah to Jawaharlal Nehru after his release from jail in 1958

Soura, Srinagar
11 April 1958

My dear Panditji,

Since my release from detention Bakshi Ghulam Mohammed and his supporters are deliberately giving publicity to false and mischievous reports about my activities in order to cover up their past misdeeds. This is extremely sad. Under cover of this propaganda hundreds of Kashmiris belonging to various walks of life – lawyers, doctors, businessmen, ex-ministers of the State and ex-members of the Indian Parliament, etc. – have been either detained without any chargesheet or involved in fictitious cases, criminal or otherwise. They are being given most shabby treatment in various lock-ups and provided with meals and other necessities of life hardly worth ten annas a day. They are not allowed to receive private beddings and are often refused eatables from their home people. In fact the treatment accorded to them is worse than a convicted criminal is receiving at the hands of the jail authorities. The police deliberately adopts delaying tactics in completing the chalans of the accused in order to cause maximum amount of mental and physical torture to them while they remain in their custody. Some of the most respectable persons have been taken to the interrogation centre of the Intelligence Bureau, Government of India, where they are being tortured in a way reminiscent of Nazi Concentration Camps in order to force them to give or sign false statements involving popular leaders in treason charges. With the promulgation of Rule 50 of the Defence Rules, prohibiting public meetings and processions, the whole Valley has become almost a graveyard. CRP, Peace Brigade, Militia and the police have been spread in the city and in all the corners of the Valley and the Doda District to spread terror in the minds of the people. Daily arrests are being affected without any rhyme or reason on absolutely false and fictitious charges, and the victims carried into various lock-ups and tortured. I am silently watching all this in order to know for myself how the Indian democracy is functioning in that part of the State which is predominantly Muslim. But even my silence and inactivity is causing the coup-stagers of August 1953 anxious sleepless nights and they are making every effort to have me back in prison.

I am amazed at the recent utterences of Bakshi Ghulam Mohammed, at Hyderabad and Bombay, in which he has accused me of organizing a force of Razakars and raising funds for the same in order to make an all-out attack on the Government at a suitable time. This is yet another fantasy of the man who has betrayed not only the people of Kashmir but also his own benefactor to gain personal power and accumulate wealth for his family through corruption and other foul means. In 1953 he succeeded in misleading you and some of your other colleagues and the result was the August tragedy. Then he charged me with having entered into a conspiracy with a foreign power to gain independence for the State. He threatened to publish my correspondence with you, the late Maulana Azad and Rafi Ahmed Kidwai, to substantiate his charge. He has not done so up till now. Having failed to prove this charge, he is again at his old game and along with his other co-conspirators, both here and in Delhi, is trying to create the most vicious atmosphere in the country about me and my activities. I hope you will not be deceived twice by the man who is devoid of all moral principles and decency.

As you very well know, I have never indulged in intrigues and falsehoods. There is no doubt that I do not agree with the policy that Government of India is pursuing regarding Kashmir. I have made no secret of my views vis-à-vis my stand. I believe that the only fair and just way of ending this ten-year-old dispute is by conceding the right of self-determination to the people of Kashmir which you once so ardently supported and for the protection of which Government of India sent her armed forces into the State in 1947. I am determined to secure this right for the people of Kashmir through all legitimate and peaceful means, whatever the cost.

I am so strongly convinced about the justness of my cause that I feel that a day will definitely come when the world conscience will force India to yield to our demand.

I am not interested in creating trouble within the State to overthrow any Government, whatever its character. Of course I do want to create an organized opinion amongst all sections of the people of Kashmir as well as of India to have this dispute over Kashmir between the two great neighbours – India and Pakistan – settled as early as possible in accordance with the wishes of the people of the State expressed freely and without any fear, internal or external.

Inspite of all what has happened since August 1953, I still believe that the key of the solution lies in your hands and I appeal to you not to be deceived by Bakshi Ghulam Mohammed and his other supporters in pursuing a policy which, in the end, is bound to prove disastrous for all.

I hope you are well.

Sincerely yours,
Sd/- Sheikh Mohammed Abdullah

Hon'ble Pandit Jawaharlal Nehru
Prime Minister of India, New Delhi

Press release issued by Mridula Sarabhai on events from 30 April to 15 May 1958.

11. Jayaprakash Narayan's article in *Hindustan Times*, 20 April 1964: 'Our Great Opportunity in Kashmir'

The story of Kashmir is an account of confused aims, unsure methods, insincere ideals. From the beginning, Kashmir has been the Prime Minister's concern. Yet when Sheikh Abdullah was dismissed from the Prime Ministership and detained, Mr Nehru happened to know of the event just as any other Indian citizen did. That is only one example of the incredible manner in which the Kashmir question has been handled. The present ballyhoo over Sheikh Abdullah's statements raises the doubt if the old story was not going to be repeated again.

After eleven years of dilly-dallying the Sheikh was at last released. But again there seems to be no well thought-out policy behind that belated decision. Surprise and pain have been expressed at Sheikh Saheb's statements. Unless the gentlemen concerned had deliberately hidden their heads in the sand, they could have saved themselves these emotional upsets. Sheikh Abdullah has said nothing that was not expected from him. Happily, the one sane voice in the ruling party is that of the Prime Minister himself.

What, after all, is the substance of Sheikh Abdullah's statements? This, that the future of Kashmir has to be decided by the people of Kashmir, and that it has to be done in a manner that the dispute about it between India and Pakistan is amicably ended. With a little imagination it was possible to see that this clear and principled stand of the Kashmir leader opened for India a wonderful opportunity that could be exploited to the advantage of all concerned. What actually is happening, however, is parrot-like reiteration of slogans that carry no conviction in any dispassionate quarters.

One of these slogans is that the accession of Kashmir to India is final and irrevocable. The Sheikh has questioned that, and it is for impartial lawyers to decide the issue. But the vital point to keep in mind is that it is not by legal advocacy that a human problem like that of Kashmir can ever be settled. Indeed, it was such realization that had prompted the original promise of the Prime Minister to ascertain the wishes of the people

At this point two further slogans are raised: (a) the people of Kashmir have already expressed their will at three general election; (b) if the people of Kashmir are allowed to express their will, it will be the beginning of the end of the Indian nation.

Both, to my mind, are baseless slogans. The elections in Kashmir after Sheikh Abdullah's arrest were neither fair nor free. If that has to be disproved, it can be done by an impartial inquiry and not just by official assertions. Delhi seems to believe that by auto-suggestion it can establish any fact it pleases.

I may be lacking in patriotism or other virtues, but it has always seemed to me to be a lie to say that the people of Kashmir had already decided to integrate themselves with India. They might do so, but have not done so yet. Apart from the quality of the election, the future of the State of Jammu and Kashmir was never made an electoral issue at any of them. If further proof was needed, it has come in the form of Sheikh Abdullah's emphatic views who, to put it at the least, is as representative of the people as any other Kashmiri leader.

Lastly, if we are so sure of the verdict of the people, why are we so opposed to giving them another opportunity to reiterate it? The answer given is that this would start the process of disintegration of the country. Few things have been said in the course of this controversy more silly than this one. The assumption behind the argument is that the states of India are held together by force and not by the sentiment of common nationality. It is an assumption that makes a mockery of the Indian nation and a tyrant of the Indian state.

Threats have been held out that should Sheikh Abdullah misbehave, the law would take its course. The law had taken its course. The law had taken its course for eleven years and the issue remained unsettled. It is not likely to achieve more in the future. It is remarkable how the freedom-fighters of yesterday begin so easily to imitate the language of the imperialists.

The last and final slogan raised in the ballyhoo is that there is no Kashmir question at all, and that if there was one at any time, it has now been settled once for all. Kashmir is a part of India and that is a fact of history, they say. That, I think, is the worst form of auto-suggestion.

The slogan-raisers forget that less than half of the State of Jammu and Kashmir is under the occupation of Pakistan. Has that been accepted as settled fact? If so, when and where? If not, how is the issue of Kashmir settled, except in the private thoughts of those who believe that 'we shall keep what we have' and 'they shall keep what they have'.

Secondly, the issue is still pending before the Security Council and UN observers are still posted in Kashmir. Thirdly, here is a leader of the stature of Sheikh Abdullah who clearly states that the issue has yet to be settled.

Therefore, as a humble servant of this country, I plead earnestly that instead of trying to take shelter in fool's paradise of our own making, let us have the courage to face facts and deal with them on the bases of the ideals and fundamental principles that guided our freedom movement. After all, Sheikh Abdullah has not said anything that shuts the door to a reasoned and amicable settlement. All he has done is to envisage the unity and integrity of the original State of Jammu and Kashmir and the ascertainment of the wishes of the people of the reunited state in a manner to be agreed upon. He has indicated that a plebiscite need not be the only way of ascertaining the people's wishes and has mentioned free and fair election as one method. That is not a stand that does not provide a meeting ground for India, Pakistan and the people of Kashmir.

It was encouraging to find that the Prime Minister in his reply to the foreign affairs debate boldly affirmed his faith in Indo–Pakistan friendship, envisaging even some kind of a constitutional tie, and was generous enough to concede that mistakes had been made by both sides. Recent events have proved that the partition of India was grave mistake and it has failed to solve any problem. However, there is now the incontestable fact of two sovereign nations.

But, at the same time, the history of the post-independence years has proved another incontestable fact, namely, that neither India nor Pakistan can live and grow unless there is friendship and co-operation between them. The lack of such relationship between them has, among other things, upset the power-balance in South and South-East Asia, depriving the sub-continent of the role that history and geography had destined it to play. The result was the tilting of the balance in favour of China – a most unhealthy state of affairs.

The Kashmir question has to be viewed in this broad perspective.

The question whether settlement of the Kashmir problem would establish friendship between and Pakistan may be debated, but it cannot be denied that it will go a long way towards that goal, as also create international conditions that will necessarily promote that friendship. I do fervently hope that our leaders would have the vision and statesmanship that this historic moment demands.

12. Jayaprakash Narayan's article in *Hindustan Times*, 15 May 1964: 'The Need to Re-think'

My recent article on Kashmir has provoked a rather fierce controversy. That is good, because after the emotional catharsis, tempers should cool down, allowing for a more reasoned approach to a question that has plagued the sub-continent for the past seventeen years. There is urgent need for re-thinking on this question, and all I had done in my article was to plead for this. It is to be regretted, therefore, that most of those who thought it necessary to preach angry sermons to me on patriotism refused to look squarely at the truths I had drawn attention to.

Yet, I have no desire to prolong this controversy, because I believe it would help if everyone concerned kept his counsel for a while. But in recent days there have been some amazing statements, and a dangerous state of mind has been revealed. Therefore, it seems necessary to deal briefly with some of these anxious matters, and point if possible a constructive way out.

When I wrote of the ballyhoo in my article, I had little imagined that there had been such a vast, organized attempt to work up a state of mind that was hysterical and closed to reason and intolerant to a violent degree of all dissent. The public temper in Delhi at the time of Sheikh Abdullah's arrival reminded one of the days when the Father of the Nation was sacrificed at the altar of a similar synthetic hysteria. Regrettably, Parliament itself helped to create that spirit of violent intolerance: recall, to give only one example, the shouting down of Mr Frank Anthony.

A rather mortifying example of the mental state of some Members of Parliament was provided by Mr A.P. Jain, President of the U.P. Congress and one-time Union Minister. He is reported to have said at New Delhi that there were men who held a different opinion from mine on Kashmir who had voluntarily imposed upon themselves 'extreme restraint'; but that 'if provocations of the type that Mr Narayan is making continue, their patience might be exhausted'.

I have no idea what Mr Jain means by that threat; perhaps he and his friends would have me put away in prison. Personally, I would welcome that as an opportunity to snatch some rest and do some reading. But the crucial point to ponder is, if a person of Mr Jain's position throws about threats in this manner, can it be surprising that irate young men should go about muttering assassination?

The pity is that when I made a reference to this mass hysteria at a public meeting in New Delhi, some friends in the Rajya Sabha turned it into an issue of personal security (I am in no need of protection), rather than giving serious thought to the dangers of the situation that had developed. May I say with due respect that in order to remedy the situation Members of Parliament might well begin with themselves by practising a little more patience and tolerance?

Of all the amazing statements made in the course of this controversy the one by the twenty-seven Congress MPs (including the Secretary of the Congress Party and other important members) would easily take the prize. First, there was the astounding assertion of the primacy of the law over moral and human values. As legislators the MPs should know the nature and limitations of law, as they are making and unmaking laws, even amending the Constitution, all the time. In human affairs law no doubt has an important role to play, but it has its limits. Morality and human values transcend the limits of law and take precedence over it.

Nor is it a question of any 'one's personal views of what is moral'. It is not at all difficult to identify what civilization in this age considers moral and human. It was Mahatma Gandhi who devoted his whole life to spiritualize politics. It is sad to find that in a decade and a half leaders (one hopes their number is limited) of the organization which he built up have come to sneer openly at morality and humanism.

Coming to Kashmir, this is how they authoritatively summed up the position: 'You can no more talk of self-determination in the case of Kashmir than in the case of, say, Bombay or Bihar.' Further on they said, 'After the Americans attained independence was any State allowed to exercise the so-called right of self-determination?' Surely, Congress MPs know better. Then why this deliberate obfuscation? Is the answer far to find?

Lest the public, who have proverbial short memories, should be led into believing that the idea of self-determination for Kashmir was a creation of Jayaprakash Narayan and his ilk, let me try to put the record straight. When partition was agreed upon, it was decided that what was known as British India would be divided according to Muslim and Hindu majority areas (without any referendum); and that in Princely India the Princes would have the option to accede to either India or Pakistan. Thus, there was no question of any referendum in Bihar or Bombay.

As to the Princely States, the accession of the Prince was to be final. So, when Maharaja Hari Singh of Kashmir acceded to India, that should have set the matter beyond doubt for all times, as indeed in strict law it actually did. But there was a snag: the accession had to be accepted. And it was precisely at that point that the idea of referendum or self-determination in regard to Kashmir was injected into the course of events. After accepting the Instrument of Accession on 27 October 1947, Lord Louis Mountbatten, in a separate letter of the same date, wrote to the Maharaja as follows:

> In the special circumstances mentioned by Your Highness, my Government have decided to accept the accession of Kashmir State to the Dominion of India. Consistently with their policy that, in the case of any State where the issue of accession has been the subject of dispute, the question of accession should be decided in accordance with the wishes of the people of the State, it is my Government's wish that, as soon as law and order have been restored in Kashmir and her soil cleared of the invader, the question of the State's accession should be settled by a reference to the people.

A few days later (2 November 1947) Mr Nehru, in a broadcast, underlined the assurance given by the Governor-General in these clear words:

> We decided to accept this accession and to send troops by air, but we made a condition that the accession would have to be considered by the people of Kashmir later when peace and order were established. We were anxious not to finalize anything in a moment of crisis, and without the fullest opportunity to the people of Kashmir to have their say. It was for them ultimately to decide.
>
> And here let me make clear that it has been our policy all along that where there is a dispute about the accession of a state to either Dominion, the decision must be made by the people of that state. It was in accordance with this policy that *we added a proviso* to the Instrument of Accession of Kashmir.

Later in the same broadcast the Prime Minister went on to declare to all the world:

> We have declared that the fate of Kashmir is ultimately to be decided by the people. That pledge we have given, and the Maharaja has supported it, not

> only to the people of Kashmir but to the world. We will not, and cannot, back out of it. We are prepared when peace and law and order have been established to have a referendum held under international auspices like the UN. We want it to be a fair and just reference to the people and we shall accept their verdict. I can imagine no fairer and juster offer.

In view of this crystal-clear position it is amazing that such frantic efforts should be made to cloud the issue.

At this point it might help to clarify matters to consider another variation of the theme – though it was not the theme of the twenty-seven MPs. Briefly, it is this: true, there was a proviso added to the Instrument of Accession, but that has already been given effect to and there is nothing further to be done about it. The proviso was carried out, it is said, when the Kashmir Constituent Assembly adopted in 1956 a constitution which declared that 'the State of Jammu and Kashmir is and shall be an integral part of India'. That was three years after Sheikh Abdullah's arrest, but that may not be considered so important. The really important point is that a decision of the Constituent Assembly cannot be equated with a referendum, which the Prime Minister had solemnly pledged.

Statements of Sheikh Abdullah are bandied about to prove that he himself had accepted the accession. But there never was any question about it. Following the Maharaja's legal act of accession, the Sheikh and the National Conference had endorsed and explicitly accepted the accession; and on many subsequent occasions their acceptance was reiterated. All that is incontestable. Yet the proviso remained and had to take effect. Neither the National Conference nor Sheikh Abdullah could take the place of the people of Kashmir, whose will had to be ascertained and not the Sheikh's or that of the National conference.

Still another argument is that since Pakistan joined SEATO and CENTO and the USA supplied it arms, and other things happened, the situation became so transformed that the offer of referendum stood no longer. But it is forgotten that it was not to Pakistan that the offer of pledge had been given but to the people of Kashmir. There could be no justification for punishing the latter for the actions of the former.

In view of all this it appears to me that the right and constructive approach is not to deny to Kashmir the *right* to self-determination, or to assert that the right has already been exercised, but to show rationally how impractical and imprudent it would be to exercise that right *now*.

The following considerations might be put forward: first, there is the hard fact of aggression by Pakistan, which they show no intention to vacate; second, a referendum might have serious consequences for the minorities both in India and Pakistan; third, a referendum might lead to further disintegration of the State of Jammu and Kashmir; fourth, the effect of the fore-going would have serious consequences for India's defence. There may be other factors; but these four are weighty and reasonable and neither Sheikh Abdullah nor any other Kashmir leader, because they are as much concerned with India's good as with that of Kashmir, would brush them aside.

Therefore, my humble plea is that we put aside all this heated controversy about the accession having been final and irrevocable, and sit down with the Sheikh and discuss practical ways of settlement. If according to us the only way of settlement is for Sheikh Abdullah to accept the finality and irrevocability of the accession, we might as well send him back to prison: he will never agree to that position. But in order to find a mutually acceptable solution, it is not necessary for either side to give up its position. The important thing is for each to understand that merely by asserting one's own position and sticking to it, the problem is not solved. No matter how aggressively we affirm that Kashmir's accession to India is final and irrevocable, the world does not accept it, the 'Azad Kashmir' area remains under Pakistan, the cease-fire line remains, the two armies remain facing each other, the minorities in both India and Pakistan continue to live in fear, discontent in Kashmir simmers and might have to be put down by force. So, what have we gained, or hope to gain in the future, by our insistent unilateral assertion? On the other hand, if Sheikh Abdullah continues to press for the right of self-determination, and the circumstances do not permit it to be exercised, what good does it do to him or anyone else?

So, let each hold on to his position, but put it aside and get down to brass tacks to find a practical solution. Let it be recalled that there were three referendums in Alsace Lorraine, and now who cares where it belongs!

I do not think anyone knows what the solution can be. Yet a few positive things might be stated about it. One, that there must be an honest desire on all sides to find a solution. Two, it should be remembered, as an English statesman said, that nothing is settled unless it is settled right. Of course, it is not easy to know what is right in a complicated situation, but one test may be that it gives satisfaction to all concerned. Therefore, the third point about the solution is that it must be such as to satisfy India, the people of Kashmir and Pakistan.

Sheikh Abdullah's insistent stress on Indo–Pak understanding as a part of any solution of the Kashmir's question has irked Indian public opinion and many have read into it his predilection for Pakistan. This, however, is a complete misreading. Sheikh Abdullah sees, as everyone else should, that if Pakistan were not a party to it, there could be no settlement. The very Kashmir question came into being on account of Pakistan, and it was India that made her a party to the dispute at the UN. Apart from Kashmir, Sheikh Abdullah also sees that the future of both India and Pakistan depends upon whether they are friends or enemies.

This is a view that will not be seriously contested in this country, and it has the support of no less a person than the Prime Minister. In a courageous and statesmanlike speech in the Lok Sabha, in reply to the foreign affairs debate, Mr Nehru was reported to have said that, 'he would have hoped that India and Pakistan would come together closer, even constitutionally, but that would annoy the Pakistan authorities'. So he would content himself to declare: 'There is no other way for us except to live in peace.' When it is recalled that the speech was made at a time of intense communal feeling, its courage and wisdom become still the more impressive.

I might remark here parenthetically – though this is not the place for it – that the Prime Minister's speech was equally remarkable for its responsive approach to the inquiry made by the Prime Minister of Ceylon. I should add, however, that it is not for China to make a 'proper approach' to us as the Prime Minister said. Now that both sides have been sounded, it is for the mediators, the six Colombo Conference powers, to make the proposal in a formal manner to both Governments. That would amount to a mutually agreed amendment of the original Colombo proposals, and enable India and China to meet at the conference table.

However, to return to Indo–Pakistan relations and Kashmir. The reference by the Prime Minister to some kind of constitutional link between the two countries is particularly interesting in the present context. And it need not be assumed that Pakistan would always be opposed to such an idea. After all, every country is concerned above all with its security and economic development. Can there be any doubt that a constitutional link between India and Pakistan would go a long way to guarantee their security as well as economic progress? Moreover, the fact that Sheikh Abdullah is also thinking on similar lines introduces a fresh element of hope into the situation. So, if the rigid positions are kept out of the way, there is every hope that a constructive line of approach will be agreed upon that might lead ultimately to a solution at once satisfying to India, Kashmir and Pakistan. Here is a task of statesmanship of the highest order.

Before concluding I wish to take a look at our secularism in relation to Kashmir. Apart from other considerations, Kashmir is deemed to be of great value to us because we wish to hold it up as an example of our secularism. I wonder if the spokesmen of secularism are aware of the irony of the present situation. The same Kashmir that is supposed to be an example of Indian secularism has occasioned a nasty upsurge of Hindu communalism. It is not easy to discern this process, because it is happening under the cover of nationalism. India being a Hindu-majority country, it is not difficult, as has been remarked by many observers, for Hindu communalism to trot out in the garb of Indian nationalism. Therefore, it is more urgent that those who believe in a truly secular and composite nationalism should be on their guard.

What is meant by Kashmir being an example of Indian secularism? It means, I believe, that the people of India have given such proof of their non-communal outlook that the Muslims of Kashmir, even though they are in a majority there, have freely decided to live with India which is a Hindu-majority but a secular country, rather than with Pakistan which is a Muslim-majority. But suppose we had to keep the Muslims of Kashmir within India by force; would that also be an example of our secularism? The very question exposes its absurdity. And yet, how widespread is the mentality today that in order to defend the secular basis of our nation, we must keep Kashmir, if necessary by force, within the Indian Union!

Therefore, I do wish most seriously to plead with the Prime Minister, the Congress President and other Congress leaders to look carefully at the cancerous process that is taking place within their party. As things are moving there would soon be little to choose at least in this matter between the Congress and the Jana Sangh. Shallow and timid Congressmen are feeling that the latter is stealing the thunder. But by and large the people's mind is sound, and they would rally round Pandit Jawaharlal Nehru (as they have always known him) if he were to give a clear and bold lead. And so would all the faint-hearted Congressmen who are eager to ride to victory on the communal wave. If some such event does not happen, I am afraid there would be vital damage done to the secular base of our nation.

13. Jayaprakash Narayan's letter to A.G. Noorani, dated 19 February 1965, and the concerned article by A.G. Noorani

Dear Noorani Saheb,

I thank you for your letter of 7 February. I greatly liked your article, on India, Pakistan and Kashmir, and found myself incomplete agreement with you. If you could send two dozen copies of the reprint of your article to J.J. Singh, he would circulate it to the members of the Group with a covering letter and seek their opinion. I am writing to J.J. on these lines.

When I next visit Bombay, I shall make it a point to meet you.

Wishing you the best,

Yours sincerely,
Jayaprakash Narayan

India, Pakistan and Kashmir

(published in *Opinion*, 12 May 1964)

Sheikh Abdullah, having proclaimed his stand several times over, has met Mr Nehru and the principal political leaders of India. His stand may be summed up in three propositions. First, Kashmir's future remains to be decided. Second, its people's vioce must be respected in arriving at the decision, to which process both India and Pakistan are also parties. Lastly, 'Kashmir should not leave its individuality', nor live in isolation. 'It will live if India lives and Pakistan lives: the State is an integral part of the sub-continent.'

These propositions have been elaborated in several corollories: the future of minorities in both countries must not be overlooked in deciding Kashmir's future, the categorical rejection of the two-nation theory, and, most significantly, the repeated hints that alternatives to a plebiscite should be explored. They all add up to a self-governing Kashmir having close relations with both its neighbours.

What shall be our response to this stand? That Kashmir is a closed chapter? That is easily said, but the next step will be none too easy. By common consent the 1962 elections in the State were far from fair or free. The demand for fresh elections cannot, therefore, be averted for long. Only last February Mr Lal Bahadur Shastri, Union Minister without Portfolio, observed that it was important that the people of Kashmir should be fully satisfied that 'they are being governed by those who are their truly elected representatives'. And what if the people return Sheikh Abdullah's men in a majority, as they, will in all probability? Repeal of Article 370 and all the rest of it will hardly help us if the State Assembly with a mandate from the people asks for a fundamental change in Kashmir's relationship with India. We shall once again be met with the choice between conciliation and repression. One is reminded here of Burke's memorable statement about the futility of the use of force, a people are not governed who are perpetually to be put down.

Nor can democratic India relish a situation in which it is at loggerheads with a determined section of the people. The one thread that runs through India's case as it has evolved over the years is that it is in the State by the consent of the people. Once that consent is clearly and manifestly withdrawn, a situation of the utmost danger to our national prestige and honour will arise. 'Ultimately the will of people will prevail', Mr Shastri remarked in the course of the same speech.

It should be the task of Indian statesmanship to avert that day. In this regard Sheikh Abdullah's release has not altered the situation as many think. It has only brought to the surface what was simmering within. The utter unreality of a situation which depended on the continued imprisonment of one man stands exposed.

In sum, it will not do to say come weal, come woe, my status is quo. If a change must come, far better that we mould it deliberately to accord with our interests than drift to an inevitability which ignores them.

Our interests in Kashmir are two-fold: the security and the peace of the sub-continent. We went there because both were in peril. We cannot accept any change which imperils either now. The interest of Kashmir is to have an order in which she is the master of her own house to as full a degree as her situation permits. Kashmir's great interest is also an end to the curse of uncertainty which has singled out her people. Pakistan's object is to have Kashmir if possible, or at least those links which will assuage the sense of injustice which has possessed her all these years.

All legitimate interests are reconcilable according to the old liberal creed. Every effort must be made to find a *modus vivendi* which achieves such a reconciliation.

It is here that Sheikh Saheb's statements assume great significance. Unlike in 1958, he no longer insists on a plebiscite as the only possible solution but is prepared for 'other methods'.

But it may be objected that Pakistan might not agree to such a solution even if India and Kashmir did. The record, happily, suggests otherwise. On 12 March 1960, the then Foreign Minister of Pakistan made a pronouncement which marked a radical break from his country's past stand on Kashmir. In an address to the Pakistan Institute of International Affairs, he said that if somebody has a solution 'other than ours, let him suggest it. We can at least start thinking about it.' Since then Pak spokesmen have consistently adhered to that line. It serves to tabulate the statements for they reveal a line which is of the utmost significance in the present context.

30 June 1960: Dr Raghu Vira, MP, said at New Delhi, after meeting President Ayub in Karachi, that the President no longer insisted on plebiscite as the only solution. Some other 'mutually acceptable' way could be found which could 'save the face' of both the countries.

22 March 1961: President Ayub said, 'If there is any other reasonable solution as would satisfy the people of Kashmir we should be prepared to listen.'

26 March 1961: Pak Foreign Minister Qadir at Calcutta said, 'In a mood of conciliation and for the sake of settlement', Pakistan was willing to consider fresh proposals acceptable to all the three parties.

8 July 1961: Lt.-Gen. K.M. told newsmen at New Delhi that Pakistan was prepared for a solution other than a plebiscite but such a suggestion should come from India.

What is this halfway house between the cease-fire line (with the Valley in Indian hands), totally rejected by Pakistan, and the plebiscite with the possibility of the Valley going to Pakistan? It can only be a Valley going to neither.

Pakistan's view that India should suggest such a proposal is understandable; for it to propose an independent Kashmir and be rebuffed is to lose all. The question is, should India accept such a compromise?

It will not disturb the peace of the sub-continent since there will be no pre-plebiscite propaganda. Nor is there any transfer of territory which would entail the movement of refugees. It boils down, simply, then to our security interests.

One can think of a particular form of independent Kashmir which will not affect our security interests. It lies in making the Valley and Azad Kashmir territory together independent as a whole, in the precise manner indicated here. India will retain the Jammu and Laddakh provinces, Pakistan only Gilgit and Hunza. The State of Kashmir so constituted will be neutralized by a treaty along the lines of the Austrian State Treaty foreclosing accession to either, such an event being deemed as a *casus belli*. The State will be fully independent but it will not have international representation. Being landlocked, it will be impossible to attack it without attacking India or Pakistan first. Defence being automatically assured by geography, foreign affairs lose their *raison d'etre*. There can thus be no fear of 'foreign intrigue'. Both neighbours will have communications with the State, India having the right of passage for her armed forces to Ladakh so long as a settlement of the border question is not concluded. For the rest, the State of Kashmir can have the fullest internal autonomy, very much like the State of Singapore under the Lim Yew Hock–Lenno Boyd agreement of April 1957 which remained in force till Singapore's merger with Malaysia. If the basic principles are accepted, the details can be filled in. There is nothing inherently impracticable about the plan. A UN guarantee can also be obtained. Unlike a condominium in which two parties join to administer a territory, here all that will be required will be a hands-off policy by both.

This suggestion is fully compatible with the interests of all the parties concerned. Neither side suffers a loss of face or hazards its interests. Azad Kashmir territory will be vacated by Pakistan and a reunited Kashmir personality will emerge.

There is every reason to believe that Pakistan will accept such a set-up. In a recent statement Mr Bhutto said that Sheikh Abdullah was the only leader acceptable to Kashmiris on either side of the cease-fire line and the best person to settle the Kashmir question in consultation with the Indian and Pakistani leaders. This is very significant, implying as it does a readiness to bypass the Azad Kashmir leaders who advocate accession to Pakistan and to deal with a politician whose constant refrain has been the development of Kashmir's separate personality.

There are those who constantly equate Pakistan and China. If you compromise with the former, what of the latter they ask. This is equation with a vengeance. Happily, Mr Nehru's outlook is different. 'I hope your disputes with Pakistan are more soluble than your disputes with China', a correspondent asked the Prime Minister at London on 17 March 1961. His reply was emphatic: 'Of course, that is patent. Between Pakistan and India whatever may happen, essentially they remain family disputes. We may be bitter against each other, but we are the same people who have lived together for hundreds of years. I think no doubt they will be solved.' Mr Nehru's reply to the Lok Sabha debate on the External Affairs Ministry's budget grants is the latest expression of the same approach. India must live in peace with its neighbours 'more particularly, Pakistan'.

Kashmir is in reality a part of the unfinished business of Partition and we shall fully settle down only when the dispute is resolved. This explains why any exacerbation of the controversy disturbs the minorities. The answer lies not in shutting our eyes to the grim reality but in facing it.

A settlement at this juncture will not be taking place as a result of international mediation or pressure. Any concession by India will not be represented as surrender, but as a response to the Sheikh's repeated appeals, as a clear act of grace.

Never were the auspices more favourable. Never again shall we have an opportunity such as this. General K.M. Cariappa reported very recently after meeting President Ayub, that he is eager to come to India and meet Mr Nehru to discuss Kashmir 'if India offered fresh alternative plans for resolving the Kashmir issue, if India ruled out the holding of plebiscite'.

The Nehru–Ayub communique of 29 November 1962, it is worth recalling, foreshadowed that after the ministerial talks, 'at the appropriate stage, direct talks will be held between Mr Nehru and President Ayub'. That stage has now been reached.

The recent and tragic history of this sub-continent has been a history of lost opportunities on the part of India and Pakistan. The latter missed an opportunity for accord in 1953 when it turned to the US. We missed an opportunity when President Ayub offered joint defence. Is history to repeat itself? If it does, posterity will say with Goethe, 'The century gave birth to a great epoch but the great moment found a petty generation.'

14. K. Radhakrishna's report of his visit to Sheikh Abdullah in internment, 1965

As was decided with J.P. and Vinobaji, both Narayan Desai and I interviewed Sheikh Abdullah on 6 and 7 October 1965 at Kodaikanal. Our interviews lasted for nearly ten hours and the discussions ranged from the historical aspects of the Kashmir issue to the present Indo–Pak conflict. Before leaving Delhi, we had a meeting with the Prime Minister, Lal Bahadur Shastri. We told him of our proposed visit to Sheikh Abdullah and delivered him a letter from J.P.

Sheikh Abdullah looked healthier than we had seen him last, although a slight swelling on the left foot was visible. Before leaving Madurai we spent some time with the Collector, Madurai and enquired about the physical comforts provided to the Sheikh. He has been moved to a bigger bungalow, the Kohinoor, which he previously used to occupy. This shifting was done on the day we met him, a few minutes before we had arrived. This was done at his own request as the earlier building had less accommodation and moving space. His posts are usually delayed, but the Collector promised us to arrange for prompt delivery. Arrangements have also been made to receive or transmit telegrams over wireless to Madurai. The south Indian newspapers are supplied to him as also journals he asks for. The Delhi papers had to be stopped because they took some days to reach him by post. He has also a radio and thus he is generally able to keep in touch with news through the radio and the press. Arrangements have also been made for medical aid and personal attendance.

The chief points regarding physical arrangements for him are:

1. If the period of his internment is to be prolonged indefinitely, he would like to be in Kashmir or near about from where he could look into his domestic affairs and his relatives also could occasionally meet him.

2. Recently [almost synchronizing with the cease-fire declaration] an order was served on him restricting his movements to the house only, while previously it was possible for him to go about in the town under police escort and under close supervision. This limits his movements and confines him to the compound. He pleads for a relaxation of the order so that he can move about as he used to do and also keep his physical frame in order.

The Chief Minister, Madras [C.M. Annadurai] explained to us that this order had to be issued to protect him from any possible violence by extremists or fanatic elements. As there is always a police guard and the war situation has considerably eased, this argument does not seem to hold much ground.

3. Begum Abdullah and his daughter Surayya who were with him till recently had to leave for Delhi. It was rumoured that there were direct and indirect hints that they might be asked to go; Sheikh Saheb himself therefore took the initiative and asked them to leave. The restrictions on the Begum need not be enforced particularly because she is a non-political figure. Further, the Sheikh also mentioned the question of a compensatory allowance for the family as he was the sole earning member. No decision seems to have been taken so far on this matter and the family is reported to be put to hardships.

We got the impression from the local authorities that the Sheikh was not at all a troublesome internee and got on fairly well with local officials.

We had free and frank discussions with him regarding the current political situation (without the interference of police officials). We reported to him the stand taken by J.P., Vinoba and the Sarva Seva Sangh on the Indo–Pak conflict. We also gave him a report which we had received about the pressure being exerted on Maulana Masoodi by the extremist elements in the Valley. We mentioned to him the investigations carried out by Vimala and Kulsum Sayani and the recent visit of Poorna Chandra Jain and other friends. The Sheikh's attitude might be summed up as under:

1. The Indian Government did not take advantage of the situation following the Sheikh's release; and the process of rethinking started by Jawaharlal Nehru towards the close of his life as well as the favourable climate created by the Shastri–Ayub meeting during October 1964 have been allowed to be

lost. On the contrary, the Governments have adopted the stiff line of achieving full integration (by persuasion if possible and by compulsion if necessary), thereby betraying the confidence of the people in Kashmir and reversing the process that was initiated in 1964. Over and above all this, now comes the oft-repeated slogan that there is no Kashmir problem; and it has been finally solved. This has only created further frustration, lack of confidence and a fear complex in the minds of the people.

2. As far as Pakistan is concerned, these steps taken by Delhi came as a breach of understanding reached in Karachi between Ayub and Shastri; and it appeared to them that all doors for the reopening of Kashmir issue and discussing or settling them in the light of understanding achieved or declarations made were slammed. The Kutch dispute, he feels, was an attempt to rake up the Kashmir question indirectly. Having failed in this effort, Pakistan supported and encouraged Azad Kashmir infiltrators so that the issue, deemed to have been closed by India, might again be raised in the international counsels. Although their action was violent and bordered on blackmail, Pakistan was left with no alternative in the situation created by India where all the openings for raising this issue were closed.

3. Thus, while tacitly admitting that Pakistan undertook unreasonable measures to force the issue, the Sheikh would not condemn them. In the first place, this situation has been forced by Indian intransigence. Secondly, the slogan which the Azad Kashmir infiltrators raised has been that of self-determination for the people in the face of Indian refusal to recognize the existence of the problem at all. ('How am I to sell this to my people', the Sheikh says, 'who have been given the promise and hope of self-determination?') He feels that it was good to be in jail during the Indo–Pak conflict as otherwise he would have been placed in a most embarrassing situation.

4. Any settlement of the Kashmir dispute, he repeats, should have the support and concurrence of India, Pakistan and the people of Kashmir. Both because of the existence of Azad Kashmir and the placing of the problem on international agenda, we cannot lose sight of the fact that Pakistan has not merely an interest but a stake in the Kashmir problem.

5. But in view of the Indo–Pak conflict, the Sheikh accepts that it would be wise for India to come to a settlement with the people of Kashmir unilaterally at the moment without invoking the Pakistan Government or the UN. He contends that it would only be thus that the Pakistani and international allegation that India has not honoured its pledge to the people of Kashmir and to the world, could be met. When normal relationships develop with Pakistan, as they must, a negotiated settlement that India reaches now with the people of Kashmir could be confirmed.

6. The initiative for the next move, in the Sheikh's opinion, rests now with the Government of India. Further negotiations could be started when the slogan that the problem does not exist at all is stopped; and sincere and

honest efforts are made to seek a solution of the problem according to the wishes of the people of Kashmir.

7. Such an action is necessary, in his view, not only because the conflict with Pakistan might not end for a considerable time (at least till the item is inscribed in the agenda of the UN Assembly and sufficient pressures are brought to bear upon India), but also for the fact that China is a strong contender for the leadership of Asia and has been cleverly conducting its diplomatic strategy and reducing India to a nearly friendless situation. The long-term consequences of the Chinese strategy for Asian leadership have to be carefully thought over and faced by cementing friendship with Pakistan. The question of our building up an armament potential to face both Pakistan and China at the cost of economic development of the country should be squarely faced.

8. With a change in the attitude of the Government of India, the Sheikh feels that it should be possible for him and other leaders of Kashmir to sit together with like-minded people outside the Government and consider solutions to the Kashmir problem under the changed context. No particular solution should be ruled out. The implications of all solutions should be fully worded out – as working papers – and the merits and demerits of each solution carefully weighed. This should further lead to a round-table conference with the leaders of the Government where a final solution might be reached. Such a solution will also have to be discussed with international powers and their concurrence also sought. When normal relationship with Pakistan is restored, the Government of Pakistan might be brought into the picture.

9. The Sheikh feels that the original proposal for referendum is no longer practical in the changed context. He was prepared to accept that de-accession was well-nigh impossible. The question of fullest regional autonomy should be examined, provided there are some guarantees that history will not repeat itself. This is a question which needs much serious consideration. The Sheikh was not unprepared to consider the question of his taking over the reins of government if need be.

10. For one who has spent more than eleven years in prison, the Sheikh spoke without any trace of bitterness. One could also notice in him a grim determination because, as he feels, he was fighting for accepted fundamental principles.

The following are some of the suggestions that have emerged out of our discussions with Sheikh Saheb:

1. Our first concern should be to help consolidation of the cease-fire line with honour to both the parties at the present moment. Both the countries are claiming military success and boosting public morale. Sooner or later, the hollowness of a military solution of the dispute should be evident.

2. An appeal to the Government of India and public to keep the Kashmir

situation fluid and not claim that it has been solved, should be made in the names of people like J.P., Vinoba, Rajaji and others after the cease-fire situation solidifies.

3. Simultaneously, we should ask for the release of Sheikh Abdullah and call for a round-table on Kashmir.

4. The Sarva Seva Sangh should take the initiative and call for a recon-sider-ation of India's foreign policy through a political seminar consisting of leading Sarvodaya workers and like-minded non-party public men.

Report provided by K. Radhakrishna of Gandhi Peace Foundation and an associate of Jayaprakash Narayan.

15. Jayaprakash Narayan's letter to Indira Gandhi, Sokhodewra, 23 June 1966

Dear Indiraji,

When I was in Delhi recently for a day, I learnt that you had asked Mr Sadiq and some of his colleagues to meet you on the 26th for a review of the Kashmir question. In view of the importance of that meeting, I am venturing to place before you some of my ideas in that connection. I hope I am not being a nuisance, and that you will not think I am trying to pressurize you.

The Kashmir question has plagued this country for nineteen years. It has cost us a great deal materially and spiritually. We profess democracy, but rule by force in Kashmir – unless we have auto-suggested ourselves into believing that the two general elections under Bakshi Saheb had expressed the will of the people, or that the Sadiq government is based on popular support except for a small minority of pro-Pakistan traitors. We profess secularism, but let Hindu nationalism stampede us into trying to establish it by repression.

Kashmir has distorted India's image in the world as nothing else has done. There is no nation in the world, not even Russia, which appreciates our Kashmir policy, though some of them might, for their own reasons, give us their support.

No matter how much and how loud and how long we doubt that Kashmir is an inalienable part of India and that, therefore, there is no Kashmir problem, the fact remains that a serious and urgent problem faces, and will continue to face, us in that part of the country.

That problem exists not because Pakistan wants to grab Kashmir, but because there is deep and widespread political discontent among the people. The people of India might be kept in the dark about the true state of affairs in the Valley, but every chancellory in New Delhi knows the truth, and almost every foreign correspondent. It would appear that all but our Intelligence know the facts; or, we too know the facts but do not wish to face them and hope that someone – maybe Sadiq Saheb or Qasim Saheb – might one day perform some miracle that would bring about a psychological revolution in the Valley.

Historical events, some without and some within our control, have narrowed down greatly the room for manoeuvrability that the Government of India may have now. For instance, any manner of de-accession of any part of the State is now impracticable – no matter how just or fair according to the principles of democracy and secularism. Whatever be the solution, it has to be found within the limitations of the accession.

It is here that Sheikh Saheb's role may become decisive. I have been pressing for his release not because he is a friend. Friendship, no doubt, counts in every human situation, but I hope I have enough moral discipline to allow without protest even my nearest and dearest one to be sent to the gallows if that were the demand of justice – I would have added 'and of national interest', had it not been for the fact that many times it is not possible to be sure what is in the national interest, and different persons, all equally patriotic, may have different interpretations of it in a given situation.

On this count too, let me say, it was not justice to have arrested and detained Sheikh Abdullah without giving him a chance to clear himself of the charges so wildly made against him. On his part, he had established his bonafides sufficiently by deciding to return to his country and answer his detractors.

Nor do I think that he is a traitor. Godse thought that Gandhiji was a traitor. The RSS thinks that Jayaprakash is a traitor. Godse was an individual, the RSS is a private organization; a democratic government represents the people and has principles and procedures according to which it functions. Nobody can be held to be a traitor by the Government of India unless it has been established in accordance with due process of law. If the government finds it difficult to do that, it is cowardly to use the DIR and continue to use it indefinitely, even when no palpable danger to the country's defence remains.

It was, I think, 'indiscreet' of Sheikh Saheb to have met Chou-en-Lai. But that is all that can be said about it. No fair-minded person would consider that as a treasonous act. When the Chinese had attacked in 1962, had he not written to the Prime Minister 'expressing our deep anguish'? Did he not, on 25 May 1964, publicly rebuke in Rawalpindi, Chaudhari Ghulam Abbas for having sought Chinese intervention? In London, did he not say at a press conference (*Times*, 19 March 1965) that China's claims on Ladakh were 'inadmissible'?

Much has been made of Sheikh's statements abroad. I doubt if, on an objective examination, those statements, as published in the foreign press and not their garbled versions in India, would amount to anything more than what he had been saying in India. I agree that it would have been better if Sheikh Saheb had spoken less and more guardedly. But Sheikh Saheb cannot be expected to be anything but himself – he just cannot keep quiet. This is a common failing of us Indians. Have not Union Cabinet members been speaking out of turn, not only in India but even abroad, even in Jawaharlalji's lifetime?

I would like to close this chapter with one more quotation from the Sheikh. Before he had left for his trip abroad this is what he had said at a farewell function at Constitution Club on 10 February 1965: 'We might have differences among ourselves. But after all India is the homeland of us all. If, God forbid, India ceases to be India and goes down, how can others be saved? We have to look at problems from that angle.'

But I have not been agitating for the Sheikh's release because he is a friend, or just because I am concerned about civil liberties. My primary concern in this matter has been to seek a solution of the Kashmir problem. As I see it, if there is any chance of this matter being settled, it is with the help of Sheikh Abdullah. I am not hundred per cent sure of this – no one can be. But the odds appear to me to be favourable enough to urge Sheikh Abdullah's unconditional release. An element of risk may be there, but there is risk in every big political or military decision, in fact in most human decisions, as even when two persons decide to wed.

Here may I digress a little? Nandaji seems to have told Shri R.K. Patil that Jayaprakash is 'completely out of touch with public sentiment' on the question of Kashmir and Sheikh Abdullah. I suspect that more of your colleagues are of that view. I, therefore, want to offer a few comments to clear the air – incidentally, that might help your colleagues to come to the right decision.

First of all, some people (mostly crypto-communists, and Hindu nationalists of all hues) have created a certain image of Jayaprakash Narayan – a silly idealist or a hidden traitor – and whatever that man says or does is twisted to fit that image. For instance, I am supposed to have advocated the giving away of Nagaland to the Nagas, Kashmir to the Pakistanis. I have never even remotely made any such suggestion. Even in the case of Aksai Chin, I had suggested a lease (an internationally recognized transaction and one that was agreed to by India in a recent Indo–Nepal deal). That lease too was suggested as a measure of give and take, i.e. if China agreed to India's counter demand, maybe in the Chumbi Valley or elsewhere along the 2500 miles of border. But having created a false image, it was easy for anyone to throw stones at it.

But that did not alienate Jayaprakash from public sentiments. Without appearing to be vain, I make bold to say that except for you personally, there is no one in your government who is as constantly and widely in touch with the people as I. Almost daily I address public meetings, and invariably my experience has been that I am heard in pin-drop silence, and afterwards people come to assure me that they had been completely misled and if that was what I meant, they were all for it. The only two meetings that were disturbed were in Delhi at the time of my visit to West Pakistan and the trouble-makers were RSS boys whose minds were closed. I am not saying that everyone who listens is persuaded, but I am saying that the views I propound – with frankness and sincerity – are far from being out of touch with public sentiments.

Lastly (on this digressive count), the leaders of this country are not doing justice to the people. It is the job of leaders to lead, but most of them are too timid and weak to speak out the truth, to advocate unpopular policies, and, if the need arose, to face the wrath of the people. For my part, I have faith in our people – they are sound and intelligent. If they are given all the facts, they can take the right decisions. May I say here, without appearing to flatter you, that by your recent bold decisions you have shown that you are attempting to give the people courageous leadership.

Returning to the main theme of this letter, why do I plead for Sheikh Saheb's release? Because that may give us the only chance we may have of solving the Kashmir problem. Why? Because, in the event of the Government of India reaching an agreement with him about the future status of Kashmir – which will have to be within the limits of accession – the Sheikh is the only Kashmiri leader who could swing Muslim opinion in the Valley towards his side. I believe it is obvious that the farthest that any status within the Indian Union can go is full internal autonomy, i.e. a return to the original terms of the accession.

Several questions arise at this point. Will Sheikh Saheb agree to any such status? If he did, would he succeed in persuading the Kashmiris to rally round him? Would not autonomous Kashmir, sooner or later, attempt to secede from the Union?

Nandaji tries to cloud the whole issue by asking for proof that the Sheikh's thinking has changed. Earlier, he seemed to think otherwise. Referring to the interview of Shri Radhakrishna and Shri Narayan Desai with Sheikh Saheb, Nandaji had stated in the Rajya Sabha on 26 November 1965, that the Sarvodaya leaders' meeting had produced a 'very positive reaction'.

Be that as it may, all this talk of the Sheikh not having changed appears puerile to me. Keeping people in jail is not the best way of inducing them to be more malleable. Nandaji should have learnt that much from his own experience in British Indian prisons.

Moreover, supposing the Sheikh were released in a fanfare of official propaganda about the Sheikh having changed, would an iota be left of his political utility for India? After that if the Sheikh were to arrive in Srinagar, would the crowds be chanting 'Sher-i-Kashmir Zindabad' or 'Bharat ka Pithu Murdabad'? What chance would he have of persuading the Kashmiris to become good Indian citizens? All this is so obvious that it is amazing that the Home Minister is unable to see it.

On the contrary, I am sure that on his release Sheikh Saheb would again reiterate the right of the Kashmiris to decide their future; he would again declare that the accession was not final and that the so-called general elections had not expressed the people's will. We should have maturity enough to understand that and not to denounce him as a Pakistani agent. He can never hope to persuade the Kashmiris to accept an autonomous position within India if he did not make it clear that it was they and not anybody else who was to take that decision. Instead of that, if he came out and declared that the issue had been settled already when he was in prison by the Kashmir Constituent Assembly and the two general elections that followed, his voice would carry no more weight than that of Bakshi Saheb did or of Sadiq Saheb does.

The more important question is, how would Sheikh Abdullah want the Kashmiris to 'decide their future'? I am sure not by a plebiscite. Then how? One way, and the best in the circumstances, would be to let the people decide at the general election in 1967. The Sheikh could do that by fighting the election on the basis of his agreement with the Government of India (envisaged above). Could the Kashmiri people be enthused over autonomy within the Union? I think they could, by Sheikh Saheb frankly telling them that was the only way they could save themselves from self-destruction as a result of their territory becoming a battle-ground for India and Pakistan; that if it could be shown that they had taken that decision freely at an election run by their genuine leaders (like himself) and that Pakistan would have no ground left to interfere in their affairs; that it was the best way to bring about Indo–Pak amity, that they would be rid of the overbearing Indian police and enjoy full freedom to order their lives as they liked. If all that were put across to the people by one in whom they had trust, I have every hope that they would acquiesce willingly.

I may be asked, what ground have I for believing that Sheikh Abdullah would accept autonomy within India? Part of the argument I had given in a press statement, which had received your and your government's notice at the time. I reproduce it below:

> It has been known these many years that Sheikh Saheb has been resolutely against Kashmir being merged with Pakistan. He did, no doubt, entertain ideas of some kind of an independent Kashmir; but I believe he is realist enough to realize that
>
> (a) no solution of the Kashmir question could ever be accepted by India, after the last war with Pakistan, that involved de-accession of the State, or any part of it, from the Union; and
>
> (b) an independent State in that part of the world could have little chance of survival in face of Pakistan's consuming hunger for the valley of Kashmir and the emergence of Chinese power in the region – a power that cannot be

expected to exercise self-denial in relation to its weak neighbours.

In addition to the above argument, I have this to say. Sheikh Saheb had told Narayan and Radhakrishna that he would be prepared even to accept the status of full internal autonomy for Kashmir, provided history were not allowed to repeat itself. By that he meant, provided the autonomy was not gradually whittled down and the Centre did not interfere in the State's internal affairs.

The last evidence I have is the report of Gul Shah, of which J.J. has already apprised you fully.

I grant that my case is not fool-proof. But no case can be. Nandaji's own case is far from it. To hold a general election in Kashmir with Sheikh Abdullah in prison is like the British ordering an election in India while Jawaharlal Nehru was held in prison. No fair-minded person would call it a fair election. Nor would that election settle any political issue more than the two earlier ones did. And if we miss the chance of using the next general election to win the consent of the people to their place within the Union, I cannot see what other device will be left to India to settle the problem. To think that we will eventually wear down the people and force them to accept at least passively the Union is to delude ourselves. That might conceivably have happened had Kashmir not been geographically located where it is. In its present location, and with seething discontent among the people, it would never be left in peace by Pakistan. China is bound sooner or later to take a hand in the sport of fishing in troubled waters. With the issue settled to the satisfaction of the great majority of the people, the external mischief makers would not find a favourable soil for sowing their mischief. Internationally, India's prestige would soar. No reasonable government would then be able to point an accusing finger at us.

Another question may be asked: will Sheikh Abdullah negotiate with the Government of India to the exclusion of Pakistan? Well, he told the two Sarvodaya friends that in the light of the Indo–Pak war and its consequences, he was quite prepared to have bilateral talks with India. He called that the 'first stage', meaning thereby that later on Pakistan would have to be brought into the picture and persuaded to accept the compact made between him and Government of India. I see nothing offensive in this approach. Sooner or later Pakistan's support to any real settlement in Kashmir will have to be obtained, so that the ceasefire line might be normalized (rationalized?), disengagement of the armed forces of the two countries could be secured and the tension between the two countries, with its terrible effect on Kashmir, might be eased. Instead of resenting Sheikh Saheb anxiety to secure Pakistan's acceptance of his compact with India, we should ourselves take the initiative and use his good offices in the manner found feasible.

I am sorry to have inflected on you such a long letter. But I felt it was my duty to my country to put these thoughts before you and your colleagues.

With kindest regards,

Yours sincerely,
Jayaprakash Narayan

From *Jayaprakash Narayan: Selected Works*, edited by Bimal Prasad, Vol. 9, Delhi: Manohar Publications, 1964: 46–52.

16. Jayaprakash Narayan's associate Narayan Desai's visit to Kashmir

Some points discussed with Mirza Afzal Beg at his residence in Anantnag on 2 and 5 October 1967.

1. Beg had expressed his earnest desire to meet the President, Prime Minister or the Home Minister of India regarding the present situation in Kashmir. Unfortunately the interview was not granted.

2. The situation in Kashmir was grave and it was worsening every day. Some members of the Plebiscite Front had started grumbling that communal harmony was not a one way traffic. Shri Beg was, however, determined to maintain communal harmony in the state. 'It could be disrupted only on our dead bodies' he said. Hindu–Muslim unity was an article of faith to him.

3. Long before the General Elections this year, he had expressed his willingness to consider participation in them, provided proper care was taken to assure the fairness of the election. This he thought could have been possible if the Government of India had accepted his proposal to hold the elections under the direct supervision of any one of the following personalities:

(a) Shri Vinoba Bhave,
(b) Dr Zakir Hussaini,
(c) Shri J.P. Narayan.

This proposal was sent through some special agency. Shri Beg did not know what happened to it.

4. He simply could not understand the Government of India's inaction about the situation in Kashmir.

5. The security of the State should not be left in the hands of the Special Reserve Police coming from different states of the country, nor in the hands of the CRP. A 'Kashmir Militia' should be raised, reflecting the different communities of the State in it and it should have some south Indian general at its command [*sic*]. It would be more desirable if some Muslim general could be found for this purpose.

6. In order to restore confidence among Muslims and prepare the ground for communal harmony, he felt that some sort of compensatory measures

should be immediately taken. He suggested the following as examples:

(a) Immediate compensation to be offered to Muslims in Jammu whose shops had been either destroyed or looted;
(b) Visit by Hindu leaders to the mosque and expressing their regrets at the destruction caused by violent mobs;
(c) Similar visits by Muslim leaders where damage was done to Hindu temples;
(d) Expression of regret regarding communal disturbances by Hindu and Muslim leaders at joint meetings;
(e) Inquiry should be made about the incidents at Jammu and Baramulla.

7. The immediate release of Sheikh Mohammed Abdullah was long overdue. 'Never in my life', he said, 'have I craved so much for his release as I do today.' Beg thought that Sheikh was the person who might be able to save the situation even now.

8. Communally fanatic papers like 'The Organizer' and 'Milap' should be banned from entering the Valley.

9. Inquiry should be ordered on the communally provocative posters said to have been seized at the customs office.

10. Restrictions on his [Sheikh Abdullah's] free movements should be lifted.

17. Record of Narayan Desai's conversation with Chief Minister Ghulam Mohammed Sadiq at his office in Srinagar, on 3 October 1967

1. The situation in the state was rather serious. It had taken a communal turn for the first time in history.

2. All efforts should be made to maintain communal harmony in the state. He [Sadiq] thought that the peace committees formed in the state were doing good work in this direction, but they should be more active in the future. He thought the majority of the members of the peace committees were non-party men.

3. Sadiq would welcome the release of Sheikh Mohammed Abdullah and discuss the question of Kashmir over a conference table, provided the Sheikh was prepared not to involve Pakistan into the picture.

4. Sadiq hesitated in commenting regarding the behaviour of the Special Reserve Police and the CRP in the state. But he felt that the clash between the CRP and the J&K Police had been unfortunate. He felt that even if the J&K Police had committed certain excesses the CRP could not take the law in its own hands. There could have been an inquiry on the alleged excesses

of the J&K Police. He favoured the idea of raising the Kashmir security force.

5. He assured support to the Shanti Sena Centre at Mendhar and had no objection in starting new centres in the Valley. The following discussion followed:

Narayan: Why only 'no objection'? Why not fullest support?

Sadiq: That is because some of you are interested in the Kashmir politics.

Narayan: Do you mean J.P.?

Sadiq: Not only him, but also others.

Narayan: Our view about Kashmir politics are clear. We do not think that the Kashmir problem is a closed one. We think it is an open question and ultimately it has to be settled between the people of Kashmir and the Government of India. We believe that Pakistan has forefeited rights, if at all she had any, of participation in the discussion on this problem, after her second aggression in 1965. Although our work is absolutely apolitical and meant for the service of the society, I must say we do have these political views. Would you still maintain your position of 'no objection'?

Sadiq: If that is your politics, then not only 'no objection' but you are assured of my support.

6. Narayan sought Shri Sadiq's support in the Gandhi Centenary programme and expressed his surprise at the absence of Congress leaders at the Gandhi Jayanti meeting. Sadiq expressed his personal apology for not having been present at the meeting and promised to give some more time to the Gandhi Centenary committee deliberations.

7. Narayan expressed his hope of being permitted to see Maulana Mohammed Saeed Masoodi when he came next to Srinagar. Sadiq showed his willingness to grant the permission.

18. Sheikh Abdullah's talks with T.N. Kaul in 1967–68: the rival versions

18(a). T.N. Kaul's record of the meetings of 10, 12 and 30 October 1967

Top Secret
Ministry of External Affairs
I had written a short letter to Sheikh Abdullah on the 3 October 1967 through the Deputy Commissioner, Delhi, enquiring about his health and asking whether I could call on him at some mutually convenient time. He got my letter on the 7th and replied the next day that he would be glad to have me for tea on 10 October. I have known Sheikh Abdullah since my student days in Kashmir and wanted to pay a purely courtesy call on him.

2. The Deputy Commissioner was good enough to send the ADM, Shri V.K. Kapoor, and Shri Marwaha of the police to take me to see Sheikh Abdullah on 10 October. They were present during my meeting with Sheikh Abdullah and I explained to the Sheikh that this was a purely personal and courtesy call and not an official call and should not be divulged to the press. Sheikh Abdullah smiled and told me that I was an old friend and there was no question of anyone talking to the press about our meeting.

3. We then went to the dining room and had tea there. The Sheikh looked quite healthy and I complimented him on his health and cheerfulness. He gave me a long history about his illness and the present state of his health.

4. I then asked him how he looked at the world situation. At first he tried to evade the question and said that it was difficult for him to take an objective view because he had not moved outside his house and he did not think newspapers or the radio gave correct reports. He, therefore, did not wish to be subjective in his approach to things. (Incidentally, he mentioned that during the 1965 Indo–Pak conflict, he had been confined to a single room and that had affected his health and blocked his imagination, but he was feeling much better now after coming to Delhi. He played badminton and went for walks, but had to be careful about his diet.)

5. After further probing Sheikh Abdullah said that the Chinese policy seemed to be getting more and more dangerous. China wanted to dominate the whole of Asia and felt that India was the main stumbling block in her ambitions. That was the reason why China had entered into an agreement with Pakistan against India. Pakistan probably saw in such an alliance a counter to her fear of India. Although this fear may be unrealistic there were many elements in Pakistan who felt that India had not reconciled herself to the fact of Partition. Certain elements in India also encouraged this feeling. Jammu and Kashmir, under his leadership, had voluntarily acceded to India without any pressure or inducement from India. The Kashmiris believed in 1947 that they had much more in common with Gandhi's and Nehru's India than with Pakistan. In spite of Hindu–Muslim massacres in the rest of India and even in areas of Jammu and Poonch, in the Kashmir Valley there had been perfect harmony between Hindus and Muslims. He had insisted in October 1947 that we should liberate the whole of Kashmir and not stop at Uri. Unfortunately, Panditji had overruled this. Even in the Security Council he had advocated that we should merely ask Pakistan not to allow facilities to the raiders to enter Kashmir and should ask them to facilitate their withdrawal. Unfortunately he was again overruled, and unnecessarily we entered into a long discussion with Pakistan in the Security Council.

6. Sheikh Abdullah had then suggested to the Prime Minister that a Constituent Assembly should be called in Kashmir to finally ratify the accession to India, but Panditji had discouraged this because he felt it would go against the Security Council's resolution. Panditji had declared to the whole world that the Act of Accession was provisional and would be subject to final

ratification by the people of Jammu and Kashmir. Later on Panditji wanted the accession ratified by the Constituent Assembly, but Sheikh Abdullah found it difficult to go back on what he had told his people earlier in accordance with Panditji's wishes, i.e. that accession would be subject to ratification by the people through a plebiscite.

7. Sheikh Abdullah had tried against very heavy odds to increase the revenues of the State and to give it a clean and efficient administration. He had taken the wind out of the sails of the Communists by introducing land reforms and setting up Debt Conciliation Boards. However, the vested landed interests and moneyed people did not like this and started corrupting his colleagues like Bakshi Ghulam Mohammad, Sham Lal Saraf and others. When he asked Sham Lal Saraf to resign because of allegations of corruption against him, Bakshi Ghulam Mohammad opposed this because he feared that he would be the next man to be asked to go. They carried false tales to Delhi and got an order issued for the Sheikh's arrest on the trumped-up charge that he was going to Gulmarg to contact the Pakistanis. Actually he was going to Gulmarg with three of his personal staff who were Kashmiri Pandits, J.K. Zutshi, R.K. Naina and one other – and there was absolutely no truth in the allegations made against him. However, he submitted to this gross injustice, quietly and without any protest, in the hope and belief that truth would come to light one day. When he met Panditji after his release, the latter told him that he was very sorry about the whole thing and the Sheikh replied, 'Let us forget the past and look to the future.'

8. With Panditji's blessings he went to Pakistan in 1964 and persuaded Ayub Khan to have a meeting with Panditji in order to bring about a peaceful and honourable settlement that would strengthen the secularism of India and at the same time provide a basis for improving Indo–Pak relations. The Sheikh did not wish anything to be done that would harm India or India's secular policy. Unfortunately Panditji passed away and the Sheikh's plans could not materialize. After Panditji's death, he said, there appeared to be a change in policy, mainly due to the pressure put by the then Home Minister (Shri Nanda) on the new Prime Minister (Shri Lal Bahadur Shastri). He was given a passport and allowed to go abroad. His statements in London were distorted and misreported to India. He had spoken to Dr Jivaraj Mehta about this and asked him to give the correct version to his Government, but the Indian press had already created the wrong impression that the Sheikh was doing anti-Indian propaganda abroad. He was not even allowed to complete his Haj pilgrimage and was asked to return. He had been offered passport and asylum by a number of countries, including Pakistan, but he refused all such offers and returned to India inspite of the fact that he had been warned that he might be arrested on landing in India. If he really had any designs of working against India, he would not have returned to India. He was not even given an opportunity to explain his activities abroad and was kept under detention. However, he felt no bitterness about

it at all except a little sorrow that things had been allowed to drift in Kashmir and the situation grew from bad to worse. He had faith in God and in his people. He still believed that Indian secularism should be strengthened and India's larger interests should not be harmed in any way. At the same time he felt that the gradual whittling of Article 370 of the Constitution with regard to Kashmir was unfortunate. It showed a lack of faith in secularism and the ability of Hindus and Muslims in Kashmir to get along with each other. He did not know what the future held in store for him, but he had his ideals and his faith.

9. I had to take his leave at this juncture although he wanted to talk more, because I had an appointment with the Burmese delegation. He said he would like to see me again and invited me to come for dinner on 12 October. I told him that it would not be possible for me to come for dinner, but I would like to see him again without any other persons being present. He readily agreed.

T.N. Kaul
11.10.1967

Strictly Personal and Very Confidential

I met Sheikh Abdullah on 10 October at his residence for one hour and a half; the Additional District Magistrate, Shri V.K. Kapoor, and Superintendent of Police, Shri V.P. Marwaha, were also present. Sheikh Abdullah's daughters and some relatives were also present.

2. I explained to Sheikh Saheb that this was a purely personal and private call and not an official call and should not be divulged to the press. He told me that I was an old friend and there was no question of anyone talking to the Press about our meeting.

3. I complimented Sheikh Saheb on his health and cheerfulness. He told me about his past illness and the present state of his health.

4. I then asked him how he looked at the world situation. He said it was difficult for him to take an objective view because he had not moved outside his house and he did not think newspapers or the radio gave correct reports. He therefore did not wish to be subjective in his assessment. I told Sheikh Saheb that there was always a subjective element in one's assessment and I would be glad to hear of his assessment of the world situation.

5. Sheikh Saheb replied that the world situation seemed to be getting worse and worse. Chinese policy appeared to be getting more dangerous. China wanted to dominate the whole of Asia and felt that India was the main stumbling block in her ambitions. That was the reason why China entered into an agreement with Pakistan against India. As for Pakistan, she saw in such an alliance a counter to her fear of India. I told Sheikh Saheb that this fear was unrealistic because India had no designs on Pakistan's territory and had accepted the partition as final. Sheikh Saheb replied that although this fear might be unrealistic, there were many elements in Paki-

stan who felt that India had not reconciled herself to the fact of Partition. Certain elements in India also encouraged this feeling. Jammu and Kashmir, under his leadership, had voluntarily acceded to India without any pressure or inducement from India. The Kashmiris believed in 1947 that they had much more in common with Gandhi's and Nehru's India than with Pakistan. In spite of Hindu–Muslim massacres in the rest of India and even in areas of Jammu and Pooneh, there had been perfect harmony between Hindus and Muslims in the Kashmir Valley. He had insisted in 1947 that we should liberate the whole of Kashmir and not stop at Uri. Unfortunately, Panditji had overruled him. Even in the Security Council Sheikh Saheb had advocated that we should merely ask Pakistan not to allow facilities to the raiders to enter Kashmir and should ask them to facilitate their withdrawal. Unfortunately he was again overruled and unnecessarily we entered into a long discussion with Pakistan in the Security Council.

6. Sheikh Abdullah proceeded to say that he had then suggested to the Prime Minister that a Constituent Assembly should be called in Kashmir to finally ratify the accession to India, but Panditji had discouraged this because he felt it would go against the Security Council's resolution, Panditji had declared to the whole world that the Act of Accession was provisional and would be subject to final ratification by the people of Jammu and Kashmir.

7. Sheikh Abdullah said he had tried against very heavy odds to increase the revenues of the state and to give it a clean and efficient administration. He had taken the wind out of the sails of the communists by introducing land reforms and setting up Debt Conciliation Boards. However, the vested landed interests and moneyed people did not like this and started corrupting his colleagues like Bakshi Ghulam Mohammad, Sham Lal Saraf and others. When he asked Sham Lal Saraf to resign because of allegations of corruption against him, Bakshi Ghulam Mohammad opposed this because he feared that he would be the next man to be asked to go. They had carried false tales to Delhi and got an order issued for Sheikh Saheb's arrest on the trumped up charge that he was going to Gulmarg to contact the Pakistanis. Actually he was going to Gulmarg with three of his personal staff who were Kashmiri Pandits and there was absolutely no truth in the allegations made against him. However, he submitted to this gross injustice quietly and without any protest, in the hope and belief that truth would come to light one day. When he met Panditji after his release, the latter told him that he was very sorry about the whole thing and Sheikh Saheb replied 'Let us forget the past and look to the future'.

8. With Panditji's blessings he went to Pakistan in 1964 and persuaded Ayub Khan to have a meeting with Panditji in order to bring about a peaceful and honourable settlement, that would strengthen the secularism of India and at the same time provide a basis for improving Indo–Pak relations. Sheikh Saheb said he did not wish to do anything that would harm

India or India's secular policy. Unfortunately, Panditji had passed away and Sheikh Sahab's plans could not materialise.

9. After Panditji's death, he said, there appeared to be a change in policy. However, he was given a passport and allowed to go abroad. His statements in London were distorted and mis-reported to India. He had spoken to Dr Jivraj Mehta about this and asked him to give the correct version to the Government of India, but the Indian press had already created a wrong impression that he was doing anti-Indian propaganda abroad. He was not even allowed to complete his Haj pilgrimage and was asked to return. He had been offered passport and asylum by a number of countries, including Pakistan, but he refused all such offers and returned to India in spite of the fact that he had been warned that he might be arrested on landing in India. If he really had any designs of working against India, he would not have returned to India. He was not even given an opportunity to explain his activities abroad and was immediately on his arrival kept under detention. However, he felt no bitterness about it at all except a little sorrow that things had been allowed to drift in Kashmir and the situation had grown from bad to worse. He had faith in God and in his people. He still believed that Indian secularism should be strengthened and India's larger interests should not be harmed in any way. At the same time he felt that the gradual whittling of Article 370 of the Constitution with regard to Kashmir was unfortunate. It showed a lack of faith in secularism and the ability of Hindus and Muslims to get along with each other. He did not know what the future held in store for him, but he had his ideals and his faith.

10. I thanked Sheikh Saheb for his frankness and expressed my appreciation of his faith in secularism in the larger interests of India. I asked if I could come and see him again and be said he would be glad to meet me.

Top Secret

After consulting Home Secretary and Home Minister, I accepted Sheikh Abdullah's invitation to meet him on 12 October 1967. I was with him for two hours from 7 to 9 p.m. He insisted on my having dinner with him, but I excused myself as I had another engagement that evening.

2. This time we were alone and Sheikh Abdullah spoke more concretely than on 10 October. The main points he made are:

(1) He stood by all he had said before his arrest in June 1953. He had not changed in any way, but circumstances in Kashmir had changed. There was a pro-Pakistani element there and there were separatist trends in Jammu Province which was dominated by the Jan Sangh and also in Ladakh. Besides this, in the rest of India also, secular forces were getting weaker and communal forces were getting stronger. What had happened in Ranchi was bound to have some effect in Kashmir. He did not know whether the Central Government was strong and determined enough to crush the forces of communalism and strengthen those of secularism. He said that the present

communal trouble in Kashmir had been aggravated by the speech of Shri Balraj Madhok who, according to him, had been responsible for inciting scores of murders of Muslims in the Jammu Province in the past.

(2) Kashmir was not like any other State of India, but held a special position, which was recognized in Article 370 of the Constitution. However, this special position had been eroded and in spite of the guarantees he had been arrested without any cause or justification in 1953. The people of Kashmir had lost faith in the sanctity of Article 370 and would ask for firmer guarantees about the autonomy of the State.

(3) Shri Jayaprakash Narayan had some time ago suggested to him that Kashmir should go back to her autonomous status at the time of accession, but Sheikh Abdullah wondered whether this was possible now in view of –

a) The opposition from Jammu province which wanted complete integration with the rest of India;
b) Opposition from Ladakh which wanted to become a separate Union territory; and
c) Opposition from pro-Pakistani elements and the Plebiscite Front in Kashmir itself.

He said that before he could accept such a proposition, Government must consider these three points and make up their mind whether they can deal with them effectively.

3. In passing, Sheikh Abdullah said that the people had lost faith in the word of the Government and even the Princes were losing faith because of the talk of doing away with Privy Purses and their privileges.

4. When I asked Sheikh Abdullah what, in his opinion, was a possible solution of the Kashmir problem, he suggested:

(1) Government should put the problem before a small body of leaders of public opinion whose patriotism and loyalty are unquestionable. He did not suggest any names. Such a body could go into the various implications and suggest a solution that should be accepted by Government. Government could include in this body some leaders of the opposition parties, if necessary. When I insisted on Sheikh Abdullah giving his own idea as to what such a body could recommend, he was disinclined to be drawn into a detailed discussion. However, he indicated that in his view if such a body recommended going back to the pre-1953 position and giving autonomy to Kashmir, such a solution might still be workable. However, there would have to be firm guarantees that Government would not whittle down Article 370 as it had done.

(2) He said some bitter things about the suppression of democratic liberty and freedom in Kashmir. He said that the CRP and BSF were treating the people of Kashmir as if it was a colony of India. He conceded that the presence of the Army was necessary to protect Kashmir against external threats, but he did not see any necessity for large scale presence of CRP and BSF for maintaining internal law and order. Their presence showed that the Govern-

ment of India did not trust the people of Kashmir. When I told the Sheikh that Kashmir Police had many pro-Pakistani and communal elements, and it behaved rather badly during the recent Kashmiri Pandits agitation, he admitted this and said the remedy was to remove such elements from the Kashmir administration and not to bring in similar elements from outside Kashmir. He affirmed that relations between Kashmiri Pandits and Kashmiri Muslims had always been cordial; a Kashmiri Brahmin girl always had a Kashmiri Muslim foster mother and foster brother in whose hands her honour was safe. This was true till recently, but now the atmosphere in Kashmir had been poisoned by the inefficiency of the local Government, corruption and nepotism of the administration and lack of a clear and far-sighted policy by the Centre. I told the Sheikh Saheb that the question of Kashmir was not merely a question of four million Kashmiris but involved the fate of fifty-five million Muslims in the rest of India and peace in the whole sub-continent. He agreed with me and said he was prepared to do his bit provided the Government had confidence in him and gave him full trust and support and did not treat him like they had in the past. He said he had confidence in the bona fides of the Prime Minister, but he was not sure whether other elements in the political parties would support her in any reasonable solution of the Kashmir question. I told him that the reaction in India was mainly due to the hostile criticism and propaganda in Pakistan. Conditions in the Pakistan-occupied Kashmir were much worse than in any part of India and in spite of Kashmir being a border State, there was considerable freedom and democratic liberty there. Sheikh Abdullah admitted this but said that India was gradually slipping into the same communal atmosphere that prevailed in Pakistan. Unless this trend was stopped effectively, Muslims in Kashmir would lose faith in India. I asked Sheikh Saheb to bear in mind that the Kashmir problem was one to be settled between the Kashmiris and the rest of India. No third party had any locus standi in it. No Government of India could afford to make any concessions on Kashmir to Pakistan nor was an independent Kashmir possible because its independence would not last more than a few days – it would only benefit China and neither India nor Pakistan. Sheikh Saheb did not contradict this, but said he would like to talk further on these matters. As it was getting late, I took leave of him and said I would come again. He insisted on my having a meal with him next time.

5. My general impression as a result of the two talks I had with Sheikh Abdullah is as under:

(a) He has probably realized that an independent Kashmir is out of the question – neither India nor Pakistan want it.

(b) He has also realized that no Government of India can afford to give the Valley to Pakistan. He has also realized that this would weaken secularism in India and the position of fifty-five million Muslims in the rest of India.

(c) Sheikh Abdullah is probably reconciled to the idea of autonomous Kashmir within the Indian Union, but with proper guarantees and safeguards against whittling down the autonomy.

(d) Sheikh Abdullah is not quite sure whether he will be able to take the people of Kashmir along with him if he gets a chance to resume his leadership and wants an assurance in advance that he will have the full support and confidence of the Government of India.

(e) He is not sure that the Congress Party alone can solve the Kashmir problem and probably has apprehensions that even the Congress Government at the Centre may change after some time. He would, therefore, like an all party assurance or solution of some sort to be evolved in order to support and strengthen the Government's stand on any reasonable solution of the Kashmir question.

(f) Sheikh Abdullah is not bitter but sad. It will not be easy to deal with him if he resumes leadership of Kashmir again. He will make demands which will not be easy to satisfy, e.g. removal of CRP and BSF. But it is possible that once he sees the reality of the situation he may become more pragmatic and reasonable. Since Mir Sadiq himself has said publicly that he is not against the release of Sheikh Abdullah, it may be worth while considering this step after having some further talks with him and making it clear to him that Government of India cannot accept any solution which gives out the valley of Kashmir. It would perhaps be worthwhile for PM or Home Minister to invite Sheikh Abdullah for a meal and to have a quiet, friendly exchange of ideas with him. I got the feeling that although he was very free and frank with me, because I have known him for the last thirty-six years, he was still holding back his final cards which he will probably reveal only to the Prime Minister.

(T.N. Kaul)
12.10.1967

Strictly Personal and Very Confidential
Record of talk with Sheikh Abdullah on 12.10.1967

I met Sheikh Saheb alone, this time for about two hours (from 7 to 9 p.m.). Sheikh Saheb said that he had given me a general appreciation of his own views and asked what my views were. I told him that I was speaking purely in my personal capacity and not on behalf of the Government. It was my belief that it was vital for peace and harmony in India and on the Indian sub-continent to strengthen India's secular base and not to allow any chance to the forces of communalism to gain strength. It was, I believed, the firm opinion of the political leaders of India that Kashmir, being a symbol of India's secularism, should remain an integral part of India. Therefore, any solution of the Kashmir question must be sought within the framework of the Indian Constitution.

2. Sheikh Saheb said that he stood by all he had said before his arrest in

June 1953. He had not changed in any way, but circumstances in Kashmir had changed. There was a pro-Pakistan element there and there were separatist trends in Jammu Province which was dominated by the Jana Sangh, and also separatist trends in Ladakh. Besides this, in the rest of India also secular forces were getting weaker and communal forces were getting stronger. It was disappointing and sad that after an experience of twenty years there was a wide gulf between the precepts and performance of the Indian leaders. Sheikh Saheb described his own personal experiences in this regard as to how the Indian national leadership was responsible for weakening the secular base of India by conniving at and sometimes even encouraging the communal forces in India. Some eminent columnists had even stated that a large number of persons believing in communal politics had penetrated into the Congress ranks at various levels. Even after the lapse of twenty years frequent communal riots in different parts of India were taking place in which the Muslim minority was generally the worst sufferer. What happened recently in Ranchi was a sad commentary on Indian secularism in practice. He said that the present communal trouble in Kashmir had been aggravated by the speech of Mr Balraj Madhok. Hs asked how was it possible under such circumstances to convince the Muslims of Kashmir that India was secular and their life and honour were safe there?

3. Sheikh Saheb said that Kashmir was not like any other State of India, but held a special position which was recognized in Article 370 of the Constitution. However, this special position had been eroded and in spite of these guarantees he had been arrested without any cause or justification in 1953. Shri Jayaprakash Narayan had some time ago suggested to him that Kashmir should go back to her autonomous status at the time of accession, but Sheikh Saheb wondered whether this was possible now in view of:

(a) The opposition from Jammu Province which wanted complete integration with the rest of India;
(b) Opposition from Ladakh which wanted to become a separate Union territory; and
(c) Opposition from pro-Pakistani elements in Kashmir itself.

He said that before such a proposition could be accepted Government must consider these three points and make up their mind whether they can deal with them effectively.

4. Sheikh Saheb said that his past experience had convinced him that the salvation of the people of Kashmir and peace and progress of the people of India and Pakistan lay in the establishment of firm understanding and friendship between the two neighbours. This, however, was not possible so long as the main dispute between them over Kashmir remained unresolved. Sheikh Saheb felt that in his opinion the disposal of the Valley was the crux of the problem and no solution will be acceptable to Pakistan which would give the Valley to India. I told Sheikh Saheb that Pakistan had no locus standi in the problem. No Government of India could agree to give independence to

the Valley or to give it to Pakistan. If there was agreement between the Government of India and the people of Kashmir, Pakistan would have to accept any such arrangement. Sheikh Saheb said in his judgment India had largely contributed to the bitterness in Pakistan and when President Ayub took over control of Pakistan he was very keen to settle all disputes with India and at one time he even offered to have joint defence. It was because of the keenness on his part that some ticklish problems like the Indus water, etc. between the two countries which had existed for a long time were successfully resolved. Pandit Nehru had rejected Ayub's offer of joint defence and did not respond to his overtures for a solution of Kashmir problem. The Pakistanis felt that India had not yet reconciled herself to the existence of Pakistan and some irresponsible utterances by leaders of some communal organizations in India off and on had lent support to this feelings.

5. I told Sheikh Saheb that his analysis was not quite correct. Pandit Nehru had been more than reasonable towards Pakistan. He had unilaterally declared that India would not use force to recover Pakistan-occupied Kashmir. He had even informally suggested internationalizing the ceasefire line with minor modifications, However, there had been no positive response from Pakistan to all these moves. On the contrary, Pakistan had entered into a provisional agreement with China giving away 2500 square miles of Indian territory in Kashmir to China. That had completely changed the situation, The 1965 aggression by Pakistan had further changed the situation. However, India was keen to improve relations with Pakistan but not at the expense of Kashmir or her secular ideal. While at Tashkent President Ayub appeared to be reasonable and willing to come to terms with India, after his return to Pakistan he had changed the tune. His recently published autobiography also seemed to show a pathological hatred towards everything Indian. Sheikh Saheb said that public statements and public postures need not necessarily reflect the real picture. If Pandit Nehru had lived on, Sheikh Saheb's efforts in 1964 might have been successful.

6. I asked Sheikh Saheb what in his opinion was a possible solution of the Kashmir problem. He said that he was not against a dialogue with Kashmir leaders, but for that the initiative rested with India. In his opinion, no fruitful dialogue was possible unless free and congenial atmosphere was created in Kashmir so that the people felt convinced that no harm would come to them if they expressed their mind freely. Sheikh Saheb added that besides stationing her Army in the State for meeting external aggression – which was understandable – India had sent into the State a large number of CRP, Border Security Police (BSP) and Armed Constabulary from Bihar, Punjab and other States of India. Many elements of these police forces were reported to be communally indoctrinated. The recent upheaval in the Valley and the part played by these police forces had amply demonstrated this sad aspect.

7. I told Sheikh Saheb that this was not quite correct. It was reported

that some elements in the Kashmir State Police were communally minded and this may have produced a few incidents in the State. All this could be and must be corrected.

8. I said that whatever might have happened in the past, there was need to look to the future. I asked him what he thought was a possible solution of the Kashmir problem. Sheikh Saheb replied as follows:

9. Government should put the problem before a small body of leaders of public opinion whose patriotism and loyalty are unquestionable. He did not suggest any names. Such a body could go into the various implications and suggest a solution that should be accepted by Government. Government could include in this body some leaders of the Opposition parties, if necessary. If such a body recommended going back to the pre-1963 position and giving autonomy to Kashmir, such a solution might still be workable. However, there would have to be firm guarantees that Government would not whittle down Article 370 as it had done.

10. Sheikh Saheb said that the people of Kashmir did not aspire for a kingdom. They wanted only peace to be able to pursue their lawful avocations. Relations between Kashmiri Pandits and Kashmir Muslims had always been cordial. A Kashmiri Pandit girl always had a Kashmiri Muslim foster mother and foster brother in whose hands her honour was safe. This was true till recently, but now the atmosphere in Kashmir had been poisoned by the inefficiency of the local Government, corruption and nepotism of the administration and lack of a clear and farsighted policy by the Centre. He said he had confidence in the bona fides of the Prime Minister, but he was not sure whether other elements in the political parties would support her in any reasonable solution of the Kashmir question.

11. I told Sheikh Saheb that the reaction in India was mainly due to the hostile criticism and propaganda in Pakistan. Conditions in Pakistan-occupied Kashmir were much worse than in any part of India (including Kashmir) and in spite of Kashmir being a border State, there was considerable freedom and democratic liberty there. Sheikh Saheb said that India was gradually slipping into the same communal atmosphere that prevailed in Pakistan. Unless this trend vas stopped effectively, Muslims in Kashmir would lose faith in India. I told Sheikh Saheb that the Kashmir problem was one to be settled between the Kashmiris and the rest of India and no third party had any locus standi in it. No Government of India could afford to make any concessions on Kashmir to Pakistan nor was an independent Kashmir possible because its independence would not last more than a few days. It was up to leaders like Sheikh Saheb who believed in secularism and peace and harmony on the sub-continent to play their constructive and positive role in this matter.

12. I expressed the hope that I might be able to see Sheikh Saheb again and he said he would be glad to meet me.

Top Secret
I had a third talk with Sheikh Abdullah on the 30 October 1967 for about two hours. His wife and daughters were in the sitting room and we talked alone in an adjoining room. I made it clear again to the Sheikh Saheb that I had seen him as an old friend, purely in my personal capacity, and had no instructions from Government to put forward any proposals; nor did my statements commit Government in any way. Sheikh Saheb said he realized this, but, at the same time, our talks could not be useless and he hoped that they will bear some fruit.

2. Sheikh Saheb asked me what were my personal views about the Kashmir question. I told him categorically that no Government of India would be prepared to lose the Valley of Kashmir or hand it over to Pakistan at any cost. The Valley of Kashmir was a symbol of India's secular ideology and vas vital for maintaining communal peace and harmony between the various communities in the country. What vas involved in the Valley of Kashmir was not merely the fate of four million Muslims of Kashmir and not only the fate of the fifty-five million Muslims of the rest of India, but peace and harmony in the whole sub-continent. Besides this, the Valley of Kashmir was vital for the defence of India and particularly Ladakh vis-à-vis China. I appealed to the Sheikh Saheb to bear these considerations in mind and play a constructive role.

3. Sheikh Abdullah replied that it would have been possible to work on these lines, if the Government of India had not eroded Article 370 and arrested him and his colleagues. They had only played into the hands of anti-secular and pro-Pakistani elements thereby. Pakistan was much stronger today, having achieved economic and political stability and international prestige which she did not enjoy before. She had also acquired support among the Muslims in this side of the ceasefire line which she did not have before 1953. This had been due to the wrong and repressive policies of the Government of India. Apart from this, the Muslims of Kashmir were facing in their own home frequent communal riots. There had been frequent communal riots in different parts of India also and the atrocities committed on the Muslim minority by the majority Hindus had shaken the confidence of the Muslims of Kashmir in the secular ideals of India. This had naturally helped the pro-Pakistani elements within the State to gain in strength. The most unfortunate fact of the matter is that the Government of India, through their stooges in Kashmir, provided all the material resources to strengthen and organize such elements not only during the regime of Bakshi Ghulam Mohammad but even today. The Sheikh had received authentic reports that the riots which took place in Kashmir recently were engineered, supported and guided by the ruling party – the Congress. Mirza Mohammad Afzul Beg was refused permission to address meetings in Srinagar and other important towns of the Valley for maintaining communal peace and harmony. The tragedy was that the Kashmir Government had placed under arrest a

large number of workers of the Plebiscite Front, whose only sin was that under the direction of their President, Mr Beg, they campaigned for communal peace and harmony, while those who had actually been indulging in fanning the flame of communal hatred, loot and arson were by and large moving freely under the protective wings of the ruling party. Perhaps communal peace and harmony did not suit the interests of the present ruling junta, who appeared to have been willing to harm India in order to maintain their own position.

4. I expressed surprise at these statements and said that I was not aware of any such thing. While some people did say that Bakshi Ghulam Mohammad, while he was in power, had boosted certain elements with the money provided by the Government of India, the present regime in Kashmir could not have any motive for following the same line. I questioned Sheikh's statement that Pakistan today was stronger and his implied statement that India was weaker. I told him that after the 1965 conflict Pakistan should have learnt a lesson that she could not take Kashmir or any other part of India by force. Sheikh Saheb answered that the motives were identical, i.e. to keep themselves in power although some people attributed other motives also, e.g. (a) to postpone the expected release of political prisoners, including Sheikh Saheb in order to prevent a rapprochement between them and the Government of India; (b) to scuttle the efforts of some elements in India who desired a settlement with Pakistan; (c) to provide justification for the continuance of repressive measures and thus continue the uncertainty in the State so that power remained in their hands; and (d) to fight the Plebiscite Front by encouraging the parties opposed to it and thereby to weaken hold.

5. Sheikh Saheb added that all those who believed in the secular ideology should realize that by allowing the ruling party in Kashmir to pursue the suicidal course, they were unconsciously helping in the creation of a Frankstein [*sic*] which would destroy the very fabric of secularism which they were expected to uphold and strengthen. He reiterated his opinion that, for fear of losing power, the present set-up in power in Kashmir would never encourage the Centre to adopt a more humane and democratic attitude towards the people of Kashmir in order to understand and meet their aspirations.

6. I told Sheikh Saheb that I could not agree with his sweeping statement. While there may be some anti-secular and selfish elements in Kashmir, as elsewhere, the present Sadiq regime had by and large a secular outlook. What was perhaps wrong in the present set-up was the failure of a strong, efficient and honest administration. I expressed the hope that Sheikh Saheb would work with secular-minded elements in Kashmir in order to strengthen secularism in Kashmir and the rest of India. I drew Sheikh Saheb's attention to a statement made by Mr Sadiq which was published on 30 October. Sheikh Saheb said that he did not attach much importance to the utterances of Mr Sadiq whose only aim was to retain power. Expressing his reluctance to work with a person who had betrayed him in the past, Sheikh Saheb said

that Mr Sadiq was brought into politics by him, given positions of trust and honour, both in the organization as well as in the Government, and often protected against the onslaughts of his rivals, yet he did not hesitate to stab him in the back to advance his self-interest. According to Sheikh Saheb, Mr Sadiq was one of the main conspirators who enacted the 1953 coup against him. Sheikh Saheb assured me that he was not a revengeful man; but how could there be cooperation with a person who had stabbed him in the back? He wanted me to put myself in his position and asked what my attitude would be under such circumstances.

7. I told Sheikh Saheb that he was a much bigger man than I, and there may have been misunderstandings and mistakes on both sides. One had to forget and forgive such things in the larger interests of the country and the secular ideology. Sheikh Saheb said that Government of India was free to deal with anybody who was ready to serve their ends, but he was not prepared to get bitten twice. His loyalty was to the ideals of secularism and democracy which, according to him, had grown much weaker through the years and particularly after Pandit Nehru's death. In any case, Sheikh Saheb thought that settlement between India and Pakistan was essential in order to solve the Kashmir problem. I told him that Pakistan had no locus standi in Kashmir, that the Kashmir problem was to be settled between the people of Kashmir and the Government of India, and once they agreed on any plan they could face Pakistan with a bold stand [*sic*]. Sheikh Saheb said he agreed with this approach to the problem, but it could only be the first step and not the last. It was possible, if the people of Kashmir and the Government of India agreed among themselves, they could isolate Pakistan and Pakistan would have to come to a reasonable settlement of the question. I told Sheikh Saheb that Pakistan's attitude had been most unreasonable and intransigent and she wanted to settle the Kashmir question only on her own terms. Panditji had been very generous and reasonable, but Pakistan had not responded at all. Even at Tashkent, Chairman Kosygin tried his best to persuade President Ayub to arrive at a reasonable solution of the problem, but President Ayub said he was not yet ready. President Ayub had admitted to Chairman Kosygin at Tashkent that an independent Kashmir would be neither in the interests of India nor Pakistan, but would only suit China. When asked by Chairman Kosygin what then he wanted in Kashmir, President Ayub had said that he would like to have the Valley for Pakistan because it had a Muslim majority and give Ladakh and Jammu to India. Chairman Kosygin had, however, pointed out to him that this could not be a basis for settlement, because on the same analogy the Soviet Union could claim Sinkiang which had only four million Uzbeks while Soviet Uzbekistan had eleven million Uzbeks. President Ayub had no answer to this. He merely said that he had certain maximum and minimum demands, but was not yet ready to reveal them. In any case, India had declared that she would not use force to recover Pakistan-occupied Kashmir; while a solution might be possible based

on the realities of the present situation, there was no question of the Valley going out of India.

8. Sheikh Saheb emphasized the necessity of creating a proper atmosphere in which talks could be held between the people of Kashmir and the Government of India. When I asked him whether he meant introduction of President's rule in order to create a proper atmosphere, he replied that before taking such a step Government should consider its implications both internal and international [*sic*]. It was possible that the people of Kashmir would not perhaps welcome such a step as it had the strong support of the Jana Sangh which had made such a move suspect not only in the minds of the Muslims of Kashmir, but in the minds of the democratic elements in the country as a whole. Sheikh Saheb could not give his own opinion unless he was in a position to find the reactions of his comrades and the people to such a proposal. He hinted, however, that such a proposal might be necessary in order to prepare the ground for further steps.

9. I asked the Sheikh what people he had in mind besides himself with whom the Government of India could talk in Kashmir. He replied that he would suggest the Plebiscite Front. I said no Government of India could talk with a body which had as its objective the holding of a plebiscite in Kashmir, which was out of the question now. It would, therefore, serve no useful purpose to talk with such a body if they stuck to this position. Sheikh Saheb warmed up at this and said that this attitude was similar to that of the British Government towards the Indian National Congress. The British in their arrogance and intoxication of power had closed their eyes to the realities of the situation, but events had forced them to seek peace and understanding from the 'naked fakir'. India was committing a similar mistake in Kashmir. According to him, the Plebiscite Front was the only organization in Kashmir which represented the urges and aspirations of the majority of the people, and which alone had the capacity and strength to mobilize public opinion behind any agreement which might finally emerge out of the talks with them. If, however, India was not willing to talk with the Plebiscite Front, it was no use to have talks with him either; he could not work in a vacuum.

10. I warmed up too and said that it was not fair or right to compare the British Government with the present Government of India. The Congress have been fighting a foreign power, but the people of Kashmir were brothers and kith and kin of the people of India. Differences could arise between brothers, but they could not be compared to the kind of differences between a foreign government and a subject people. Sheikh Saheb remarked that the people of Kashmir had never suffered such atrocities during the British or even the Maharaja's regime as they were suffering now. I challenged the accuracy of this statement.

11. Sheikh Saheb then informed me that although he supported the Plebiscite Front's basic stand, he was not himself a member of that organization.

As far as he knew, their stand on plebiscite was not rigid. Its leaders had repeatedly declared their willingness to consider any alternative method of ascertaining the will of the people of Kashmir. Sheikh Saheb expressed surprise that the Government of India should refuse to talk with the Plebiscite Front, whose only crime apparently was that it demanded the fulfilment of the commitments and solemn pledges given repeatedly by India not only to the people of Kashmir but to the whole world. I told Sheikh Saheb that the commitment to ascertain the will of the people was made unilaterally by the Government of India to the people of Kashmir and it had been fulfilled a number of times, even according to the statements of Sheikh Saheb himself, before 1953. I told him however that if the Plebiscite Front was not rigid in its demand for holding plebiscite, perhaps talks could be held with them. Sheikh Saheb said it was very strange that while the Government of India had no hesitation in talking to the underground Nagas who had opened armed revolt against her, they should refuse to meet the real representatives of the people of Kashmir. I told Sheikh Saheb not to compare Nagaland with Kashmir. The Nagas had been deliberately kept out of touch with the rest of India by the British and had not been emotionally integrated with the rest of India, but the Kashmiris were so close and near to the rest of the people of India and the situation is not similar.

12. I asked Sheikh Saheb who were the people besides Mr Beg in the Plebiscite Front with whom talks could be held. Sheikh Saheb replied that Mr Beg was the President of the organization and it was for him to suggest the persons. I told Sheikh Saheb that I was going out on tour for about a week and would like to see him again on my return if he so desired. Sheikh Saheb was hesitant to commit himself because he had said what he had to say. When I asked him whether my meeting him caused him any embarrassment, he assured me that there was no such thing, but he did not like to have political talks with anybody while in detention; it was only because of his past relations with me that he had agreed to meet me.

13. I asked Sheikh Saheb whether he would like to see Shrimati Gandhi or any other leaders. He replied that despite what he had suffered all these years, his affection and regards for Indiraji had not lessened and when he was free from detention he would be glad to meet her.

(T.N. Kaul)
7.11.1967

18(b). Sheikh Abdullah's record of the 30 October 1967 meeting

3, Kotla Lane
3 November 1967

Shri T.N. Kaul,
Secretary, Ministry of External Affairs,
Government of India,
New Delhi

My dear Tikki,
I was surprised to receive your letter dated 30 October 1967, and wondered why you felt 'distressed' when you read my Note. If you did not find its content 'quite correct' you could send me your own version of talks. After all it was not an idle chat between two friends but a serious one concerning the destinies of millions of people of the sub-continent and therefore, I thought it was necessary that they should go on record.

To the best of my memory, I put down on paper what had actually transpired between us but if you found certain 'inaccuracies' you are welcome to correct them and straighen the record. It is important that we understand each other clearly if these talks have to serve any useful purpose.

I attach herewith a note on the talks that took place between us on 30 October. With regard to our further meetings I have explained my position to you when we met last.

With kindest regards.
Yours sincerely,
Sheikh Abdullah*

* This letter presumably refers to Sheikh Abdullah's record of the meetings on 10 and 12 October 1967 which he had sent under a letter dated 30 October 1967. It also contains the Sheikh's record of the meeting on 30 October 1967.

On the 30 October 1967, Shri T. N. Kaul had another talk (third in the series) with Sheikh Saheb for about two hours.

After exchange of usual courtesies, Sheikh Saheb asked Shri Kaul that now that he had heard his views how was Government of India going to resolve the problem? Shri Kaul replied that India was not prepared to lose the Valley to Pakistan at any cost. Apart from defence strategy, India considered the retention of the Valley vital for maintaining communal peace in the country and for the preservation of secular ideology. [India was, however, willing to come to a settlement with Pakistan on the basis of the present Ceasefire Line.] She was also prepared to have a rapproachment with the people of Kashmir [on the basis of the relationship that existed between them and the Government of India before 9 August 1953]. Mr Kaul asked Sheikh Saheb if he would help. Sheikh Saheb's reply was that it would perhaps have been possible to work on those lines if Government of India had not torpedoed that relationship by force. Now the position was quite different. Pakistan, today, was much stronger, having achieved economic and political stability and international prestige which she did not enjoy before. She had also acquired a powerful support amongst the Muslims on this side of the Ceasefire Line which she did not have before 1953, and for which the wrong and repressive policies of the Government of India and dishonouring of pledges repeatedly given to the people, were entirely responsible. Apart from what the Muslims of Kashmir were facing in their own home State, frequent communal riots in different parts of India and the atrocities committed on the Muslim minority by the majority community, often with the connivance and support of the law and order agencies, had completely shaken their confidence in the secular ideals of India. This had, naturally, helped the pro-Pakistan elements within the State to gain in strength beyond expectation. The most unfortunate fact of the matter was that the Government of India, through her stooges in Kashmir, provided all the material resources to strengthen and organize such elements not only during the regime of Bakshi Gulam Mohammed but even today. Sheikh Saheb informed Shri Kaul that he had received authentic reports that the riots which took place in Kashmir recently were engineered, supported and guided by the ruling party – the Congress. Mirza Mohd Afzal Beg was refused permission to address public meetings in Srinagar and other important towns of the Valley for maintaining communal peace and harmony. The tragedy was, added Sheikh Saheb, that the Kashmir Government had even put under arrest a large number of Plebiscite Front workers whose only sin was that, under the direction of Mr Beg, their president, they campaigned for communal peace and harmony, while those who had actually indulged in fanning the fire of communal hatred, loot and arson were, by and large, moving freely under the protective wings of the ruling party; perhaps communal peace and harmony did not suit their interests. To spite the Plebiscite Front, which stood like a rock for communal harmony, the ruling junta appeared even willing to cut its own nose and that of India too. Shri Kaul expressed surprise and said that he did not know about it. [He agreed with Sheikh Saheb that] Bakshi Gulam Mohammed, when in power, did boost up anti-social and communal elements with the money provided by India in order to find a base for work and advance his own interests. But what could be the motive of the present regime to follow the same line, he asked. Sheikh Saheb answered that the motives were identical, although people attributed some others also, which according to them were:

(a) To postpone the expected release of political prisoners including Sheikh Saheb in order to prevent a rapproachment between them and Government of India;

(b) To scuttle the efforts of some elements in India who desired a settlement with Pakistan;

(c) To provide justification for the continuance of repressive measures and thus to continue the uncertainty in the State so that the power remained in their hands;

(d) To fight the Plebiscite Front politically by encouraging the parties opposed to it and thereby weaken its hold upon the people.

Sheikh Saheb told Shri Kaul that all those who believed in secular ideology should realize that by allowing the ruling party in Kashmir to pursue this suicidal course, they were unconciously helping in the creation of a Frankenstein which will destroy the very fabric of secularism which they were expected to uphold and strengthen. He reiterated his opinion that, for the fear of losing power, the present set-up in power would never encourage the Centre to adopt a more humane and democratic attitude towards the people of Kashmir in order to understand and meet their aspirations.

Mr T. N. Kaul enquired whether imposition of President's rule would help. Sheikh Saheb replied that before taking such a step the Government of India should carefully consider its implications, both internal and international. In his opinion people of Kashmir would not, perhaps, welcome such a step as the strong support given to it by Jana Sangh and other Hindu communal organizations had made such a move suspect, not only in the eyes of Muslims of Kashmir but other democratic elements in the country as well. Sheikh Saheb told Mr Kaul that he could not give his own opinion unless he was in a position to find the reactions of his comrades and the people to such a proposal.

Mr T. N. Kaul expressed a wish that Sheikh Saheb would combine and lead again all those elements who believed in secularism. In this connection he said that while he did not know much about the views of Bakshi Gulam Mohammed or Mir Qasim, but with regard to G.M. Sadiq he knew that [though a weak man] he sincerely believed in the ideals of secularism and, therefore, it would not be difficult to work with him. Mr Kaul made an oblique reference to the statement of Mr Sadiq published in the *Hindustan Times* of 30 October 1967 [which, according to him, showed identity of views between Sheikh Saheb and Mr Sadiq]. Sheikh Saheb said that he did not attach much importance to the utterances of Mr Sadiq. The only aim being to retain power, he could be made to say anything without actually believing in it. Expressing his reluctance to work with a person who had betrayed him in past, Sheikh Saheb informed Mr Kaul that Mr Sadiq was brought into politics by him, given positions of trust and honour both in the organization as well as in the Government and often protected against the onslaughts of his rivals, yet he did not hesitate to stab him in the back to advance his self-interests. He was one of the main conspirators who enacted the 1953 coup against him. Sheikh Saheb assured Mr Kaul that he was not a revengeful man but asked: 'How could there be any cooperation with a person of such a character?' He wanted Mr Kaul to put himself in his position and tell him what his attitude would be under such circumstances. Mr

Kaul replied that he would have the same feelings but Sheikh Saheb was a much bigger man and could be expected to forget and forgive such lapses in the larger interests of the country. Sheikh Saheb told Mr Kaul that the Government of India was free to deal with anybody who was ready to serve their ends but he was not prepared to get bitten twice. His loyalty was only to the ideals of secularism and democracy, which, to his sorrow and misfortune, the Indian leadership, by and large, had failed to uphold.

Mr Kaul told Sheikh Saheb that the Government of India would prefer to explore a settlement with the people of Kashmir before initiating talks with Pakistan, to which Sheikh Saheb replied that that could also be an approach to the solution of the problem. But it would only be the first step not the last. [Nobody should overlook the fact that a permanent peace in Kashmir or between India and Pakistan was impossible of achievement unless Pakistan was made a party to any settlement that might be arrived at between India and the people of Kashmir.]

Mr T. N. Kaul said that it was very unfortunate that Pakistan was not willing to agree to any solution of the Kashmir dispute except on her own terms. He informed Sheikh Saheb that the late Lal Bahadur Shastri tried hard at Tashkent to pursuade President Ayub Khan to accept a reasonable solution based on the present Ceasefire Line but he would not agree. When Mr Kosygin asked if independent Kashmir would satisfy him, his reply was that that would help neither India nor Pakistan, but only China.

Sheikh Saheb again emphasized the necessity of creating a proper atmosphere in which talks could be held. Thereupon Mr Kaul asked him what steps he had in mind which needed to be taken to improve the atmosphere. Sheikh Saheb replied that he had already indicated the steps in his earlier talk. 'Who are the people with whom the Government of India should negotiate besides him', asked Mr Kaul. Sheikh Saheb replied that he would suggest the Plebiscite Front. Mr Kaul said that the Government of India was not prepared to talk with the representatives of that organization as its objective was plebiscite in Kashmir, which India had rejected. Therefore, it would serve no useful purpose to talk with them. Sheikh Saheb was annoyed to hear this and told Mr Kaul that this showed the same attitude which the British Government had once adopted towards the Indian National Congress and, contemptuously, called its accredited leader, Mahatma Gandhi, 'a naked faqir'. The British, in their arrogance and intoxication of power, closed their eyes to the realities of the situation but events forced them to beg peace and understanding from the same 'naked faqir'. India was committing similar mistake in Kashmir [*sic*]. The Plebiscite Front was [admittedly] the only organization in Kashmir which represented the urges and aspirations of the majority of the people, and which alone had the capacity and strength to mobilize public opinion behind any agreement which might finally emerge out of the talks with them. If, however, India had finally decided not to deal with this organization, it was no use then to have talks with him as well. He could not work in a vacuum. Shri Kaul replied that it was not right to compare the British Government with the present Government of India. The Congress, he said, was fighting a foreign power, but the people of Kashmir were their own brethren and sometimes difference did arise even between brothers. Sheikh Saheb remarked that the people of Kashmir had never suffered such atrocities during the British and Maharaja's regimes as they were suffering now.

Sheikh Saheb informed Mr Kaul that although he supported its (Plebiscite Front's) basic stand, he was not himself a member of that organization. As far as he knew, their stand on plebiscite was not rigid. Its leaders had repeatedly declared their willingness to consider any alternative method of ascertaining the will of the people of Kashmir, provided India convinced them that holding of plebiscite was impracticable and fraught with difficulties.

Sheikh Saheb expressed surprise that Government of India should refuse to talk with the Plebiscite Front whose only crime, apparently, was that it demanded the fulfilment of the commitments and solemn pledges given repeatedly by India not only to the people of Kashmir but to the whole world. It was very strange, said Sheikh Saheb, that while the Government of India had not hesitation in talking to Nagas who were in open armed revolt against her, they should refuse to meet the real representatives of the people of Kashmir. Mr Kaul remarked that Nagaland had never been a part of the Indian administrative machine like Kashmir, and anyhow, nothing came out of the talks held so far with them. Sheikh Saheb replied that the position of Kashmir was not different.

Mr Kaul said that he was glad to know that the attitude of the Plebiscite Front on the question of plebiscite was not rigid and enquired as to who were the people from this organization, besides Mr Beg, with whom Government of India should talk. Sheikh Saheb told him that Mr Beg was the president of the organization and it was for him to suggest the personnel.

Mr Kaul expressed a desire to meet Sheikh Saheb again on his return from a tour of Bhutan and some other places, but he told him that further meetings would not serve any purpose as he had said what he had to say and it was now for the Government of India to move. Upon this Mr Kaul enquired if his meetings caused him any embarrassment but Sheikh Saheb assured him that there was no such thing, but generally he did not like to have political talks with anybody while in detention. It was only because of his past relations with Mr Kaul that he could meet him.

[In the end Mr Kaul expressed a desire that Sheikh Saheb should have direct talks with Mrs Indira Gandhi, to which Sheikh Saheb replied that, despite what he suffered all these years, his love and regard for Indiraji had not lessened. When he was free from detention he would gladly respond to her invitation for talks.]

COPY FORWARDED TO SHRI T.N. KAUL FOR RECORD

STRICTLY PERSONAL AND CONFIDENTIAL

12 Tughlak Lane, New Delhi
17 November 1967

Thank you for your letter of 3 November which I received on my return from tour a few days ago.

2. As I made it clear on all the three occasions I had the pleasure of meeting you, I was speaking purely in my personal capacity without any instructions from or commitment by the Government. It was not my understanding that a record would be kept of our talks. Since, however, you have taken the trouble of recording your impressions, I am enclosing detailed Notes of all the three conversations which, to the best of my knowledge and recollection, contain both what you said and I said. This is strictly personal and confidential and not to be divulged to any third party.

3. I had requested to see you with a view to renewing my contacts with an old and respected friend who had played a leading role in strengthening Panditji's ideal of secularism in India and who, I believe, can still play that role in the larger interests of the country. The talks were carried on mainly in Kashmiri and Urdu but I have tried to put them down in English retaining the language used by you most of the time. I hope you will find the record useful and it will remove misunderstandings and not create any controversies.

4. I spoke to you as an old friend who has respect and admiration for you. I spoke as an Indian citizen born and bred in Kashmir. I must, however, clarify again that I was speaking purely in my personal capacity and not on behalf of the Government.

With kindest regards,

[T.N. Kaul]

3 Kotla Lane,
C/o Deputy Commissioner,
Delhi, 22 November 1967.

My Dear Tikki,

Thank you for your letter dated 17 November, and the Note attached to it. I have carefully gone through the contents, you have left out some topics, added others and at some places given your own interpretation to what I had stated. However, I do not want to enter into any controversy with you. You are welcome to hold on to your own version, but, I see no reason to doubt the veracity of my own record.

I hope you are doing well.

With best wishes,

Yours sincerely
Sheikh Abdullah

Shri T.N. Kaul, 12 Tughlak Lane, New Delhi.

18(c). T.N. Kaul's record of the 6 January 1968 meeting

As I mentioned to PM, I invited Sheikh Abdullah and his wife and daughter to a quiet dinner at my house last night. Begum Abdullah was unable to come as she was not well, but Sheikh Saheb and his unmarried daughter came. Apart from my wife and daughter, Shri and Shrimati P.N. Haksar were also present. Sheikh Saheb and his daughter left at 12:30 midnight.

2. It was a friendly social function and I told Sheikh Saheb that I hoped he would not record any Note about this meeting as it was a purely social, private and informal one. He agreed.

3. He talked most of the time, though I had to prod him now and then to draw him out. He repeated the same old arguments as before, but my impression was that his general attitude was less bitter than before and he seemed to be aware of the 'realities of the situation' and that he would have to 'face the facts'. He was also less bitter against Sadiq Saheb. Although he talked against Bakshi Ghulam Mohammad, he also admitted some of his dynamic qualities. As for Syed Mir Qasaim, he did not seem to have a very high opinion of him and pooh-poohed his claim that he had enrolled seven lakhs of Congress members in the State. He also mentioned that Mir Qasim had received a certificate signed by Jinnah when, as a student at Aligarh University, he had campaigned for the Muslim League during the elections.

4. I am not mentioning the arguments I used with him, but following are the main points Sheikh Saheb stressed:

(1) It is for the Government to take the initiative in setting right the wrong trends appearing throughout the country. He referred in this connection to the situation in West Bengal, Haryana, Punjab, etc.; the language question; the students' unrest; and last but not least, the anti-secular forces led by the Jana Sangh and communal-minded elements in the Congress Party.

(2) He was directly concerned only with Kashmir because he was partly responsible for the present situation there. He would, therefore, concentrate on his 'base' in Kashmir and thereby help in setting right the trends throughout India by improving the situation in Kashmir.

(3) As he put it, 'Government must face the facts, and if they cannot handle the situation, they should get out and let others take the reins of power in their hands, or else the Prime Minister should bring people who are known for their integrity, honesty and intelligence into the Government whether they belong to any political party or not.'

(4) Only a bold leadership could set right things in the country.

5. He made the following points, in particular, with regard to Kashmir:

(1) The economic situation in the Valley was bad because people were unemployed for four to six months in the year. Communications must be improved and more employment provided for educated Kashmiris in the rest of India.

(2) In spite of the efforts of the Jana Sangh, which wanted to wipe out secularism and considered the secularism in Kashmir as their main stumbling block, communal harmony had been by and large maintained throughout Kashmir, in contrast with what had happened at Ranchi and elsewhere. Secularism could be further strengthened in Kashmir and the rest of India if the Government was prepared to support really secular elements and take strong action against communally-minded elements. As he put it, 'a surgical operation is necessary to cut off the diseased limb'.

(3) Kashmiri accession to India was 'provisional' and was based on the three subjects mentioned in the Instrument of Accession. As the Government of India had eroded the autonomy of Kashmir, Kashmir's accession had also been eroded. It was difficult to say whether this accession could be revived or finalized by going back to the 1952 position. However, the will or the people had to be determined and the Government was committed to this.

(4) As for the demand for a separation or complete integration of Jammu Province with the rest of India, and the demand for making Ladakh into a Union Territory, Sheikh Saheb said, 'we should settle this problem by persuasion and not by force. No section of people can be kept within India by force of arms and bayonets, but if they can be persuaded, that is the only way of keeping them within India. If they cannot be persuaded, then they have the right to go their own way.' When asked whether this would not lead to the disintegration of the country, he said, 'if the leaders cannot persuade the people, naturally the country will disintegrate. The fault therefore lies with the leadership and not with the people. The Central Government had encouraged the wrong kind of leadership which was communal minded and was exploiting the situation to keep themselves in power.'

(5) If the Kashmir problem is settled amicably, it can have a tremendous influence in creating friendship between India and Pakistan which is most essential for both countries. As Sheikh Saheb put it, 'India should try to create friendly neighbours and not enemies.' He blamed Shri V.K. Krishna Menon for having misled Panditji and provoked the Chinese through his forward policy.

6. Sheikh Saheb said he stood by Panditji's ideals and the policies he had propounded after great thought and introspection. He said, 'Our present leaders must look within and make a self-analysis and find out where they have gone wrong. If they are prepared sincerely to follow Panditji's path, I shall go along with them too.' He said that he felt Shrimati Indira Gandhi naturally wanted to follow the path laid down by Panditji, but he was not sure of 'others in the crowd'. As for Shri Jayaprakash Narayan, he said, 'he is an honest man and a man of integrity, but he is a visionary and not a practical man'. He blamed Dr Lohia for having reduced the Parliament to a fish market. He thought, however, that there were people in the country who had honesty, integrity and intelligence, and if Shrimati Gandhi had the

courage she could take a bold step in getting them together and asking them to give a lead to the country. The people at large were sound, but bold and imaginative leadership is lacking. Asked whether he would cooprate in this task, he said, 'I cannot take the leadership; let Shrimati Indira Gandhi give the lead on the right lines and I will go along with her'. Beyond this he would not commit himself.

(T.N. Kaul)
7.1.1968

18(d). Record of Sheikh Abdullah and Mirza Beg's talks with T.N. Kaul on 15 February 1968

Top Secret
Most Immediate
Sheikh Mohammad Abdullah had invited about 50 people to a Kashmiri lunch at No. 3 Kotla Lane today (15 February 1968). My family and I were also invited. I am reporting briefly the following points which were made to me by various people present.

Shri S. Moolgavkar and Shri J.J. Singh: They pointed out the danger of letting Sheikh Saheb go back to Kashmir without some direction or understanding from the Government of India. They said that once he went to Kashmir without any such understanding, he might be carried away by what he sees in Kashmir and a settlement of the Kashmir problem may become even more difficult. They suggested therefore that PM or some other responsible person should send for Sheikh Saheb and tell him that a settlement within the Indian Union with maximum autonomy possible could be agreed to and the details worked out. Their impression is that Sheikh Saheb is willing to bite on this although he may not commit himself immediately.

Shri Afzal Beg: He told me that people were maliciously dubbing him and Sheikh Saheb as Pakistani agents. He swore to me that neither he nor Sheikh Saheb had met the Chinese Chargé d'Affairs recently as reported in the press. I asked him what kind of a settlement of the Kashmir problem was likely in his view. He said that if there was an understanding, both Sheikh Saheb and the Government of India would work out details pointing to the conclusion that Kashmir would remain an autonomous unit within the Union of India. I told him that the difference in his approach and mine was that I wanted to work within the framework of the Indian Union and fill in the details within that framework, while he wanted to work out the details first and then draw the framework. He said I was correct in this analysis, but via media could be found.

Sheikh Saheb: Sheikh Saheb told me that he was waiting for a signal from the Prime Minister for a dialogue. He had not heard anything after Shri G. Parthasarathi had met him, although the latter had promised that he would hear further from PM. He said that he was anxious to go back to Kashmir as soon as the road was clear and in any case before the end of this month. He appeared to be keen on having a talk with PM.

Shri Mulgavikar told me that according to his information, when Sheikh Saheb had asked PM, in his last meeting, what were the possibilities that the Prime Minister had referred to in her Press Conference, the Prime Minster had indicated that she was merely answering a question from a press correspondent and had nothing particular in mind. This had disillusioned Sheikh Saheb. I told him that it was for Sheikh Saheb to come forward with some proposals and not expect merely the Government of India to commit themselves.

2. I would respectfully suggest that PM may consider sending for Sheikh Saheb again and asking him to work out a solution within the framework of the Indian Union in consultation with all concerned. It seems Sheikh Saheb is not prepared to go to Kashmir House to meet Sadiq Saheb, but I feel confident that if PM gives him the above indication, it is more than likely that he may be willing to talk to Sadiq Saheb. PM may like to consider this suggestion and either send for Sheikh Saheb herself or ask Home Minister or someone else to talk to him.

T.N. Kaul
15.2.1968

From *T.N. Kaul Papers* (I and III Instalments), Subject File No. 12 and 15, Nehru Memorial Museum and Library, New Delhi.

19. Jayaprakash Narayan's article on Kashmir, 3 March 1968: 'Kashmir, a Human Problem'

Though India had attained her Independence 20 years ago, the problem of Kashmir has remained as unresolved as before. There are several questions that arise in connection with Kashmir. The official view holds that Kashmir's accession to India has been final and irrevocable. Neither the question of de-accession nor the right to self-determination of the Kashmir people would now arise. Alas, I wish this had been true! But it is saddening beyond words to find the same old policy of confusion and ambivalence being again pursued in the case of Kashmir.

There are a few basic historical facts which need to be brought to the light at the beginning. First, the question with regard to the right of self-determination to the people of Kashmir has wrongly been dealt with in this country. I should however make it clear that the idea of self-determination is not my creation although many severe and bitter criticisms in the past have been heaped on me as if I am out to disrupt the country's integrity. But there is not the slightest grain of truth in it. While I hold that Pakistan, by her repeated acts of aggression, has forfeited what right she had earned from historical circumstances to have a say about the future of Kashmir, I would consider it politically to be dangerous delusion and morally wrong to believe that there is no further problem left to tackle in Kashmir.

These facts notwithstanding stem from India's own commitments to the people of Kashmir. When Partition was agreed upon, it was decided that what was known as British India would be divided according to Muslim and Hindu majority areas (without any referendum); and that in Princely India the Princes would have the option to accede to either India or Pakistan. Thus there was no question of any referendum in Bihar or Bombay.

As to the Princely States, the accession of the Prince was to be final. So, when Maharaja Hari Singh of Kashmir acceded to India, that should have set the matter beyond doubt for all times, as indeed in strict law it actually did. But there was a snag: the accession had to be accepted. And it was precisely at that point that the idea of referendum or self-determination in regard to Kashmir was injected into the course of events. After accepting the Instrument of Accession on 27 October 1947, Lord Louis Mountbatten, in a separate letter of the same date, wrote to the Maharaja as follows:

> In the special circumstances mentioned by your Highness, my Government have decided to accept the accession of Kashmir State to the Dominion of India. Consistently with their policy that, in the case of any State where the issue of accession has been the subject of dispute, the question of accession should be decided in accordance with the wishes of the people of the State, it is my Government's wish that, as soon as law and order have been restored in Kashmir and her soil cleared of the invader, the question of the State's accession should be settled by a reference to the people.

A few days later (2 November 1947) Nehru, in a broadcast, underlined the assurance given by the Governor-General in these clear words:

> We decided to accept this accession and to send troops by air, but we made a condition that the accession would have to be considered by the people of Kashmir later when peace and order were established. We were anxious not to finalize anything in a moment of crisis, and without the fullest opportunity to the people of Kashmir to have their say. It was for them ultimately to decide.
>
> And here let me make clear that it has been our policy all along that where there is a dispute about the accession of a State to either Dominion, the decision must be made by the people of that State. It was in accordance with this policy that we added a proviso to the Instrument of Accession of Kashmir.

Later in the same broadcast the Prime Minister went on to declare to all the world:

> We have declared that the fate of Kashmir is ultimately to be decided by the

> people. That pledge we have given and the Maharaja has supported it, not only to the people of Kashmir but to the world. We will not, and cannot, back out of it. We are prepared when peace and law and order have been established to have a referendum held under international auspices like the UN. We want it to be a fair and just reference to the people and we shall accept their verdict, I can imagine no fairer and juster offer.

In view of this crystal-clear position it is amazing that frantic efforts should be made to cloud the issue.

There is still another self-complacent view in the country. Briefly it is this; true, there was a proviso added to the Instrument of Accession, but that has already been given effect to and there is noting further to be done about it. The proviso was carried out, it is said, when the Kashmir Constituent Assembly adopted in 1956 a Constitution which declared that 'the State of Jammu & Kashmir is and shall be an integral part of India'. That was three years after Sheikh Abdullah's arrest, but that may not be considered so important. The really important point is that a decision of the Constituent Assembly cannot be equated with a referendum, which the Prime Minister had solemnly pledged.

Statements of Sheikh Abdullah are bandied about to prove that he himself had accepted the accession. But there never was any question about it. Following the Maharaja's legal act of accession, the Sheikh and the National Conference had endorsed and explicitly accepted the accession; and on many subsequent occasions their acceptance was reiterated. All that is incontestable. Yet the proviso remained and had to take effect. Neither the National Conference nor Sheikh Abdullah could take the place of the people of Kashmir, whose will had to be ascertained, and not the Sheikh's or that of the National Conference.

Still another argument is that since Pakistan joined SEATO and CENTO and the USA supplied it arms, and other things happened, the situation became so transformed that the offer of referendum stood no longer. But it is forgotten that it was not to Pakistan that the offer or pledge had been given but to the people of Kashmir. There could be no justification for punishing the latter for the actions of the former.

It is therefore wrong to say that there is no problem of Kashmir; the problem is still there and that is between the Government of India and the people of Kashmir. This problem can never be solved by treating it more as one of law and order. It is a human problem. The important point to keep in mind is that it is not by legal advocacy that a human problem like that of Kashmir can ever be settled.

In view of all this it appears to me that the right and constructive approach is not to deny to Kashmir the right to self-determination, or to assert that the right has already been exercised, but to show rationally how impractical and imprudent it would be to exercise that right now.

The following consideration might be put forward: first, there is the hard fact of aggression by Pakistan which they show no intention to vacate; second, a referendum might have serious consequences for the minorities both in India and Pakistan; third, a referendum might lead to further disintegration of the State of Jammu and Kashmir; and fourth, the effect of the foregoing would have serious consequences for India's defence. There may be other factors, but these four are weighty and reasonable; and neither Sheikh Abdullah nor any other Kashmir leader, because they are as much concerned with India's good as with that of Kashmir, would brush them aside.

Therefore, my humble plea is that we put aside all this heated controversy about the accession having been full, final and irrevocable, and sit down with the Sheikh and discuss practical ways of settlement.

The more important question is, how would Sheikh Abdullah want the Kashmir to decide their future? I am sure not by a plebiscite. Then how? One way, and the best in the circumstances, would be to let the people decide at the election. The Sheikh could do that by fighting the election on the basis of his agreement with the Government of India (as envisaged above). Could the Kashmiri people be enthused over autonomy within the Union? I think they could, by Sheikh Saheb frankly telling them that that was the only way they could save themselves from self-destruction as a result of their territory becoming a battle-ground for India and Pakistan; that if it could be shown that they had taken that decision freely at an election run by their genuine leaders (like himself), Pakistan would have no ground left to interfere in their affairs; that that was the best way to bring about Indo–Pak amity; that they would be rid of the overbearing Indian police and enjoy full freedom to order their lives as they liked. If all that were put across to the people by one whom they trust, I have every hope they would acquiesce willingly.

It has been known these many years that Sheikh Saheb has been resolutely against Kashmir being merged with Pakistan. He might have, no doubt, entertained ideas of some kind of an independent Kashmir; but I believe he is realist enough to realize that (a) no solution of the Kashmir question could ever be accepted by India, after the last war with Pakistan, that involved de-accession of the State, or any part of it, from the Union; and (b) an independent State in that part of the world could have little chance of survival in face of Pakistan's consuming hunger for the Valley of Kashmir and the emergence of the Chinese power in the region – a power that cannot be expected to exercise self-denial in relation to its weak neighbours.

The question arises, what kind of a settlement would Sheikh Saheb want. Clearly he cannot be expected to agree to the present status of the State and may want to go back to the original position of limited accession. In other words, he may want full internal autonomy for the State with the Centre exercising authority and control in defence, external relations and communications. That will need to be considered with an open mind on both sides, particularly in view of the developments since 1947. Dr Karan Singh's imaginative suggestions about reorganization of the State might also be examined in this context. Finally, there is the possibility of Sheikh Saheb's playing a constructive part in preserving and promoting the spirit and aims of the Tashkent declaration. Indo–Pak friendship has been his passion. Now that both the countries have accepted friendship as their common aim, Sheikh Saheb's services might prove to be invaluable.

From Sarva Seva Sangh Monthly Newsletter, Vol. 2, No. 3, March 1968: 6–8. Also see *Jayaprakash Narayan: Selected Works*, edited by Bimal Prasad, Vol. 9, Delhi: Manohar Publications, 1964: 240–44.

20. Jayaprakash Narayan's inaugural address at the J&K State People's Convention organized by Sheikh Abdullah to discuss the state's future, Srinagar, 10 October 1968

Friends,
I am thankful to Sheikh Abdullah for asking me to inaugurate this important convention. As you perhaps know, I have come after some hesitation, indeed after an initially negative decision. Two main considerations finally persuaded me to come. One, my affection and regards for Sheikh Saheb, and two, the hope that my plain words, spoken from the heart, might on the one hand help you to reach a practical decision, and on the other, influence Indian public opinion also to take a realistic and constructive view of the situation. . . .

Before dealing with some of the vital issues before this Convention, I should like to speak briefly to those in this State and the rest of the country who claim that there is nothing left to settle in Kashmir, that the State is as irrevocably a part of India as, let us say, Uttar Pradesh. All those who give expression to this view are not really of one mind on the question. There are, for instance, the Bharatiya Jana Sangh and elements in the Congress and the Government of India who hold that Article 370 of the Constitution of India should be abrogated and the State fully 'integrated' with the Union of India, and further, that Indian citizens should be able freely to buy land and settle down in the State. There are others, like Chief Minister G.M. Sadiq, who assert that the State is truly an integral part of India, though they concede that the quantum of autonomy that the State should enjoy is a negotiable matter. There are also several variations of this general theme, such as that (a) Jammu should be separated from the state, or that (b) the area should be given a measure of regional autonomy within the State. There are also intermediate views between these proposals.

On the other hand, Sheikh Abdullah and many people associated with him do not agree that the State's accession was final and irrevocable. Had Sheikh Saheb been just an individual of little consequence, surrounded by a handful of other similar individuals, his opinions could have been ignored. But if one does not want to indulge in wishful thinking, it has to be recognized, however unpleasant and inconvenient it might be to some, that Sheikh Abdullah continues to be a key-figure in the State because he still commands impressive mass support in the Valley as well as in certain other parts of the State. That being so, for a large number of people the question of Kashmir cannot be deemed to have been settled unless the Sheikh is also a party to the settlement.

It is not necessary to remind you that if there was one man more responsible than anyone else for the accession of the State to the Indian Union in 1947, it was Sheikh Mohammad Abdullah. Another historical event deserves mention in this context: at the time of Independence, while overwhelming numbers of Muslims throughout undivided India had rallied to the banner of Mr Jinnah and subscribed to his two-nation theory, two shining exceptions stood out in bold dissent: the North-West Frontier Province and the State of Jammu & Kashmir. The Muslim masses in these two regions refused to be swept off their feet by the cry of a separate Muslim nation. That was due, let it be remembered, to the leadership of two deeply religious and towering, charismatic Muslims: Khan Abdul Ghaffar Khan and Sheikh Abdullah. . . . There is another salient fact about this State to which I should like to draw the attention of those who assert that there is nothing left to settle in regard to Kashmir. That is the fact of widespread and persistent discontent in the Valley. Part of the discontent is undoubtedly of the same nature that one finds, in some measure or other, all over the country. But there is also no doubt that the greater part of it is peculiar to this State and stems from the political situation: in particular, from the lack of agreement with Sheikh Abdullah and the absence of genuine democracy and good government in the State. Some of the recent judgements on the election petitions in the State provide a significant commentary on the working of democracy here.

It seems to me that all those who loudly proclaim that Kashmir is an inalienable part of India should feel deeply concerned over this persistent discontent. But, regrettably, one does not find such concern in these quarters. The majority of them believe in a policy of drift and pathetically trust to time to settle all problems. It does not occur to them that time has not settled this particular problem in 21 years. Another 21 years are hardly likely to settle it along the path of indecision and opportunism. Indeed, if the situation is allowed to drift further and Sheikh Abdullah continues to be ignored, extremism would keep on growing apace and the consequences might well be incalculable.

There are, of course, those for whom the solution of every problem lies in force. To them it is of little significance how popular Sheikh Abdullah is and how disaffected are his followers. Force in their reckoning will take care of all that. Such a naïve and reactionary view appeals naturally to a certain type of mind. But the large-scale use of force, especially in such a sensitive spot of the world as Kashmir is, carries with it immense risks. There is also a real danger that the continued reliance on force in Kashmir may erode democracy in other parts of India, create and feed communal conflict, and become a running and festering sore in the body politic and economic of the country. . . .

Let me also remind you that the world of 1968 is far removed in outlook and mood from the world of 1947. In these intervening years, new factors have emerged which have radically altered the essential nature of issues involved in a solution of the problems of Kashmir. The right to self-determination, viewed against such a changed background, needs to be interpreted afresh in keeping with today's needs of the people of Kashmir.

There is, of course, a broader implication in the right to self-determination, namely, the inherent right of every people to determine their ways of life and the form and character of their institutions. But this is an extremely complicated matter; and in the context of the modern nation-state, the complications are further compounded. Now, I am not an admirer of the nation-state and in fact regard it as an already outmoded and outdated concept. But it exists and does seem to arouse the strongest sentiment that moves and united men today. It cuts across the boundaries of religion, race, language, culture and ideology, including the ideology of communism.

In the context of the nation-state, it is extremely difficult to define and geographically demarcate 'a people'. Are the Kashmiris a people? Then, what about the Dogras and the Ladakhis? Where will you draw the line? You can look around the world and see for yourselves how doggedly the existing nation-state, no matter how haphazardly created, fights against any of their 'people' wanting to break away or to exercise their right to self-determination.

This is a hard fact of which due notice must be taken. Whether one likes it or not, the Indian nation-state, also a haphazard creation owing to the tragedy of Partition, has its geographical boundaries demarcated. India is no more prepared than Pakistan, or for that matter any other nation-state, willingly and peacefully to let any part of the country break away on any plea whatsoever. Let this fact be duly appreciated. No doubt military means can be used to enforce the right to self-determination, but a breakaway part of a nation-state is never likely to achieve its end or maintain it for long by such means – unless it is helped by other powerful nation-states for their own selfish ends. However, such a possibility is entirely irrelevant to the discussion here, because I am not aware that there is anyone present who is advocating a military or a violent solution. . . .

These are unpleasant but inescapable realities; and as your friend and well-wisher I am bound to speak the truth as I see it. This Convention must understand clearly that after the 1965 conflict, no Government of India can accept a solution that places Kashmir outside the Union of India. Or, to put it positively, a solution has to be found within the framework of the Union. This statement should not surprise any of you, because this is not the first time that I am making it publicly. As some of you at least must know, this also happens to be the view of many others in the country who have been trying over the past several years to create public opinion in favour of an agreed settlement in Kashmir. . . .

The main issue that I would place before you today is, how can the people decide these complicated and grave issues without clear and unambiguous advice from their leaders? I feel strongly, and wish to say to you with all the emphasis I can command, that this is the occasion when you owe it to yourselves and to the people to make up your minds and advise them unambiguously on these vital issues. I donot think it will be difficult for the leaders gathered here to go to the people and convince them that the decisions reached here are the best possible solutions in the circumstances and would guarantee them peace, happiness and honour. If this Convention is not to be a mere exercise in political debate but represents an earnest and constructive effort to find a practical way out of the present impasse, I am convinced that this is the wisest course open to it.

Another large question that my suggestion raises is, how will Pakistan react to a settlement within the limits pointed out by me? It is often urged that unless Pakistan is at least tacitly reconciled to the situation here, there can be no guarantee of peace and security in the State. This is true. So, let us see what possible Pakistani reaction there could be. Pakistan's public stand has always been that the people of this State should themselves decide their fate. Therefore, if you take a decision here and persuade the people to endorse it, as I have no doubt that you will be able to do, Pakistan will have no valid grievance or cause for complaint. World opinion too would acclaim a settlement acceptable to the people of Kashmir and restrain Pakistan from the pursuit of any policy but that of an acceptance or acquiescence. Should that happen, it may prove to be the beginning of a new and happy chapter in the history of India–Pakistan relations.

The last question, and the most important, is what about the possible reaction of the Government of India to the course I am advocating here? While I cannot speak for the Government of India, I have no doubt that your acceptance of this line would clear the ground for a meaningful dialogue between your leaders and the Government of India. In that event, even other leaders of the State, who have stayed away from this Convention, may join forces with you. It seems to me that a new day would have truly dawned then.

Such questions as the constitutional status of the State within the Indian Union, a guarantee that that status would not be unilaterally altered, etc., will remain to be discussed. But the proper place for such discussions is not here but at a later stage, with the Government of India's representatives at the conference table. I am aware that in some quarters there is a view which is opposed to any State being given a special position, but I doubt if such a view can be maintained in the changing circumstances of India. For historical reasons modification will have to be made in the general pattern. . . .

From *Jayaprakash Narayan: Selected Works*, edited by Bimal Prasad, Vol. 9, Delhi: Manohar Publications, 1964: 293–301.

21. Jayaprakash Narayan's letter to the Editor, *Hindustan Times*, 1 February 1972

Since I read your preceptive and perspicacious editorial on the forthcoming elections in Jammu & Kashmir, in your issue of 13.1.1972, I had been wanting to write to congratulate you with all my heart. I agree with every word that you have said in that editorial. In fact, when rumours were thick in Delhi in the first week of January 1971 that some action was imminent against Sheikh Abdullah and some of his colleagues aimed to deny them the opportunity of participating in the (last) elections to the Lok Sabha, I had raised my voice of protest and also pleaded personally with the Prime Minister and Mr P.N. Haksar. But to no effect. As a result, India's image as a democracy grievously suffered in the eyes of the world and the people in the Valley were further alienated from the rest of us. Referring to the externment order served on the Kashmiri leaders, I had deplored *inter alia* that we had foolishly thrown away 'the first chance that had occurred since 1953 of drawing Sheikh Abdullah and his colleagues into the *mainstream of Indian public life* and of letting the healing capacities of participation in the democratic process produce their beneficient results'. I am glad that these words find such a powerful echo in your editorial in the present context.

The context again is that of elections – this time to the Jammu & Kashmir State Assembly. And once again the new Chief Minister, Mr Mir Qasim, with the concurrence, I am sure, of Delhi, has announced that the externment orders will remain in force because the conditions that obtained before have remained unchanged. That surely is an amazing statement to be made by a responsible political leader. One should have thought that the independence of Bangladesh and the defeat of the Pakistan army have completely changed the situation in the subcontinent. If no change has occurred in the minds of the Muslims of Jammu & Kashmir, it is an admission of the complete bankruptcy of Mr Qasim's party and his leadership. Personally I do not accept his assessment of the situation, however, and he seems to be motivated more by personal power considerations than reconciliation in the Valley and the good of its people. I hope I am wrong, but I can find no other reasonable explanation for his action.

But let me go back to the question of democracy. For the past ten months we have been presenting ourselves to the world as ardent champions of democracy and the rights of man in Bangladesh. What are we going to tell the world when we deny the same rights to our own citizens in one of our States? Whatever government spokesmen might have said before or may say now, there has never been a free and fair election in the State of Jammu & Kashmir. As you have so rightly pointed out in your editorial, freedom and democracy are indivisible. But if Sheikh Abdullah and his externed colleagues are not alowed to return to their State sufficiently before the elections, and the political prisoners yet in prison, barring those guilty of proven acts of violence, continue to be held in prison – I know some have been released but many are still behind the prison bars – how can our loud professions of democracy be squared with our acts and the world convinced that we do not follow a double standard: one at home and another abroad?

Let me at this point make my position clear on one important relevant point. There was a time when I used to plead persistently for negotiations with Sheikh Abdullah so as to reach an agreement with him and satisfy his amour propre. That was because I had felt convinced after my prolonged talks with him at Kodaikanal that he would be agreeable to his State remaining within the Indian Union, irrespective of Pakistan's wishes, provided we made some face-saving concessions to him. But, unaccountably, talks with him were never seriously held except in fits and starts. I believe the most serious series of talks held were between him and Shri G. Parthasarathi some time after the Sheikh's release from Kodaikanal and his return to Delhi from his State where he had made some rather ambiguous and unfortunate statements. Yet, I believe the nearest point ever reached between the Indian and the Sheikh's views was reached then. But for some inexplicable reason, when the issues were about to be clinched and Shri Parthasarathi was scheduled to meet the Sheikh again in a day or two, Shri Parthasarathi was hastened out to New York without a word of explanation to the Sheikh. Since then there has never been a serious effort made to explore the possibilities of a political accommodation with the Kashmiri leader.

My purpose in relating this past bit of history is not to suggest that the Government of India should once again enter into any negotiations with the Sheikh so as to create the requisite conditions for a credible, democratic election in the Valley. I have to confess with a heavy heart that Sheikh Saheb's attitude towards the freedom struggle of Bangladesh and his attempt to draw a parallel between the Kashmir and Bangladesh issues have sorely disappointed and disillusioned me. After all that has happened since 1947, it is futile for any Kashmiri leader to keep on harping on Jawaharlal Nehru's assurance to hold a plebiscite in the State when normalcy was restored there. The plebiscite issue is dead for ever. Even the Sheikh cannot put back the clock of history. No question can be raised now about the accession of Jammu & Kashmir to India. Anyone who thinks otherwise is living in a fool's paradise and has failed to grow with times and grasp the historic significance of the tremendous changes that have taken place in the Indian sub-continent. In fact, I doubt if there are many left in the Valley itself who are any more concerned about it. The only question that may still be considered to be relevant is that of the quantum of autonomy that Jammu & Kashmir should enjoy within the Union of India, and Jammu and Ladakh regions, in their turn, should enjoy within the constitutional framework of the State. But this is not a question in any way peculiar to Jammu & Kashmir. There are several States in this country which have been demanding a larger measure of autonomy. There is, for instance, the Rajamannar Committee's report in regard to Tamil Nadu. But at the same time it must be recalled with pride the ringing words of Chief Minister Shri Karunanidhi which he is recently reported to have spoken at a public meeting at Thanjavur: 'The demand for greater autonomy to the States', he declared, 'was never meant to divide the country but only to promote the welfare of the people. . . . The Prime Minister, Mrs Indira Gandhi, herself could examine the demand for more powers to the States for advancing the people's interests without in any way affecting unity and integrity of the country.'

There is enough flexibility in our Constitution and our Central and State leaders have been wise enough to appreciate the limits within which the demand for autonomy may be pressed. I myself have been a consistent advocate of a much larger measure of autonomy to the States in view of the vastness of our population and the diversity of our problems. I have also felt that smaller States would make for better government and bring democracy nearer to the people and give them a better sense of participation, and, further, that smaller States would also help in removing regional disparities with far less tension and at a faster pace. At the same time I have also been consistently emphasizing that the strength and authority of the Union Government should not be impaired in any way, nor should the territorial integrity of the country be allowed to be weakened. I believe that within these limits there is enough scope for mutual adjustment, accommodation and give and take.

For these reasons I have never doubted that there was any danger whatever to the integrity of our nation. I am sure India would continue to remain united and keep growing from strength to strength. We have colossal problems, but I am confident that we shall conquer them. Happily, the independence of Bangladesh, the second largest Muslim nation in the world, and the role of so-called 'Hindu' India in the liberation of the new nation have driven the last nail into the coffin of both Hindu and Muslim communalism in this country. Habits die slowly, but I am sure even the most bigoted will not fail to get the message of the recent historic events. Incidentally, may I suggest to the Government of India to take a leaf out of the book of Bangladesh and ban at least those political parties in this country who still flaunt unabashed their communal character by their very name and action, such as the Hindu Mahasabha and the Muslim League. Casteism, of course, will continue as a terrible blight, but it is more a product of socio-economic backwardness than anything else. Caste as a basis of social organization has lost whatever validity it might have possessed before, and I am sure that as the country marches forward, casteism will die a natural death. This is not to suggest that there is no need to carry on a ceaseless and enlightened war against this outdated relic of the past, which politics more than anything else is keeping alive.

It is because of this faith in India's fature that I am pleading for a free and fair election in the State of Jammu & Kashmir, and am trying to convince all concerned that no election in that State can ever be considered by impartial observers as free and fair unless its externed leaders are allowed to go back in time to participate in it if they so desire. I must admit, however, I am not so sure about lifting the ban on the Plebiscite Front. The very word 'plebiscite' has become meaningless and even treasonous in the present context. I do hope that Mirza Afzal Beg and his colleagues would have courage enough to face the present realities as even Mr Bhutto seems to be doing, though reluctantly and slowly, and would reconsider the situation and transform themselves into a real Indian party. In this connection, I find myself in complete agreement with you, Mr Editor, when you ask the question: after all what are we afraid of? The existing laws are enough to deal effectively with any treasonous anti-national activity. I am also sure that the people of the Kashmir Valley have gone through a sincere heart-searching, and whatever affinity they might have felt before with Pakistan on grounds of religion must have been shattered by the events in Bangladesh. The people of Jammu & Kashmir, particularly its Muslim citizens, are in a position to make a valuable contribution to the establishment of harmonious relations between India and what is left of the old Pakistan. As the Prime Minister and many others, including myself, have been repeatedly saying in the past months, India bears no ill-will towards the people of Pakistan and has no wish to see it break up and disintegrate. Disintegration of the residuary Pakistan will make for endless trouble, not only for themselves, but also for India and the entire subcontinent, allowing great power politics to continue to fish in the troubled waters.

As I had said in my very first statement on Bangladesh when Sheikh Mujibur Rahman had launched his remarkable Non-Cooperation movement on 7 March 1971, the territorial integrity of the erstwhile Pakistan depended not on the Bangabandhu, whose demand was only for autonomy, but on Yahya Khan and his government. I should like to quote the relevant words because they are so pertinent to the present crisis in Pakistan:

Let me make it clear that just as I believe in the territorial integrity of my

> country, I do not wish to see the break-up of Pakistan. Sheikh Mujibur Rahman himself has been asking for nothing more than full autonomy for his State and in spite of acts of genocide on the part of the West Pakistan military rule, he has desisted from taking the last irrevocable step of secession. That is a measure of his statesmanship. The responsibility of pushing him beyond his self-imposed limit would be entirely upon the civil and military powers in West Pakistan. Let us hope that they would be wise enough not to push him that far.

Alas, as events have shown, they did not possess that wisdom, and tried instead, along with such of their perverse friends as Mr Nixon and Mr Kissinger, to make India the villain of the piece. The integrity of residuary Pakistan depends in the same manner, not on India, which has repeatedly made its position clear, nor on Khan Abdul Wali Khan or Abdus Samad Khan, the Baluch Gandhi, but on President Bhutto himself. He is faced with an identical question: will he have the wisdom to respect the democratic aspirations of the different peoples of Pakistan? Pakistan is not a homogeneous country and the cry of Islam alone cannot keep it united. By refusing to agree to President Yahya Khan's order for the execution of Sheikh Mujibur Rahman, Mr Zulfiqar Ali Bhutto, who by then had become the Foreign Minister of his government, has given proof of his political resilience and far-sightedness. I hope he will show the same qualities in dealing with the autonomy demand not only of Baluchistan and NWFP, but also of his own State, Sind. His reported refusal to hand over power in the NWFP and Baluchistan to the National Awami Party, which in alliance with the Jamiat-ul-Ulema-e-Islam has a clear majority in the Provincial Assemblies in those States, sounds ominous and pregnant with great deal of mischief. He seems to be repeating the blunder committed by Yahya Khan.

If in this situation the Muslims of Jammu & Kashmir finally make up their mind and accept the realities of the situation, and decide sincerely to live as loyal citizens of India, they will not only be contributing to their own rapid progress, development and welfare, but also to the integrity of Pakistan itself by scotching the likely mischief-makers there and denying them the opportunity to divert their people's mind from the urgent tasks of national reconstruction, establishment of sub-continental (not excluding Bangladesh) peace, goodwill and cooperation so essential for all concerned.

Be that as it may, the Government of India would be making a great contribution to national integration and our cherished ideals of secularism and democracy if it took courage in both its hands and allowed the externed Kashmiri leaders to return home and play their rightful role as equal citizens of this country in the forthcoming elections. Any other course at this moment would be short-sighted, petty-minded and fraught with future dangers.

As you said in your editorial, the Naga rebels who had been waging an armed struggle against India were brought to Delhi and the Prime Minister herself had held negotiations with them, and in spite of continued disturbed conditions in that State, free and fair elections were held which have borne such rich fruits. I apprehend no trouble in Sheikh Abdullah and his friends returning home before the elections. And India would then be able to hold its head high and prove to the world that when it supported the cause of democracy in Bangladesh at such great cost and risk, it did not hesitate to uphold the same ideals in one of its own States.

One last point, though not strictly relevant to the elections in Jammu & Kashmir, yet of vital importance in the context of the vexatious dispute regarding Kashmir, deliberately nurtured over the years by Pakistan and some of the great powers. The point is about the 'ceasefire' line. After so many years and at least three Pakistani overt and covert aggressions across that line, and particularly after the recent Indo–Pak war, the old ceasefire line has no reality or relevance left at all. This is a point on which I find there is general agreement in the country, including its official circles. Nobody, I think, baring some on the lunatic fringes, is wanting to take back by force the whole Pakistan-occupied part of the original State of Jammu & Kashmir. But there is general agreement that the old ceasefire line and the presence of the UN observers, whose contribution to assuring peace along that line has been nil, have become anachronisms now. It follows, therefore – and on this point too a national consensus has emerged – that the so-called ceasefire line should be rationalized and re-drawn and converted into a well-defined permanent international border so as to guarantee India's security in that region and make it difficult, if not impossible, for Pakistani adventurers to create any further mischief. If that were done, any UN presence in that area would become unnecessary and contrary to international law. I believe, outside India also it is now recognized that the original ceasefire line was irrational and hastily drawn up without any regard to geography and the requirements of stability and security and the wishes of the people of the area, particularly those of the Maharaja and the then Prime Minister of the State, Sheikh Mohammad Abdullah.

This is a matter on which some amount of give and take may be necessary. One hopes that President Bhutto is sincerely concerned about establishing firm and friendly relations with India, which is so obviously essential in the interests of both the nations, besides eliminating at the same time the possibility of international intrigues which have wrought so much mischief in the past. I am sure that if Mr Bhutto rises to the occasion, refuses to be anybody's tool, accepts the facts of history and desires lasting peace with India and mutual cooperation between the two countries, he will not find the Government of India to be unresponsive.

From *Jayaprakash Narayan Papers*, Nehru Memorial Museum and Library, New Delhi. Jayaprakash Narayan contributed this specially to *The Hindustan Times* which published it in a letter form on 1 February 1972.

22. Letters by Sheikh Abdullah to Mirza Mohammed Afzal Beg, president of the then Plebiscite Front, and Syed Mir Qasim, then leader of the Congress Legislature Party, inviting them to join the revived National Conference

Srinagar,
May 23, 1975

My dear Beg Saheb,

You would recall that during our talks with the Central Government, preceding the Accord, the future of the Plebiscite Front came under discussion a number of times; and it was our agreed stand that the right of decision with regard to the future of the Front, its shape and its political programme, lay with its Working Committee and General Council. It was also our assertion that all these questions would be taken up in proper time; and even though we accepted the necessity of changing the name of the Front under the new circumstances, we made it amply clear that this could not be made a basis or a condition precedent for any accord between us and the Centre. I was happy that our stand was taken in its proper perspective and that Mrs Gandhi and her associates did not insist on a hurried change in the nomenclature, form or the pattern of activities of the Front.

During the last few months you and other leading members of your party have had opportunities of deliberating over this question of a new name and fresh political aims; and I am grateful to you for having kept me informed about your views and the trends in the party. It appears now, as is revealed by your latest statements in this regard, that the Front has decided to disband itself and, in its place, form a new party. I am sure that this decision has the support of a sizeable majority of the members, and that you and your comrades will show the same magnanimity of approach, foresight and large-heartedness in adopting a name and a programme for the new party as had always been characteristic of the Front.

This vexing problem of substituting the Front with a new political forum has naturally occupied my mind also. Indeed, as you know, we have been exchanging ideas on this issue. But now, as you have made an explicit pronouncement about the end of the Front, the question, important as it always was, has assumed an urgency which forbids any further ramblings in our search and calls for our immediate attention, so that the present political vacuum is filled, and a positive programme for economic uplift and a healthy political set-up is placed before the people of the State. This was our purpose for assuming responsibilities of the Government.

While drawing the contours of our new party, we have to be careful not to lose sight of our basic aims, the history of our struggle to achieve them, the importance of our distinctive role and the compulsions of the present-day circumstances. At no cost should we forget that we are the inheritors of a great past; and it should be our anxiety not to take a false step that might disturb the historical continuity which, in turn, forms a base for the edifice of our pride. If we break away from our past, we will have no foundation to erect our future upon. I do not think we should wash our hands completely from our past heritage only because some userpers succeeded in sabotaging us at a very important juncture of our struggle. Indeed, after considering the matter in all its aspects and in depth, I have come to the conclusion that it is time that we all gather under the same flag which fluttered over our heads during all the great days of our crusade against tyranny and exploitation. It is this flag which symbolized our struggle for thirty years, and it is with this that all our memories and the blood of our martyrs is associated. At this time particularly, when we have turned an important corner in the history of our struggle, it would look odd if we brushed aside the very symbol of sacrifice that blazed our trail and heralded all our steps for honour and pride. It should certainly not be our part to deprive ourselves of this great legacy. It is my considered opinion, therefore, and also my decision that we should revive our bonds with the old values of that name – National Conference – and move forward with renewed determination to achieve our aims and fulfil the dreams which stand documented in 'Naya Kashmir' and to which are dedicated the thirty long years of our movement.

You would agree that even though the scope for activities of the National Conference as a political party was restricted to the State, it was veritably a part and parcel of the freedom movement of India, in its undoubted ideological affinity with it and in its practical participation. It was for this reason that great leaders of our country were deeply associated with all the events and movements of the National Conference, and among these were the illustrious names of Mahatama Gandhi, Jawaharlal Nehru, Abul Kalam Azad and Badshah Khan. Acting with perfect understanding, we had evolved methods of participation without belonging to one organization. In that memorable period of harmony the need of a merger with the Indian National Congress was never felt by anybody. On the other hand, Pandit Nehru and his colleagues did not only approve the idea of keeping the individuality of the National Conference intact but also felt happy about it. Such an attitude towards our particular needs and problems only proved that the Central leaders were positively in favour of letting us retain our identity; and at this juncture, when, after a span of twenty two years, Mrs Indira Gandhi and her colleagues have also conceded, in their latest Accord with us, the importance of the peculiar problems which we face in the State, I think it should be most appropriate that the same organization is reborn in the State with which is associated a golden period of friendship and cooperation, a time which could be regarded as the most pleasant in terms of our relations with the Central leaders. I think even today there is considerable scope of active participation by other progressive forces of the country with our political movement, and that we can stand in company in our fight for secularism, democracy and social justice. The revival of the National Conference will certainly pave many ways to purposeful and coordinated activities and I am sure that we will succeed, once again in establishing mutual trust and confidence.

At the State level, I intend to invite all the friends who continued to struggle for the principles, upholding which you and I and many of our comrades suffered the misery of incarceration. I intend to invite them all to join the National Conference. It is my intention also to invite even those friends who got severed from our movement after 1953 under misunderstanding and the pressure of times, and those also who renounced politics or joined other political parties after power was captured by a self-seeking and unscrupulous coterie. In my anxiety to impart a truly representative character to the organization and to make it a party of the State's people, I will request those friends also to join it who had formed the Congress, considering it to be as an alternative to the National Conference. It is towards this end that I am writing separately to Syed Mir Qasim in detail.

Before I make a formal announcement in this regard, however, I would like you to consult your colleagues and enlighten me about your reaction so that I could lay down my future course of action. To those of our friends who are still haunted by the post-1953 image of the National Conference we have to explain that inherent values and the sanctity of institutions do not get affected by temporary desecrations. During the bloody days of 1947 numerous temples, mosques and other places of worship were forcibly occupied by inhuman looters. But the history of these places did not get altered, nor did their worth diminish in any way. In the same manner, the National Conference passed through an ugly time, a miserable period, under the enemies of our movement, but that could not and should not be expected to cast a lasting shadow on the inherent power, status or the sanctity of the organization. It is indeed our occasion to feel satisfied in our pride of having succeeded in regaining a paradise lost.

S/d S.M. Abdullah

May 23, 1975

My dear Qasim Saheb,

You might be aware that for some time past a debate has been going on in our ranks regarding the constitution of a new political organization. The President of the Plebiscite Front, Mirza Mohammed Afzal Beg, has announced the decision to dissolve the Front and set up a new party. Along with this, some of our colleagues are considering the pros and cons of joining the Congress. My personal interest in the issue notwithstanding, I kept myself aloof from the debate so far simply for the reason that everyone should have the full freedom of expressing his opinion. Everybody should be able to express the dictates of his conscience, regardless of my likes and dislikes in this issue. I had also the opportunity to talk to my old colleagues and friends during this period, and I tried to ascertain their views. You will recall that I also discussed the subject with you. In this process, I tried to listen to and understand various viewpoints on the issue, and now I am in a position to express my final and well-considered opinion.

You will agree with me that no political organization can become live, purposive and strong unless it has the resolute popular backing. This is possible only when this political organization has behind it the rich asset of a movement, a history and a struggle, whereby people have a sense of association. According to this standard, National Conference is the only organization in our State with which the history of our struggle, our dreams and aspiration are linked. Every soldier and commander of our freedom movement will bear testimony to this fact that it is under the banner of National Conference alone that we fought decisive and invigorating battles against despotic and feudalistic regimes. I hardly need reminding you that after the conversion of Muslim Conference into National Conference in 1938, it was the National Conference alone which sympathized and guided the people of the State, on every turn of its political history. Thus, this organization became the valuable heritage of our movement and history. The tragedy of 1953 is a black chapter of this beautiful history, the mere mention of which is sufficient to injure our mutual trust and confidence. I want to forget this unpleasant period like a nightmare and revive the National Conference – with which is linked the blood of our martyrs, sacrifices of our people, fidelity of our friends and the conspiracies of our enemies. This invaluable asset of our thirty years of labour and hard work cannot be re-created even in 100 years. This is the reason why I have, after careful deliberation, chosen National Conference as my instrument for fulfilment of our political ends, execution of economic plans and establishment of a progressive and welfare society. I would like that all our friends subscribing to the political ideals of secularism, democracy and social justice should, by joining National Conference, once again work shoulder to shoulder with determination, unity and zeal, and take Kashmir on the road of fulfilling the dream of 'Naya Kashmir'. I sincerely and affectionately invite you, your other friends, to forget individual differences, personal preferences, past bitterness and imaginary apprehensions, to join the National Conference and become inheritors of this great heritage, which to all of us is a matter of great pride and confidence. I am confident that the resurrection of the National Conference will restore the great historical continuity which, due to some unpleasant situation, had been snapped for some time, and which had produced an ominous vacuum in our political history. I am aware that you are presently associated with a political organization which, because of its proud past and great traditions, has a great standing in the political history of our country. I also affirm the role played by the Indian National Congress in the freedom struggle and subsequent economic reconstruction of the country. There can be no denying of its greatness and capacities. But, in spite of this, if I invite you and your colleagues to the National Conference, it is due to the reason that cooperation and not confrontation have marked the relationship between the National Conference and Congress. These two organizations, though organizationally separate, always worked together on the ideological level. That is why in its struggle against the despotic rule of Maharaja, National Conference could always elicit the practical support and active cooperation of the commanders of the Indian freedom struggle. In the 'Quit Kashmir' movement of 1946 Shri Jawaharlal Nehru, despite his heavy preoccupations, came to our assistance, and was arrested by the then Prime Minister, Mr R.C. Kak. Similarly, in 1944 Mr Nehru, Maulana Abdul Kalam Azad and Badshah Khan came to participate in the Annual Session of the National Conference at Sopore. In this way, a climate of mutual unity and cooperation was established between the National Conference and the Congress, and it was never felt necessary that the two parties should merge. I can recall vividly that the top leaders of Congress were so much satisfied with this ideological affinity that they always encouraged us to maintain our individual identity.

Regarding the role of the National Conference after 1953 and its subsequent merger with the Congress in 1965, I would only say that it was motivated not by political considerations but by the experience of time. Now, fortunately, that climate has changed and the compulsions which kept us apart no longer exist. We should do everything to strengthen the new atmosphere and endeavour to eliminate all possible bitternesses and obstructions which can weaken our mutual cooperation. For this reason, we should no longer delay the rejuvenation of the National Conference and its high values with which are linked our past history and bright future. All of us are pledged to the dream of 'Naya Kashmir' and the people of this State for the last 25years are restive for the fulfilment of this dream. Much valuable time has been wasted and we cannot afford to waste more. Therefore, I invite you and your colleagues sincerely to join the National Conference and play your historical role in the decisive fight against poverty, illiteracy and backwardness. I am confident that you and your colleagues will seriously deliberate upon my appeal, and intimate me with your decision. I hope that the Central leadership of the Indian National Congress will, keeping in view the special problems of the State and the larger interests of the country, permit you to join the National Conference, and thus fulfil a historical necessity.

I have also invited the President of the Plebiscite Front, Mr Mirza Mohammed Afzal Beg, and his colleagues to join the party. I do hope that he and his party will accept my invitation. I am also inviting all other leading political workers of Jammu, Kashmir and Ladakh who have somehow been associated with the freedom struggle, so that the National Conference attains the same public support at the State level which it enjoyed before 1953 as the premier political voice of the people.

Yours sincerely
(S.M. Abdullah)

Jenab Syed Mir Qasim,
Srinagar.

Copies of the letters by courtesy of Sheikh Abdullah.

23. Correspondence between Sheikh Abdullah and leaders of the Janata Party

Camp Srinagar,
17 April 1977

Dear Sheikh Saheb,
Yesterday evening, I did not like to interrupt your fascinating exposition of your view-point. Later, lack of time prevented us from pursuing the subject. There is, however, one point that I must clarify immediately. You made references to the question of trust. May I point out that when you were in Delhi last, all of us independently and spontaneously urged upon you to take the lead in organizing the Janata Party in the State. For various reasons you could not respond to the proposal.

In determining our approach to the State we have to be guided by the fundamental urges that have shaped the Janata Party. Next only to our dedication to democracy and human rights is our conviction for consolidation of political parties. Without the sacrifice of the separate identities of our parties, we could never have evoked the historic response of the people. For us the need for political consolidation remains imperative. I hope when you think about trust or lack of it, you will keep before you our considerations and convictions.

Yours sincerely,
Sd/- (Ashok Mehta)

Sheikh Mohammad Abdullah,
10, Maulana Azad Road,
Srinagar.

Camp Srinagar,
18 April 1977

Dear Sheikh Saheb,
I am deeply grateful to you for the warmth that you showed for me this morning. I shall cherish the cordiality of our talk. In order to be sure that I

have understood your point of view properly, I am briefly summarizing our talk:

1. The special conditions of Kashmir need to be remembered, so also the historic role of, and the struggle waged by, the National Conference. You were particular that I should remind my colleagues about the purposeful consideration extended to these matters by Pt. Jawaharlal Nehru and even Sardar Patel.

2. The National Conference also shares the objective of conciliation of the democratic forces in the country.

3. The Conference, however, believes that the formation of the Janata Party should be put off till after the elections. The Conference should be allowed to contest the elections with the good-will and support of the Janata Party. Where the Conference may not be able to put up its own candidates, which can happen in some constituencies in Jammu, candidates may fight as Independents but who will later be eligible for holding Ministerial offices. Thus, in fact, it will be a coalition Government led by the National Conference.

4. After the elections the spokesmen of the two parties can sit down and consider the modalities of merger, care being taken that the process is not hustled.

5. I was anxious to know from you as to what would happen to various elements unconnected with, and perhaps opposed to the National Conference. Both of us seem to agree that they were unlikely to gravitate as a Congress which is likely to crumble. I, therefore, requested you to give me your assessment about these forces. After they come together what are they likely to do, what would be their stance and what would be its implications and repercussions on the politics of the State. This assessment is of importance in determining the likely pulls and pressures for or against merger of the National Conference with the Janata Party. You very kindly agreed to let me have your assessment before I left for Delhi.

Please convey my respects to Begum Sahiba,

Yours sincerely,
Sd/- Ashok Mehta

Sheikh Mohammad Abdullah,
10, Maulana Azad Road,
Srinagar

10, Maulana Azad Road,
Srinagar, Kashmir,
18 April 1977

My dear Ashok Ji,

I acknowledge the receipt of your letter dated the 18th April.

With regard to point 4 of your summary wherein you have referred to the consideration of ‘the modalities of merger’ by the spokesmen of our two parties after the elections, I would like to clarify that the modalities can only be considered after the question of merger is settled.

In answer to point 5 of your summary, I am of the view that the elements referred to by you as being opposed to the National Conference would be averse to functioning under a communal dispensation, but would rather put up a posture of being genuinely secular to make election gains. Once the elections are over they will appear in their true colours. You may have noted that Maulvi Farooq has publicly said that he is putting aside the question of self-determination (i.e., plebiscite) only for about three months. This is an instance in point. The elements opposed to the National Conference will endeavour to create obstacles and difficulties in the efforts made by us to arrive at a mutually amicable and workable relationship between the Janata Party and the National Conference. It will be in the overall interests of national solidarity not to give any succour to these elements. For the present their avowed aim is to attempt to forestall any meaningful conclusion to our talks so as to create a stalemate between us. They will do their utmost to play the Janata Party and the National Conference against each other to gain their nefarious ends. We shall have to guard against this most of all.

With kindest regards,

Yours sincerely
Sd/- (S.M. Abdullah)

Shri Ashok Mehta
Camp Srinagar.

10, Maulana Azad Road,
Srinagar, Kashmir
26 May 1977

My dear Chandra Shekhar ji,

I was happy to read in today's national papers your clarification on the status of Kashmir in the Indian Union wherein you have unambiguously stated the official position of your party on the issue. You are also alleged to have deplored attempts by some, including myself, to create confusion over your party's position in this regard.

The confusion, doubts and misgivings that have been created in the minds of the people of Jammu and Kashmir with regard to the position of Article 370 are due to the seemingly conflicting pronouncements made by some leading members of the Janata Party and my friend, Shri J.P. Narayan. It is true that soon after assuming office at the Centre, Shri Vajpayee as Foreign Minister stated that Article 370 would not be altered without consulting the people of Kashmir. However, hardly any time had elapsed after his statement when another important member of your party, Shri Subramaniam Swamy, MP, stated in a press conference in Jammu that he would press for the complete abrogation of this Article.

Everybody in the country is aware of my relations with Shri J. P. Narayan and the pre-eminent position he holds as the main inspiration behind your party. I was, I must confess, shocked when I read in the press the contents of his letter addressed to Shri Ghulam Mohiuddin Kara in which the former stated: 'Kashmir, so far, has tended to maintain some kind of separateness from India and its politics has been, more or less, not in line with the main political developments in this country. Now I find that you are active in forging the Janata Party in Jammu and Kashmir.' Shri Narayan expressed the hope that the Janata Party would bridge this 'political gulf'.

In April last, your party deputed a fact-finding mission to the State led by Shri Ashok Mehta who had with him Shri Bhanu Pratap Singh, Member of Parliament and Shri Nanaji Deshmukh, MP. It pains me to say that instead of finding facts and assessing the situation in the State objectively, they lost no time in collecting all sorts of persons to form the Janata Party unit, many of whom were rejected by the people because of their dubious past. Their only qualification was their anti-Abdullah stance. Shri Mehta and his colleagues came to see me as well and had dinner with me. I made it quite plain to them that if this was the real intention of their fact-finding mission, then it would hardly serve any useful purpose to seek understanding with me. Shri Mehta came to see me for the second time before his departure for Delhi. He sprang another surprise by categorically stating in the presence of my colleagues, Mr Mirza Mohammad Afzal Beg, Mr Ghulam Mohammad Shah and Mr D.D. Thakur, that his party was fundamentally opposed to the Kashmir policy of the late Jawaharlal Nehru.

As everybody knows, this policy was jointly evolved by Shri Nehru and his important colleagues, Sardar Patel, Maulana Azad, C. Rajagopalachari and Gopalaswami Ayyangar, on the one side, and myself, Mirza Afzal Beg and the late Bakshi Ghulam Mohammad, on the other, and unanimously endorsed by Parliament and the Constituent Assembly of the State.

While presenting the Delhi Agreement to the State's Constituent Assembly on 11 August 1952 for its approval, I said: 'I would like to make it clear that any suggestions of altering arbitrarily this basis of our relationship with India would not only constitute a breach of the spirit that letter of the Constitution, but it might invite serious consequences for a harmonious association of our State with India.' Mere reference to my well-known position in my speech at Mujahid Manzil, Srinagar on 23 May 1977 should not have caused confusion in anybody's mind.

Shri Nehru and his above-named colleagues are not alive to defend their policies on Kashmir, but I and Mr Beg are still living. How does, if I may ask, your party expect us to denounce and jettison those policies which were evolved after great thought and care? If one of your front-rank colleagues makes such a bold statement in denunciation of these policies in our presence, should we not take it seriously? If your party, according to Shri Mehta, is fundamentally opposed to Nehru's policy on Kashmir, then where do the people of the State stand? And if I, on their behalf, press for clarification by the Janata Party as well as by the Central Government of their stand on these policies, then how can one call this as 'unfortunate'?

I quite understand that your party is yet in the formative stage and the greatest task facing you is to evolve an agreed policy on many matters of state, including that of Kashmir. Therefore, if the leading lights of your party speak in differing terms on various policy matters, it is understandable. However, you will undoubtedly agree with me that this discordance is not helpful and the trend has got to stop before irreparable damage is caused to the supreme and overall interests of the country as a whole. It is in these circumstances that I was compelled to draw the attention of the ruling party at the Centre to the doubts and misgivings caused in the minds of the people of Jammu and Kashmir concerning the Janata Party's ambiguous position on Article 370.

I may add here for your information that the Congress Party has always had reservation about the special relationship between the State and India. We were pressurized to accept the complete merger of the State with India, and when we did not yield, coercion and suppression were taken recourse to in order achieve their aims. But all their efforts proved a failure. The people of Jammu and Kashmir did not agree to surrender their autonomy. With this confrontation between the people of the State and the Government of India, the situation in the State drifted towards total chaos. It was then that I was invited by Smt. Indira Gandhi to lend my helping hand to save the situation from further deterioration. I accepted the offer on the condition made explicitly clear to her emissary, Shri G. Parthasarathi, in my letter to him dated 23 August 1974, wherein I stated:

> Apropos our talks yesterday and the day before, I hope that I have made it abundantly clear to you that I can assume office only on the basis of the position as it existed on 8 August 1953.
>
> With regard to the provisions of the Constitution or the Union Laws and Entries applied to the Jammu and Kashmir State after 9th August, 1953, judgement thereupon will be deferred till the newly-elected Assembly comes into being.

It is with this spirit that I undertook the heavy and seemingly insurmountable task of improving the situation in the State, and all will bear witness to it in Jammu and Kashmir except those who have eyes but cannot see, ears but cannot hear, and whose entire power of reasoning is befuddled by their personal jealousies, hatred and rancour towards my person.

In all fairness, I would like to ask you that if the Janata Party can make alliances with the Akali Dal, the DMK, the CPI(M), and many other national and regional parties, then why should the Janata Party appear so —— to insist on the winding up of the National Conference and seek its merger with your party? It is not understandable that while Shri Nanaji Deshmukh stated categorically recently that the Janata Party —— no alliance with the

National Conference, —— unit of his party in the State is keenly —— avowedly communal and anti-national parti —— Awami Action Committee and the Jamaat-I —— you agree with me if I may ask, that adop —— hostile attitude towards the National Conference —— has had an undoubtedly brilliant record of national service and which made it possible for the Sheikh to accede to India, is unmeritted by my party?

It will not, I hope, be too presumptuous of me to say that I claim many friends in your party including of course yourself, and I also hope and trust that they will consider my point of view with equanimity, sympathy and understanding, and will not attribute ulterior motives if I seek clarification from the party which has just taken the destiny of the country in its hands so that Indo–Kashmir relationship is strengthened and consolidated. Since the manner in which my views on Article 370 have been presented to the people by the national press have created a controversy and misgivings, I am releasing this letter to the press.

With kindest regards,

Yours sincerely,
Sheikh Abdullah

Shri Chandra Shekhar
President of the Janata Party,
Jantar Mantar Road, New Delhi.

Note: Chandra Shekhar did not reply to this letter. The missing words are due to the damaged condition of the letter.

Copies of the letters, courtesy Sheikh Abdullah.

24. 'Muslims a Minority in JK Services', *Greater Kashmir*, 7 May 2007

Srinagar, May 6
While the Sachar Committee Report has painted a dismal picture of the condition of Indian Muslims, the plight of the community in Jammu and Kashmir, according to senior government officials, is no better. Muslims figure at the bottom when it comes to their share in the state administration. And to top it, they are a distant minority in the top bureaucratic positions.

Official sources said that out of 63 IAS officers – both direct and indirect – 30 are Muslims, 28 Hindus, 3 Sikhs and 2 Buddhists. Muslim representation in the present top bureaucratic line-up is zero. Most of the Financial Commissioners and Principal Secretaries of the State happen to be non-Muslims. No Muslim bureaucrat heads important departments like Home,

Finance and Planning, Health, Industry, and Works. The only seniormost Muslim IAS officers are Iqbal Dhandey and Khursid Ahmed Ganai. While Ladakh region has had its first Chief Secretary in the shape of the incumbent C. Phunsong, only 8 of the 24 Chief Secretaries since 1947 were Muslims.

The situation in the police department is worse. Since 1914, when the post of J&K Police Chief was first created by then Maharaja of Kashmir, the state has had only two Muslim police chiefs. In fact from 1914 to 1979 no police chief was Muslim. The situation was no different till last year. The State's 7 DGP and 5 ADGP rank officers are non-Muslims, and only 4 out of 15 IGP rank are Muslims. And down the line in the police, there are only 6 Muslims among the 15 DIGs and only 26 among 87 SSPs. Muslims form less than one-third of the IPS officers. Out of 111 IPS officers, only 33 are Muslims including an IPS officer of Bihar cadre, Abdul Gani Mir, who was repatriated to that State last year.

Though the figures for the State's civil service, the Kashmir Administrative Service (KAS), show a different picture, it won't remain the same for long. Out of 343 officers, 217 are Muslims. But if the last two KAS results are anything to go by, this will also change soon. Muslims form a small percentage of the candidates who passed the two KAS exams held in the past five years. In 2001, for example, only 80 out of the 208 successful candidates were Muslims. Similarly in 2004, of a total of 137 successful candidates only 62 were Muslims.

The question is not only how many Muslims there are at higher positions, but how many there are from the Jammu and Kashmir State at decision-making levels. Of course the Chief Secretary is from Ladakh but what about the rest of the top-level bureaucracy?

The top two officers presently holding Principal Secretary position are non-locals. They are Ajit Kumar and SB Mathur. The Financial Commissioner, B.R. Singh, and Principal Secretary Agriculture, Satinder Singh, too are non-locals. Manu Des Lupin, Additional Secretary Agriculture, Government of India, is on deputation in the State, and Sham Singh Kupur, presently Principal Secretary Planning, is also a non-State subject.

A.S. Sidhu, Samuel Vergese, Makav Lal, Babu Lal Navesh, Pankaj Jain, Dr Arun Kumar, Sonali Kumar and P.G. Dharchakerverty are Principal Secretaries heading different departments; they are all non-State subjects.

Now take a look at the Commissioner Secretaries who are from the State: Brij Raj Sharma, Promod Jain, Atul Dulu, Basharat Ahmad Dhar, Devender Nagrotra and Mehbood Iqbal. The number of Commissioner Secretaries from other parts of India is 10. They are: K.B. Agarwal, B.B. Vyas, Lokesh Jha, Suresh Kumar, Pradeep Tripathi, Sudesh Panday, Sandeep Naik, Arun Kumar Malhotra, Umang Narola and R.K. Goel.

The non-local Secretaries are: Shant Munu, Shailendra Kumar, Vipul Pathak, A.K. Parimar and Dheeraj Gupta.

However, some officials of the Public Service Commission attribute the growing low percentage of candidates from the Valley in administrative services to 'lack of interest' among the Valley candidates in the KAS examination. A senior PSC official said that in July 2005, some 7,000 candidates from the Valley appeared for the preliminary examination. From Jammu, 11,000 appeared. Some even attribute the low percentage of Muslims in government services to 'lack of Muslim educated class' in the State.

But this opinion runs contrary to the findings of the Sachar Committee Report which paints an encouraging picture of the educational status of the Valley's Muslims. According to the Report, the primary class enrolment of Muslim children exceeded 5.3 lakh last year with the boy–girl ratio a healthy 50.3:49.7. The number of Muslim male literates has increased by 25 per cent and women by 23 per cent over the past two decades, revealed the Sachar Committee findings.

Besides, Kashmir produces more than 16,000 Muslim graduates every year and the number of postgraduates crosses 3,000 annually. The figure for female students pursuing higher education is also encouraging. Of the 57,000 students enrolled in colleges, more than 25,000 are girls.

On the contrary, despite the hullabaloo about the proliferation of Islamic seminaries across the Valley, only 2,691 students – 950 of them girls – are enrolled in the Darul Ulooms.

LIST OF IAS OFFICERS OF J&K CADRE AS ON 11.11.2005

S. No.	Name of the officer
1	Ajit Kumar
2	Amit Kushari
3	Vijay Bakaya
4	Sohan Behri Mathur
5	Birinder Raj Singh
6	Gurmukh Das Wadhwa
7	Chewing Phunsog
8	Balwant Raj Kundal
9	Sadanand V. Bhave
10	Satinder Singh Sahni
11	S. Maria Desalphine
12	Sham Singh Kapur
13	Azmer Singh Sidhu
14	Samuel Verghese
15	Madhab Lal
16	Parvej Dewan
17	Babu Lal Nimesh
18	Anil Goswami
19	Pankaj Jain

20	Mohammead Iqbal Khanday
21	Dr Arun Kumar
22	Mrs Sonali Kumar
23	Prabodh Gopal Dhar Chakraborty
24	Dr Rave Kulbushan Jerath
25	Ashok Kumar Angurana
26	Khurshid Ahmed Ganai
27	Brij Ram Sarma
28	Krishan Ballabh Agarwal
29	Pramod Kunar Jain
30	Bharat Bushan Vyas
31	Rakesh Kumar Gupta
32	Lokesh Dutt Jha
33	Suresh Kumar
34	Praip Kumar Tripathi
35	Sudhanshu Pandey
36	Sandeep Kumar Nayak
37	Arun Kumar Mehta
38	Khurshid Ahmed Malik
39	Najamus Saqib
40	Atal D. Ulloo
41	Umang Narulla
42	Basharat Ahmad Dhar
43	Devinder Nargotra
44	Mohammad Manzoor Bhat
45	Sham Lal
46	Raj Kumar Goyal
47	Mehboob Iqbal
48	Dr Mohammed Deen
49	Shant Manu
50	Shaleen Kabra
51	Bipul Patgak
52	Ashok Kumar Parmar
53	K.R. Padha
54	A.K. Garyali
55	S. Charanjit Singh
56	Dheeraj Gupta
57	Asgar Jassan Samoon
58	N.K. Verma
59	K.M. Wani
60	Khalid Habib
61	Ms. Naseem Lanker
62	Dalip Singh

63	P.S. Betab
64	M.H. Samoon
65	Abdul Hamid
66	Navin Kumar Choudhary
67	Dr Pawan Kotwal
68	Rohit Kansal
69	Shalender Kunar
70	Sheikh Nisar Ahmad
71	M.S. Khan
72	K.B. Jandial
73	Ghulam Ahmad Peer
74	R.K. Thusu
75	A.K. Raina
76	Ms. Tanveer Jehan
77	Syed Fazalullh
78	Azad Ahmad Lone
79	Jeet Lal Gupta
80	V.K. Bakshi
81	Bisan Das Sharma
82	BashirAhmad Khwaja
83	Gowhar Ahmed
84	Pradeep Gupta
85	B.A. Runiyal
86	Sheikh Ejaz Iqbal
87	Farooq Ahmed Pir
88	Yedullah
89	Mrs Sunita Sharma
90	Abdul Hamid Wani
91	Bua Ditta
92	Kachoo Isfandyar Khan
93	Tashi Dorjee
94	Manoj Kumar Dwivedi
95	Hirdesh Kumar
96	Mrs Sarita Chauhan
97	Sanjeev Verma
98	Dr Mandeep K. Bhandari
99	Saurabh Bhagat
100	Sujeet Kumar Sahu
101	Ghulam Hassan Tantray
102	Mandeep Kaur
103	Pandering Kondabarao Pole
104	M. Raju
105	Shalini Singh

LIST OF IAS OFFICERS OF J&K

Cadre on Central Deputation as on 01.01.2005

S. No.	Name of officer
1	Chewang Phunsog
2	Shiben Lal Bhat
3	Pankaj Jain
4	P.G. Dhar Chakraborty
5	Ashok Kumar Angurana
6	Krishan Ballabh Agarwal
7	P.K. Tripathi
8	Suresh Kumar
9	Sudhanshu Panday
10	Sandeep Kumar Nayak
11	Raj Kumar Goyal
12	Shant Manu
13	Shaleen Kabra
14	Bipul Pathak
15	Navin Kumar Choudhary

INCUMBENCY POSITION OF SOME OF THE IAS OFFICERS OF J&K

S. No.	Name of the officer	Date of retirement
1	Khurshid Ahmad Malik	30.04.2006
2	Mumtaz Afzal	30.03.2005
3	Basarat Ahmad Dhar	31.12.2011
4	Harbhajan Singh	31.05.2005
5	Davender Nargotra	31.10.2001
6	Mohd Manzoor Bhat	30.06.2006
7	Najamus Sadiq	30.11.2006
8	Sham Lal	31.03.2006
9	Feroz Ahmed	31.10.2011
10	Mehboob Iqbal	30.11.2011
11	S. Mahajan	31.01.2005
12	Dr Mohammad deen	31.12.2006
13	K.R. Padhu	30.06.2007
14	A.K.Garyali	31.08.2007
15	S. Charanjit Singh	31.05.2006
16	N.K. Verma	31.05.2010
17	Khazir Mohd Wani	31.03.2009
18	Khalid Habib	31.07.2009
19	Naseem Lanker	08.02.2012
20	Dalip Singh	08.02.2009
21	Pritpal Singh Betab	31.05.2009
22	M.H. Samoon	31.08.2009

23	Abdul Hamid	31.05.2011
24	Sheikh Nisar Ahmed	31.10.2007
25	M.S. Khan	31.01.2007
26	K.B. Jindial	30.11.2009
27	Ghulam Ahmed Peer	31.03.2012
28	R.K. Thushu	31.03.2010
29	A.K. Raina	30.04.2012
30	Tanveer Jehan	31.08.2015
31	Syed Fazalullah	
32	Azad Kumar Lone	31.03.2014
33	Jeet Lal Gupta	31.08.1013
34	V.K. Bakshi	31.01.2010
35	Bisen Das	31.10.1012
36	Bashe Ahmad Khawaja	31.12.2010
37	Gowhar Ahmaed	31.05.2012
38	Pradeep Gupta	31.07.2013
39	B.A. Runiyal	31.03.2013
40	Sheikh Ejaz Iqbal	31.10.2013
41	Farooq agmed Pir	30.04.2014
42	Yedullah	31.05.2013
43	Sunita Sarma	31.08.2012
44	Abdul Hamid	31.03.2012
45	Bua Ditta	31.05.2012
46	Kachoo Isfandtar Khan	31.01.2012
47	Tashi Dorjee	31.05.2011
48	Ghulam Hassan Tantray	30.04.2013

25. K.C. Pant's efforts as Interlocutor in 2001

No. 1/JK/Inv/2001 Date: 14.4.2001

Dear Shri Shabir Ahmed Shah,

Consequent to the announcement of unilateral 'cease-fire' by the Government of India in November 2000, the need for a meaningful forward movement was felt by all sections of people of J&K and outside. In pursuance of this objective, the Prime Minister has nominated me to initiate a political dialogue, which could lead to permanent peace in J&K. This casts a responsibility on all of us who are genuinely interested in ending the strife and suffering of the Kashmiri people, and I seek your fullest cooperation to this end.

I am enclosing the text of the announcement made by the Government of India on April 5, 2001. In this context, keeping in view your concern for the people of J&K, I take this opportunity to invite you for a discussion. I am asking my office to contact you to fix a mutually convenient date and time for a meeting.

With regards,

Yours sincerely
(K.C. Pant)

Shri Shabir Ahmed Shah
President,
J&K Democratic Freedom Party
Srinagar.

STATEMENT ISSUED ON 05 APRIL 2001

1. The Government of India had declared unilaterally a policy of Non-Initiation of Combat Operations in J&K with a view to lowering the levels of violence and creating an atmosphere conducive to commencement of a peace process in the troubled state. Despite the continuing violence on the part of some predominantly non-Kashmiri terrorist groups, the Government is gratified to note that there is an unmistakable groundswell for peace among the people of J&K. In order to promote a vigorous movement towards establishment of peace and tranquility, the Government have decided to embark upon a political dialogue with all sections of the peace loving people of the State including those who are currently outside it.

2. The dialogue from the side of the GOI will be held by Shri K.C. Pant, Deputy Chairman, Planning Commission. It is hoped that representatives of all walks of life from among the people of J&K will be partners in this dialogue. More specifically it is expected that, besides the J&K Government, all political parties, non-government organizations, trade unions, social and religious bodies from all the regions of the state will participate. The Government invites people of goodwill who desire restoration of peace and normalcy in the State to come forward to participate in the dialogue.

3. The Government notes that the All India Hurriyat Parties Conference (APHC) has all along taken the position that talks should be unconditional. Now that the Government has agreed to hold talks in the interest of early restoration of peace, it is for the APHC to consider whether it would not be inconsistent for them to set pre-conditions for the dialogue. The doors are open for them to join in the talks. The doors are also not closed for Kashmiri organizations which are currently engaged in militancy in the State but are desirous of peace. The agenda for the dialogue, briefly stated, is 'Peace and how it may be attained in the troubled State'. All aspects bearing on this theme will be relevant to the dialogue.

4. The GOI takes notes of the frequently repeated requests from Pakistan that they are eager for a dialogue with India on J&K. The GOI re-affirms its faith in such a bilateral dialogue and hopes that Pakistan will help in its resumption by curbing cross-border terrorism and putting an end to the

vicious anti-India propaganda emanating from Pakistan. This will be in accordance with the Shimla Agreement and the spirit of the Lahore Declaration.

5. The road to peace is not without serious obstacles; and such is continuing violence against the innocent people of J&K. To reduce this violence, security forces have been directed to vigorously conduct operations against those who disturb the peace and victimize the innocent people of J&K, while at the same time ensuring that the population at large is spared undue hardships or harassment. The Government expects that all right thinking people in the state will join hands with the Government and march purposefully in quest of the peace which has eluded them for the last 12 years. It is only in on atmosphere of peace that an agreed solution for the J&K issue can be evolved.

Ref. No. DFP/ P/506 Date 1.05.2001

Respected Mr K.C. Pant Saheb,

In response to your letter dated 14 April 2001, I will draw your attention to the following.

That my party has all along been desirous of seeking a peaceful political resolution of the Kashmir problem through a dialogue which considering the gravity of the conflict around it, has to be meaningful and purpose-oriented under all circumstances.

There can be no denying to fact that Kashmir conflict has now assumed dangerous proportions threatening peace not only in South Asia, but a conflagration at a much wider scale. Peace in South Asia is delicately hinged on an amicable settlement of the Kashmir issue which has, in its very historical perspective three parties to it: India, Pakistan and people of the Jammu and Kashmir. By not involving any of these three parties in parleys to eke out an acceptable solution to all three of them, will be, according to my opinion, hoping against hope. History bears ample witness to it that bilateralism, in this regard, has throughout the fifty years of this dispute borne no fruit at all. It will utterly be an exercise in futility to hope for permanent peace through the mechanism of bilateralism. However, keeping in view the complexity of Kashmir problem, a serious, well-meaning beginning has to be made to a gradual peace process aimed at final settlement of the issue for which bilateralism, without losing precious time, should evolve into a comprehensive dialogue involving each one of the three parties to the dispute. If Government of India (GOI) is serious and sincere enough, then it has to engage the genuine representatives of the people of Jammu and Kashmir in a constructive dialogue to search for a viable solution of the Kashmir tangle. Who they are is not hard to imagine. If the problem could be sorted out and resolved accordingly by engaging the in-line-with-India insignificant elements in Kashmir, then it would not have to come to the explosive level at all at which it right now is. One does not really understand the motive behind your proposition of diluting the proposed dialogue to that sundry level. Even if they are presumed to exist as one of the determining factors to focus on the contours of the peace process, I believe that their view point will be present by the chief negotiator himself from GOI in due course of the parleys that will follow. This factor will surely advocate upholding of status quo in a peaceful atmosphere. Obviously enough, Kashmir is not a law and order problem whose resolution lies in maintaining the status quo. Sincerity on the part of GOI to resolve the issue, without missing the need to meet Kashmiri desires, would demand that at this critical juncture out-of-place redundant elements be discarded if the road map to permanent peace is to chalked out.

It needs to be said here that JKDFP believes in a genuine political dialogue to find a lasting solution to the Kashmir issue. In this connection it believes that the basic initiative lies with the Government of India. Despite the constrained nature of your letter, it views a dialogue offer in a broader perspective. It will await the response accordingly from your good self.

Yours sincerely
Shabir Ahmad Shah

K.C. Pant, Deputy Chairman, Planning Commission 13 May 2001

Janab Shabir Shah Saheb,
I was pleased to meet your colleagues on May 3 and I thank you for your letter of May 1. I appreciate your and your party's resolve to seek a peaceful political resolution of the J&K problem through a process of dialogue.

I share your approach that in view of the complex scenario in Kashmir, a serious and well-meaning beginning needs to be made through a graduated peace process. In the meanwhile, as suggested by you, it would be desirable to make a beginning without losing any precious time. It is important to emphasize peace because it is necessary to alleviate the sufferings of the people, and not because the Kashmir problem was being treated as a mere law and order issue. It is only in an atmosphere of peace that an agreed solution for the J&K problem can be evolved. An agreed solution should, indeed, be the end result of a dialogue. I will have the benefit of your views in the matter when we meet.

The Government of India is not averse to engage Pakistan in meaningful talks on J&K, and is hopeful that Pakistan will cooperate with India and initiate measures that would facilitate the process. The GOI has taken and is willing to take such steps as would contribute to a meaningful dialogue; being the initiators, we are committed to its success. It was in this spirit that the Prime Minister had taken various initiatives like the Lahore visit, announcement of unilateral cease-fire, etc.

I value the democratic spirit evident in your holding discussions with persons drawn from different regions of J&K and representing different viewpoints reflecting the pluralistic ethos of Kashmiriyat. At this stage, we are keen to understand the concerns of all sections of the people of J&K. It would have been against the spirit of democracy not to give those who have a stake in the future of J&K a chance to express themselves.

The issues you have raised in your letter are not amenable to summary disposal through an exchange of letters. May I suggest that we should now meet to discuss these and other issues? We should move ahead in search of peace and of an agreed and peaceful solution of the J&K problem.

With regards,

Yours sincerely,
K.C. Pant

Shri Shabir Ahmed Shah,
President, J&K Democratic Freedom Party
Kursoo, Raj Bagh, Srinagar

Ref.No. DFP-507 29 May 2001

Respected Mr K.C. Pant Saheb,

The latest development of the offer of dialogue on part of Government of India to the Chief Executive of Pakistan is, prima facie, positive. Peaceful settlement of Kashmir issue is what each of the three parties to the dispute has been coveting ever since. Which possibility, logically speaking, is bound to remain unachievable without a genuine dialogue involving the parties to the dispute. As such, J&K Democratic Freedom Party appreciates the move on part of GOI to invite Pakistan's Chief Executive to New Delhi for this purpose. You will kindly recall that in my letter I had said that to resolve the issue peacefully, GOI has to persuade itself to agree to a meaningful dialogue with Pakistan without attaching any condition to it. The letter further said that 'the initiative to settle the Kashmir tangle lies with India'. By inviting General Parvez Musharraf to New Delhi for holding talks on all outstanding issues between the two countries, and primarily on the most contentious issue of J&K, I am of the view that the same has been taken in consequence of serious deliberations over the matter by the Hon'ble Prime Minister of India and his colleagues. May I restate that DFP stands for a negotiated, peaceful resolution of the problem of J&K.

Now that a seemingly serious step has been taken by the GOI in this direction, what else can the people of J&K hope and pray for than a result-oriented dialogue. The alleviation of our sufferings depends on the success of this dialogue. Let narrowly conceived perceptions be abandoned so that the high road to peace yields itself to sight. Needless to mention that without involving the third party to the dispute in the dialogue, mists will continue to hover over the high road to peace to obliterate it from the view. We hope that in due course of its run the dialogue will become comprehensive.

Meanwhile, for the very smooth run of the dialogue a conducive atmosphere would seem to be a basic perrequisite. In this area also GOI may have to come forward with yet another positive step. It will be optimally reducing the level of human rights violations in J&K. While the offer of dialogue to Pakistan is appreciable, the withdrawal of cease-fire is not, even though it was not really working on the ground. Its connotation for the whole process of dialogue can be taken as negative. We feel that even this semblance of a process for peace has been withdrawn by India and it appears only as a contradiction in terms. But now that the dialogue has been started at the highest level it will, as of necessity, involve a gradual follow-up policy and the creation of a conductive atmosphere so that it may not have to face a rough sea.

India's offer of dialogue to Kashmiris on the one hand and to Pakistan on the other contradicts with the deteriorating situation of human rights in J&K. This is not in conformity with what has been professed in the dialogue offer. Since the time the offer of dialogue has come about the violation of human rights in the Valley has considerably increased whereas it ought to have been the very opposite of it. In this regard the level of increase in the far-flung rural areas of J&K can only be imagined, considering the level of increase it has touched in the city of Srinagar. To substantiate the truth of my statement, I refer to some horrendous events. One of my own party activists, namely Aijaz Kitab, was arrested in front of my office at Rajbagh in Srinagar on 19 May 2001 by the security forces and soon after killed. His murder is a glaring case of custodial killing. In fact, the rate of custodial killing has increased in geometrical progression since the time GOI made the offer of dialogue to the cross-section of the people in J&K. From Chattabal, an area which falls in the heart of the city of Srinagar, two young men were taken into custody by the security forces and killed at Harwan, which is a suburban locality of Srinagar. Only a couple of weeks before, two young students of class XII of the higher secondary school in Shopian – a town 52 km distant from Srinagar – were bulleted by these so-called security forces [*sic*]. Each of these gruesome events was reported by the local as well as the Indian print media. With these horrifying killings happening day in and day out, how can the dialogue evoke credibility from the people in J&K and proceed constructively to the desired end? I would, with all emphasis at my command, propose that GOI take measures to stop these flagrant violations of human rights and humanitarian law at the hands of the security forces and STF if at all a conducive atmosphere to a constructive dialogue is to be built. The security forces need to be restrained and the State Task Force, which is an instrument of torture and murder in cold blood on the model and pattern of the Gestapo of Nazi Germany, needs to be disbanded. For more than a decade young Kashmiris have been suffering illegal and immoral detention in the Indian jails. They shall have to be released. I may say that more of such positive measures shall have to be taken by the GOI to make possible a congenial atmosphere in which a comprehensive dialogue to resolve the Kashmir conflict can thrive.

With regards,

Yours sincerely
Shabir Ahmad Shah

K.C. Pant
Deputy Chairman
Planning Commission India

Copies of the letters circulated by Government of India.

26. Brinda Karat's intervention in Parliament, 15 March 2011

The House met at eleven of the clock; Mr Deputy Chairman in the Chair.

Matters raised with permission of the Chair: Denial of justice to the families of those killed and injured in Kashmir Valley.

Shrimati Brinda Karat (West Bengal): Sir, I would like to draw the attention of the House to the continuing denial of justice to the people of Jammu and Kashmir and, in particular, the denial of minimum norms of justice to the families of those whose children were killed in the unfortunate incidents last year. Four Members of Parliament had an occasion to attend the Women's Conference held in Srinagar, organized by the Central Government-appointed Interlocutors. Women from all the regions of Jammu and Kashmir and Ladakh were present in that Conference. Unlike some of the attempts to project the differences between different regions, what we saw in this Conference was the unanimous outrage against the fact that even though 117 young people were killed in the Valley, not a single official, not even a constable has been punished. Sir, whenever this type of a police firing takes place in other parts of India, we know actions are taken to make the forces accountable. But, here, Sir, leave alone being punished, even FIRs have not been registered. Out of 117 deaths, only 37 FIRs have been registered. No inquiries have been made. Therefore, Sir, the first demand that the women have made is to have some process to ensure justice. I, myself, feel that an independent inquiry commission, with impartial people, to take strong action against those responsible, in a time-bound way, be set up.

Secondly, Sir, you will be shocked to know, the House will be shocked to know, that even today, young people are being called to *thanas,* threatened and arrested. Indiscriminate arrests are taking place in the Valley. This is very unfortunate. You cannot have peace and calm without justice. We demand: 'Stop those indiscriminate arrests.'

Sir, the third point that I would like to make is that women were saying that at every corner there are bunkers. It seems that there is militarization of the entire Valley. Sir, you will be shocked to know that every time young university girls, students and lecturers going to the university, enter the university or college, they have to show their identity cards. They asked us: 'Is this not our land?; is this not our State; is this not our college?; every time I walk into my college, do I have to be humiliated to show my identity card?' That is why, Sir, we demand that justice be geven to the women and children of Kashmir and also to the people in the Valley. Stop behaving like an occupying power. That is my demand, Sir.

Srimati Viplove Thakur (Himachal Pradesh): Sir, I also associate myself with the point made by the Hon. Member.

Note: Three other Members of Parliament also associated themselves with these views.

27. 'Kashmir: manufacturing ethnic conflict', by Jean Dreze, *The Hindu*, 29 March 2000

Kashmir has often been described as a paradise, and the term strikes the visitor as appropriate in more ways than one. The description usually refers to the landscape, which is indeed stunning, especially the panoramic view of the Himalayas in their full glory. On a less predictable note, Kashmir looks refreshingly prosperous and civilized compared with other parts of north India.

The Valley, where a majority of the Kashmiri population lives, boasts a vibrant rural economy that combines wide-ranging farm products (rice, apples, vegetables, saffron, milk, meat, fish) with a diversity of manufactures, from carpets to cricket bats. Living conditions are good by Indian standards, and so is the public infrastructure. What is more, most families own at least some land, so that extreme poverty is rare. '*Yahaan roti, kapada aur makaan sab ke paas hai*', I was told in the villages, and the statement has a ring of truth. It is all the more tragic that economic development in Kashmir is now stifled by armed conflict.

On a similar note, Kashmiri society and culture look anything but 'backward' (as often implied in the Indian media). One gets the impression of a well-integrated society with a fine blend of tradition and modernity. Most villages have a mosque as well as an 'English-medium' school. Even Kashmiri women seem to enjoy a higher social status than their north Indian counterparts, in many respects. Of course, gender relations in Kashmir are quite conservative, with clearly demarcated gender roles and little tolerance for sexual liberation. However, the Kashmiri way of life also has much to offer by way of women's freedoms: purdah is uncommon, female infanticide and bride-burning are virtually unknown, married women retain a strong bond with their parents and siblings, widow remarriage is viewed in a positive light, and sexual harassment is regarded as a serious matter. There also seems to be a positive attitude towards girls' education.

Such are the initial impressions I formed of Kashmir when I visited it for the first time earlier this month. Curious to learn more, I hired a bicycle in Srinagar and spent a few days riding around the Valley and talking with local residents. My initial purpose was to study the schooling situation, but it turned out to be difficult not to focus on people's overwhelming concern: the endless *zulm* (repression) unleashed by the security forces.

The security forces were rarely out of sight, even in remote villages. As far as the local population is concerned, Kashmir is 'occupied' by a foreign army. Everywhere I went, there were sobering tales of harassment at the hand of the Indian Army and paramilitary forces: curfews, searches, interrogations, killings of suspected militants, and accidental as well as intentional killings of innocent civilians, to name a few complaints. In one village, I was told that a father and son had recently been shot in the knee before being pushed into a house in flames. In several villages, shops and houses had recently been burnt in retaliation against recent killings of Army personnel – a prime example of 'collective punishment', proscribed by international conventions. Physical hardships are compounded by constant humiliation. 'Imagine how we feel when a Bihari or a Madrasi asks us for our identity card in our own country, when we should be asking them for their papers', said one. In a similar vein, a middle-class woman in Srinagar complained that her house had recently been searched by a '*Chambal ka daku*' in uniform.

Most people trace the beginning of this nightmare to 1989, when violence first spread in the Valley. The situation that has prevailed since then is referred to as 'militancy'. This does not mean that people hold militants – local or foreign – responsible for the problem. 'Militancy' is simply the situation. As for the militants, they seem to enjoy varying degrees of popular support, partly due to their decent behaviour towards the people (often contrasted with the brutality of the security forces), partly because they are seen to be upholding the common cause – *azadi*. *Azadi* has come to be identified with an independent state, but the main concern of ordinary people is to be able to lead their life without harassment, and to be free from Delhi's yoke. Interestingly, one person said that 'before 1989, there was *azadi*'. He added, however, that things have come to a point where *azadi* cannot be achieved short of an independent state. Of course, it is possible that most people would in fact be willing to accept a compromise, for the sake of ending *zulm*, if it involves the substantive freedoms they aspire to. Those who are unlikely to compromise are the hard-core 'militants', whose power and influence has been greatly enhanced by the Indian Government's iron-fist approach to the situation.

Asked whether the ongoing conflict was in part a Hindu–Muslim conflict, people emphatically said 'no'. Some respondents even had difficulty understanding the question: it simply had not occurred to them to think in those terms. They insisted that it was simply '*azadi ki ladai*'.

Considering that this is a situation where, effectively, a predominantly Muslim population is brutally policed by a predominantly Hindu army (which takes its orders from a BJP-led Government), it is remarkable that the conflict has not taken a more communal turn. Asked about the flight of Kashmiri Pandits in 1990, most people said, '*Jagmohan ne unko bhaga diya*' (Jagmohan sent them away). This is probably a mixture of truth and propaganda, but the perception is interesting. In one remote village, I met Hindu and Sikh families; they were quite happy there and felt secure.

Kashmiris come across as deeply peace-loving people, and they are even said to take pride in their non-violent nature. 'People here used to hate guns', one teacher told me. Folklore has it that Kashmiri men used to be capable of little more violence than throwing their *kangris* at each other. While these cliches should not be taken literally, there is at least one tangible indication that they contain a grain of truth: Kashmir used to have one of the lowest murder rates in India.

The non-communal and peace-loving outlook of the Kashmiri people, however, is in danger of subsiding as Army repression pushes them into the hands of foreign-sponsored, fundamentalist groups. Soon after I returned to Delhi, news came of the massacre of 35 Sikhs in Chani Singhpore. No doubt this incident will be seen by some as confirmation that the Kashmir conflict is rooted in ethnic hatred. It is possible to take the opposite view: that ethnic animosity in Kashmir is so weak that the most gruesome provocations are needed to incite communities against each other. The incident reminded me of a comment made a few years ago by a bemused resident of war-torn Bosnia: 'The war had to be so bloody because the ties between us were so strong.'

On the train back to Delhi, I talked with members of the Border Security Force (BSF) who were going home for Holi. In Kashmir, I had often felt a tinge of pity for the jawans, seeing how they had to stand for hours in the biting cold, bored to death, looking nervous if not frightened. Asked about Army brutality, one of them said, 'We don't like to beat them up, but they don't talk straight, so we have to do it.'

There is no simple solution to the Kashimir impasse. What seems clear is that the present stand of the Indian Government is a trifle contradictory. In international fora, mediation is rejected on the grounds that Pakistan and India have agreed to resolve the Kashmir dispute bilaterally. When Pakistan approaches India for talks, it is told that Kashmir is an internal matter (despite India's own claim to 'Pakistan-Occupied Kashmir'). Within India, however, Kashmir is treated like a colony, unworthy of democratic rights. It is no wonder that the Indian Government's attempt to entice the State into the national fold has failed to strike a chord with the Kashmiri people.

28. Faiz Ahmad Faiz's solution to the Kashmir dispute

The great poet Faiz Ahmad Faiz had a strong Kashmir connection. Sheikh Mohammed Abdullah performed his *nikah* at Srinagar when he married a young English girl, Alys George, in 1941. The *nikahnama* (deed of marriage) was signed by G.M. Sadiq, Bakshi Ghulam Mohammed and Dr Noor Husain as witnesses. 'In this sense my *nikahnama* bears the character of a historic document', Faiz told Shamim Ahmad Shamim, M.P. from Srinagar and editor of the weekly *Aina* when he called on the poet in Lahore in 1969. The interview, first published in *Aina*, was reprinted in the Srinagar weekly *Chattan*, edited by Tahir Mohiuddin, on 18 April 2011.

> Shamim: When did you last visit Kashmir?
> Faiz: I went there last in 1947. I was in Srinagar on 15 August 1947 when the sub-continent was partitioned and left on 24 August. Thereafter the Kashmir problem erupted which, far from being resolved, gets worse by the day.
> Shamim: How in your opinion can this problem be solved?
> Faiz: Bhai, the problem has become so complex that it is very difficult to devise any easy solution to it. Unfortunately both sides have adopted extreme positions, with the result that the possibility of resolving it through dialogue is receding day by day. The governments of both countries seek to score points over each other through extremism. In such a situation, it has become meaningless and difficult to try to devise any solution. One course is quite possible. While reserving their respective positions, both countries can enter into talks in confidence, very much like the continuing talks in Warsaw between the United States and China despite their deep differences. In the same way India and Pakistan can enter into talks in a third country for a sustained dialogue.
>
> But the current position is that Pakistan asks for a solution to the Kashmir dispute, while India says that a Kashmir dispute simply does not exist. It is really wrong to deny the existence of the dispute and I have often told my friends in India that this is a wrong position to adopt. Only recently, during a brief visit to India, some friend said: well the Kashmiris are satisfied – to which I replied, let the Kashmiris themselves declare that they are satisfied. They rejoined: 'We will satisfy them, but even then Pakistan will not be satisfied.' I replied, you are right. Pakistan will be dissatisfied still. But in that event Pakistan's stand will not be as strong as before.

Faiz was speaking with great calm, Shamim noted:

> His sincerity and seriousness made his personality all the more appealing. He was not saying anything new. But he spoke as if he was unravelling a deep secret. I felt that his heart was pained at the plight of Kashmir. I heard from him remarks on Kashmir which I never heard from any other Pakistani.

Faiz said:

> The best solution for Kashmir is that both countries should leave Kashmir alone and, as a self-governing ('khudamukhtar') State, Kashmir should establish friendly relations with both countries. Eventually this is what will happen; but after suffering much harm and damage. People like you on both sides should jointly press such a proposal.

Faiz and Shamim proceeded to discuss other matters. Sixty years later the Four Point formula was accepted by both India and Pakistan. The train blasts in Mumbai in 2008, besides the crisis in the judiciary in Islamabad in March 2007, delayed finalization of, and signature on, the agreed draft.

The Mumbai blasts of 26 November 2008 considerably retarded perhaps the most promising dialogue on Kashmir since December 1947. The draft should not be shelved. Before long, the package must be dusted and the draft retrieved for signature. Only if the Four Points are implemented, in the spirit in which Faiz propounded his solution in 1969, will the Kashmir dispute be well and truly solved.

Translated by the author from the Urdu text.